THE MERTON ANNUAL

Studies in Culture, Spirituality, and Social Concerns

Volume 26	2013

Edited by

David Joseph Belcastro   Joseph Quinn Raab

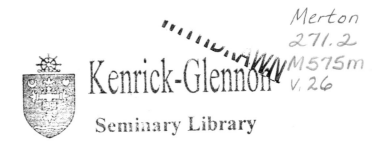

THE MERTON ANNUAL
Studies in Culture, Spirituality, and Social Concerns

THE MERTON ANNUAL publishes articles about Thomas Merton and about related matters of major concern to his life and work. Its purpose is to enhance Merton's reputation as a writer and monk, to continue to develop his message for our times, and to provide a regular outlet for substantial Merton-related scholarship. *THE MERTON ANNUAL* includes as regular features reviews, review-essays, a bibliographic survey, interviews, and first appearances of unpublished or obscurely published Merton materials, photographs, and art. Essays about related literary and spiritual matters will also be considered. Manuscripts and books for review may be sent to the editors.

EDITORS

David J. Belcastro
Dept. of Religion and Philosophy
Capital University
Bexley, OH 43209
mertonannual@gmail.com

Joseph Quinn Raab
Religious Studies Department
Siena Heights University
Adrian, MI 49221
mertonannual@gmail.com

EDITORIAL COMMITTEE

William Apel (McMinnville, OR), Deborah Kehoe (Oxford, MS), Victor Kramer (Decatur, GA), Roger Lipsey (Garrison, NY), Gray Matthews (Memphis, TN), Patrick F. O'Connell (Copy Editor) (Erie, PA), Paul M. Pearson (Louisville, KY), Malgorzata Poks (Koszecin, Poland), Lynn Szabo (Vancouver, BC), Bonnie B. Thurston (Wheeling, WV), Monica Weis (Rochester, NY).

Grateful acknowledgement is expressed to The Merton Legacy Trust and the Thomas Merton Center at Bellarmine University for permission to reproduce the calligraphy by Thomas Merton for the cover artwork.

PUBLISHED BY:
Fons Vitae
49 Mockingbird Valley Drive
Louisville, KY 40207
502.897.3641
Fonsvitaeky@aol.com
http://www.fonsvitae.com

SPONSORED BY:
International Thomas Merton Society
Thomas Merton Center
Bellarmine University
2001 Newburg Road
Louisville, KY 40205
502.272.8187 or 8177
merton@bellarmine.edu
http://www.merton.org/ITMS/

Further details about membership and subscribing to *The Merton Seasonal* and *The Merton Annual* are available at http://www.merton.org/ITMS/membership.aspx or by contacting the Thomas Merton Center at the above address.

For members of the International Thomas Merton Society, available for $15.00, plus shipping and handling. Individual copies are available through bookstores and directly from the publisher for $19.95. Institutions $39.95. *Copyright:* All rights reserved.

ISBN 978-1891785-580   ISSN 0894-4857

Printed in Canada

The Merton Annual

Volume 26	2013

Joseph Quinn Raab
Introduction: Sophia's Romancing   7

Peggy L. Fox
James Laughlin and Thomas Merton:
"Louie, I Think This Is the Beginning of a Beautiful Friendship"   12

James Laughlin
An Interview about Thomas Merton
Conducted by *Paul Wilkes*
Edited by *Paul M. Pearson*   24

Ian S. MacNiven
More Than Scribe: James Laughlin, Thomas Merton
and *The Asian Journal*   43

* * * * * * *

Christopher Pramuk
"She Cannot Be a Prisoner":
The Lure of Wisdom as Bearer of Hope   54

Edward K. Kaplan
Personal Bridges, Spiritual Communities:
The Correspondence of Thomas Merton
and Zalman Schachter-Shalomi   74

Gordon Oyer
Louis Massignon and the Seeds
of Thomas Merton's "Monastic Protest"   84

Michael Plekon
"The Immense Mercy of God Was upon Me":
Thomas Merton's Reading of the Russian Émigré Thinkers   97

Patrick F. O'Connell
"The First Cistercian and the Greatest Trappist":
Thomas Merton's Poems on John the Baptist   107

Monica Weis, SSJ
"With My Hair Almost on End":
Le Point Vierge and the Dawn Birds　　140

Robert Weldon Whalen
Thomas Merton and Pierre Teilhard de Chardin:
"The Dawning of Divine Light"　　147

Fiona Gardner
Thomas Merton and the Concept of the Child-Mind:
"The Only One Worth Having"　　157

Mark C. Meade
From Downtown Louisville to Buenos Aires:
Victoria Ocampo as Thomas Merton's Overlooked Bridge
to Latin America and the World　　168

Raymond Carr
Merton and Barth in Dialogue on Faith and Understanding:
A Hermeneutics of Freedom and Ambiguity　　181

David Joseph Belcastro
2012 Bibliographic Review Essay:
Thomas Merton, Escape Artist　　195

Reviews

Bonnie Bowman Thurston
The Life of the Vows: Initiation into the Monastic Tradition 6
by Thomas Merton edited by Patrick F. O'Connell　　211

Mark C. Meade
On Christian Contemplation by Thomas Merton
edited by Paul M. Pearson
On Eastern Meditation by Thomas Merton
edited by Bonnie Thurston　　213

Jonathan Montaldo
*Precious Thoughts: Daily Readings from the Correspondence
of Thomas Merton* edited by Fiona Gardner　　216

Patrick F. O'Connell
Thomas Merton on Contemplation; *Finding True Meaning and
Beauty*; *Thomas Merton's Great Sermons*; *Vatican II: The Sacred
Liturgy and the Religious Life*; *Thomas Merton on Sufism*; *Ways*

of Prayer: A Desert Father's Wisdom; *Thomas Merton on the 12 Degrees of Humility*; *Solitude and Togetherness*; *The Prophet's Freedom* (CDs)   220

Deborah Kehoe
Thomas Merton and Thérèse Lentfoehr:
The Story of a Friendship by Robert Nugent, SDS   233

Christine M. Bochen
Thomas Merton—The Exquisite Risk of Love:
The Chronicle of a Monastic Romance by Robert G. Waldron   236

Patrick Thomas Morgan
Returning to Reality: Thomas Merton's Wisdom
for a Technological World by Phillip M. Thompson   241

Richard Weber, OCSO
Thomas Merton: Monk on the Edge
edited by Ross Labrie and Angus Stuart   246

Margaret B. Betz
It Draws Me: The Art of Contemplation by Mary M. McDonald   249

Erlinda G. Paguio
A Miracle of Grace: An Autobiography by E. Glenn Hinson   251

Deborah Kehoe
Denise Levertov: A Poet's Life by Dana Greene   255

Donald Grayston
I'm Your Man: The Life of Leonard Cohen by Sylvie Simmons
The Holy or the Broken by Alan Light   259

Contributors   265

Index   271

The International Thomas Merton Society   276

Introduction: Sophia's Romancing

Joseph Quinn Raab

"In every generation she passes into holy souls
And makes them friends of God, and prophets."
Wisdom 7:27b

"There is a mystic thread of life
So dearly wreathed with mine alone,
That destiny's relentless knife
At once must sever *both* or *none*."
Lord Byron

We don't often apply the term "philosopher" to Thomas Merton but perhaps he was first and foremost *a lover of wisdom*. He knew his beloved by many names and faces, but he preferred her as she appears passionately in the poetry of Jerusalem rather than in her formal dress—the clean abstractions of Athens. I like to think that he so loved Sophia that the two became one. He surrendered his voice to her and discovered his true freedom. The Thirteenth General Meeting of the International Thomas Merton Society, whose fruit largely comprises this current edition of *The Merton Annual*, was an occasion for many to reflect collectively on Merton's call to transform *our* hearts by *Living Together with Wisdom*. For this sophianic love is not jealous and possessive but inclusive and meant to be shared. Fittingly then, a common discernable thread running through this collection of fine essays is the tug of Sophia, the nameless *substance* we call *love*, romancing us into an ever-deepening friendship with God, a fruitful union producing prophecy.

This collection begins with three pieces focused on the relationship between "Tom" Merton and his longtime editor from New Directions, James "J" Laughlin. **Peggy Fox** explores the personal dimension of that friendship in "James Laughlin and Thomas Merton: 'Louie, I Think This Is the Beginning of a Beautiful Friendship.'" In this engaging piece Fox shows the relationship to be a symbiotic one where the worldly editor offered the monk a way "to free himself of his self-imposed shackles and engage in the world's struggles and as an artist to break conventional molds and recreate himself as a poet." Conversely, the monk and poet offered J a way of retaining his personal authenticity while finding a connection to God—a "spiritual balm in a world that seemed to be fracturing."

The next piece in this volume is Paul Wilkes' interview with **James Laughlin** about Thomas Merton, which was conducted on March 18, 1983. While a redacted version of this interview appeared in Wilkes' book *Merton: By Those Who Knew Him Best*,[1] this is the first time the interview appears in full, carefully transcribed and edited by Paul M. Pearson. This version includes the specific questions Wilkes had asked Laughlin, which are omitted in the book, and helps the reader contextualize Laughlin's illuminating reminiscences. Laughlin's intimate recollections portray Merton as an ebullient and humble genius, a friend of God and prophet, whose enthusiasm for life and for God was irresistibly contagious, even for Laughlin, the self-described "heretic."

The third piece in this introductory trio is **Ian S. MacNiven**'s "More Than Scribe: James Laughlin, Thomas Merton and *The Asian Journal*." As the title suggests, this fine piece of scholarship convincingly portrays Laughlin's herculean work that stands behind *The Asian Journal*. J spent almost three years painstakingly deciphering three separate notebooks, much of the content of which was nearly illegible, and some entirely so. In order to render the content intelligible to a New Directions audience J also compiled an impressive glossary. Beyond that, J had to track down some of Merton's interlocutors who appear in the journal to clarify the content and meaning of those ciphered texts. This is all the more impressive because J was simultaneously working through his own grief over the untimely death of his dear friend Tom. MacNiven presents J as nearly a co-author of this text since the fact that there is a golden narrative thread running through *The Asian Journal* is mostly due to J's loving labor.

Following that featured friendship this volume moves to ten articles, nine of which were originally presented in some form at the ITMS conference in Fairfield. The first of these is **Christopher Pramuk**'s "'She Cannot Be a Prisoner': The Lure of Wisdom as Bearer of Hope." This beautifully compelling piece helps to frame many of the essays in this volume that follow. It offers a glimpse of divine Wisdom that begins with Merton's *Hagia Sophia* and moves on through holocaust narratives and post-holocaust theology, unveiling the One who can bestow a sacramental appreciation of the world as full of God, healing and "rushing out to us from every pore" as Fr. Alfred Delp put it, even in the midst of evil and suffering. Pramuk, through his struggles to understand "the music of divine mercy," has acquired or received a rare ability to help others glimpse the "diffuse shining of God."

In "Personal Bridges, Spiritual Communities: The Correspondence

---

1. Paul Wilkes, ed., *Merton by Those Who Knew Him Best* (San Francisco: Harper & Row, 1984) 3-13.

of Thomas Merton and Zalman Schachter-Shalomi," **Edward Kaplan** offers an astute interpretation of an inter-contemplative friendship that gets underneath doctrinal divides to an ineffable reality grounding both gentile and Jew. Kaplan's reading of the latter part of their dialogue raises the haunting question: is this ineffable reality indifferent or personal, static or dynamic, dead or alive? The correspondence of these two men reaches a rare and intimate sharing at what a Christian would call the foot of the cross. Their letters to one another expose a mutual vulnerability when they openly discuss doubt, dread and fear of annihilation. Yet through it all their humor and love prevail. This humor and love, percolating up from our deepest human weaknesses, looks like Sophia's romancing—the trace of the One for whom both devotedly yearn.

Gordon Oyer's piece breaks new ground by highlighting the influence of Louis Massignon on Merton's peace activism. Merton readers readily recognize Massignon's influence on Merton in other areas, introducing him to *le point vierge* and many Sufi writers, but in "Louis Massignon and the Seeds of Thomas Merton's 'Monastic Protest,'" Oyer highlights Massignon's profound influence on Merton the peace activist—a sustained influence that helped Merton recognize the humanity of those on both sides of a conflict and to maintain a self-deprecating humor that disarms self-righteousness. Oyer shows how Massignon, not only through his writing but through his own living example, helped to ground Merton's pacifism in Wisdom rather than ideology.

The next piece in this collection, "'The Immense Mercy of God Was upon Me': Thomas Merton's Reading of the Russian Émigré Thinkers" by **Michael Plekon**, is the only one of these ten articles that was not originally presented at the conference. In it, Plekon helpfully shows how writers like George Fedotov, Sergius Bulgakov and Paul Evdokimov, among others, impacted Merton. These thinkers whom Merton had "devoured in roughly the last decade of his life" inform and support Merton's theological vision of God as *Philanthropos*, the One who loves all without limitations, and Merton's understanding of the contemplative as one who lives a realized eschatology—eroding the artificial divide between the sacred and the secular and becoming a bearer of this immense mercy.

In "'The First Cistercian and the Greatest Trappist': Thomas Merton's Poems on John the Baptist," **Patrick F. O'Connell** provides a masterful reading of three of Merton's earlier poems all focused on the "contemplative prophet" whom Merton called his "great patron, friend and Protector." This substantive study elucidates Merton's creative interpretation of the New Testament texts that inform his powerful poetic homage to St. John. O'Connell's agility recognizing Merton's biblical allusions, and understanding the implications of how he arranges and connects them, bears witness to his skill both as a theologian and as an expert interpreter of poetry. Through his sustained meditation on these poems O'Connell shows us that in St. John, even while still in the womb of Elizabeth, Merton finds a model for himself as "hidden in the very womb of the Church" yet prophetically pulsating throughout the body.

In a less formal, more lyrical reflection, **Monica Weis, SSJ** explores Merton's experience of awakening to the "*full meaning* of lauds" when the birds began to sing very early on that June morning in 1960.[2] This experience is the focus of Weis' probing piece "'With My Hair Almost on End': *Le Point Vierge* and the Dawn Birds." Weis invites us to appreciate the significance of this powerful experience, and to allow Merton's metaphors expressing it to entice us and dare us into a withdrawal in the hope of finding ourselves living together with Wisdom in the paradise of the present moment.

Robert Weldon Whalen brings us an enriching comparison of "Thomas Merton and Pierre Teilhard de Chardin" in terms of each one's insight into the "The Dawning of Divine Light"—as the subtitle reads. Whalen adeptly lifts up common readings of our perpetually dawning future offered by the poet and the paleontologist. He illustrates how both herald a new mysticism, firmly rooted in the past, "intensely incarnational and sacramental," yet broadened and deepened as it emerges within a new context of a religiously plural, scientific era, consciously accountable to whatever lies ahead.

Revelation asserts, of course, that this divine light perpetually dawns as the new creation awakening in the newly born because Sophia delights in the presence of children (Proverbs 8:31). **Fiona Gardner**'s piece follows then with a reflection both broad and deep on "Thomas Merton and the Concept of the Child Mind: 'The Only One Worth Having.'" Centering her work on Merton's poem "Grace's House," which was inspired by a child's drawing, Gardner draws from a wide range of resources in her interpretation. In this insightful unpacking of Merton's poem, Gardner celebrates the only mind worth having, which far from being childish is nonetheless truly childlike in its simplicity, trust and unfettered imagination.

Returning to the bridge metaphor already encountered in Kaplan's

---

2. See Merton's journal entry of June 5, 1960 in Thomas Merton, *Turning Toward the World: The Pivotal Years. Journals, vol. 4: 1960-1963*, ed. Victor A. Kramer (San Francisco: HarperCollins, 1996) 7; see also the opening pages of "Part Three: The Night Spirit and the Dawn Air" in Thomas Merton, *Conjectures of a Guilty Bystander* (Garden City, NY: Doubleday, 1966) 117-18.

piece, **Mark Meade** offers "From Downtown Louisville to Buenos Aires: Victoria Ocampo as Thomas Merton's Overlooked Bridge to Latin America and the World." Meade introduces us to the fascinating person of Victoria who looks to be a kind of Argentinian counterpart to Fox's portrait of Laughlin. Like J, Victoria opens Merton to new worlds. In this engaging and educational essay, Meade pieces together a portrait of their friendship from remaining fragments of their correspondence. It is a friendship between pilgrims who courageously and confidently bridge barriers of nationality, religious affiliation and political contexts to reclaim their shared humanity in their common search of God.

The tenth and final piece in this central series of articles is **Raymond Carr**'s theologically astute "Merton and Barth in Dialogue on Faith and Understanding: A Hermeneutics of Freedom and Ambiguity." In his autobiographical introduction Carr recalls his first impressions of these intellectual giants from denominationally diverse worlds, and his own surprise at how similar they would prove to be. Carr then elucidates the quality of each one's intellectual and spiritual humility which accounts for their receptivity to the word of God, and grounds their shared "theological hermeneutics." Carr deftly argues that grace, and this resultant humility, frees both Merton and Barth from literalism and rationalism, permitting each to transcend the false dichotomy of faith and reason, and to be at home with the ambiguity of divine mystery.

Following these central pieces and serving as a segue into the review section of this journal, **David Joseph Belcastro** skillfully and lucidly reviews the world of Merton-related literature in 2012. To frame his review of a topically diverse landscape Belcastro relies on the compelling image "Thomas Merton, Escape Artist." Delighting in the paradoxical image of the avowedly stable monk who is yet a kind of spiritual Houdini, Belcastro elucidates how we learn from Merton that the freedom of the children of God requires an escape. This is not an escape from reality or an escap*ism* of obstinate refusal to accept things, but an escape from illusion and slavery *into* reality. So much of our continued fascination with Merton, evinced by publication after publication, has to do with our desire for the kind of freedom Merton obviously enjoyed, even amid the countless snares of our modern world. Belcastro's piece celebrates Sophia's call to escape these snares and to live together with her and with Tom in this transformative freedom.

And last, a word of gratitude: David and I wish to thank our editorial review board members for all of their help in producing this current volume. We especially thank Paul M. Pearson for his constant support and Patrick F. O'Connell for his patient and expert copyediting. And now, to you, happy reading.

James Laughlin and Thomas Merton: "Louie, I Think This Is the Beginning of a Beautiful Friendship"

Peggy L. Fox

You are reading this volume of *The Merton Annual* because of your appreciation and love of Thomas Merton as monk, contemplative, spiritual writer, ecumenical guide, activist. We all have some idea of the trajectory of Merton's life from young reprobate, would-be poet and journalist, through his conversion to Catholicism and eventually his entry into Gethsemani, becoming Brother and then Father Louis. Perhaps you have read *The Seven Storey Mountain*[1] and many of Merton's other works, from the purely spiritual such as *Bread in the Wilderness*[2] to those touching on Asian religion such as *The Way of Chuang Tzu*[3] to his poetry, most recently showcased in *In the Dark before Dawn*,[4] expertly edited by Lynn Szabo. Just look up a title by Merton on Amazon and the author bio says: "Thomas Merton is arguably the most influential American Catholic author of the twentieth century."

But in this article devoted to exploring Merton's relationship with one person who occupied a special role in his life, you will meet James Laughlin, founder and publisher of New Directions, and some of you will say, "James who?" New Directions began publishing Merton's poems in 1944[5] and continues to publish and now keeps in print all of Merton's poetry[6] plus a wide variety of titles from *New Seeds of Contemplation*[7] to *The Wisdom of the Desert*.[8] When Laughlin died in 1997, the very best obituary appeared in *The Nation* magazine by the elegant and provocative essayist Eliot Weinberger. It began: "Every consideration of James Laughlin and New Directions must begin with The List: a list numbing to recite, overwhelming in its whole and astonishing in its particulars.

---

1. Thomas Merton, *The Seven Storey Mountain* (New York: Harcourt, Brace, 1948).

2. Thomas Merton, *Bread in the Wilderness* (New York: New Directions, 1953).

3. Thomas Merton, *The Way of Chuang Tzu* (New York: New Directions, 1965).

4. Thomas Merton, *In the Dark before Dawn: New Selected Poems*, ed. Lynn R. Szabo (New York: New Directions, 2005).

5. Thomas Merton, *Thirty Poems* (Norfolk, CT: New Directions, 1944).

6. Thomas Merton, *The Collected Poems of Thomas Merton* (New York: New Directions, 1977); subsequent references will be cited as "*CP*" parenthetically in the text.

7. Thomas Merton, *New Seeds of Contemplation* (New York: New Directions, 1961).

8. Thomas Merton, *The Wisdom of the Desert: Sayings from the Desert Fathers of the Fourth Century* (New York: New Directions, 1960).

New Directions was the publisher—and almost always the first publisher in the United States—of . . ."—and here follows a very long list from Borges to Tennessee Williams, Nabokov to Sartre, Pound and W. C. Williams to W. G. Sebald. Weinberger continues, "Laughlin was more than the greatest American publisher of the twentieth century: His press *was* the twentieth century."[9] Two extraordinary men receiving extraordinary praise—how did their paths cross and what drew them into a close, almost symbiotic friendship?[10]

In this volume of the *Annual*, Ian MacNiven, whose biography of James Laughlin will be published in 2014, writes as a scholar and biographer who has devoted many years to studying Laughlin, his authors and associates, about Laughlin's editing of Merton's *The Asian Journal*,[11] but I am here to give you a more personal perspective, as someone who knew Laughlin and who understood, on a day-to-day basis, the role that Merton played in his life and he in Merton's. When I first came to New Directions in 1975, *The Asian Journal* had been published just two years earlier, *The Collected Poems* was in the process of being assembled, and one of my jobs was to make sure that Laughlin's voluminous correspondence concerning something called the "Merton Legacy Trust" was properly filed. And I learned firsthand the intensity of Laughlin's devotion to Merton and to the proper publishing of his work. When *The Collected Poems* went to well over a thousand pages and production costs mounted far in excess of revenue expected from sales, it simply didn't matter. He would do right by his friend Tom, Laughlin said, or he wouldn't do it at all!

James Laughlin was born into the Laughlin steel family of Pittsburgh in 1914, the year before Merton's birth in France. He had a privileged

---

9. Eliot Weinberger, "James Laughlin," *The Nation* 265.846 (15 Dec. 1997) 38-39.

10. In addition to the usual published sources, I will be quoting from James Laughlin's unpublished 1982 typescript of 49 pages, simply called "Thomas Merton" (in the Laughlin Literary Executor files of Peggy L. Fox; subsequent references will be cited as "Laughlin, 'Thomas Merton'" parenthetically in the text), from which is derived the essay "Thomas Merton and his Poetry," published in James Laughlin, *Random Essays: Reflections of a Publisher* (Mt. Kisco, NY: Moyer Bell, 1989) 3-31 (subsequent references will be cited as "Laughlin, *Random Essays*" parenthetically in the text); it also provided the raw material for Laughlin's March 18, 1983 interview with Paul Wilkes, published in full in this volume of *The Merton Annual*, and in edited form as "Thomas Merton—A Portrait," in Paul Wilkes, ed., *Merton by Those Who Knew Him Best* (San Francisco: Harper & Row, 1984) 3-13, reprinted as an appendix to Thomas Merton and James Laughlin, *Selected Letters*, ed. David D. Cooper (New York: W. W. Norton, 1997) 373-84 (subsequent references will be cited as "*SL*" parenthetically in the text).

11. Thomas Merton, *The Asian Journal*, ed. Naomi Burton Stone, Brother Patrick Hart and James Laughlin (New York: New Directions, 1973).

and somewhat pampered childhood in a wealthy Presbyterian family with the casual anti-Catholic and anti-Semitic prejudices of its time and class; but unlike his forebears he, through annual excursions to the mill, soon developed an aversion to the fiery furnaces of the family business, Jones & Laughlin Steel. He was an early rebel against his *haute bourgeois*, strait-laced Calvinist upbringing as well as most of the conventions of the society led by Andrew Carnegie and "Uncle Andy" Mellon. But once his intellectual attention was engaged at the Le Rosey School outside Geneva, where he and his brother were sent to escape exposure to their father's mental breakdown in 1929, he began to excel in his studies. Subsequently enrolled in schools near his highly opinionated but indulgent Aunt Leila Laughlin Carlisle in Norfolk, Connecticut (where he would live for the rest of his days), he emerged as the winner of four of five major prizes in his final year at Choate Academy—graduating three years ahead of John Fitzgerald Kennedy.

Influenced by his literary mentor at Choate, Dudley Fitts, he matriculated at Harvard rather than the "family" school of Princeton. Having been introduced by Fitts to the "moderns," Ezra Pound and T. S. Eliot, James Joyce and Gertrude Stein, he found the more traditional reading list at Harvard rather a bore and took off for the Continent in 1933, where he *did* meet Pound. He subsequently returned to Europe in 1934, where he *did* stay with Gertrude Stein and studied with Pound at the "Ezuversity" in Rapallo, Italy. The curriculum at this unconventional and utterly informal academy was reading what Pound recommended (his friends' works), listening to Dorothy Pound read Henry James in her cultivated English accent (her mother had been W. B. Yeats' special friend, Olivia Shakespear), learning Italian at the local cinema, and playing tennis with the Boss (as he called Pound).

In describing how he came to publishing, J (as he preferred to be called—just the initial, no period) often told the tale of Pound's rejection of his poetry and how Pound thought he "might" be able to manage doing something "useful" like being a publisher (of Pound's friends of course) and how as a result he founded New Directions. As Ian MacNiven's biography clearly shows, this is probably not literally true. Even when I came to know him in his early sixties, J was in perpetual doubt about his own abilities. Before he met Pound, he had already written a short story about a painter who asked his mentor if he should continue despite the master's belief that the young man would never reach the highest ranks of artistic achievement. The master replied: "There is always work."[12]

---

12. James Laughlin, "Melody with Fugue," *Random Stories* (Mt. Kisco, NY: Moyer Bell, 1990) 27.

But while Laughlin often embellished the New Directions "origin myth" (as we liked to call it), the basic outline is true: Laughlin returned to the U.S. to finish at Harvard (eventually) and, at Pound's urging and with introductions to authors as supplied by Pound, he settled into his "work"—publishing. He began his publishing venture out of his Harvard lodgings in 1936 with *New Directions in Prose and Poetry*, the first New Directions anthology, whose contents page still reads like a Who's Who of twentieth-century literary greats.

My telling of the Laughlin/Merton story is, by necessity, highly compressed, so we will fast forward to 1943, when New Directions was still a fledgling operation, but one becoming increasingly respected. Meanwhile Thomas Merton had not only entered the Abbey of Gethsemani, but was now Brother Louis. What brought these two men together was unrequited desire—Merton's to be a poet and be recognized as such and Laughlin, in Merton's words (written after his first face-to-face meeting with Laughlin), "because he [was] looking for God."[13] Before he entered Gethsemani in December of 1941, Merton, in late 1940 or early '41, sent a few poems to New Directions, hoping to be published in the annual anthology. Publishing secret: knowing how such things work, I can almost guarantee that Laughlin never saw the submission. It would have been given ten minutes, at most, by one of young writers who constituted the office staff in those days. This is how things really work: Mark Van Doren, who had been Merton's favorite teacher at Columbia, owned a farm near Laughlin's home in Connecticut, and J, an avid fly fisherman as well as fisher of poets, would sometimes exchange a catch of brook trout for a drink and literary conversation. So in 1943, Van Doren, still in contact with his star pupil, Brother Louis, sent Laughlin a "small sheaf" of Merton's poems. With Van Doren's *imprimatur*, Laughlin was able to overcome his admitted prejudice against Merton's non-experimental style and overtly religious content. Laughlin later wrote: "Now, religious poetry has never been one of my enthusiasms. But I was quickly caught up in this young man's vividness of language and freshness of imagination" (Laughlin, "Thomas Merton" 2). J was also captured by Merton's accessibility and found his poetry "extremely likable." J immediately decided to publish what became *Thirty Poems* in his Poet of the Month series.

But another reason that J took to Merton's poetry, and then to Merton himself, was his own spiritual longing. Although he had long since given up on church-going, he was drawn not only by Merton's acceptance of the strictures of monastic life, but also by his joy in this highly controlled

---

13. Thomas Merton, *The Sign of Jonas* (New York: Harcourt, Brace, 1953) 53; subsequent references will be cited as "*SJ*" parenthetically in the text.

environment. In *Byways*, Laughlin's poetic "autobiography," he writes in
the "Tom Merton" section about his first visit to Gethsemani:

> How wrong I had been about the inhabitants!
> These brothers and monks
> Were warriors of joy.
> Happy and friendly, laughing
> And joking, rejoicing in the
> Hard life of work and prayer
>   . . .
> These chantings of supplication
> For the whole world, even infidels
> Not just for the monks.
> Such brightness, *lux in aeternitate*.[14]

J spoke to Merton about his chronic doubts and Merton replied, "You
are not at all made for the misery of the cannibal world you have to live
in" (*SL* 20). Merton recommended prayer "in a simple way" (*SL* 20)
and supplied titles that might help J advance "my desire to increase the
spiritual component in my life" (*SL* 22). Merton instinctively understood
J's needs and wrote of their first meeting on June 12, 1947 in *The Sign
of Jonas*: "Laughlin is a fundamentally simple person. He is basically
religious because he is clean of heart . . . I like him very much. He is the
kind of person I can understand" (*SJ* 52-53).

As their relationship deepened through correspondence and repeated
visits by J to Gethsemani, each man came more and more to depend on
the other: Merton on Laughlin for the support he needed as a poet and
writer (as an artist as opposed to a religious thinker)—I will show how by
developing Merton's contacts with other writers and artists (sometimes
by rather devious means), Laughlin was able to spur a remarkable change
in Merton's poetic style and even substance, leading to his flowering
as both an activist against segregation and the Vietnam War and as an
ecumenical writer looking to other world religions for a deepening of
his own Christian faith. Likewise, Merton's belief in his friend's goodness, loyalty and utter reliability led him to trust Laughlin with not only
the responsibility for his literary legacy after his death, but with a very
personal responsibility for the individual who had touched his heart most
deeply. And in return Laughlin, by undertaking these tasks, received his
own most profound religious experience in editing *The Asian Journal* as
well as a source of focus and stability at a time of crisis in his health and

---

14. James Laughlin, *Byways: A Memoir*, ed. Peter Glassgold (New York: New
Directions, 2005) 219-20.

psychological well-being.

After *Thirty Poems,* New Directions published three more books of Merton's poetry in what, for publishing, amounted to rapid succession (*A Man in the Divided Sea*[15] in 1946, *Figures for an Apocalypse*[16] the following year, and *The Tears of the Blind Lions*[17] in 1949). During this poetic flowering, Merton was ordained a priest on Ascension Day, May 26, 1949. Laughlin confessed that he "cried through most" of the solemn high mass and that "heretic as I am," he took communion from an "exalted" Tom's own hands the next morning when Merton said his first Mass (Laughlin, "Thomas Merton" 18). But after *Blind Lions* was published, Merton went dormant as a poet, and New Directions branched out to publish other Merton titles such as *Seeds of Contemplation*[18] and *Bread in the Wilderness.* Merton responded to Laughlin's devotion to his work with an equal measure of loyalty. In 1951 Robert Giroux made an attempt to corner the exclusive rights to all of Merton's literary output for Harcourt, Brace where he then worked. Giroux might have succeeded had Merton not personally intervened with his agent Naomi Burton (who had sided with Giroux), Merton saying that despite the fact that Laughlin was not "a very orderly businessman," he "is a good guy. He likes to come down here. It does him good to come down here. He has a soul and a destiny to work out for himself which is more important than books" (*SL* 85). Abbot James Fox, who like Laughlin had attended Harvard, supported J, and J and Tom agreed between themselves that the poetry and certain hard-to-define prose works would be ND's province while "major" projects would go to Harcourt.

The dust-up seemed to solidify the personal connection between J and Tom. As J sensed in Merton a desire to expand his horizons beyond the monastery walls, Laughlin began to supply Merton with a steady stream of New Directions books: in the letters, thanks abound for volumes by Kafka and Rilke, Camus and Faulkner. But some books didn't get past the abbot and, according to J, it was Tom who suggested, "Let's try Jim Wygal," consulting psychiatrist for the monastery. In his essay on Merton's poetry, Laughlin explained, "Gethsemani needed a psychiatrist because after Tom's *Seven Storey Mountain* became a bestseller there was a flood of applicants for admission, many of whom were not sufficiently stable for the hard monastic life. Dr. Wygal screened these postulants. 'Send the books to Jim Wygal's office and when I take a batch of novices up

---

15. Thomas Merton, *A Man in the Divided Sea* (New York: New Directions, 1946).
16. Thomas Merton, *Figures for an Apocalypse* (New York: New Directions, 1947).
17. Thomas Merton, *The Tears of the Blind Lions* (New York: New Directions, 1949).
18. Thomas Merton, *Seeds of Contemplation* (New York: New Directions, 1949).

there I'll pick them up.' That is how Tom received Henry Miller, Djuna Barnes, and half a dozen others not usually to be found in a monastic library" (Laughlin, *Random Essays* 6). So during the time that Merton had sworn off poetry, Laughlin, by feeding him a steady stream of the more iconoclastic and technically experimental poets (and other writers), many published by New Directions, was shaping the poet that Merton was to become. When Merton resumed sending poems in 1956, Laughlin noted "the beginning of the secularization of Merton's poetry" (Laughlin, *Random Essays* 10-11) in the poems written between 1948 and 1956 that were to appear in *The Strange Islands*.[19]

As an indication of Merton's shifting attitudes during this time, I will cite the example of the notorious Henry Miller, author of *Tropic of Cancer* and other banned books. In 1950, Merton showed some alarm at appearing in a New Directions annual that would also include Miller (*SL* 73). But within the decade, Merton and Miller had become not only pen-pals but, as the young would say, best buds. When Henry wrote to ND, "I feel closer to him [Merton], his way of thinking, than any American writer I know of," Tom responded, "Well, that is a testimonial. I am really warmed by it. To me that is an indication that I am perhaps after all a Christian" (*SL* 189).

Laughlin also noted Merton's belief that the community and particularly the novices under his care (Merton was Novice Master for ten years: 1955-1965) "should have more access to secular books and know more about the injustices of the outside world and its problems. What good was prayer if you didn't know what to pray for?" (Laughlin, "Thomas Merton" 19). As Merton's reputation as a writer and religious thinker grew, he started corresponding with the Berrigans and other progressives both in the Church and beyond. He became more outspoken about segregation and the peace movement as demonstrated by poems like "And the Children of Birmingham"[20] and the strange and chilling *Original Child Bomb*,[21] published by New Directions in 1962, a prose poem about the bombing of Hiroshima about which J commented: "What sets the poem apart is the new verbal tone, a mixture of satire and irony, fused into black humor" (Laughlin, *Random Essays* 11). Merton was moving away from his earlier conventionally religious poetic persona not only in content but in form.

And when Merton began writing articles for magazines against the,

---

19. Thomas Merton, *The Strange Islands* (New York: New Directions, 1957).

20. Thomas Merton, *Emblems of a Season of Fury* (New York: New Directions, 1963) 33-35; *CP* 335-37.

21. Thomas Merton, *Original Child Bomb* (New York: New Directions, 1962); *CP* 291-302.

as J commented, "business-military complex, against the Pentagon and even against Kennedy" (Laughlin, "Thomas Merton" 24), protests came in to Gethsemani from various American bishops and other Catholics, and Dom James Fox, after consultation with the Abbot General in France, was forced to tell Father Louis basically to SHUT UP—he was to stick to religion and religious poetry, PERIOD. J continued: "But wiley [*sic*] Tom got around the ban. He had the absolute loyalty of the novices and they were willing to mimeograph things in many copies. Tom inaugurated a series of 'Cold War Letters' which kept up his drumfire against war and social evils and these were sent out to his large mailing list of editors, friends, and admirers" (Laughlin, "Thomas Merton" 24). What J didn't mention in this passage from the long essay he wrote on Merton in 1982 is the role that he himself played in the *samizdat* circulation of these in-fluential "letters" to a wide mailing list by introducing Tom to his friend at the Ford Foundation, W. H. "Ping" Ferry (*SL* 381).

In the midst of being told to cease and desist, Tom proposed to J the publication of a peace paperback and, to the astonishment of all, New Directions published a political polemic on the nuclear arms race, *Breakthrough to Peace*,[22] to which Merton contributed. (He also edited the book though he was not named as the editor to avoid further controversy.) J had always striven for pure political neutrality on the ND list—the fascist Céline and the communist Neruda were both equally welcome *as artists*—but in *Breakthrough* he helped Tom Merton to storm the establishment citadels, with his encouragement and full backing. These last few "snap-shots" of J and Tom illustrate to me the nature of their relationship—they completed each other. J pushed Tom to open himself to the world, to free himself of his self-imposed shackles and engage in the world's struggles and as an artist to break conventional molds and re-create himself as a poet. Meanwhile, Tom offered J, always something of an aesthete, existing beyond the fray, a way to participate in the struggles of his time without being drawn too directly into conflict. He also offered J spiritual balm in a world that seemed to be fracturing.

Another sign of Merton's increasing openness, not only to the secular world but also to other religions, was his interest in Zen Buddhism, which goes back at least to 1955 when Tom asked J for books by D. T. Suzuki. By 1959 Merton and Suzuki were corresponding and J was excited by the idea of publishing their letters around the centerpiece of Suzuki's essay on *Wisdom of the Desert*. Unfortunately the Abbot General of the time (Dom Gabriel Sortais) forbade publication of the exchange as an "inappropriate"

---

22. [Thomas Merton, ed.], *Breakthrough to Peace: Twelve Views on the Threat of Thermonuclear Extermination* (New York: New Directions, 1962).

linkage with a non-believer. Protesting, J wrote Tom that "It seems to me that it is a good thing for members of one religion to learn about others, in order to develop sympathy and understanding" (*SL* 151). So, cleverly side-stepping, J published "their dialogue between East and West" as the profound "Wisdom in Emptiness" in the annual, *New Directions 17* (1961), where it was less conspicuous than as a stand-alone title. Several years later in 1964, Merton was allowed a rare trip out of Gethsemani to meet Suzuki in New York, which J comments was one of the high points of Tom's intellectual life (Laughlin, "Thomas Merton" 12-13). Suzuki gave Tom one of his own Japanese brushes, which led to the hundreds of beautiful brush abstracts that Tom was to do in the next few years, illustrating, among other things, his *Raids on the Unspeakable*.[23] Merton's tribute to Suzuki is the lovely *Zen and the Birds of Appetite* published by New Directions in 1968 which, coming full circle, included "Wisdom in Emptiness."[24]

J, as Merton's co-conspirator in global outreach, was more acutely aware than most that Tom had become "intensely ecumenical." Laughlin wrote that "He knew that the great religions of the world must come to terms with each other. For years he had been reading all he could about the religions of Asia, the Muslims, the Sufis, various cults, even primitive tribes. . . . As these interests grew, so did Tom's urge to get out to Asia to meet religious thinkers there. But this was not possible in the reign of Dom James. However, with the accession of Dom Flavian [Burns] everything changed" (Laughlin, "Thomas Merton" 35-36). (Laughlin doesn't mention that Merton, while deflecting all talk about putting himself forward for election as abbot, quietly championed Burns, his friend and former student.) This led to the invitation Tom received through Dom Jean Leclercq, the influential Benedictine, to attend a conference in Bangkok of leading Asian Catholic monastics interested in monastic renewal. (See the essay in this volume Δby Ian MacNiven on that fateful trip and the great act of personal devotion and tribute that was Laughlin's editing of *The Asian Journal*.) While there has been speculation about Merton's attraction to Buddhism, J was quite clear about the purpose of the trip: "He would try to get to as many of the holy places in the Orient that he had always wanted to visit as he could and talk with spiritual leaders of all faiths, particularly those which practiced contemplation. He wanted to see what these practices might have to offer for Christian contemplation" (Laughlin, "Thomas Merton" 36).

---

23. Thomas Merton, *Raids on the Unspeakable* (New York: New Directions, 1966).

24. Thomas Merton, *Zen and the Birds of Appetite* (New York: New Directions, 1968) 99-138; see also Merton's essay, "D. T. Suzuki: The Man and His Work" (59-66).

So far I have been concentrating on the ways in which Laughlin was helping Merton to stretch and extend himself intellectually and in his breadth of sympathy. What is not as clearly documented, but something that I know from J's casual comments, was how much Merton kept J grounded, through his friendship and his faith in J and his publishing enterprise. J couldn't subscribe to particular religious beliefs, but he did have faith, a faith that "word workers" could make a difference and that writers like Tom could cross the boundaries that so often seemed to keep people in armed and separate camps. If Merton could make common cause with Henry Miller, what other walls might come tumbling down? Fostering such relationships, building such bridges was what Laughlin saw as his own spiritual mission.

But J didn't expect (in MacNiven's words) to become confessor to a monk. You have all read or heard about the young nurse "M" who captured Merton's heart and mind while he was in a Louisville hospital following a back operation in 1966. I say it that way rather than "fell in love" because both Merton's subsequently published journal of this period[25] and the private journals he gave into J's keeping, reveal that what Merton experienced was a feeling of complete spiritual union with another human being, something that, despite his closeness to the Infinite, had eluded him previously.

Tom wrote letters to M, he wrote a journal in which he tried to analyze what had happened, and he wrote poems to and for M. Merton obviously wanted these records of the most important episode in his emotional life to endure, but whom could he trust for their safekeeping? It was to J he immediately turned. In the 1982 manuscript J wrote, "He did not want these papers in his hermitage so he arranged for me to keep them safe for him. Every so often, usually through an intermediary, I would receive an envelope marked for the 'Menendez file' and I would put it in my bank box" (Laughlin, "Thomas Merton" 32; Frank Menendez was the chef at the Alta Lodge, part of the ski resort J owned in Alta, Utah, and he unwittingly lent his name to the coded file). The poems were eventually published (in 1985) as *Eighteen Poems*[26] in an edition limited to 200 copies after J carefully consulted with M—Tom had wanted these poems published, but J was ever respectful of M's privacy and feelings in the matter and thereby tried to limit the circulation of the book as much as possible. My instructions at New Directions were that the book was *never* to be reprinted, *never* to be done in a trade edition, and that permission

---

25. Thomas Merton, *Learning to Love: Exploring Solitude and Freedom. Journals, vol. 6: 1966-1967*, ed. Christine M. Bochen (San Francisco: HarperCollins, 1997).

26. Thomas Merton, *Eighteen Poems* (New York: New Directions, 1985).

to reprint individual poems was to be denied. However, by the time of the publication of the new edition of selected poems, *In the Dark before Dawn*, so many of the poems had appeared in the journals or in unauthorized places that New Directions and the Trustees of the Merton Legacy Trust jointly decided that any poems which had been published elsewhere could be included in that volume.

Merton was also concerned about his literary legacy in general and in 1964, well before the trip to Asia was planned or M had appeared in his life, he had asked J and Naomi Burton Stone to be his literary and artistic executors. And before he embarked on his travels in 1968 he set up the Merton Legacy Trust. J describes the impetus for the Trust this way: "[Tom] was aware from the great success he had had with his books that he was a writer of consequence and he was convinced that certain of his writings would have influence on monastic reform in the future. So he had his friend John Ford, a good lawyer in Louisville, incorporate, as a non-profit trust with the monastery as beneficiary, The Merton Legacy Trust, of which Naomi Burton, Tommie O'Callaghan and myself were the initial trustees. What Tom feared was that at his death his papers might just be packed in cartons and stored in the corner of the monastery library, from where someday some over-zealous housecleaner might throw them away" (Laughlin, "Thomas Merton" 40-41). When word came of Merton's death, Merton's Louisville friend Tommie O'Callaghan drove to Gethsemani and filled her station wagon with these papers, which she soon deposited at Bellarmine College for the collection that has become the Thomas Merton Center at Bellarmine University.

Also before he left, with a sense of tidying affairs, Tom sent J two poetry manuscripts, one of which was the unfinished and ongoing *The Geography of Lograire*[27] (a map of Merton's mind, J liked to say). With an eerie prescience Merton made up a list of things J was to take care of should he die during his travels: finish the notes for *Lograire*, publish any journals or writings from the trip (these became *The Asian Journal*), watch over M's welfare. When the unimaginable happened, J carried out each of these mandates as if it were a sacred commandment. He maintained a watching brief over M, writing to her (in a letter included by David Cooper as an epilogue to the Merton/Laughlin correspondence): "I don't think you should feel, as you say in your letter, that Tom didn't know how devoted you were to him. As I reread the poems and journals, it seems clear to me that he did understand, and that you were as close to him as any mortal person could be. He always spoke to me of you with the deepest affection and gratitude for what you brought to his life" (*SL*

---

27. Thomas Merton, *The Geography of Lograire* (New York: New Directions, 1969).

371). M and J continued to correspond until J's death. Both agreed that Tom had radically changed their lives.

Father Louis and James Laughlin, Tom and J—two unlikely friends who were two parts of a linked story, each representing a road not taken by the other. Tom could not have had a more faithful servant to carry out his wishes, and in fulfilling those mandates, J felt that his own soul had been purified and saved. He ends his rambling 1982 manuscript that became the basis for more polished pieces in an unpolished but heartfelt way: "Dear Tom, if I have said anything in these pages to offend you, please just laugh at me as you always used to do when I said something silly, your laugh that no one could ever forget. Wherever you are, in the heaven for jolly monks, in the 'palace' that Chatral Rimpoche told you about, even a tulku in Tibet, know that our friendship goes on and always will" (Laughlin, "Thomas Merton" 49).

An Interview with James Laughlin
about Thomas Merton

Conducted by Paul Wilkes, March 18, 1983[1]
Transcribed and edited by Paul M. Pearson

Paul Wilkes: Why don't we begin with your describing your first contact with either Thomas Merton or Thomas Merton's words.

James Laughlin: Well, the first contact with his words came through Mark Van Doren and that would have been sometime, I think, in the very late thirties or the early forties and at that time I had been publishing my New Directions books for perhaps four or five years. And I had been a friend of Mark Van Doren who was one of the greatest teachers we have ever had in this country and he was a professor of literature at Columbia. I'd been a friend because he lives just over the mountain from where we are now talking[2] and he of course was one of Thomas Merton's principal professors at Columbia and there was a deep friendship between them. Tom, by then, was down in the monastery and he was continuing to write poetry. He had written poetry since he was quite young. His work at that time was chiefly religious in character because that was about all that the abbot wanted him to write. But he sent a group of these poems—there were thirty poems to be exact—up to Van Doren asking for his advice and criticism. Van Doren liked them very much and thought of me as a possible publisher because I was interested in poetry and I had just done a pamphlet of Van Doren's work a little bit earlier. He sent them to me and I liked them immediately. I thought this was a very exciting and fresh talent.

PW: How did Mark Van Doren recommended this young Trappist poet to you?

JL: Mark Van Doren said he thought this was a very promising poet, that he had a lot of talent, and that he had deep spiritual feeling, and he said that he thought that this was someone I would probably not find out about in the normal course of business, which was certainly true. As I have said, I liked these poems very much; there was a freshness there, there was a

---

1. This interview was conducted by Paul Wilkes in the course of shooting his 1984 film *Merton: A Film Biography*, and parts of it appear in the film; an abbreviated, reordered and rewritten version of the interview is included in Wilkes' volume *Merton by Those Who Knew Him Best* (San Francisco: Harper & Row, 1984) 3-13.

2. Laughlin's home, "Meadow House," was just outside Norfolk, Connecticut.

24

liveliness, there was kind of a verbal sprightliness that was very attractive to me, and they were not like anything that any of the other New Directions poets were writing. There was almost an ingenuous character about them which was very appealing.

PW: You're not an especially religious man—why did they strike you?

JL: It wasn't the Catholic message, which in those early poems was quite strong—I mean there were poems about the night the monastery barn burned up or the portrait of the Virgin in the cloister—I mean this sort of thing didn't really move me very much. What I liked was his imagery and the way he would take a subject like that and then carry it into other metaphors so to speak, and make it colorful and interesting so that I as a heretic, a benighted Calvinist, was able to get some feeling as I never had before of what the Catholic faith was about.

PW: Then came the day when you saw this man for the first time in person—what did you expect to see and what did you see?

JL: When I first met Merton I went down after we had published his first book *Thirty Poems*[3] for him and we corresponded quite a lot and talked about other books that he might write. The abbot invited me to come down to Gethsemani in Kentucky to visit him. This was a very novel experience for me, going into a monastery which, if I followed the precepts of my mother, I would have considered practically a place of the devil. It wasn't at all, it was a wonderful place. It was full of fun and good feeling. I had expected in Merton to meet a somber-faced monk who strode silently through the cloister and into the church muttering prayers under his breath. It wasn't like that at all! From the moment I first came to the monastery gate and was greeted by a very jolly brother gate-keeper I saw that I had been completely misinformed about monasteries; this was a very happy place and Tom Merton was very happy. He was—I suppose this is a word which one may not use anymore—but he was gay, that is to say he had a wonderful gaiety about himself and about life.

PW: How would you express that—I mean what was the quality of it? How did his face look, how did he move?

JL: He wasn't the handsomest man but he was nice looking and he had this wonderful smile and a lovely laugh and he was smiling most of the time. And what I liked about him was his capacity to put himself immediately in touch with you. I mean, when I got down there he was asking me all sorts of questions about what I was doing, and what my background

---

3. Thomas Merton, *Thirty Poems* (Norfolk, CT: New Directions, 1944).

was like, and what I had been involved with in the publishing business. Tom was interested in everything; there was practically no subject at all which he didn't want to know about. He was bubbling with this wonderful enthusiasm. One of the problems, of course, was that he bubbled so much. Not in any stupid or foolish way. Tom would arrive in my cell—he had put me up in the guest house at the monastery—at six o'clock in the morning when I was just about getting my eyes open, with a green sack full of books and all sorts of notes and things that he had thought about during the night that he wanted to discuss with me, and this would go on really all during the day. His correspondence in the archive at Bellarmine shows that he was corresponding with almost every kind of person that you can think of all over the country and even abroad. He would correspond with the young people, young beats and hippies. He would correspond with them about jazz and about all sorts of these subjects. As well he would try to help them solve their spiritual problems.

PW: Let's move to *The Seven Storey Mountain*.[4] When that came out you were a very established publisher at the time; I'm wondering, why was that book such a phenomenal success at that time? It went onto the best seller list—what did it have?

JL: I would say that *The Seven Storey Mountain* had something to say that people were at that moment in our social history ready to hear. It presented an answer to spiritual problems that many people, particularly young people who were upset by the way things were going in the country, who were upset by the threat of the atomic holocaust and all the rest of it, they wanted to hear that and they liked the way Merton put it, so simply and so directly.

PW: What was he saying and what were they hearing from him? What was his message?

JL: Well, at that time, of course, his message was very different from what it later became. Let's see, it would have been twenty years later, he was writing much more as the French would say, *au point*. Later on he was responding directly to Vietnam and the Pentagon and all those things. At that early time, in *The Seven Storey Mountain*, he was responding in personal terms to a kind of spiritual angst, a kind of a spiritual doubt which so many of the young people had. That was his appeal. And it was all done so gently and without any proselytizing. That's the thing that always interested me about Tom. In all the years that I knew him he never tried to convert me to Catholicism, never once did he ever try. If I wanted

---

4. Thomas Merton, *The Seven Storey Mountain* (New York: Harcourt, Brace, 1948).

to ask him a question, and often I did about Catholic doctrine, he would give me a good short answer, but never once was there any attempt to sell me on Catholicism.

PW: That point is very interesting because here was a man who did in fact convert many—millions, hundreds, thousands—and yet never tried to do it in person. How do you reconcile those two things? He would write to your soul but not talk to you?

JL: Well, he wrote what was in his heart and his mind. The things that he felt he wanted to say and also what God wanted him to say. I mean this comes out in his journals, the private journals which are at Bellarmine, which haven't been published yet. In those journals you find some wonderful little [passages], written almost as dialogues where he talks to God and asks God whether he is doing the right thing, and asks for guidance so that he will do better as a writer. Now he doesn't put this in terms of, you know, buying more recruits for the Pope. He puts it, in the sense of, is he communicating to others as it is his desire and his duty to communicate.

PW: Do you think he was a God-inspired man . . . could we say that about Thomas Merton?

JL: Yes, I would say so.

PW: Returning to *The Seven Storey Mountain* and talk within the publishing industry . . .

JL: I think that everybody in the publishing industry was quite amazed that the book had done as well as it did do, and of course it became a great best-seller and has been translated into languages all over the world. I did not publish *The Seven Storey Mountain* for an interesting reason. Tom's agent, Naomi Burton, sent in the manuscript just as I was going off skiing and I didn't think it would make good reading in the mountains so I left it on my desk in New York and told Tom that I would read it when I got home. Well, Tom became a little impatient over that, because I think he realized that he'd written a very important book and so he sent to, I guess it was Bob Giroux then, his old friend from Columbia days at Harcourt, Brace and they published it. But I've always thought that this was really a very good thing for Tom and all concerned because New Directions was a terribly small press in those days and we had almost no promotional facilities, we had very few salesmen and I'm afraid that if we had done the book it simply wouldn't have gotten around and wouldn't have been seen.[5] But, being done by a big firm like Harcourt, it was beautifully

5. This insight is borne out by the *New York Times* Best Seller list for 1949. After

promoted and did get around and had this chance and became a great best-seller so that overnight Tom was famous. It was sort of like what happened to Tennessee Williams the morning after *The Glass Menagerie* was published—suddenly he was famous. And Tom was famous.

PW: Within the publishing industry what was the talk? I mean was it utter amazement or what at the success of this book?

JL: The way *The Seven Storey Mountain* became a bestseller, I don't think it was utter amazement in the publishing industry. I think there was amazement. I'm sure if one looked up the old records at Harcourt, Brace you would find that the first printing was a small one because they simply did not anticipate, they hadn't you know, tested the water, they didn't realize that there was this hunger for a book of what you might call self-redemption, or finding one's way on life's path in a difficult ambiance, or however you want to put it.

PW: We are going to deal with two things now; one is his growth as a writer, and then as a poet. As a writer was *The Seven Storey Mountain*, as you look back on it, kind of a green book? It seems a little too effervescent or something as I read it now. I read it twenty years ago. How do you feel about it? Was this a book that was good in its time and stayed there and the beat went on from it, or is it a classic that will go on forever?

JL: I think that *The Seven Storey Mountain* is certainly a classic. Whether it is a literary classic of the same level say, as *The Confessions of St. Augustine*, or something of that kind, I can't judge, and only time can judge it. There are faults in the book. There are points where it becomes a little bit preachy, which I just skip when I reread it. What is good is his story—the story of his life, of his heart, of his mind. And this is told vividly and compactly and effectively. And I think that's what put the book across. Now you ask whether *The Seven Storey Mountain* was a "green" book—I don't know quite what you mean by a "green" book. It certainly had, as I say, these little faults. But his writing took off and grew from that point. One might say that *The Seven Storey Mountain* is in some respects slightly undisciplined. Later, in his later books, particularly in the journal books, which came after, he disciplined himself a bit more, and held

---

entering the list in December 1948 *The Seven Storey Mountain* would remain on the list for every single week of 1949 and into 1950. *The Waters of Siloe*, also published by Harcourt, Brace, would enter the list at the beginning of October 1949 and remain on it for the rest of the year, spending three weeks in second position. In comparison, *Seeds of Contemplation*, published by New Directions, would only spend two weeks on the list, reaching only fourteenth place.

closely to the track. He also gained greatly in writing style. Merton was a natural writer. He had written at Columbia, and perhaps even before that. I have read the dissertation which he wrote at Columbia for his Master's degree, an essay on Blake.[6] It's very well written, very well thought out. There's a control of language there. There's a knowledge of what he is doing with language and what he wants to do. Now, this grew consistently throughout his life—what one would call his professionalism, his craft as a writer grew continually. And he got better and better as he went on. And that was why I felt it was so, just tragic, and I couldn't understand it, when he died as young as he did, because his powers were increasing all the time. And if he'd only lived, he would have written more really great books. But, God's will . . .

PW: These private journals that you talked about—why aren't they published and what's their special quality.[7]

JL: Tom's private journals—and I should say, he did two kinds of journals. He was a prodigious worker, and a very fast writer. And at any time you would find—when I would go down there to visit him—that he'd be working on two sets of journals. One would be the journals which would later be made into books, with a good deal of cutting and polishing, and then the others were these private journals which he kept in big, as I remember, they were black ledgers. And these were his very personal thoughts, like his diary. The public journals were written for publication, the private journals were written just for his own dialogue with himself.

---

6. "Nature and Art in William Blake: An Essay in Interpretation" (1939), in *The Literary Essays of Thomas Merton*, ed. Patrick Hart, OCSO (New York: New Directions, 1981) 385-453.

7. In Merton's Legacy Trust agreement he instructed his Trustees that "after the completion of my biography . . . and after twenty-five years from the date of my death, the Trustees are to publish said holographic notebooks, journals and diaries in whole or in part, according to their judgment." Beginning in 1995, the private journals referred to here have now all been published: *Run to the Mountain: The Story of a Vocation. Journals, vol. 1: 1939-1941*, ed. Patrick Hart (San Francisco: HarperCollins, 1995); *Entering the Silence: Becoming a Monk and Writer. Journals, vol. 2: 1941-1952*, ed. Jonathan Montaldo (San Francisco: HarperCollins, 1996); *A Search for Solitude: Pursuing the Monk's True Life. Journals, vol. 3: 1952-1960*, ed. Lawrence S. Cunningham (San Francisco: HarperCollins, 1996); *Turning Toward the World: The Pivotal Years. Journals, vol. 4: 1960-1963*, ed. Victor A. Kramer (San Francisco: HarperCollins, 1996); *Dancing in the Water of Life: Seeking Peace in the Hermitage. Journals, vol. 5: 1963-1965*, ed. Robert E. Daggy (San Francisco: HarperCollins, 1997); *Learning to Love: Exploring Solitude and Freedom. Journals, vol. 6: 1966-1967*, ed. Christine M. Bochen (San Francisco: HarperCollins, 1997); *The Other Side of the Mountain: The End of the Journey. Journals, vol. 7: 1967-1968*, ed. Patrick Hart (San Francisco: HarperCollins, 1998).

The quality of them is, as I say, very free, very frank—he's often, quite often talking to God, and asking advice from God. He's often in them worrying about whether he is a good contemplative. More than that, he is worrying about when is he going to get a great mystical experience.

PW: Did he ever?

JL: He did. If you read the end of *The Asian Journal*, when he got to Polonnaruwa—which is that place in Ceylon[8] where there are these enormous hundred-foot long reclining Buddhas—I think, if you read those pages in *The Asian Journal*, you will be convinced, as I was, that he had had his great mystical experience. Now, it's ironic that it was Buddhism, and the art of Buddhism, which brought him these experiences, and not something in the monastery or in the Catholic faith. But that's how things happen. And he was so ecumenical, you see, he was interested in all religions. He was interested even in Islam, and Sufism and all kinds of different religions. And to me it's rather beautiful that this great experience came to him as a result of his ecumenism, because he would never have gone to Ceylon unless he had read Buddhist texts at the monastery.

PW: What do you think the message is in that? You know, you talk about ecumenism, and usually you have the Protestant minister come to the Catholic Church, but this is really way out there. What do you think that means, that he had it within that whole other culture and experience that we don't really know much about?

JL: Well, I think it was several things. Merton had this mystical experience at Polonnaruwa in Ceylon, I think, because he had always been so open to spiritual forces of all kinds. In his readings, as you read the journals and other books, you see this constant openness to other traditions. And then, beyond that, it was simply that he had read a great many Buddhist texts. I mean, he knew the *Dhammapada*, the great Buddhist text, almost by heart—he was completely open to these things. And then, when he saw this place—I wish I had time to read to you just a paragraph or two from that part of *The Asian Journal*—because I can't begin to express what he told us happened to him with his beauty of phrase and his nobility of utterance. I mean it is simply a lovely passage where looking at these Buddhas in their massive tranquility, he felt that he had at last come to the place where time stopped. And he was a part of the larger spiritual universe. He felt that as he saw these figures. This is the beautiful passage

---

8. Upon renouncing its status as a British Dominion and becoming a republic in 1972 Ceylon became known as Sri Lanka.

from *The Asian Journal* where Merton talks about his mystic experience at Polonnaruwa in Ceylon:

> I am able to approach the Buddhas barefoot and undisturbed, my feet in wet grass, wet sand. Then the silence of the extraordinary faces. The great smiles. Huge and yet subtle. Filled with every possibility, questioning nothing, knowing everything, rejecting nothing, the peace not of emotional resignation but of Madhyamika, of sunyata, that has seen through every question without trying to discredit anyone or anything—*without refutation*—without establishing some other argument. For the doctrinaire, the mind that needs well-established positions, such peace, such silence, can be frightening. I was knocked over with a rush of relief and thankfulness at the *obvious* clarity of the figures, the clarity and fluidity of shape and line, the design of the monumental bodies composed into the rock shape and landscape, figure, rock and tree. And the sweep of bare rock sloping away on the other side of the hollow, where you can go back and see different aspects of the figures.

Lovely, isn't it?

> Looking at these figures I was suddenly, almost forcibly, jerked clean out of the habitual, half-tied vision of things, and an inner clearness, clarity, as if exploding from the rocks themselves, became evident and obvious. The queer *evidence* of the reclining figure, the smile, the sad smile of Ananda[9] standing with arms folded (much more "imperative" than Da Vinci's Mona Lisa because completely simple and straightforward). The thing about all this is that there is no puzzle, no problem, and really no "mystery." All problems are resolved and everything is clear, simply because what matters is clear. The rock, all matter, all life, is charged with dharmakaya . . . everything is emptiness and everything is compassion. I don't know when in my life I have ever had such a sense of beauty and spiritual validity running together in one aesthetic illumination. Surely, with Mahabalipuram and Polonnaruwa my Asian pilgrimage has come clear and purified itself. I mean, I know and have seen what I was obscurely looking for. I don't know what else remains but I have now seen and have

---

9. Merton was mostly likely following an older guide book which would have described the seven-meter-high standing image of the Buddha as an image of Ananda, the Buddha's disciple, mourning the Buddha's departure for Nirvana. But with more recent discoveries of other images with the same unusual arm positions, it is now generally accepted that this is also an image of the Buddha.

pierced through the surface and have got beyond the shadow and the disguise. This is Asia in its purity, not covered over with garbage, Asian or European or American, and it is clear, pure, complete. It says everything; it needs nothing. And because it needs nothing it can afford to be silent, unnoticed, undiscovered. It does not need to be discovered. It is we, Asians included, who need to discover it.[10]

Now there of course we have in Tom Merton's magnificent language—and with always his sense of the poetry of the language present—we have his statement of this very deep spiritual and aesthetic experience which occurred to him in Ceylon, and which I think profoundly altered the last parts of his life.

PW: Now you knew him as a man and a writer—what did it really mean to him? What really happened there?

JL: Well, he had, I'm convinced, a mystical experience. The sort of thing that other mystics have had—St. John of the Cross, Sister Teresa, the lady down in Spain—they all had these great mystical experiences, and other mystical writers in many faiths have had these experiences. It is an experience which unfortunately I never expect to have, where you suddenly lose your identity in the greater identity of the spiritual cosmos. And this can happen in any religion. It happens to Hindus, it happens to Buddhists, it happens in Islam, it can happen in any culture.

PW: It's interesting in his writings that he always said, "Don't seek that mystical experience; it will find you." Had he sought it do you think?

JL: Oh, I'm sure that he sought it. Every contemplative who prays a lot, who meditates a lot—that's what they are seeking. But I think if they are humble and they know the literature of mysticism, they will know that this is something you can't reach out and take. You can prepare for it— through many years you can prepare for it. After all, the Tibetan monk training to be a monk in his cave in Tibet, used to prostrate himself a hundred thousand times, a complete prostration, calling out "Om Mani Padme Hum," which means "the jewel at the heart of the lotus." And you can seek it, but you only get it if God or Buddha or whoever is the power, wants you to have it. I know that Tom wanted it, but he was also humble, and he knew his place, and he talked a great deal about grace. Grace is the Catholic term, I think, to describe when a person is granted this sort of illumination.

---

10. Thomas Merton, *The Asian Journal*, ed. Naomi Burton Stone, Brother Patrick Hart and James Laughlin (New York: New Directions, 1973) 233, 235-36.

PW: Throughout his life and in so many of the books, he writes of having come home. "I've found my home in Gethsemani." Tell us about Merton's continual coming home and never being home?

JL: Yes, Gethsemani was his home. You see, I think he'd lost all his family early, except for his grandparents. He'd had a good home with the grandparents in Long Island, but it wasn't quite the same thing as a final home, a place where you stay for the rest of your life. And that's what he wanted Gethsemani to be for him. And I remember I talked with him a few times about this when we were on my visits there; I would rent a car and the abbot would let him go off for the day, and we'd drive through the country, and talk about things, or take walks or go to visit some good friend of his. And I once asked him—Tom had been grousing a little bit, he could grouse—about the restrictions at the monastery, and how he disliked the cheese business, and how he disliked the junky stuff in the store which sold little crucifixes or rosaries to the tourists, and you know, he was grousing a bit about the monastery. And I said, "Well, Tom, if it gives you this much pain, why do you stay there? After all, you're a brilliant writer, you could go out in the world, you could still do your spiritual teaching, you'd be a very successful writer, why do you stay there?" And he said, "You don't understand—that's where I belong. That is my home." And even at the end, following later than that in his life, there were many times when he got annoyed with things at the monastery, with the conditions. I know that he used to complain a lot about all the conversation in the monastery. Now we think of the Trappists as not talking, but that isn't so, not necessarily so, as the song says. These Trappist monks, they talk sign language to each other, and they're going all day with this sign language, and he said he didn't want to be bothered with that. It was interfering with his meditation and his work, so that he wanted to get off and be a hermit. Of course, there's a curious contradiction there, kind of a dichotomy, or you might almost say a split personality, that this man was constantly wanting to be a hermit, to get further and further away from everything. At one time he tried to get to be a hermit down in, I think it was in Cuernavaca, Mexico, and he was corresponding with a bishop who had invited him to come down there. He was going to live in a cave with the ravens, you know, and administer to the poor Indians. Well, I just wonder if he had done that, how much he would have missed these interesting intellectual visits that he had from Catholic churchmen such as Maritain, and writers from all over the country who would come to see him. From people such as Nicanor Parra, the Chilean anti-poet. I don't think he would have stuck it out very long if he were really a hermit. But this was a constant obsession with him and that's why after Father Flavian became abbot, and was more permissive in trips, he went out to California where he and Ping Ferry and his wife drove him around to see places there on the Redwoods shore where he might have a hermitage.

PW: We talked a bit about the changes in his life, and how at first he was very, very humble and then, as he became successful, there was a different Thomas Merton.

JL: There was a definite change in the, sort of the inner climate of Merton's life. When he first came to the monastery, he had all the proper attitudes of a postulant, and then as a novice, and then as a young priest. He was humble, he was obedient, he fully believed that whatever the abbot said was what he should do. But later on as he became more mature, in my view, and he had his success and realized his powers as a writer—you see, I don't think that early on he knew whether he was going to be a good writer or not. I think that he smelled in the success of *The Seven Storey Mountain*, a certain element somehow of sensational publicity. You know, wicked young man runs off to monastery to save soul. But as he, with his other books, realized what he could do with his writing, this gave him more confidence to be himself. So that he was less willing to put up with restrictions, or some bishop writing in to the abbot and telling him what he could write and what he couldn't write. Now, this never took, at least with me, the form of vanity, or of arrogance. It was just a kind of an inner determination that he was going to, in his writings, work out what was still God's will, more than his will. As Merton matured and became more self-confident, there was—I wouldn't call it a personality change—it was rather a change in his adjustment to his surroundings and to life. He never became, to me at least, he never seemed vain, he never seemed arrogant; it was rather a change in his self-evaluation and how he would best work out, through his writings, what he had decided God wanted him to do. Now, here of course came up one of the considerable battles with the abbot. It was also my battle. That is, when Tom began to get interested in social conditions. You see, he was a leader in the non-segregation movement. He was a leader against the Vietnam War. I mean he was speaking for possibly, I don't know, hundreds of thousands, millions of Catholics, who didn't like the way things were going. He got interested in these movements. Well, then there was a big friction, because when he would write these articles attacking the Pentagon or something the Catholic bishops, who were not then like they are now— I mean now they are, you know, they've seen the light, and they're quite marvelous—they would write in to the abbot and say, "You must restrain this man; he's a monk. All he's supposed to do is pray, and he has no business to be concerning himself with social movements and the Vietnam War" and so forth. And Tom didn't like this very much at all. I had, not an argument, but I just accosted the abbot one day as he was coming across the field, his robes were blowing in the wind, he looked very handsome and beautiful, he looked like something out of a Winslow Homer painting—and I said, "Father Abbot, could I have a word?" and he said, "Yes, James," and I said, "Father, now you've really got to let Tom"—Father Louis, I would have called him to the abbot—"you've got to let him go on being slightly political." And Dom James said to me: "James," he said, "you don't understand. Tom's work and the work of all of us monks is to pray, and our prayers will go up to heaven and God will hear them, and God will fix up the troubles in the world." Well, I was polite, and I didn't say the short word. I just said, "OK." But that was his problem, and you see the Catholic bishops did bring all this heat on the abbot, and so the abbot—they had quite a long discussion and Tom agreed—that he would stop attacking the Pentagon and stop this political writing. But of course he had a very ingenious way to get around this, which was that he didn't publish publicly, but he published privately. And there's a whole series of marvelous writings which are called the "Cold War Letters."[11] Now, these are letters on all these controversial subjects. And Tom would write these things, and then he would get his friends in the novitiate to type them out and mimeograph them and then he would send them to a large and increasingly growing mailing list of people all around the country who would get his views and his word on these subjects. So they had quite a circulation because people would quote from them, you see, and they would have an influence. But he did in the form, if not in the substance, he obeyed the rules.

PW: Why do you feel that his works, *The Seven Storey Mountain*, of course, being the beginning, touched and continue to touch people? What's the quality of it that you, as an editor, would see in them? Why did people keep reading him? What did he have?

JL: Well, once you've been bitten by Merton, you will go on reading him, and read everything you can—that's the secret. Now, how he actually did it, who knows? I mean, do any of us know what is the particular magic that a great or even a fine writer has? This is something that is combusting inside of him. And it is coming out in fine language, clear thought and persuasive communication. He is touching people's minds and hearts. Now, I can't analyze his works and tell you how he did it. If I did know

---

11. Thomas Merton, *Cold War Letters*, ed. Christine M. Bochen and William H. Shannon (Maryknoll, NY: Orbis, 2006).

how he did it, I would write the same kind of books and become famous myself. But, this is something again that we get, or that we are born with, and then we can do it if we are writers.

PW: How would you place him in the writers of that mystical tradition—spiritual writers, social prophets—what is his place? What kind of company should he be in?

JL: Well, he comes out, let's see, he comes out of a long tradition of religious writers who were more than commentators. People who had something original and personal to say which raised them above the lump of just commentary writers about religion or theologians quibbling over this small point or that small point, whether the Athanasians were right, or whether the Albigensians were right, or that sort of thing. He belongs in a more personal tradition, and I would have to give you those names, I would have to go down and look at the shelf to pick them up again. Well one man that he liked very much was St. Clement of Alexandria. He translated him.[12] And it was that type of mystical theological writer who interested him. It isn't limited to the Catholic tradition. I mean, there are many in England, there are many mystical writers who were extremely powerful: George Herbert, for example, a poet, and there are a number of others. That is the tradition that he belongs in, and which he learned from, because he read all those people early on.

PW: At the end of his life you felt he was coming back to the world in some way. Tell us about what was happening in his own life and what that was about?

JL: Well, I would say that definitely with this change in self-confidence, there came a tendency to find out more about what was going on in the world. You see, in the early days, the only news of the world that the monks got from Dom James was at chapter in the early morning when Dom James would relay to them anything that he had heard over the radio, or read in the paper, that he thought was proper for them to hear. Well, this was not, shall we say, a complete journalistic coverage of the world situation. As he grew in self-confidence and grew in his interests of the other things that he wanted to know about, Tom went toward, what I would call a more open life. Now this was difficult, really until Dom Flavian became abbot—an old friend of Tom's who had similar views—who believed that the monks should know what was going on in the world and then should have some intellectual contact with what

---

12. Thomas Merton, *Clement of Alexandria: Selections from* The Protreptikos (New York: New Directions, 1962).

good writers were reading.

PW: Tell us about the other Thomas Merton and being a friend?

JL: Thomas Merton was a wonderful friend. One reason was that he was truly interested in his friends and he would bring them out more than talk to them. He wasn't at all a lecture-y person in any way. I mean, he'd tell you something if you asked, but he really was interested in people. He was deeply interested in people. And I loved to go down there and visit him in the monastery because frankly, we just had such good times. And when I'd go down there I'd usually pick up a car, at the rental car at the Louisville Airport, and then I'd drive down, and the next day Father Abbot would have given him permission to go out with me for the day. Tom would usually start out very circumspectly; he would go into the old bishop's store room and he would find an old bishop's suit and he would put that on and he would exit from the monastery, so as not to shock the gate-keeper, looking very ecclesiastical. Then we would get out a few miles and he'd stop by the woods and he'd say, "Stop here"; then he would go into the woods and he would take off his bishop's suit and he would put on his blue jeans and his old sweater and his beret. And then we would head east, stopping, I must say, at a few beer parlors on the way, where Tom always was very popular with the local farmers. He knew how to talk to all kinds of people and they found him funny and they liked him. So we'd usually then head on over to Lexington where we would visit with and have lunch with his wonderful old friend, the great Austrian artist and philosopher, and the great hand-printer, Victor Hammer, and that was always a great occasion. Carolyn Hammer, Victor's American wife, would put on a superb little gourmet lunch for us and, again, there would be an excellent bottle of wine which Tom would down with evident relish and would never seem to feel any effects of it. I mean, I would walk out of the Hammers' barely able to stand up and Tom would stride ahead straight on the lawn. It was very curious—he had no allergy to alcohol. Then we would usually stop on our way back, we'd stop at other places, often at that beautiful Shakertown where he loved the old buildings and the old Shaker furniture and the stories about those people.

PW: Let's move to his poetry for a minute, which is something which is, of course, very close to your heart. Tell me about his growth as a poet, moving on up to that period when he really started talking about peace and justice in the world and stuff like that?

JL: I think there must have been earlier childhood poems that I haven't seen, and I think he also did some humorous writing for the *Columbia*

Spectator,[13] I believe it was called, the magazine at Columbia College. He started writing poetry before he was converted to Catholicism, but it wasn't religious poetry. And then, after he got into the monastery, the only kind of poetry that the abbot wanted him to write, thought it proper for him to write, was religious poetry. Now, these early religious poems, as I've said earlier, are not quite my dish because, I suppose, just because I'm not a Catholic, and they were certainly not as good as somebody like George Herbert or somebody like Hopkins. But they have a lot of passion, a lot of feeling for what he is writing about. And of that period, I suppose, the most famous one and the most beautiful, is the poem in memory of his brother who was killed in the war.[14] And this is a very beautiful and great poem by anybody's standards. However, later as he matured and became more secular in his interests, and as the censorship on him, or to put it rather, the direction on him, was diminished from on top, he began to write a different kind of poetry, which was more concerned with what was happening outside the monastery than what was happening inside the monastery and inside him. There is a profound and notable change in Merton's poetry about 1963 when his book *Emblems of a Season of Fury*[15] was published. This was the first time he felt that he could write about social and political themes and get away with it. But in writing about these themes his treatment was always extremely metaphorical and extremely poetic. Now, there was one very great poem, it's a long poem, I can't read all of it, but I'd like to read a little bit of it for you. It is called "Chant to Be Used in Processions around a Site with Furnaces." Now, this is his poem about the German concentration camps and about the Holocaust. And it is written with a wonderful kind of ingenuous irony, such as he later used in his political poem "Original Child Bomb,"[16] which was about the atom bomb. He's using a technique here which Pound used in his "mask form"[17] where he is speaking through the mouth of one of the Nazi executioners in a concentration camp. This is the Nazi speaking:

---

13. Merton contributed a small number of news items to the *Columbia Spectator*; however, his humorous writing, including poetry, and his cartoons would appear in the *Columbia Jester*.

14. "For My Brother: Reported Missing in Action, 1943." *The Collected Poems of Thomas Merton* (New York: New Directions, 1977) 35-36; subsequent references will be cited as "*CP*" in the notes.

15. Thomas Merton, *Emblems of a Season of Fury* (New York: New Directions, 1963); subsequent references will be cited as "*ESF*" in the notes.

16. Thomas Merton, *Original Child Bomb* (New York: New Directions, 1962); *CP* 291-302.

17. In much lyric poetry the poem is in the voice of the author. With Pound's "mask form" the speaker is another character with whom the poet did not necessarily identify.

How we made them sleep and purified them

How we perfectly cleaned up the people and worked a big heater

I was the commander I made improvements and installed a guaranteed system taking account of human weakness I purified and I remained decent

How I commanded

I made cleaning appointments and then I made the travellers sleep and after that I made soap

I was born into a Catholic family but as these people were not going to need a priest I did not become a priest I installed a perfectly good machine it gave satisfaction to many

When trains arrived the soiled passengers received appointments for fun in the bathroom they did not guess

It was a very big bathroom for two thousand people it awaited arrival and they arrived safely

There would be an orchestra of merry widows not all the time much art

If they arrived at all they would be given a greeting card to send home taken care of with good jobs wishing you would come to our joke

Another improvement I made was I built the chambers for two thousand invitations at a time the naked votaries were disinfected with Zyklon B[18]

You see you get in there already a touch of what was to come later in the anti-poetry of *Cables to the Ace*[19] and of *The Geography of Lograire*,[20] where you get the humor, and you get him suddenly throwing a word out saying that the prisoners in the concentration camp would write home to their families, invite them to come to their "joke." This kind of black humor crops up consistently in his later work.

PW: Tell us a little about *The Geography of Lograire.*

JL: Yes, the transitional step between *Emblems* and *The Geography of Lograire* was the book *Cables to the Ace*. Now, here he was very much

---

18. *ESF* 43-47; *CP* 345-46.

19. Thomas Merton, *Cables to the Ace* (New York: New Directions, 1968).

20. Thomas Merton, *The Geography of Lograire* (New York: New Directions, 1969); subsequent references will be cited as "*GL*" in the notes.

influenced[21] by my friend, the Chilean poet Nicanor Parra, known as the anti-poet, whom I took down to Gethsemani to meet Merton and they became great friends and corresponded. Now, I have never quite understood what Parra is talking about when he's an anti-poet because it sounds to me just like an ordinary vitriolic poem. But Merton was right on wave-length with him and [we see] the great influence of this chap Parra in the *Cables to the Ace*. But the poem of his which I find the greatest, and the most liberated, and the most extraordinary, is the first book of his long poem *The Geography of Lograire*. Now this was going to be his work in progress, it was going to be his *Cantos*, such as Pound wrote; it was going to be his *Paterson*, such as W. C. Williams wrote; and he expected to be working on it for the rest of his life and it might be a thousand pages long. The title *Lograire* is a code word that he made up. It comes of course from *Logos*, the Greek for "the word," the poet speaking. It comes also from Villon,[22] the French poet's family name, *Des Loges*. It also comes out of Arthurian romance, where it might have been a mythical country in the Arthur legend. The geography is simply his mind. What he is going to tell us in this poem is everything that went on in the geography of his mind, everything that he had read, everything that he remembered, but all distilled into these marvelous, compact, almost symbolic poems. He only completed the one volume, of course, because he died. When he went off to Asia he left the first volume with me and he said, that if anything happens to me, I want you to publish this, and we did. I think it's a superb long poem. It's very varied in its content. He had read widely in history, in anthropology and all sorts of subjects. But the point is what he could do with this material, how he could shape it to his own ends, and the really great use that he made of parody, where he would parody some earlier writer. Or the use that he made with myth, when he would take anthropological myths, such as the stories about the cargo cults in Melanesia, and make marvelous, tight, little but rich poems about them. And I think that this poem will eventually be recognized as one of the great modern personal epics along with the *Cantos* and *Paterson*.

PW: As the last thing could we have a little reading from *The Geography of Lograire*?

---

21. In a June 1965 letter to Parra Merton writes, "you will find that before knowing your work I had written some antipoems, for example 'Chant to Be Used in Processions...'" (Thomas Merton, *The Courage for Truth: Letters to Writers*, ed. Christine M. Bochen [New York: Farrar, Straus, Giroux, 1993] 213). This suggests that Merton's antipoetic style, certainly initially, developed independently of Parra's influence.

22. François Villon was born in Paris in 1431. He was banished from Paris in 1463 for brawling and never heard from again.

JL: Merton used parody in a very effective way in *The Geography of Lograire*. He used it for humor and he also used it for satirical comment and one of the funniest ones, I think, is a section of the poem about the old Mexican Indians which he based on the books of Covarrubias[23] mostly, and here he does something that was typical of him. In writing about these beautiful ladies in ancient Mexico he went to copies of *The New Yorker* magazine. I don't know how exactly *The New Yorker* magazine got into the monastery, but it must have, because I have checked through and I find that many of the lines in what I am going to read you I can find in old advertisements in *The New Yorker* for ladies' clothes, perfume and other female finery. So here's a little section from "The Ladies of Tlatilco":

> The ladies of Tlatilco
> Wore nothing but turbans
> (Skirts only for a dance)
> A lock of hair over the eyes
> Held only by a garland
> Tassels and leaves
> They bleached their black hair
> With lime
> Like the Melanesians.
>
> Feminine figurines with two heads or with four eyes and ears
> Two noses or doublemouth on the same head
> "Reminiscent of Picasso
> Perhaps connected with idea of twins."
>
> A most provocative perfume
> Wicked wicked charms
> Natural spray dispenser
> A special extract
> For four-eyed ladies of fashion
> MY SIN
> "And my most wicked provocative lewd
>   dusting-powder excitements."
> (Two noses on the same head)[24]

Now, you see what he's doing there, is that he is playing off those wonderful one-eyed or two-eyed ladies of Picasso with the ads from *The New Yorker* magazine, and he was an expert at doing this. This is what we call,

---

23. Miguel Covarrubias [1904-1957], *Indian Art of Mexico and Central America* (New York: Knopf, 1957).
24. *GL* 28; *CP* 484.

in the beanery trade,[25] the juxtaposition of incongruities, but Merton does it with more humor than ever a Pound or Williams or any of the others did it with. This is one of Merton's funny poems—it's about the cheese business down at the monastery which he never liked very much. It's modeled, as you'll see, on Joyce Kilmer's poem "Trees," and there's a very nice typographical touch, when he is spelling cheese in the title he has not an "S" but a dollar sign.

CHEE$E

Joyce Killer-Diller

I think that we should never freeze
Such lively assets as our cheese:

The sucker's hungry mouth is pressed
Against the cheese's caraway breast

A cheese, whose scent like sweet perfume
Pervades the house through every room.

A cheese that may at Christmas wear
A suit of cellophane underwear,

Upon whose bosom is a label,
Whose habitat:—The Tower of Babel.

Poems are nought but warmed-up breeze,
Dollars are made by Trappist Cheese.[26]

---

25. Laughlin referred to universities and colleges as "beaneries." Therefore "the beanery trade" would have referred to academe in general. I am grateful to Peggy Fox, former President of New Directions, for clarifying Laughlin's use of this term.

26. *CP* 799-800.

More Than Scribe: James Laughlin, Thomas Merton and *The Asian Journal*

Ian S. MacNiven

James Laughlin was the founder of the New Directions Publishing Corporation that, by the time of Thomas Merton's death in 1968, had already published all of his poetry and many of his prose works. The role that Laughlin assumed in the case of *The Asian Journal* was far more than that of amanuensis, of scribe: in fact, his creative hand forged the text as it would be published. Each New Directions book includes the chaste notation, "published for James Laughlin"; but Laughlin would step in as editor or designer or publicist, or indeed any other role, whenever he thought it necessary. Given the chaotic state of the Asian travel writings handed over to Laughlin, this would prove his most intensive involvement on a Merton volume during their long association.

Before setting out on his Asian journey, Merton, Father Louis—Tom to his old friend, whom he called J—had told Laughlin that, in the unlikely event that anything catastrophic happened, any drafts and manuscripts written during the trip were to be handed over to him. When Merton was accidentally electrocuted outside Bangkok on December 10, his body was returned to America on a U.S. Air Force jet that also contained, ironically yet fittingly, the bodies of American service personnel killed in Vietnam, in a conflict that Father Louis had vigorously opposed. With his body came a small brown traveling case containing the notebooks and other papers that he had written on his trip. This case was turned over to J Laughlin.

Ordinarily, Laughlin was content to remain anonymously on the sideline, his work on a book unmentioned. But when Brother Patrick Hart, the editor of *The Other Side of the Mountain*, the seventh and final volume of Merton's *Journals*, which incorporates three previously published Merton texts, *Woods, Shore, Desert*,[1] *Thomas Merton in Alaska*[2] and *The Asian Journal*,[3] mentioned Laughlin in what struck him as a bit too perfunctory a tribute, he was upset. Brother Patrick had written:

---

1. Thomas Merton, *Woods, Shore, Desert: A Notebook, May 1968*, ed. Joel Weishaus (Santa Fe, NM: Museum of New Mexico Press, 1982).

2. Thomas Merton, *Thomas Merton in Alaska: The Alaskan Conferences, Journals, and Letters*, ed. Robert E. Daggy (New York: New Directions, 1989) 1-36.

3. Thomas Merton, *The Asian Journal*, ed. Naomi Burton Stone, Brother Patrick Hart and James Laughlin (New York: New Directions, 1973); subsequent references will be cited as "*AJ*" parenthetically in the text.

43

"James Laughlin in particular must be singled out for a word of special thanks, since he did the lion's share of the research and negotiations on the original manuscript of *The Asian Journal*."[4] To J, who had spent the better part of three years on the text, this seemed a very small portion indeed for the lion. His lifelong habit of self-deprecation and his modesty prevented a more forceful assertion of his claim on the final text, but to his then vice-president at New Directions and his literary executor, Peggy Fox, he typed out a crisp note on December 12, 1994, under the impression that *The Asian Journal* would become the entire seventh and final volume of the *Journals*. "I can't stand in the way of this project," he wrote in some distress, "but it is perhaps an opportunity to state my claim that I *wrote* the book, page by page, turning Tom's jumbled notes into his style, doing the glossary and notes." The vehemence of J's claim of authorship arose in part because he felt that his work on *The Asian Journal* had been *the* major accomplishment of his entire literary career. "Perhaps I'm being petty," he continued, "but it galls me that I've never had any recognition from Catholic academics, and precious little from Gethsemani."[5]

It was not a case of mere petty professional jealousy on J's part: it was as if his friendship with Tom had been somehow undervalued. And there was more to it than that. Laughlin had been devastated by Tom's death, so much so that he had found himself unable to face his burial service at Gethsemani. Instead, he came to the monastery soon after it to hold his own private communion with the spirit of his friend. A lapsed Presbyterian, J had hitched his attempts to resolve his religious quest for salvation onto Tom's faith, telling Father Louis of his own chronic doubts and seeking his advice on prayer and religious meditation.

In the traumatic weeks that followed, Dom Flavian Burns, the Abbot of Gethsemani, had Merton's cassocks burned because he was afraid that relic hunters would break into the abbey. For J, the most bizarre happening was the appearance in his New York office of a wild-eyed woman who announced that Merton had been reborn as a *tulku*, a reincarnated master of Tibetan Buddhism, and that Laughlin must leave at once for Tibet to find the baby and bring him to America.

Much has been written about Merton's supposed premonition of his death in Asia—"If I just die of amebic dysentery on the banks of the Ganges, that in itself would be superb," Tom wrote gaily to J, adding as

    4. Thomas Merton, *The Other Side of the Mountain: The End of the Journey. Journals, vol. 7: 1967-1968*, ed. Patrick Hart (San Francisco: HarperCollins, 1998) xi; subsequent references will be cited as "*OSM*" parenthetically in the text.

    5. James Laughlin to Peggy L. Fox, December 12, 1994 (New Directions [ND] correspondence files).

an afterthought, "Though doubtless unpleasant."[6] Predictably, given the sensational aspect of his actual death, a quantum of conspiracy theories sprang up. But the circumstances of Merton's life in the years and months preceding his journey point rather to his eagerness for new knowledge and new experiences than to a desire to escape from the Cistercians. His wish to study Asiatic modes of meditation had been given great impetus through his meeting in 1964 with the aged Zen philosopher Daisetz T. Suzuki,[7] and their important collaboration, *Zen and the Birds of Appetite*,[8] had been published by New Directions in January, 1968. With his ever-increasing fame, the three years of Merton's private hermitage on the grounds of Gethsemani had proved a disappointment when it came to solitude and meditation. Some of it was his fault: he found it difficult to refuse writing and speaking engagements, and his innate politeness made him susceptible to drop-in visitors who hiked in from the highway, and to the four college girls who came by appointment in a group to interview him (which led to beer, and a bottle of bourbon—probably Heaven Hill—bought by Father Louis) (see *OSM* 75-76 [April 6, 1968]). Then too, there was the noise problem: local hunters and gun enthusiasts had set up an impromptu shooting range at a lake adjacent to the abbey property, and his last journal records incessant barrages of gunfire, unsettling especially to pacifist Tom.

Finally, there was a real opportunity for him to break loose, to travel. Abbot James Fox had kept Merton on a short leash for two decades; now he was succeeded by Father Flavian Burns. Merton had campaigned for Father Flavian's election—Father Louis had been afraid that his more conservative colleagues would never accept Father Flavian. "What a difference between Father Flavian, as abbot, and Dom James," Merton wrote; "I get a real sense of openness. . . . One slowly comes back to life, with the realization that all things are possible" (*OSM* 139 [July 5, 1968]).

Suddenly so many ventures became possible: a hermitage in Alaska (the Bishop of Alaska offered help); meetings with Buddhists in Nepal, India, Thailand; even a visit to Merton's elderly Aunt Kit in New Zealand. At the very outset of Tom's excited speculation about attending a conference in Bangkok and then traveling widely in the Orient, a family

---

6. Thomas Merton and James Laughlin, *Selected Letters*, ed. David D. Cooper (New York: W. W. Norton, 1997) 356 [September 5, 1968].

7. See Thomas Merton, *Dancing in the Water of Life: Seeking Peace in the Hermitage. Journals, vol. 5: 1963-1965*, ed. Robert E. Daggy (San Francisco: HarperCollins, 1997) 113-17.

8. See Thomas Merton, *Zen and the Birds of Appetite* (New York: New Directions, 1968) 99-138; see also Merton's tribute, "D. T. Suzuki: The Man and His Work" (59-66).

tragedy occurred when Agnes Gertrude Merton—dear Aunt Kit who had knitted a sweater to keep her nephew warm—had drowned in the sinking of a huge ferry in Wellington Harbor. At length, Tom mused on the true nature of death, not a "comfortable" death with loved ones at the bedside, but death "naked and terrrible," making one "remember what death really is" (*OSM* 85 [April 25, 1968]).

If anything, Aunt Kit's death gave Merton an enhanced urgency. The writing in his several trip notebooks shows his exuberance, his haste to get *something* down before the next set of rich impressions—or even his extinction—fell upon him. And therein lay the minefield that he was to leave for Laughlin to navigate. J would type to Anne McCormick, on the same day that he wrote to Peggy Fox of his claim of having authored *The Asian Journal*, that in his haste Tom "would lapse into a kind of shorthand in which [he] put down only nouns and verbs." Then J added in longhand: "I rebuilt his style" (ND correspondence files). I might interject that from an early age J had been a natural literary chameleon: he met Gertrude Stein in 1934, stayed with her for eight days, and in his next several letters to his parents he imitated her style and diction perfectly. During the same period he was corresponding with Ezra Pound, and he mimicked Pound's language, fractured syntax and spelling. In writing, J had perfect pitch.

Oblivious to future disaster and as excited as Huck Finn setting off down the Mississippi on a raft, Tom suffered impatiently through countless preparatory details that included many painful inoculations, and posted the draft typescript of his final volume of poetry, *The Geography of Lograire*, to Laughlin. Merton had told Sister Thérèse Lentfoehr that he had "created" the land of Lograire, deriving the name from Des Loges, the real name of the poet François Villon.[9] Having entrusted the "geography" of his fictional country to J, Tom set off for real Asia.

Some weeks after Merton's death, J pulled himself together and set out to complete the notes for *The Geography of Lograire*. This did not prove to be too difficult, since J had Merton's introduction to guide him. "The 'geography' of the poem," Laughlin would write much later, "simply is that of Merton's mind," and this opening fragment, J thought, was his poetry "most liberated from convention." "The originality of *Lograire*," J continued, "lies in Merton's use of parody and reconstructed myth."[10] Tracing Tom's many references, J was soon deep in early Mesoamerican

---

9. See Thomas Merton, *The Geography of Lograire* (New York: New Directions, 1969) 140-41.

10. James Laughlin, "Thomas Merton" draft essay (Carol Jane Bangs private collection; subsequent references will be cited as "Laughlin, 'Thomas Merton'" parenthetically in the text).

history and cultural anthropology, reading *The Book of Chilam Balam*, Bernardino de Sahagún, Bishop Diego de Landa and Miguel Covarrubias on the Maya and Aztecs; Ibn Battuta's *Travels in Asia and Africa*; studying the Ranters of seventeenth-century England and the Ghost Dances of the Dakota Indians. J thought that some cuts were advisable, "But I didn't feel I had the right to do it after he was gone."[11] In J's opinion, *Lograire* was "far and away the best thing he ever did in poetry."[12]

Now to look at *The Asian Journal*, by Thomas Merton but as constructed by James Laughlin—no longer a mere editor, but a literary archeologist, recreating as faithfully as he knew how the author's intention, guided by the armature, the central narrative, the skeleton of nouns and verbs left behind by Merton.

Laughlin's varied experiences had in fact suited him to edit Merton's writings, both about what went on in his mind and about his experience of vast Asia. Laughlin had corresponded with Merton since 1944, and visited him with some regularity beginning in 1947. From 1952 through 1957 J had worked for the Ford Foundation, and during this period had made four extended trips to Asia. He possessed first-hand knowledge of Calcutta, New Delhi, Madras, Mahabalipuram, Ceylon and Thailand. (By sheer coincidence, I too have visited many of the places Merton saw, including the mountain areas that Laughlin missed: Merton's descriptions of Pathankot, Dalhousie, Kurseong, Ghoom and Darjeeling are to the life, even to the street sounds, which J chose to render exactly as Tom had written them: "Taxi call kids. Sharp cries spread rev motor whisper pony feet Hoo! Hoo!" [*AJ* 158].) J had helped edit and had published a number of books by Indian authors, and was widely if rather haphazardly familiar with the religions of the Orient. Moreover, he had come away with a great love for the Far East and the sub-continent. When Merton had been planning his trip, J had provided him with advice on everything from obtaining a credit card to what enterovioform tablets to take against intestinal bacteria.

Laughlin's task was indeed formidable. For one thing, Tom Merton had not, as he traveled, attempted to create a coherent manuscript for his *Asian Journal*, but had left three notebooks and a couple of address books, along with postcards and notes on loose scraps of paper. The spiral bound "Notebook A"—the notebook designations were added by the Bellarmine University Thomas Merton Center—has a fairly coherent

11. James Laughlin to Kay Boyle, December 30, 1969 (Houghton Library archives, Harvard University).

12. James Laughlin to Kay Boyle, November 10, 1969 (Houghton Library archives, Harvard University).

structure indicating that Merton probably intended it eventually to evolve into a publishable text. "Notebook B," a bound ledger with a page number printed on the top outside corner of each page, turned out to be a "private" journal, partly duplicated in "Notebook A." "I have no special plans for immediate new writing," Merton had written in his "September 1968 Circular Letter to Friends" (*AJ* 296) before his departure for Asia, but he seems to have changed his mind as the significance of his experiences became evident to him. The third notebook, "C," a small pocket one, was filled with hastily scrawled words: travel schedules and trip details; Pali, Sanskrit and Tibetan words spelled phonetically; phrases and short passages. J's edited text is primarily a collation of notebooks A and B, with Notebook C providing occasional hints.

J created a main editorial troika: himself, Naomi Burton Stone and Brother Patrick Hart, with Amiya Chakravarty as Consulting Editor. Stone had been Merton's literary agent from 1940 through 1959, and continued to advise him on publishing matters subsequently. Brother Patrick had been Dom James Fox's secretary for ten years, and on the abbot's retirement his successor, Dom Flavian, had asked Brother Patrick to serve as Merton's secretary. Laughlin had known Amiya Chakravarty as far back as 1953, when the Bengali poet and professor of philosophy and religion had been on the faculty of Boston University; and in 1966 Chakravarty had visited Merton at Gethsemani. These, then, were the four people most responsible for forming Merton's drafts and notes into a coherent text, each of them with strong though differing personal ties to Merton.

The basic text would involve the editors in delicate, nuanced decisions—for instance, the Dalai Lama had spoken to Father Louis off the record about the Tantra, and Merton's notes on these talks, if not sensitively edited, could be taken for Buddhist dogma, to the embarrassment of the Tibetan Buddhist leader. Complicating everything was Tom's rapid handwriting, legible on the whole but rendered problematic at times by the jerks and jolts of Indian trains and taxis. Brother Patrick now set about typing a fair copy of every scrap of manuscript in the brown case, employing his skill as a typist and his familiarity with Merton's "rather difficult handwriting."[13] Having an unblemished typescript to work from greatly simplified the editors' task.

Soon Laughlin was in correspondence with many of the Buddhists Merton had met in his travels. The "English Buddhist monk," Bhikku Khantipalo, "was especially helpful," even writing an essay on "mindfulness" (*AJ* 297-304) to complement the brief notes Merton had scribbled

---

13. Brother Patrick Hart to Ian S. MacNiven, October 29, 2011.

after their meeting.[14] Despite the hard work, J Laughlin said, "It was a happy time because I felt that Tom was at my side urging me on and lending a helping hand" (Laughlin, "Thomas Merton" 49). Toward the end of 1969 J estimated that completing the editing of *The Asian Journal* "looks like a three or four months' job."[15] He was off by almost three years. "My work on the editing of the Merton 'Asian Journal' goes much more slowly than I would wish," he said later; "I have to sandwich it in with my own regular work, but I get through a few pages every day."[16]

A special problem was presented to the editors in the matter of Merton's many quotations, passages that he tended to write on the left-hand pages of his notebooks. Often incomplete or written in fragments clearly intended to jog his memory later, these had to be tracked down and checked for accuracy. His reading on his journey had been extensive—he said that he was chagrined and humiliated at being forced to pay overweight on his flights, so that he kept discarding books, giving them away or mailing them to Gethsemani. Laughlin drew upon Purusottama Lal in Calcutta, whose translations of Sanskrit plays New Directions had published; he corresponded with Gary Snyder, a New Directions poet, who had studied for ten years at a Zen center in Japan; he consulted Lobsang Lhalungpa of Tibet and scores of others. Drawing upon their knowledge and his own now-considerable focused reading, J compiled the fifty-five page glossary, mainly of terms pertaining to Eastern religion, that concludes *The Asian Journal* volume as New Directions would publish it (*AJ* 363-418).

Laughlin's editorial decisions were guided by two principles: he wanted to maintain the appearance of a trip diary—this was, after all, the story of a journey of personal discovery. But Laughlin was a seasoned publisher who knew that the readers of *The Asian Journal* would expect a coherent narrative and standard punctuation. Merton had in the main followed the *chronology* of his travels, but he had not necessarily recorded his impressions at the time he experienced them, nor had he always written out all that he had to say about a subject at one time, but might return to it in another notebook and at a later date. The manuscript journal page headed "Dec 5—Singapore," begins with notes on Merton's avid newspaper reading. Merton's words in the "Dec 5" entry were transcribed almost verbatim for the *Asian Journal* text, except for changing ampersands to the written *and*, adding a few marks of punctuation, and

---

14. James Laughlin to Gary Snyder, May 12, 1971 (Houghton Library archives, Harvard University).

15. James Laughlin to Kay Boyle, November 10, 1969 (Houghton Library archives, Harvard University).

16. James Laughlin to Laurence Pollinger, April 7, 1970 (ND correspondence files).

changing "at full moon the ovaries of sea urchins *reached an unusually large size*" to "are unusually large in size" (*AJ* 230; italics added) (this change is hardly an improvement). Not knowing how or whether Merton would have incorporated such randomly encountered news items into his final text, J elected to include them, as he had when he was editing *The Geography of Lograire*. Merton was grimly amused that a soldier on a "crow eradication team" had been reprimanded by a magistrate for "rashly discharging his shotgun" in the streets, injuring ten children. Merton does not comment further on the incident, and while realizing that he might well have cut it in a future editing of the text, J simply left it in as written.

The editors got into trouble, however, when they placed the "Dec 5" section under December 4 in the published book without changing the single word needed to prevent an apparent error. Merton had written in Notebook A, "Polonnaruwa was such an experience that I could not write hastily of it & cannot write now, or not adequately." Nonetheless, Merton returned to the drive across Ceylon in the next paragraph: "Polonnaruwa—that was Monday. Today is Thursday. Heavy rain in Kandy." This presented J with a problem: Merton was in Singapore when he wrote this entry, but for good thematic coherence it seemed preferable to round out his visit to Ceylon with his climactic contemplation of the Buddha statues of Polonnaruwa. Also, while there is no entry in Merton's private journal, the black bound Notebook B, for the *day* of his trip to Polonnaruwa, he wrote in it at some length about the trip in an entry headed "Dec 3 Colombo." What to do? Laughlin fused together the two main texts dealing with Polonnaruwa, editing them for coherence, and inserted them into the entry for December 4. He changed the sentence, "Polonnaruwa—that was Monday," to read, "I visited Polonnaruwa on Monday" (which would have been December 2) and retained the next sentence unchanged, "Today is Thursday" (*AJ* 231). The insertion of the first person "I" was completely in keeping with Merton's practice throughout; however, J created an error by allowing Thursday to remain as the day of the journal entry, since the fourth was a *Wednesday*. Perhaps J never checked a calendar for 1968.

The Gal Vihara, or rock temple, at Polonnaruwa consists of four statues of the Buddha, standing, seated and reclining—at the time of Merton's visit the standing Buddha was thought to be of the monk Ananda, the Buddha's disciple—carved from a single immense rock of grey granite. The largest of these is forty-six feet in length, and most powerfully depicts the Buddha prone, either in sleep or death. Laughlin reproduced Merton's Notebook A text on Polonnaruwa for the length of about two manuscript pages with almost no changes beyond regularizing punctuation. Then, just before the paragraph in Notebook A describing the departure from Polonnaruwa, J abruptly shifted to Notebook B, the "private notebook," in which Merton explains what had so struck him about the site.

I consider this Merton's epiphany, perhaps the most important single *revelatory* moment of his life. I am not arguing that this was more important than the attaining of faith that led to his conversion to Catholicism, a long build-up in time, the time described in the many pages of *The Seven Storey Mountain*.[17] Polonnaruwa was, in contrast, a *moment of revelation*, and Merton describes it as such, writing in Notebook B: "When looking at this I was suddenly, almost forcibly, jerked clean out of the habitual, half-tied vision of things, & an inner clearness, clarity, as if exploding from the rocks themselves, became evident, obvious." J rendered this as follows, dropping the *When* and supplying the bridging phrase *at these figures*, so that the published text reads, "Looking at these figures I was suddenly, almost forcibly jerked clean out of the habitual, half-tied vision of things, and an inner clearness, clarity, as if exploding from the rocks themselves, became evident and obvious" (*AJ* 233, 235). J followed the text as Merton wrote it, except for adding "and" between "evident, obvious." In any case, Merton wrote here with the consciousness of having achieved the mystical experience that he long felt had eluded him: "I don't know when in my life I ever had such a sense of beauty and spiritual validity running together in one aesthetic illumination," he continued. "Surely with Mahabalipuram and Polonnaruwa my Asian pilgrimage has come clear and purified itself. I mean, I know and have seen what I was obscurely looking for" (*AJ* 235-36). Then J turned back to Notebook A, to get Merton away from Polonnaruwa, back to Kandy, and on the road to Bangkok: "The whole thing is very much a Zen garden . . . . We . . . started on the long drive home to Kandy" (*AJ* 236).

And so J continued, adding, deleting, changing: smoothing the text as he thought his friend Tom would have done had he lived. Even more than rebuilding Merton's style and fleshing out the "nouns and verbs," J's inspired juxtapositions of the various texts become a creative act of great significance.

Merton accomplished his revelation, wrote about it, and within a week he would have departed from the world of the living. His words to the audience at nearly the end of his December 10 talk in Bangkok on "Marxism and Monastic Perspectives," are chillingly appropriate, as a premonition: "So I will disappear" (*AJ* 343).[18]

---

17. Thomas Merton, *The Seven Storey Mountain* (New York: Harcourt, Brace, 1948) 169-225.

18. This dramatic conclusion was apparently not given this focus by Laughlin's

Two years later J threatened to disappear himself, into mental ill-ness. In the summer of 1970, his work on the *Asian Journal* nearing completion, Laughlin began to feel out of sorts, an ill-defined malaise characterized by periods of lethargy, aboulia, loss of will. Convinced that it was more than mere imagining, J's wife, Ann Resor Laughlin, bullied him into seeing Dr. Benjamin Wiesel, the head of psychiatric medicine at the Hartford General Hospital. Rather like a woman who has endured a long and difficult childbirth, J seemed near total collapse. As if to sug-gest parturition, J described himself as "laboring" on the editing of *The Asian Journal*. Dr. Wiesel diagnosed the onset of bipolar mania, a mental affliction influenced in Laughlin's case by genetics—it had attacked his grandfather, father and two uncles—and stress. It was perhaps no mere coincidence that the onset of bipolar illness followed not so very long after the sudden death of J's religio-psychic double. Fortunately for J and for the *Asian Journal* editing, Wiesel was a pioneer in using lithium to treat bipolar disease. He put J on the drug, his condition was stabilized, and he was able to resume intensive work on the book.

J worked most of the time in his home at Norfolk, Connecticut, in those days. In January 1971 Naomi Burton Stone and Brother Patrick came for four days of intensive effort, with Brother Patrick playing tunes from *Fiddler on the Roof* on the piano when they needed a break. They went over the text line by line, sometimes arguing. Merton had described the sky above Kanchenjunga peak, seen from Darjeeling, as having "a few discreet showings of whorehouse pink" (*AJ* 156); Naomi wanted to change this, but was over-ruled. "We were having a devil of a time," Brother Patrick told me, deciphering one particular entry that Tom had written on a bus trip. "Any brandy in the house?" Naomi asked J. He found a dusty bottle in the kitchen and poured her a glass. She took a great swallow, returned to the notebook, turned it upside-down, and immediately read out the passage that had stumped them all.[19]

Realizing that Tom might well have edited out many of the impres-

---

editing, but was rendered thus in the transcript of the talk as he received it. The transcript at the Bellarmine Merton Center, which is probably identical to the one that Laughlin worked from, ends with an ellipsis: "So I will disappear . . ." In a recording of the conclusion to the actual address, as presented in Paul Wilkes' and Audrey Glynn's *Merton: A Film Biography* (1984), Merton's voice is heard ending with the words, "So I will disappear from view and we can all have a Coke or something. Thank you very much." At some point, the final fifteen words were cut from the transcript to make the ending startlingly more telling in prophetic retrospect. It is my belief that Laughlin, having the transcript to work from, would not have gone through the bother of obtaining the recording and listening to it.

19. Brother Patrick Hart, interview by Ian S. MacNiven (September 25, 2007).

sions and observations that he jotted down, J still felt that he and his co-editors should not presume to make excisions except where absolutely required for clarity. The result was what may be the most *all-inclusive* of Merton's major books: metaphysics and esoteric philosophy jostle against phrases from comic strips and newspaper stories. Everything is there in *The Asian Journal* for all to read.

In his *Man in the Sycamore Tree*, Edward Rice, Merton's friend since his young manhood at Columbia, maintained that Merton had died a Buddhist.[20] J would have none of this. He responded angrily that it was a "complete fabrication" and that *The Asian Journal* made it clear that Tom was merely interested *as a Christian* in learning from the Tibetan *rimpoches*.[21] J yearned toward generalized *faith*, yet he could not countenance a defection from Christianity by his spiritual double. Laughlin needed the reassurance of a *Christian* agency. Merton, secure in his faith, was not threatened by the great unbounded expanse of religious thought.

J might have missed publishing *The Seven Storey Mountain*, but in editing and publishing *The Asian Journal* he achieved the other bookend to Merton's writing career, a book that is *extrospective*, a looking outward, as well as introspective, his account of the revelation that capped the *seeking* begun in his first great book of introspection. Of course, we can only speculate what Merton would have thought of his *Asian Journal*, where he might have placed it in comparison with his first major prose work. The edited text of *The Asian Journal* is open-ended in the sense that in it Merton exposed himself to the entire universe of religious belief. As such, it should provoke inquiry, and, like the Dead Sea Scrolls, the unedited notebooks deserve to be and indeed have been puzzled over and interpreted into a canonical text by devoted and inspired collaborators, not least among them James Laughlin.

---

20. Edward Rice, *The Man in the Sycamore Tree: The Good Times and Hard Life of Thomas Merton* (Garden City, NY: Doubleday, 1970) 139; but see 13 for Rice's more qualified evaluation of Merton's relationship with Buddhism.

21. James Laughlin to N. Smallwood, July 13, 1971 (ND correspondence files).

"She Cannot Be a Prisoner":
The Lure of Wisdom as Bearer of Hope

Christopher Pramuk

> Sometimes when I stand in some corner of the camp, my feet planted
> on earth, my eyes raised towards heaven, tears run down my face,
> tears of deep emotion and gratitude.
>
> Etty Hillesum, *Letters from Westerbork*, 1942

I'd like to preface this exploration into Wisdom with a brief remembrance
of Fr. Alfred Delp, a Jesuit priest who was executed on February 2, 1945,
for his resistance to Nazism. In a letter to his friends from prison, Fr. Delp
wrote about the beauty and the cost of a life lived ever more freely under
the horizon of grace. If we keep in mind the historical and anguishing
personal context in which these words were written, the following passage intensifies all the more the theme I'd like to consider in this essay,
which is the theme of hope. Fr. Delp writes:

> One thing is clear and tangible to me in a way that it seldom has been:
> the world is full of God. From every pore, God rushes out to us, as
> it were. But we're often blind. We remain stuck in the good times
> and the bad times and don't experience them right up to the point
> where the spring flows from God . . . . In everything, God wants to
> celebrate encounter and asks for the prayerful response of surrender.
> The trick and the duty is only this: to develop a lasting awareness and
> a lasting attitude out of these insights and graces—or rather, to allow
> them to develop. Then life becomes free, in that freedom which we
> have often looked for. [1]

The witness of mystics, sages and ordinary people of faith down through
the ages suggests that rising up from within creation there pulses an un-
containable Love, coming toward us in all things. Indeed, their witness
says to us, "God rushes out to us from every pore." But can we believe
it? Perhaps this is Thomas Merton's particular gift: he helps us to believe
it, that God is everywhere and desires in all things to be known. Or better, Merton helps us to *feel* it, and therefore, to feel hope, which is the

---

1. Alfred Delp to Luise Oestreicher, November 17, 1944, cited in *Ultimate Price: Testimonies of Christians Who Resisted the Third Reich*, selected by Annemarie S. Kidder (Maryknoll, NY: Orbis, 2012) 65-66.

capacity to be able to imagine again.

In this essay I look to Wisdom-Sophia as a lyric memory and name of God who brings hope for human beings and for suffering creation. The irruption of Sophia into Merton's consciousness and life of prayer in Part I will serve as a doorway to explore God's presence and promise in existential situations often presumed by rational and even religious discourse to be "God-forsaken." A consideration of Holocaust narratives and Jewish post-Holocaust theology in Part II will open onto a wider view of Wisdom in Part III as a universal mode of the divine Presence that is by no means "automatic," "inevitable" or "coercive," but which hinges on our acts of deep attention, loving freedom and compassionate participation in the divine initiative in history.[2] Part IV concludes with the question of the living remembrance of God and sophianic spirituality that frames many of the essays in this volume. What does it mean to live together with Wisdom?

In sum, my aim in what follows is to draw forward in a somewhat narrative and poetic way the following thesis: hope in the key of Wisdom awakens "that freedom which we have often looked for," intensifying our receptivity in the present moment and unveiling hope toward the hidden future of God's own imagining. I begin with *Hagia Sophia*, Merton's strangely beautiful and disarming prose-poem of 1962,[3] the text from which I take my title.

"My Creator's Thought and Art within Me"

Dawn. The Hour of Lauds.
There is in all visible things an invisible fecundity, a dimmed light, a meek namelessness, a hidden wholeness. This mysterious Unity and Integrity is Wisdom, the Mother of all, *Natura naturans*. There is in all things an inexhaustible sweetness and purity, a silence that is a fount of action and joy. It rises up in wordless gentleness and flows out to me from the unseen roots of all created being, welcoming me tenderly, saluting me with indescribable humility. This is at once my own being, my own nature, and the Gift of my Creator's Thought

---

2. In provocative ways that elude systematic categorization the Wisdom tradition bridges both the Jewish and Christian memory and future expectation of God's initiative in history. On the convergence of Wisdom and apocalyptic hope and immanent expectation in Merton's sophianic writings, see Christopher Pramuk, "Apocalypticism in a Catholic Key: Lessons from Thomas Merton," *Horizons* 36.2 (2009) 235-64.

3. Thomas Merton, *Hagia Sophia* (Lexington, KY: Stamperia del Santuccio, 1962); Thomas Merton, *Emblems of a Season of Fury* (New York: New Directions, 1963) 61-69 (subsequent references will be cited as *"ESF"* parenthetically in the text).

and Art within me, speaking as Hagia Sophia, speaking as my sister, Wisdom. (*ESF* 61)

The poem has haunted me for years, and I have struggled and broken my head (and perhaps many other heads!) trying to get behind and inside the text of the poem and its genesis to explain its particular magic.[4] But there is nothing to explain, and no magic; there is only the music of divine Mercy, realized in each of us according to our willingness to receive it.

> O blessed, silent one, who speaks everywhere!

> We do not hear the soft voice, the gentle voice, the merciful and feminine.

> We do not hear mercy, or yielding love, or non-resistance, or non-reprisal. In her there are no reasons and no answers. Yet she is the candor of God's light, the expression of His simplicity. (*ESF* 63)

If it is true, as the late Fr. Andrew Greeley once observed, that "the artist is a sacrament maker, a creator of emphasized, clarified beauty designed to make us see,"[5] then Merton in *Hagia Sophia* is the consummate artist, helping us to see—that is, to *feel in our whole person*—that while the world is stricken deeply by sin, it is also limned in the light of resurrection. Sophia is the invitation to the wedding dance; she is "the Bride and the Feast and the Wedding" (*ESF* 67); she is the mercy and co-creativity of God, ever luring, never compelling, coming to birth in us whenever we risk saying yes to "the dawning of divine light in the stillness of our hearts."[6]

The lure of Wisdom-Sophia throughout Merton's corpus is just this, a *lure*, if I can be permitted the rather mundane fishing metaphor. I invite the reader to picture with me a lure from the fish's perspective: you see it flashing and dancing and singing in the waters just out in front of you, inviting and drawing you forward. *She is God's call from the future breaking ever into the present.* And just when you think you've got her,

---

4. For a close study of Wisdom-Sophia in Merton's life and thought see Christopher Pramuk, *Sophia: The Hidden Christ of Thomas Merton* (Collegeville, MN: Liturgical Press, 2009) (subsequent references will be cited as "Pramuk, *Sophia*" parenthetically in the text); a compact overview and crystallization of the book's major themes is found in Christopher Pramuk, "Wisdom Our Sister: Thomas Merton's Reception of Russian Sophiology," *Spiritus* 11.2 (Fall 2011) 177-99.

5. Andrew Greeley, "The Apologetics of Beauty," *America* 183.7 (2000) 8-12.

6. Thomas Merton, *The Hidden Ground of Love: Letters on Religious Experience and Social Concerns*, ed. William H. Shannon (New York: Farrar, Straus, Giroux, 1985) 46 [letter to Abdul Aziz, 1/30/1961].

lunging forward to capture her in your teeth, you find that it is you who have been gotten by her. She captures you, your whole self, and will not let you go. We style ourselves as the one pursuing, and discover with a jolt that it is she, God Herself, who initiates and sustains the pursuit from before the very beginning. She is the Love of love itself in the Heart of God spilling over into the creativity of life unfolding over deep, deep time. Perhaps she is more like the water itself that bears and animates both fish and lure, not "that which" we see but that "through which"[7] we see, the veil of Love and Light enlivening. And still she dances and sings before us, shining from within all things, refusing to be domesticated.

I have just called Merton an artist, a sacrament maker; and yet I qualify. It is *God* the Artist, the Gift of the Creator's Thought and Art who speaks in and through him in *Hagia Sophia*. Merton is like the poet Yurii whom he celebrates in Pasternak's novel, *Dr. Zhivago*, the poet who "felt that the main part of the work was being done not by him but by a superior power that was above him and directed him. . . . And he felt himself to be only the occasion, the fulcrum, needed to make this movement possible."[8] For me and for countless others, Merton's writings have served as a kind of "fulcrum" making a little more possible in our lives the movement of spirit between heaven and earth, matter and spirit, freedom and grace.

The former Archbishop of Canterbury, Rowan Williams, an astonishingly sensitive poet and theologian in his own right, reinforces this point if rather more provocatively when he likens Merton to "the 'poverty' of the priest who 'vanishes into the Mass.'"[9] Williams writes:

> Merton's genius was largely that he was a massively unoriginal man: he is extraordinary because he is so dramatically absorbed by every environment he finds himself in—America between the wars, classical pre-conciliar Catholicism and monasticism, the peace movement, Asia. In all these contexts he is utterly 'priestly' because utterly *attentive*: he does not organize, dominate, or even interpret, much of the time, but responds. It is not a chameleon inconsistency (though it could be so interpreted by a hostile eye), because all these influences flow in to one constant place, a will and imagination turned Godward. (Williams 19)

---

7. The distinction is taken from St. Thomas Aquinas's discussion of God as "Light."

8. Thomas Merton, *Disputed Questions* (New York: Farrar, Straus and Cudahy, 1960) 21.

9. Rowan Williams, *A Silent Action: Engagements with Thomas Merton* (Louisville, KY: Fons Vitae, 2011) 19 (subsequent references will be cited as "Williams" parenthetically in the text), citing Thomas Merton, *The Sign of Jonas* (New York: Harcourt, Brace, 1953) 191.

These are points really worth pondering! How many would think to describe Merton as a "massively unoriginal man"? What is Williams driving at?

"The great Christian," Williams continues, "is the man or woman who can make me more interested in God than in him or her." Merton is a great Christian because he "will not *let* me look at him for long: he will, finally, persuade me to look in the direction he is looking," toward a world everywhere haunted by God. "I don't want to know much more about Merton," Williams confesses; "he is dead, and I shall commend him regularly, lovingly, and thankfully to God. I am concerned to find how I can turn further in the direction he is looking, in prayer, poetry, theology, and encounter with the experience of other faiths; in trust and love of God our saviour" (Williams 19). For all the fascination and inspiration Merton's life story has been for me, I basically agree with Rowan Williams: "being interested in Thomas Merton is *not* being interested in an original, a 'shaping' mind, but being interested in God and human possibilities" (Williams 19).[10] Merton models the "costly openness" (Williams 49) demanded by Christian love, and, I would add here, the costly openness demanded of Christian theology in every new generation. The alternative is what Williams calls the "politics of the self-enclosed world" (Williams 64), a real danger and temptation in our times, not least for the church and its theology.[11]

Thus, for me, the question of the meaning and significance of Wisdom-Sophia in Merton's life is not primarily a psychological question, though it is surely that; nor is it a strictly literary or poetic question, though it is certainly that. At its core it is the question of God, which many others of his time were asking, and which people today are asking with great urgency. Where is God? Who is God? Or simply: *Is* God? And if God is, then why is the world in such a damn mess? More precisely, how do we distinguish the true God, the One who is real and trustworthy, from the idols of sinfulness, violence and death of our time?[12]

10. For a more sustained discussion of *A Silent Action* see Christopher Pramuk, "Poetic Priest to Poetic Priest," *The Living Church* 245.2 (July 15, 2012) 21-24.

11. In a marked shift in substance and style from his two immediate predecessors Pope Francis frequently warns of the dangers of a "self-referential" Church and speaks of the need to cultivate an outward-looking "culture of encounter."

12. Of course this is the most serious of questions for the religious believer. And yet with Merton somehow it is also a playful question, a joyful question, and not-so-serious. See Rowan Williams, "'Not Being Serious': Thomas Merton and Karl Barth" (Williams 71-82). Few contemporary theologians have retrieved the biblical theme of idolatry more cogently than Jesuit theologian Jon Sobrino: see, e.g., Jon Sobrino, "Atheism and Idolatry," in *Juan Luis Segundo—Uma Teologia com Sabor Devida*, ed. Afonso Soares

In her sensitive exegesis of *Hagia Sophia* the poet Susan McCaslin observes that Merton was aware that the sophiological tradition "had been marginalized within Western Christianity" and with *Hagia Sophia* he "attempts to restore it."[13] This much is clear to me and quite significant. Merton sought to retrieve a memory and experience of God largely lost in the West, at great price. Yet for me an even more significant assertion follows, as McCaslin concludes: "While Merton recognizes the limitations of language, he assumes a metaphysical and ontological ground of being beyond language; that is, the 'real presence' of Wisdom behind and within the signs" (Dieker & Montaldo 253). What can it mean to affirm "the real presence" of Wisdom behind and within the signs?

When Jesus of Nazareth prefaced his enigmatic sayings with the words, "let those with eyes to see, see; let those with ears to hear, hear," scholars tell us he was speaking as a teacher of Jewish wisdom, appealing not just to the head but to the whole person of his listener: heart, body, mind, senses, imagination.[14] Like a lure, his words dance and play before the imagination, breaking open our habitual assumptions about "the way things are." This too is Merton's gift, but it is not necessarily an easy or pleasant gift to receive, neither from Jesus nor from Merton. To be "born again" is to break free of the stultifying womb of conventional wisdom; it is to risk the vulnerability of a covenantal faith that holds no guarantees. *Listen to the silence, hear the forgotten histories, let the music of things unseen and hidden speak to you, awaken you from slumber. Nothing is impossible with God.* Can you believe it?

Now the Wisdom of God, Sophia, comes forth, reaching from "end to end mightily." She wills to be also the unseen pivot of all nature,

---

(São Paulo: Paulinas, 1997) 66-76.

13. Susan McCaslin, "Merton and 'Hagia Sophia,'" in Bernadette Dieker and Jonathan Montaldo, eds., *Merton & Hesychasm: The Prayer of the Heart* (Louisville, KY: Fons Vitae, 2003) 252; subsequent references will be cited as "Dieker & Montaldo" parenthetically in the text.

14. Biblical scholars have long recognized the Hebrew Wisdom foundations of New Testament Christology and almost certainly of Jesus' self-identity. For a sensitive and highly readable introduction see Marcus Borg, *Meeting Jesus Again for the First Time: The Historical Jesus and the Heart of Contemporary Faith* (New York: HarperCollins, 1995) 69-118. Amid an enormous body of scholarly literature, James D. G. Dunn provides a balanced summary of the issues and texts at play in his *Christology in the Making: A New Testament Inquiry into the Origins of the Doctrine of the Incarnation* (Grand Rapids, MI: Eerdmans, 1996) 163-212; on Wisdom and apocalypticism, see John J. Collins, "Wisdom, Apocalypticism, and Generic Compatibility," in *In Search of Wisdom: Essays in Memory of John G. Gammie*, ed. Leo Perdue *et al.* (Louisville, KY: Westminster/John Knox, 1993) 165-85.

the center and significance of all the light that is *in* all and *for* all. . . .
But she remains unseen, glimpsed only by a few. Sometimes there
are none who know her at all. (*ESF* 65-67)

The imagination that bears hope, hope in the key of Wisdom, sees promise
rising in life itself and in life's protest, the sacred longing for life and
communion that pulses in the very substance of things, beckoning freedom forward, daring us to imagine and make room for another possible
future. By contrast the imagination that produces despair and world-weary
cynicism is like a tightening barbed-wire circle, a series of closing doors
that promise nothing new but only more of the same, the same horizontal
flight across the dull surface of history. Despair cannot see beyond or
imagine a way out. It infuses life with a dread weariness.[15] And still she
dances before us—"Sophia, the feminine child, is playing in the world,
obvious and unseen, playing at all times before the Creator" (*ESF* 66).

All of this is to suggest that Merton is not just painting pretty pictures
in *Hagia Sophia*. Immersed body and soul in the tradition, he writes as
a mystical theologian, a poet of the presence of God. His task is not to
defend a traditional understanding of God but rather to articulate a mode
of divine presence responsive to the crisis of his times, at once a mode
of presence faithful to the revelation of God and humanity fully alive in
Jesus, and at the same time, if real and authentic, a mode of presence and
a kind of God-talk (i.e. a theology) that will resonate in a key familiar to
others beyond Christianity and Catholicism. To grasp the "real presence"
of Wisdom implies no magic, literary or otherwise. It does imply that we,
like Merton, must learn patiently and prayerfully to discern the signs of
our times, across all boundaries, "with penetration."[16]

Building from this point I would like to leave Merton behind for a
few moments and embark on a kind of experiment in sophianic imagination. In the spirit of Rowan Williams' call to turn "further in the direction
[Merton] is looking," I'd like to chase after the lure of Wisdom-Sophia

---

15. See William Lynch, *Images of Hope: Imagination as Healer of the Hopeless*
(Baltimore: Helicon, 1965).

16. The phrase is taken from M-D. Chenu, whose analysis of "the symbolist
mentality" in medieval monastic theology goes far in illuminating Merton's own sapiential
sensibilities. See Marie-Dominique Chenu, *Nature, Man, and Society in the Twelfth
Century*, trans. Jerome Taylor and Lester Little (Chicago: University of Chicago Press,
1957) 99-145, at 99. Chenu shares with Merton the basic premise of the theologians
of the Catholic *ressourcement* prior to Vatican II that if theology aims to discern "the
profound truth that lies hidden within the dense substance of things" its scope cannot be
merely parochial or contextual but must reach toward the universal, both in its literary
and metaphysical dimensions (see Pramuk, *Sophia* 107-10).

in other places, beginning with the Jewish community, a community of critical importance to Merton in the last decade of his life. Of course the memory of the Jewish people is painfully replete with the problem of God in the twentieth century. Where was God through these unspeakably dark passages of Jewish and world history? We begin with the witness of a young Jewish woman named Etty Hillesum whose story intensifies the question of God during the Holocaust. Her story and the stories of other women like her compel us to ask not only "Where was God?" but perhaps more significantly, *"Who was God* during the Shoah?"

"To Defend Your Dwelling Place in Us to the Last"

Etty Hillesum was a Dutch Jew who lived in Amsterdam during the Nazi occupation and was murdered in Auschwitz at age 29. Her diaries, which survived the war, give witness to a spirit in humanity that defies rational explanation. In May of 1942, just before Etty was arrested and sent to the transit camp of Westerbork, she wrote the following passage in her diary, lines that have haunted me since I first read them some twenty-five years ago.

> *Saturday morning, 7:30.* The bare trunks that climb past my window now shelter under a cover of young green leaves. A springy fleece along their naked, tough, ascetic limbs.
>
> I went to bed early last night, and from my bed I stared out through the large open window. And it was once more as if life with all its mysteries was close to me, as if I could touch it. I had the feeling that I was resting against the naked breast of life, and could feel her gentle and regular heartbeat. I felt safe and protected. And I thought, How strange. It is wartime. There are concentration camps. . . . I know how very nervous people are, I know about the mounting human suffering. I know the persecution and oppression and despotism and the impotent fury and the terrible sadism. I know it all.
>
> And yet—at unguarded moments, when left to myself, I suddenly lie against the naked breast of life, and her arms round me are so gentle and so protective and my own heartbeat is difficult to describe: so slow and so regular and so soft, almost muffled, but so constant, as if it would never stop. That is also my attitude to life, and I believe that neither war nor any other senseless human atrocity will ever be able to change it.[17]

---

17. Etty Hillesum, *An Interrupted Life and Letters from Westerbork* (New York: Henry Holt, 1996) 135-36; subsequent references will be cited as "Hillesum" parenthetically in the text.

Notice what Robert Ellsberg has called the "earthy and embodied" sense of the divine that saturates Hillesum's diaries. "For Etty, everything—the physical and the spiritual without distinction—was related to her passionate openness to life, which was ultimately openness to God."[18] Our bodies, the trees, the earth—even the hard soil beneath the camps—pulses with the whisper and protest of life itself, enfolding us "in her gentle and regular heartbeat."

Etty was no naïve romantic. She felt the noose tightening, the impending "cruelty and deprivation the likes of which I cannot imagine in even my wildest fantasies." Yet there pulses throughout her diaries an enduring sense of grace and consolation:

> I don't feel [caught] in anybody's clutches; I feel safe in God's arms, to put it rhetorically, and no matter whether I am sitting at this beloved old desk now, or in a bare room in the Jewish district, or perhaps in a labor camp under SS guards in a month's time—I shall always feel safe in God's arms. . . . [All] this is as nothing to the immeasurable expanse of my faith in God and my inner receptiveness. (Hillesum 176)

The key image may be the last: her determination to maintain an "inner receptiveness" that no amount of barbed wire or ideological fury could contain. Indeed Etty's journals reflect an inner freedom and faith that seem to flow much more from sensual receptivity and wordless silence than from any explicit religious creed or ritual action. "Such words as 'god' and 'death' and 'suffering' and 'eternity' are best forgotten," she writes. "We have to become as simple and as wordless as the growing corn or the falling rain. We must just be" (Hillesum 171). Etty's sensual openness to God included her closest friendships and intimate sexual relationships. With lovers no less than with friends, family and children, we must learn to "just be," attentive and unconditionally present, whether in passing ecstasies, in evening laughter around the dinner table, or long passages of dryness and mutual loneliness. So is the way of friendship with God, who shares our desire, our solitude, our companionship, our loneliness.

Two weeks before her internment at Westerbork, Etty speaks directly to God, confessing her growing realization that the felt presence or absence of the divine in the world depends considerably upon us, on our "safeguarding" God's hidden dynamism within creation.

---

18. Robert Ellsberg, *All Saints: Daily Reflections on Saints, Prophets, and Witnesses from Our Time* (New York: Crossroad, 1997) 522 (subsequent references will be cited as "Ellsberg" parenthetically in the text). Ellsberg notes that Etty's diary, published four decades after her death, "was quickly recognized as one of the great moral documents of our time" (521).

Sunday morning prayer. "Dear God, these are anxious times. Tonight for the first time I lay in the dark with burning eyes as scene after scene of human suffering passed before me. I shall promise You one thing, God, just one very small thing: I shall never burden my today with cares about my tomorrow, although that takes some practice. Each day is sufficient unto itself. I shall try to help You, God, to stop my strength ebbing away, though I cannot vouch for it in advance. But one thing is becoming increasingly clear to me: that You cannot help us, that we must help You to help ourselves. And that is all we can manage these days and also all that really matters: that we safeguard that little piece of You, God, in ourselves. And perhaps in others as well. . . . You cannot help us, but we must help You and defend Your dwelling place inside us to the last." (Hillesum 178)[19]

Like many other stories of courage and resistance during the Holocaust, what most defies rational explanation in Etty's story was her willingness to take suffering upon herself "in solidarity with those who suffer" (Ellsberg 522). As Ellsberg notes, this was not a masochistic embrace of suffering for its own sake but rather a vocation "to redeem the suffering of humanity from within, by safeguarding 'that little piece of You, God, in ourselves'" (Ellsberg 522). *To redeem the suffering of humanity from within*: black or white, Jew or Christian, Hindu or Muslim, Buddhist or atheist, is this not what it means to live in solidarity with friends and strangers alike in the merciful womb of Love? For Christians, does this not describe the very person, life and teaching of Jesus Christ?[20]

No matter how often I read the diaries of Etty Hillesum, when I turn the final pages I am overwhelmed both with wonder and sadness. So much vitality, so much erotic warmth and humane goodness, snuffed out by the fury of racist ideology, set into motion with a technocratic efficiency and scope beyond all imagining. Etty's last known writings were scribbled

---

19. Compare to the preface of *Raids on the Unspeakable*, in which Merton describes the book's central message: "Be human in this most inhuman of ages; guard the image of man for it is the image of God" (Thomas Merton, *Raids on the Unspeakable* [New York: New Directions, 1966] 6; subsequent references will be cited as "*RU*" parenthetically in the text).

20. For Etty, to share in humanity's suffering meant accepting the contradictions of good and evil within ourselves, no less than in our enemy or persecutor. "Yes, we carry everything within us, God and Heaven and Hell and Earth and Life and Death and all of history" (Hillesum 154). She also writes of the freedom from fear that comes through embracing life's gratuity from moment to moment, a freedom the Germans could not take away (144-45). In many such passages Etty sounds remarkably like a *satyagrahi*: one who has wholly internalized the truth-force of loving nonviolence as taught and lived by Mahatma Gandhi and by Jesus' life and teachings in the Sermon on the Mount.

on a postcard thrown from the train that delivered her to Auschwitz. "We left the camp singing," she wrote (Hillesum 360).

It is not for me or any Christian to claim the victory for love, and thus for God, by Etty Hillesum's witness. And yet an almost miraculous spirit endures and comes to life again in our remembering her. Here I want to linger a moment longer with the striking feminine imagery that Etty reaches for to express her sense of God's presence, "her arms round me" so close and protective that she can scarcely distinguish it from her own heartbeat.

Of course Etty is not the first Jew to express the divine encompassing Presence in such vividly feminine terms. From the Books of Proverbs and Wisdom to the wisdom sayings of Jesus and much of the earliest christological hymns of the New Testament, the feminine face of God haunts the Bible itself, even where she has largely been marginalized or banished from institutional Judaism and Western Christianity. She saturates Jewish kabbalism's mystical narrative of *zimzum* (Hebrew: "contraction") in which God creates and nurtures the world not through sheer omnipotence or dominating power but rather more like a mother, freely and lovingly opening a space in God's very self for the emergence of the material cosmos, and consummately for human freedom. Paradoxically, it is the emptiness or womb-like openness of God's expansive love that sustains the ripening fullness of a vibrantly unfolding creation.[21] But what can such feminine imagery have to do with racist genocide or the collective horrors of human history?

In her breathtaking study *The Female Face of God in Auschwitz*, Jewish theologian Melissa Raphael joins other contemporary feminist theologians in arguing that patriarchal or exclusively male images, discourses and practices in synagogue and church have sanctioned a great deal of injustice, misogyny and violence in society, in no small part by obscuring the female face of God: God's nurturing, indwelling Presence known in the Hebrew Bible as Wisdom, Shekinah, Sophia or Spirit.[22] Patriarchal

---

21. From the teachings of Isaac Luria (1534-1572), or the *Lurianic Kabbalah*. Among Christian theologians the notion of *zimzum* has been linked with Sophia-Shekinah and the theme of divine *kenosis* by Jurgen Moltmann (*God in Creation: A New Theology of Creation and the Spirit of God—The Gifford Lectures 1984-1985*, trans. Margaret Kohl [Minneapolis: MN, Fortress Press, 1993]) and, albeit more implicitly, the great Russian Orthodox theologian Sergius Bulgakov in his dogmatics of the humanity of God, or divine-human Sophia.

22. Melissa Raphael, *The Female Face of God in Auschwitz: A Jewish Feminist Theology of the Holocaust* (New York: Routledge, 2003); subsequent references will be cited as "Raphael" parenthetically in the text. The literature on biblical Wisdom-Sophia in the Jewish and Christian traditions is vast, rich, and not without controversy. For a superb

forces have veiled the feminine divine "to the point of disappearance," argues Raphael, perhaps nowhere more horrifically than in Auschwitz. Indeed it is not altogether surprising, she suggests, that traditional Jewish theology, with its own patriarchal imagination, could not conceive how the all-powerful God of Moses and the prophets would have been so utterly powerless, so *impotent*, in the face of Auschwitz. In effect traditional post-Holocaust approaches accuse God, as Raphael notes, for *not being patriarchal enough* (Raphael 35).[23]

In truth God was not wholly eclipsed in Auschwitz, Raphael suggests, but became incarnate in women who turned in compassion and bodily care toward one another, defying the most inhumane and desperate circumstances. With unsparing detail, Raphael unearths the largely ignored and forgotten stories of women in the camps who maintained the practices of Jewish prayer and ritual purification with whatever resources were available to them—not excluding their own bodily fluids where water was nowhere to be found (Raphael 68). Within the barbed-wire enclosure of the camps one woman's body bent in compassionate presence over another woman's or a child's body formed an encircling space where the divine Presence could dwell, where God could be bodily reconciled with humanity over against the patriarchal god of raw power, the false and idolatrous god of nation-states and National Socialism. Even (and especially) in Auschwitz, the most basic gestures of compassion constituted "a redemptive moment of human presence, a *staying there* against erasure" (Raphael 157)—not only for women in the camps, but through them, for God.

Raphael tells the story of a woman who, torn from her husband and children by SS guards immediately after arriving at the camp, falls weeping on the frozen ground "with the flaming crematoria before her," when she suddenly feels two hands lay a garment around her shoulders. An old Frenchwoman had stepped forward, wrapping her in her own cloak, whispering, "It will be over and done soon, it will be over" (Raphael 58). Raphael recalls another now-iconic story of an old woman who is remembered "for holding in her arms a motherless 1-year-old child as she stood at

---

and balanced overview see Leo D. Lefebure, "The Wisdom of God: Sophia and Christian Theology," *Christian Century* 111.29 (October 19, 1994) 951-57; in Western Christian feminist retrievals the definitive study is Elizabeth Johnson's magisterial *She Who Is: The Mystery of God in Feminist Theological Discourse* (New York: Crossroad, 1992).

23. Raphael's thesis, rendered with considerable apophatic humility and deference to the inexplicable horrors of Auschwitz, hinges on the need to challenge patriarchal assumptions about how God's power and presence are (and are not) manifest in the world: "There has been too much asking '*where* was God in Auschwitz?' and not enough '*who* was God in Auschwitz'" (54).

the edge of the communal pit, about to be shot with the rest of her village by Nazi troops. The old woman sang to the child and tickled him under the chin until he laughed with joy. Then they were shot" (Raphael 58).

Clearly Raphael's case for the divine presence in Auschwitz does not hinge on numerical or otherwise logical analyses, as if hints and gestures of the good could cancel out the overwhelming weight of evil. Hers is not "a quantitative theology, contingent upon circumstance"; it is "a qualitative, ethical theology" (Raphael 71) in which "the truly numinous spectacle was not the horror of the flaming chimneys but the *mysterium* of human love that is stronger than death, the *tremendum* of its judgment upon demonic hate, and the *fascinans* of its calling God back into a world which had cast her out" (Raphael 74).[24] Indeed, the sacramental imagination, as I would call it here, whether Jewish or Christian, is an impulse that "attaches very large meanings to very small signs" (Raphael 139).

Let me risk a personal example much closer to home. Several years ago my wife and I adopted two children from Haiti. Immediately after our adopted son Henry was born, somewhere in the vast slum of Cité Soleil in Port-Au-Prince, his mother abandoned him in a latrine, believing she had been impregnated by an evil spirit. My wife and I were told this story when we held Henry for the first time at the age of 6 months. We also learned that sometime after he was abandoned—we don't know whether it was minutes or hours—another woman from the area heard his cries and found the newborn struggling in the latrine, half-submerged in feces. The neighbor retrieved him, brought him back to his mother, and insisted that she take him to the orphanage. She did. The rationalist may hear this story and call it a happy accident of circumstance. I call it a miracle of grace, which brought Henry crying and fighting *for life* from one woman's womb into another's sheltering arms, and, less than a year later, into my family's embrace.

Of course for every story like ours there are ten thousand (and six million) more that defy theological meaning. Even ours is haunted by ambiguities. Can grace rise from the horror of an earthquake? Since the earthquake in Haiti of January 2010 I have often thought of Henry's birth mother, and I pray that God has freed her from whatever dark spirits, or abusive men, may once have overshadowed her. Even still, when I contemplate this beautiful child who came to us "in the fullness of time," from a chain of events and innumerable acts of selflessness well beyond my capacity to understand, I cannot help but fall mute in wonder.

---

24. Raphael draws on Rudolph Otto's famous description of religious experience as the *mysterium tremendum et fascinans* (Rudolf Otto, *The Idea of the Holy* [New York: Oxford University Press, 1958]).

There is a beautiful teaching in the Jewish tradition called *tikkun olam*, a Hebrew phrase meaning "the reparation," the "making good," "the rescuing to make good of what is left of this smashed world."[25] The wellspring of *tikkun olam* is love received and love freely given, a fierce love that seeks justice and the flourishing of life for all God's children. In her study of Auschwitz Melissa Raphael gets it exactly right, I believe, when she concludes that the restoration or *tikkun* of the world "does not occupy a quantity of space and time; it is the theophanic possibility of a moment" (Raphael 80). The fearful mystery of grace hinges precisely on the moment—the accumulated constellation of moments—in which we, and people we will never meet, say yes or no to love.

Collectively what such moments reveal is a picture of God's power as manifest in the vulnerability and weakness of incarnate love. "Where the communal fabric of the world was being torn apart, human love was anticipating its renewal" (Raphael 142). Where racist ideology sought to obliterate God as God-incarnate in the Jews there were nevertheless women (and certainly there were men) who "made a sanctuary for the spark of the divine presence that saved it from being extinguished" (Raphael 79). Here is a central Jewish insight that Christian theology has too often obscured: God asks, God invites, God needs our participation in the indwelling drama of love. We encounter that same flash of incarnate presence in Etty Hillesum. The realization of God's own hope for the world, what Jesus calls the Reign of God, hinges on our inner receptiveness, our *fiat*, our participation.

For Catholics, of course, and for Thomas Merton, not only Christ but Mary stands as our model for the call to such participation. Thus from *Hagia Sophia*: "Through her wise answer, through her obedient understanding, through the sweet yielding consent of Sophia, God enters without publicity into the city of rapacious men" (*ESF* 68). But we must never forget that Mary's *fiat*, her deep attunement to the divine presence, had long been prepared in her, as it was for Jesus, by the people Israel, whose stories resound everywhere with the call of covenant relationship in history. Note how the word "Presence" evokes a gift that is both spatial and temporal: *I am here with you now, in this place, in this moment*—not just with you, but *in* you, and you in me. God awaits, as it were, our bodily surrender to a communion that is deeper, yet more hidden and tenuous (because free) than any earth-shaking or army-defeating theophany. Like the deep bass note of a minor triad, *Be still and know that I am God* resounds with *Be still and know that I am a human being*, and more inef-

---

25. George Steiner, "To Speak of Walter Benjamin," in *Benjamin Studies: Perception and Experience in Modernity* (Amsterdam: Rodopi, 2002) 13-23, at 22.

fably still, beneath the din of war, *Be still and know that I am the Earth*.

From a sophianic perspective the Earth indeed is "the silent memory of the world that gives life and fruit to all"; she who "preserves everything in herself" and in whom "nothing perishes," not even the smallest and most forgotten of creatures.[26] Etty Hillesum frequently describes a sense of divine presence consoling her from within the silences of nature, as in "the jasmine [outside] and that piece of sky beyond my window" (Hillesum 152). Likewise Melissa Raphael notes that when no person was capable of a kind word or compassionate touch amid the dehumanizing conditions of the camps, "inanimate natural objects could take on the functions of divine presence for women." Here she recounts Victor Frankl's story of a girl who told him as she lay dying that a bare chestnut tree "was the only friend she had in her loneliness and that she often talked to it." When Frankl asked the girl if the tree replied, she answered, "It said to me, 'I am here—I am here—I am life, eternal life.'" Raphael concludes: "If God has chosen Israel as God's vehicle of self-revelation then [such stories] must tell us something about the nature and posture of God's presence among us. It may seem little more than a tree stripped of its leaves by an untempered wind" (Raphael 58).[27]

---

26. Sergius Bulgakov, cited in Bernice Rosenthal, "The Nature and Function of Sophia in Sergei Bulgakov's Prerevolutionary Thought," in *Russian Religious Thought*, ed. Judith Kornblatt and Richard Gustafson (Madison: University of Wisconsin Press, 1996) 154-75, at 167. Rosenthal notes that in the Russian Bible, Genesis 3:19 reads: "for earth thou art and to earth shalt thou return." Bulgakov's celebration of the mutual relationship between the "holy flesh" of humanity (Adam) and "matter-mother" (the Earth) is often hymnic—"In you we are born, you feed us, we touch you with our feet, to you we return"—yet never sentimental or merely bucolic. Indeed his constructive theological justification of the natural world presages contemporary environmental theologies by some fifty years. "The fate of nature, suffering and awaiting its liberation, is henceforth connected with the fate of man . . . the new heaven and new earth now enter as a necessary element into the composition of Christian eschatology."

27. Raphael cites Victor Frankl's *Man's Search for Meaning: An Introduction to Logotherapy* (Bsoton: Beacon Press, 159) 78. For some Christian readers the image of divine presence in a tree stripped bare may evoke patristic and medieval meditations on the Cross as linked with the Tree of Life in the book of Genesis. Raphael is careful to draw a distinction between the Jewish memory and experience of Shekhinah as "the real presence of a suffering God" and a "quasi-Christian incarnation of God crucified in Auschwitz." She cites Jurgen Moltmann's theology (*The Crucified God*) as a Christian depiction "that is close but not identical" to her own, noting that in Jewish understanding "the suffering is that of one who, being among us, suffers with us, but does not suffer vicariously *for* us" (54-55). To be sure, great care must be taken not to simply conflate Jewish and Christian interpretations of a suffering God, particularly in the case of the Shoah. Much depends from the Christian side on precisely *how* we understand Jesus' crucifixion to be redemptive.

"She Cannot Be a Prisoner"

We might think of other places today, mostly hidden and marginal places, where the protest of Life itself, of Earth, and a Mother-Love's rebellion against cruelty and arbitrary violence, seeks to break through into a world increasingly engineered for war, violence of an Unspeakable kind especially against women and children, and planetary destruction. She rises from the threatened rainforests of the Amazon river basin, not least in their mournful lament for the memory of Sr. Dorothy Stang. She speaks to us in the "Mothers of the Disappeared" who dance together in the Plaza de Mayo of Buenos Aires in silent remembrance of their missing sons and daughters, husbands and grandsons, sisters and granddaughters. She weeps and rises defiantly in the story of Somaly Mam and countless other Cambodian women and children sold into the horrors of sexual slavery, often by their own families. She whispers in the resplendent sophianic icons of the Russian Orthodox tradition, in Georges Bernanos' mournful classic *The Diary of a Country Priest*, and from almost every page in Sue Monk Kidd's resplendent first novel, *The Secret Life of Bees*, where the image of the Black Madonna infuses hope into the life of a young white girl who has none. She sings in the musical artistry of Joni Mitchell, Billy Holiday and Fannie Lou Hamer, in the soulful storytelling of Bill Withers' "Grandma's Hands," live at Carnegie Hall in 1973, and in Sojourner Truth's still-electrifying "Ain't I a Woman?" She cries out in the silent aftershocks of destroyed natural landscapes and in the faces of the global poor and victimized women and children of color.[28]

What binds these diverse narratives into one wondrous yet troubling mosaic is the affirmation of divine presence precisely, urgently, and most intensely, in those persons and places written off by conventional wisdom as inhuman and God-forsaken. Indeed where conventional wisdom about the real world registers no disconnect between our complacent worship of "God" and the systematic violation of women, children and the planet itself, divine Wisdom cries out from the crossroads in protest, identifying herself especially with the little, the hidden and forgotten ones, and

---

28. See Rosanne Murphy, *Martyr of the Amazon: The Life of Sister Dorothy Stang* (Maryknoll, NY: Orbis, 2007), and *They Killed Sister Dorothy*, dir. Daniel Junge and Henry Ansbacher (First Run Features, 2009); Somaly Mam, *The Road of Lost Innocence: The True Story of a Cambodian Heroine* (New York: Spiegal and Grau, 2008); Georges Bernanos, *The Diary of a Country Priest*, trans. Pamela Morris (New York: MacMillan, 1937); Sue Monk Kidd, *The Secret Life of Bees* (New York: Penguin, 2003); Sojourner Truth, "Ain't I a Woman" (http://www.fordham.edu/halsall/mod/sojtruth-woman.asp); Nicolas Kristof and Sheryl Wu Dunn, *Half the Sky: Turning Oppression into Opportunity for Women Worldwide* (New York: Vintage, 2010).

with suffering earth, the Mother of all God's children. Neither blood, nor political boundaries, nor religion can contain the reach of God's loving presence. "She smiles, for though they have bound her, she cannot be a prisoner. Not that she is strong, or clever, but simply that she does not understand imprisonment" (*ESF* 63-64).

"She cannot be a prisoner," Merton writes, in a singular flash of hope. Yet we know that she can, and is. Surely the unraveling of the world in our time is bound up with our ongoing violence against and willful sundering *of God*. As Jewish theologian Rita Gross puts it: "When the masculine and the feminine aspect of God have been reunited and the female half of humanity has been returned from exile, we will begin to have our *tikkun*. The world will be repaired."[29]

Who is Wisdom-Sophia? She is the divine Child in us who *refuses to be accommodated* to reality as dictated by "the people with watch chains,"[30] the men who make the trains run on time: trains loaded with priests and intellectuals steaming north into Siberia for the Gulag; trains bulging with Jews like so many cattle destined for the efficient slaughter; or closer to home, trains loaded with metals stripped from the earth lumbering into the sprawling GE plant outside Louisville, Kentucky, running three shifts night and day to feed our collective appetite for new refrigerators and washing machines, or the latest generation of drone aircraft now swarming the skies in the East, piloted by some kid sitting behind a computer screen in New Mexico. She is the Child in us who rejects the logic of the businessman, a bit drowsy after lunch, who says over his steak and martini: "Look kid, the sooner you grow up and learn to live in the real world the better."

She is the perplexity of a young Benjamin Braddock played by Dustin Hoffman in *The Graduate* when the husband of his ill-fated lover, Mrs. Robinson, corners him after graduation and says to him with utter conviction: "I've got one word for you, son: *plastics*." And she is Sylvia in Peter Weir's brilliant film *The Truman Show*, breaking onto the set to tell Truman, played with perfect, poignant innocence by Jim Carrey, that the world he lives in is a completely manufactured fiction. Sylvia's is the face

---

29. Rita Gross, cited in Raphael 150. In a similar spirit Kristof and Wu Dunn open their study of global women's oppression with a Chinese proverb: *Women hold up half the sky*. When Kristof and Wu Dunn ask "Is Islam misogynistic?" (149-66) they pose one of the pivotal theological questions of our time with far-reaching social and political implications. Of course whether Christianity or Catholicism is misogynistic also continues to be well worth asking.

30. See Thomas Merton, "Boris Pasternak and the People with Watch Chains," in Thomas Merton, *Selected Essays* ed. Patrick F. O'Connell (Maryknoll, NY: Orbis, 2013) 39-51.

that haunts Truman and will not let him go; she is the one who reveals to Truman that he is not living, in fact, because he is not free. Wisdom-Sophia is that spirit of creativity and celebration *written into our very being*, yet feared and starved dead for oxygen by an institutional Church determined to rigidly choreograph and control every move in the dance. After all, as the logic of clericalism goes, the people in the pews "are not theologically trained."[31]

Hope in the key of Wisdom refuses to accommodate itself to the lock-tight logic of "the way things are" as preached by the powers and principalities in society or church. This is the meaning of her innocence, and ours, when we open our hearts and imaginations to possibilities never before seen yet dancing right before our eyes.[32] In an atmosphere marked painfully by impasse and despair, Wisdom injects a word of unity and hope, of revelatory wonder and beauty, and above all, the call to freedom in community and full participation in the human life story of God.

---

31. To cite one of far too many examples of such clericalism in practice, several years ago pastors at Catholic churches in Arizona, Michigan and Virginia forbade altar girls during *all forms* of the Mass—not just the reinstated Tridentine or Latin form, which does not permit girls to serve at the altar—under the logic that "replacing girls with boys as servers leads to more vocations to the priesthood." Facing objections from parishioners, a Phoenix pastor says he did not consult the parish council "because they are not theologically trained." One (female) Catholic blogger applauded the move, describing girl altar servers as a "liturgical aberration" and "one more example of the devastating feminization of worship which has contributed in no small measure to the prevalence of effeminate priests and the sex abuse scandal." A Virginia mother whose pastor reinstated a boys-only policy says, "That's when I knew, in my heart, that we couldn't stay any longer at this parish." She and her husband and daughters have since "floated around" between area parishes, feeling "heartbroken by our church." The diocese of Lincoln, NE, has forbidden girl servers since 1994. See Editors, "Save the Altar Girls," *America* (10/10/2011); Tom Gallagher, "No Girl Servers at Latin Masses," *National Catholic Reporter Online* (6/9/2011; available at: http://ncronline.org); Alice Popovici, "Catholics Protest Altar Server Policy," *National Catholic Reporter Online* (12/3/2011; available at: http://ncronline.org). Though it is still very early in his papacy Pope Francis has been an outspoken critic of clericalism and has suggested that "we don't yet have a truly deep theology of women in the church."

32. The theme of innocence figures significantly in Merton's theological anthropology: see "Message to Poets" (*RU* 155-64); also Pramuk, *Sophia*, 200-202. By "innocence" Merton does not mean to suggest a regression to the freshness of childhood, in a naïve or narcissistic sense, still less a denial of sin. Negatively it evokes the refusal to be accommodated to the common-sense view of things in mass society or a passive acceptance of "the way things are"; positively it speaks to "a new birth, the divine birth in us" that grounds our freedom and creativity in history as co-creators before God.

"To Say Something Worthy of God"

One of the earliest clues to the impact of the Russian Sophia tradition appears in Merton's journal of April 25, 1957: "Bulgakov and Berdyaev are writers of great, great attention. . . . They have dared to accept the challenge of the sapiential books, the challenge of the image of Proverbs where Wisdom is 'playing in the world' before the face of the Creator." If there is a clear thread running through Merton's notes on the Russians, it is his admiration for their theological creativity, their willingness to make mistakes "in order to say something great and worthy of God." "One wonders," he muses, "if our theological cautiousness is not after all the sign of a fatal coldness of heart, an awful sterility born of fear, or of despair."[33] Indeed, one wonders!

In Merton's case the embrace of Wisdom-Sophia marked a protest against the "flight from woman"[34] wounding his own past, and perhaps even crippling the prospects for renewal in the Catholic Church, a wound that cuts ever deeper today. But no less prescient was his protest against the deadly "seriousness" of American power and its Promethean grasping for life that plays out tragically, in fact, as an addiction to death. Under a reigning consciousness bent on war and its endless preparation, the sophianic Child—and real children everywhere—lay forgotten, dead, buried. Christian "eschatology" in such an atmosphere becomes little more than "the last gasp of exhausted possibilities" (*RU* 75), our secret desire to get it all over with.

What does it mean, then, to live together with Wisdom? It is to live fully awake in the center of these contradictions of our times while refusing to be *defined* by them, to accommodate ourselves to them, as Merton puts it, like an "essence" fed into a computer. "For when I am home with her I can take my ease, for nothing is bitter in her company" (Wis. 8:16).[35] Citing Julian of Norwich, Merton calls this the true "*eschatological secret*" of Christian hope, and the very "heart of theology: not solving the

---

33. Thomas Merton, *A Search for Solitude: Pursuing the Monk's True Life. Journals, vol. 3: 1952-1960*, ed. Lawrence S. Cunningham (San Francisco: HarperCollins, 1996) 85-86.

34. For the impact on Merton's consciousness of psychologist Karl Stern's book *The Flight from Woman* see Jonathan Montaldo's seminal study, "A Gallery of Women's Faces and Dreams of Women from the Drawings and Journals of Thomas Merton," *The Merton Annual* 14 (2001) 155-72, at 156. For me an important companion piece with many rich cross-resonances to Montaldo's study is Margaret Bridget Betz, "Merton's Images of Elias, Wisdom, and the Inclusive God," in *The Merton Annual* 13 (2000) 190-207, at 195.

35. See Merton's remarkable fiftieth birthday journal, January 31, 1965: Thomas Merton, *Dancing in the Water of Life: Seeking Peace in the Hermitage. Journals, vol. 5: 1963-1965*, ed. Robert E. Daggy (San Francisco: HarperCollins, 1997) 200-201.

contradiction, but remaining in the midst of it, in peace, knowing that it is fully solved, but that the solution is secret, and will never be guessed until it is revealed. . . . The wise heart lives in Christ."[36]

---

36. Thomas Merton, *Conjectures of a Guilty Bystander* (Garden City, NY: Doubleday, 1966) 192. The affirmation of covenantal promise and non-coercive divine presence even "in the valley of the shadow of death" (e.g., Psalms 22-23) seems to me the profoundest seed of biblical good news that both Jews and Christians must embrace and bring into dialogue with others in an increasingly fragmented and violent world. Whether Muslims might have recourse to such analogical or sacramental imagination through Sufi mysticism, for example, or elements of the Qur'an, I cannot say with certainty. Certainly Merton's extensive dialogue with Muslim and Sufi practitioners has much to teach us on this question. See Bonnie Thurston, "Brothers in Prayer and Worship: The Merton/Aziz Correspondence, an Islamic-Christian Dialogue," in James Conner, David Scott and Bonnie Thurston, *The Voice of the Stranger* (Stratton-on-the-Fosse, UK: Thomas Merton Society of Great Britain and Ireland, 2008) 17-33; and Rob Baker and Gray Henry, eds., *Merton & Sufism: The Untold Story* (Louisville, KY: Fons Vitae, 1999). But on this point hinge, I think, a great many theological and political difficulties, which converge on the realization of humankind's ontological unity and freedom in God, the deep ground for dialogue, justice and peace. For Islamic perspectives on divine-human relationality and the divine feminine see Seyyed Hossein Nasr, "The Male and Female in the Islamic Perspective," *Studies in Comparative Religion* 14:1-2 (Winter-Spring, 1980) (available at: http://www.studiesincomparativereligion.com/uploads/ArticlePDFs/351.pdf); and Laurence Galian, "The Centrality of the Divine Feminine in Sufism," *Proceedings of the 2nd Annual Hawaii International Conference on Arts and Humanities* (2004) (available at: http://www.hichumanities.org/). For an expanded discussion of hope and the sacramental theological imagination building from the experience and memory of God as Wisdom-Sophia see Christopher Pramuk, "Presences," in *Hope Sings, So Beautiful: Graced Encounters Across the Color Line* (Collegeville, MN: Liturgical Press, 2013) 105-21.

Personal Bridges, Spiritual Communities: The Correspondence of Thomas Merton and Zalman Schachter-Shalomi

Edward K. Kaplan

Issues of personal and spiritual integrity dominate Thomas Merton's correspondence with Zalman Schachter-Shalomi, a rabbi and teacher formed by Hasidism, the Jewish pietistic movement inspired in eighteenth-century Poland by the miracle worker known as the Baal Shem Tov.[1] Hasidism is a form of traditional Judaism that emphasizes prayer, inwardness and celebration over rote obedience to religious law (or halacha). Both Merton and Reb Zalman (as we will call him informally) sought to renew their respective traditions by emphasizing self-transformation and a concrete relationship with the living God. Seen in the abstract, their correspondence traces a deep friendship between a Jew and a Catholic, but more so a surprisingly comfortable sharing of their inner struggles with the ultimate goal of forming communities.[2]

In the 1960s, Rabbi Schachter-Shalomi founded the Jewish Renewal movement, whereas Merton donated his various writings (both intimate and official) to enable generations of scholars and activists to learn from his insights. The ITMS (International Thomas Merton Society) is the Catholic version of Jewish Renewal, a community of dissidents who are both progressive and devout. All readers can benefit from the abundant, well-organized resources of the Merton community. Merton's letters to

---

1. Rabbi Israel ben Eliezer (1700-1760), Master of the Good Name (the Name of God). Some Jewish terminology will be helpful: a Hasidic *Rebbe* is the charismatic leader of a traditional Jewish community (in a shtetl or Jewish neighborhood in a town, as close to a monastic environment as modern Jews can get). A *Rav* or Rabbi is an ordained authority who interprets sacred Law (or halacha) to the community or individuals. Hasidism emphasizes joy and celebration as well as study and meticulous observance of sacred Law. The Hasidic Rebbe derives spiritual authority from his closeness to the living God. The name Zalman Schachter is a Jewish name, comprised of Zalman (or Solomon, or Shlomy) and Schachter, which refers to a ritual slaughterer or shohet. Because of the horrendous conflicts in the Middle East between Israel and the Palestinians and other Arab countries, Zalman added the name Shalomi (from Shalom), which he would remove after peace was attained. I sometimes refer to him as Reb Zalman; *Reb* is simply an honorific term in Yiddish, like Mister.

2. My thanks to Susanne Jennings for pointing out the difference in tone between Merton's letters to Abraham Joshua Heschel and those to Zalman Schachter and her insightful suggestions for improving this article.

Zalman are collected in *The Hidden Ground of Love*,[3] edited by William Shannon, and Zalman's letters to Merton in *Merton and Judaism*,[4] edited by Beatrice Bruteau. That volume also contains papers delivered at the 2002 Louisville Conference on the topic, virtually all articles relating Merton and Judaism, along with a transcription of an interview with Reb Zalman that demonstrates the rabbi's own pluralism, his gift for fitting experiences specific to Jews and Roman Catholics into modern English, even a hip American idiom.[5]

Schachter himself completed a journey from traditional, even medieval, Judaism to modernity. Born in 1924 and educated in Vienna, he immigrated to the United States in 1941, where he joined the Lubavitch (or Chabad) Hasidic movement. In 1956 he became Hillel rabbi and professor of Judaic Studies at the University of Manitoba in Winnipeg, Canada, a period which he described as "a hothouse for the spirit."[6] The friendship of Rabbi Zalman Schachter-Shalomi with Father Louis developed with their correspondence from 1960 to 1966, and included at least one visit to the Abbey of Gethsemani.

Forming a Spiritual Alliance

Merton and Reb Zalman formed a special bond because of their common vision as prophets, or even as "heretics of modernity," in the astute formulation of Shaul Magid.[7] At first, they exchanged information, books and essays. As preparation for his conferences (or lectures) to the novices, Merton began by asking Zalman for Hasidic or Jewish sources. But quite soon their communication took on an intimate, friendly and informal tone. As the conversation began, Zalman immediately reached out to Merton in a Christian idiom sensitive to their shared liturgical calendars.

---

3. Thomas Merton, *The Hidden Ground of Love: Letters on Religious Experience and Social Concerns*, ed. William H. Shannon (New York: Farrar, Straus, Giroux, 1985) 533-41; subsequent references will be cited as "*HGL*" parenthetically in the text.

4. Beatrice Bruteau, ed., *Merton & Judaism: Holiness in Words—Recognition, Repentance, and Renewal* (Louisville, KY: Fons Vitae, 2003) 198-207; subsequent references will be cited as "Bruteau" parenthetically in the text.

5. Edward K. Kaplan and Shaul Magid, "An Interview with Rabbi Zalman Schachter-Shalomi" (Bruteau 301-23); a videotape of the interview, in which Zalman traces his relationship with Merton and other Catholics, is available at the Thomas Merton Center, Bellarmine University, Louisville, KY.

6. Zalman Schachter-Shalomi with Edward Hoffman, *My Life in Jewish Renewal: A Memoir* (Lanham, MD: Rowman & Littlefield, 2012) xiii; subsequent references will be cited as "Schachter-Shalomi, *Life*" parenthetically in the text.

7. Shaul Magid, "Abraham Joshua Heschel and Thomas Merton: Heretics of Modernity" (Bruteau 233-51).

On personal stationary whimsically decorated with images of dancing Hasidim, Zalman's first preserved letter to Merton, dated December 12, 1960, was a Christmas greeting: "Xmas continues through the feast of the *b'rith* ['covenant,' written in Hebrew in the original] the circumcision on to Epiphany. . . . Please pray for my intention—you and all your other religious problems have been on my intercession list for a while," said the rabbi, with playful seriousness (Bruteau 198).

Acknowledging receipt of Zalman's pedagogical booklet on Hasidic meditative prayer, "The First Step,"[8] Merton answered on January 18 of the New Year (1961):

> *The First Step* seems to me to be very practical and well done, and I especially like the work of Rabbi Nachman and his message of fervor and hope. Too often today the idea of "hope" is presented in a totally untheological and secular form, as a kind of pious optimism that "everything will be all right" . . . In the dark night through which we travel it is good to hear the voices of those who have not forgotten the Holy and Merciful God Who seeks to save us from ruin. . . . I am very much interested in the Hasidim and respond to their fervor very readily. (*HGL* 533)

Already Merton is thinking well beyond his personal curiosity. His inwardness, and his teaching, lead him to reflect upon possibilities of community beyond the monastery. In that same letter of January 1961, Merton expresses interest in arranging a yearly group visit to Gethsemani with Zalman and other Jewish friends, "perhaps some kind of annual event" (*HGL* 533). (The abbot discouraged Merton from inviting visitors to his hermitage.)

They shared even deeper aspirations. Merton's internal conflict between conversation versus settling into a life of silence and solitude in his hermitage was something that the busy Zalman understood quite well. For the rabbi was forced to use his driving time between home and his classes at the university not only to dictate letters but also to pray.

These friends were bothered by external obstacles to spontaneous communication. Again around Christmastime, they exchanged substantial letters relating to their quest for holiness. On December 15, 1961 it was Merton's turn to transpose Judaic concepts into Christian spirituality as he evoked Hannukah, the Jewish festival of lights: "And you know

---

8. "The First Step" began as a photocopied document. For the latest revision, see Zalman Schachter-Shalomi with Donald Gropman, *The First Steps to a New Jewish Spirit* (Woodstock, VT: Jewish Lights Publishing, 2003); see also the website "Aleph: Alliance for Jewish Renewal."

that whether I write or not, it makes no difference to the profound union between us in the glory of Him in Whose service we are hidden. And the lights are lit one by one outside the door of our Church, week by week. And we plunge more into the cold and the darkness. I wish I knew more about doing T'shuvah [metanoia or penance]. It is the only thing that seems to make much sense in these days" (*HGL* 534). T'shuvah or repentance is indeed the central goal of Jewish spiritual discipline, and not only during the ten "Days of Awe" (between Rosh Hashanah, the "Jewish New Year" and Yom Kippur, the "Day of Atonement"). While Merton insisted upon the spiritual congruity of the two religions, he recognized some theological difficulties, as he continued: "Anyway, we need to make straight the paths for the coming of the Consoler. And I think the Christian needs to wait with the longing and anguish of the Jew for the Messiah, not with our foregone-conclusion, accomplished-fact-that-justifies-all-our-nonsense attitude" (*HGL* 534). True to the spirit of a progressive Church, soon to be publicly debated, Merton affirms the enduring theological necessity—and autonomy—of Judaism.

Merton followed up these tentative reflections on messianic theology on February 15, 1962, as he anticipated Zalman's visit to Gethsemani. (During his stay in the monastery Zalman would also meet the radical Jesuit Daniel Berrigan and form another Jewish/Catholic friendship.) Merton wrote Schachter that he was inspired by *The Last of the Just*,[9] a French novel by André Schwartz-Bart about centuries of Jewish suffering and the thirty-six men who redeem the evil world through their anonymous righteousness: "I think it is a really great book. It has helped crystallize out a whole lot of things I am thinking about" (*HGL* 535). Merton elaborated on this in his journal entry of February 13, 1962 which concludes: "Pity as an absolute, more central than truth."[10] In another journal entry he wrote: can one "look attentively at Christ and not see Auschwitz?"[11] See also Merton's letter of February 24, 1962 to Rabbi Steven Schwartzschild, which continues this eschatological train of thought:

Certainly I think the unutterable pity of the fate of the Jews in our time is eschatological, and is a manifestation of the loneliness and dejection of God, that He should bring upon Himself so much sorrow and suffer it in His Beloved People. In this He is speaking to us

---

9. Andre Schwartz-Bart, *The Last of the Just* (New York: Atheneum, 1960).

10. Thomas Merton, *Turning Toward the World: The Pivotal Years. Journals, vol. 4: 1960-1963*, ed. Victor A. Kramer (San Francisco: HarperCollins, 1996) 202.

11. Thomas Merton, *Dancing in the Water of Life: Seeking Peace in the Hermitage. Journals, vol. 5: 1963-1965*, ed. Robert E. Daggy (San Francisco: HarperCollins, 1997) 98 [4/20/1964].

who believe ourselves, in His mercy, to have been adopted into His Chosen People and given, without any merit, the salvation and joy promised to the Sons of Abraham. But we on the other hand have been without understanding and without pity and have not known that we were only guests invited to the banquet at the last minute."[12]

Merton continued by evoking his own sensitivity to world crisis: atomic war, poverty, racial injustice, etc. in which Judaism should play a crucial role. Merton's preoccupation with the end of days, as expressed in his February letter to Schachter, affirms the necessity of both traditions:

Chief of these is of course no news to anyone: that the Jews have been the great eschatological sign of the twentieth century. That everything comes to depend on people understanding this fact, not just reacting to it with a little appropriate feeling, but seeing the whole thing as a sign from God, *telling* us. Telling us what? Among other things, telling Christians that if they don't look out they are going to miss the boat or fall out of it, because the antinomy they have unconsciously and complacently supposed between the Jews and Christ is not even a very good figment of the imagination. The suffering Servant is One: Christ, Israel. There is one wedding and one wedding feast, not two or five or six. There is one bride. There is one mystery, and the mystery of Israel and of the Church is ultimately to be revealed as One. As one great scandal maybe to a lot of people on both sides who have better things to do than come to the wedding. (*HGL* 535)

An analysis of these complex theological thoughts from both the Jewish and Christian perspectives is beyond the scope of this paper. Yet we can recognize that Merton is struggling to accept the difference of faiths (especially, the persistent autonomy of Judaism), while attempting to acknowledge, perhaps unconsciously, a supercessionist view: "Each on our side we must prepare for the great eschatological feast on the mountains of Israel. [I repeat: "Each on our own side."] I have sat on the porch of the hermitage and sung chapters and chapters of the Prophets in Latin out over the valley, and it is a hair-raising experience is all I can say" (*HGL* 535). Father Louis singing the Hebrew prophets is practicing what Abraham Joshua Heschel calls "depth theology," a shattering, ineffable intuition of God's reality beyond creed and dogmas.[13] It is indeed through "depth

---

12. Thomas Merton, *Witness to Freedom: Letters in Times of Crisis*, ed. William H. Shannon (New York: Farrar, Straus, Giroux, 1994) 36. (Thanks to Susanne Jennings for these quotations.)

13. See Abraham Heschel, "Depth Theology," in *The Insecurity of Freedom* (New York: Farrar Straus & Giroux, 1966) 115-26; for a comprehensive study see John C.

theology" that Merton and Schachter will achieve their fullest mutuality.

Merton then gives voice to those Hebrew visionaries, inspired in large part by Heschel's recent book, *The Prophets*.[14] Merton shared his hope with Zalman that his own recent book, *The New Man*,[15] could provide a way for Jews and Christians to affirm together the essential holiness of humankind. As Merton responded to his Jewish friend:

> Therefore I am not at all surprised that you like *The New Man*, the best parts of which are Old Testament parts. When the Christians began to look at Christ as Prometheus. . . . You see what I mean? Then they justified war, then they justified crusades, then they justified pogroms, then they justified Auschwitz, then they justified the bomb, then they justified the Last Judgment: the Christ of Michelangelo is Prometheus, I mean the Christ in the Sistine Chapel. He is whipping sinners with his great Greek muscles. (*HGL* 535-36)

Merton concludes this vigorous letter by affirming what we might call an "open tent policy." Merton writes: "Enough. More some other time. May we enter into the Kingdom and sit down with Abraham and Isaac and Jacob and the Holy One, Blessed be His Name, to Whom Abraham gave hospitality in the Three Strangers" (*HGL* 536).[16] These were tumultuous years, not only for Merton, but for the entire Church. On 15 October 1962, Catholics—and Jews—together looked with trepidation toward the opening of the Ecumenical Council, soon to be called Vatican II.

A Gritty Spirituality

The correspondence fostered other moments of intimacy, often leavened with humor. These teachers confided to each other their problems with prayer, study and mindfulness—Merton in his hermitage versus his desire to organize visits; Zalman in his increasing involvement with the American 1960s counterculture, which sought him out for Sabbath workshops around the country, and even for guidance for experimentation with LSD. Curiosity notwithstanding, Merton did not have much sympathy with Zalman's association with Timothy Leary and the drug counterculture. Zalman wrote on February 6, 1964: "I am sending you a transcript of a

Merkle, *The Genesis of Faith: The Depth Theology of Abraham Joshua Heschel* (New York: Macmillan, 1985).

14. See Merton's January 11, 1963 letter to Schachter: "I have Heschel's *Prophets*—it is magnificent" (*HGL* 537).

15. Thomas Merton, *The New Man* (New York: Farrar, Straus and Cudahy, 1961).

16. Cf. Edward K. Kaplan, "The Open Tent: Angels and Strangers," in *Hosting the Stranger: Between Religions*, ed. Richard Kearney and James Taylor (New York: Continuum, 2011) 67-72.

talk I gave on *LSD and the Ascent of the Soul of the Ba'al Shem Tov* to a group of colleagues at Oconomowoc, Wisconsin. There are so many Hebrew words, and I could not just clean the thing up, yet I think you will glance though this thing" (Bruteau 202).[17] Merton did not find time to explore his friend's documentation.

A year or so later Merton explained to Linda (Parsons) Sabbath:

> I know my friend Zalman Schachter is quite enthusiastic about [psychedelics]. I of course cannot judge, never having had anything to do with them. . . . Theologically I suspect that the trouble with psychedelics is that we want to have interior experiences entirely on our own terms. This introduces an element of constraint and makes the freedom of pure grace impossible. Hence, religiously, I would say their value was pretty low. However, regarded merely psychologically, I am sure they have considerable interest. (*HGL* 521 [12/1/1965])

Fast forward to February 1964: two powerful epistolary exchanges expose the sometimes frightful depths of spiritual friendship. Merton first thanks Zalman for his last note and apologizes for disturbing his inner equilibrium: "I am sorry to learn that some of the inevitable grit and grime of my spirit is trickling into your prayer life. But thanks anyway for the support. I suppose I am a bit more gritty than usual, but nothing exceptional. Just a great deal of work and struggling with small and futile tasks and interferences" (*HGL* 538).[18]

Zalman was touched and answered Merton immediately on February 6, confessing to his own shortcomings:

> It is so difficult to think about G-d, always being His errand boy, then I say to myself: "I didn't ask for the errand. It was sent to me. Maybe He wants my errands more than my meditations." Even the time I used to have for intercession, while driving to and from Campus, which is thirteen miles out of town, on my windshield visor there being a long list of people and I would glance up from time to time, and wherever I would feel for a moment arrested, I would take that name and offer a few rounds of favorite psalms or something for them, as well as make up my mind to offer charity on their behalf; but even this has been taken away from me. . . . So, I will pray for

---

17. See Schachter-Shalomi, *Life* 141-53 for the text of Zalman's LSD report, and the photograph of Merton holding a book with the title, *The Psychedelic Experience*, taken in 1968.

18. Merton continues: "For one thing I have not even had a chance to get to your rebbe's *Treatise on Ecstasy* [ed. Louis Jacobs], because I have had a string of books on interlibrary loan (and still do) and have now to get them back at certain times."

you and please do pray for me, and we will keep in mind, won't we, that whatever curve we get pitched, we will try to bat. And after all, what is that business of the cross all about if not that. (Bruteau 202)

Responding a week later to Merton's essay on "The Climate of Monastic Prayer,"[19] which develops existentialist insights, Zalman focuses upon dread and emptiness. Dread and emptiness, two preoccupations at the heart of their conversations, surpassing the intellectual formalities of interfaith dialogue: "Your latest thing on dread coincides with much that has been happening to me lately, and if you would not be at Gethsemani, that is to say, at a monastery in which silence is important, I would want to send you a tape in which I could express myself to you, without the medium of a secretary transcribing things" (Bruteau 203 [2/13/1964]). Zalman's letter continues with a detailed meditation on dread (as a form of awe and reverence). Now the mystery of Christ enters the dialogue. Zalman judged that "our problem is not so much to come to terms with the Jesus of the Gospels—that is easy. Midrash and the early fathers of the Jewish faith parallel the Gospels so closely that we have no problem whatsoever in that." The real problem for Jews is the Passion, which cannot be handled conceptually.

Here is where Reb Zalman's personal experiments with LSD create an analogy with the Passion. Zalman finds in Merton's essay on monastic prayer the abyss of mysticism or despair:[20]

In fact, there is not even the momentary support that a Kierkegaardian begins [with], and in this you are close to Kierkegaard but not that close, and surely not identical. In Kierkegaard at least you have the security that comes from committing oneself to leap, and so the initial impetus comes from man's own leaping. What you are describing is a falling in which suddenly the ground from one's feet has been ripped and one falls into a vertigo in which not a single coordinate remains where it is, where every bit of security and sureness is gone, and one falls, falls, falls, if only one were sure, into the hands of the living G-d.

---

19. Thomas Merton, "The Climate of Monastic Prayer," *Collectanea Cisterciensia* 27 (1965) 273-87; this article was later expanded into the book of the same title: Thomas Merton, *The Climate of Monastic Prayer* (Washington, DC: Cistercian Publications, 1969), also published as *Contemplative Prayer* (New York: Herder & Herder, 1969); see especially chapters 16-18 on dread. See also William H. Shannon, "*Climate of Monastic Prayer*" and "Dread" in William H. Shannon, Christine M. Bochen and Patrick F. O'Connell, *The Thomas Merton Encyclopedia* (Maryknoll, NY: Orbis, 2002) 64-65, 120-21.

20. See Edward K. Kaplan, "Mysticism and Despair. The Threshold of Revelation," in *Holiness in Words. Abraham Joshua Heschel's Poetics of Piety* (Albany, NY: State University of New York Press, 1996) 61-74.

At the moment one falls one is under no assurance that underneath there are the Eternal Arms. How gladly one would exchange this for the greatest awe that comes from certitude. (Bruteau 204)

Then, in the next paragraph, Zalman cites the story of Reb Zusheh of Anipoli who "loved G-d and said: 'Dear L-rd, grant me some of the awe that your angels experience,' which G-d granted him, whereupon Reb Zusheh crawled underneath the bed; unable to take any more of this, he implored G-d: 'Please give me back the love that Zusheh has, and take away the angels' awe.'" Zalman explains to Merton, "this is not what you are talking about, because this too would be welcome, and much more easily endured than the dread of utter emptiness which you describe. In Reb Zusheh's awe, you have at least the consensus of the angels, you have a radiance of light and not darkness" (Bruteau 204-205). Merton and Zalman have reached a moment of excruciating spiritual intimacy, of shared vulnerability and mutual trust—human trust, I mean. Reb Zalman's letter is far too intense for our brief analysis, but I will cite the rabbi's recognition of solidarity with the Christian experience:

There is a mighty pull to build around that moment of love so that I, too, will not be alone but with you, and maybe in my tumbling. I'm like Dismas [the penitent thief crucified with Jesus] looking for assurance in the last moment of dying, and even if you were to give it to me, . . . you and I would have to bear our own total abandonment, being unprotected by *our* G-d, in fact, being completely unsure of [there] ever existing a covenant between us and G-d, so that we frantically can look for the covenant policy so that we can put in a claim. (Bruteau 205)

These two brothers, a Jew and a Catholic, become one in this agonizing anticipation of either disbelief or mystical death. The question of faith, of trust in God, looms large. Are there at least two covenants—or none? Merton responded more succinctly, and with more focus, about one month later, on April 7, 1964:

Many thanks for your Easter note and I have not forgotten the long good letter dictated in the car about the prayer of dread, etc. Actually, according to Abbot Ammonas, my latest discovery, the prayer of dread is prelude to the gift of the Holy Spirit, after a "last purification" in which one seems to be in hell. I am not exactly looking forward to that kind of thing, as the minor purifications I am getting are hot enough for me right now. (*HGL* 539)

After two more years, in addition to these theological and prophetic issues, Zalman's last preserved letter to Merton (December 1, 1966, a transcribed taped communication) exemplifies the essence of contemplative friendship: "Shalom—Pax—Enchanté—Om—'tah-tah'—and all the good! Today is a day. Yesterday was freezing rain and a blizzard. Driving is really terrible. I'm not quite with you then, so have to watch driving a bit. This week is loused up something terrible" (Bruteau 206). After telling Merton about a discussion he had with Jewish college students in Montreal, Zalman expresses his own perplexities about political activism: "I wanted them to share with me my struggles of the difficulty of making any kind of 'pronunciamento' especially that they felt the basic unsaved exilic condition in which we are and the conviction that says that, before the Messias, the body of the world has to bleed a little some place. Maybe that all the peace efforts ought to be directed to keep the bleeding down to a minimum" (Bruteau 207).

We have finally returned to the ITMS community of which we are all a part. Zalman's letter of 1 December 1966, dictated when driving in a blizzard, ends with this plea for more communication:

> You never answered me since I sent you that thing on *Life* magazine. I'd like to get a word, just hello, or goodbye, or "go to hell," or something from you. So at least I know you are alive. Otherwise I get all kinds of schemes in my head—like Thomas Merton is a prisoner in a Catholic cookie factory or cheese and every noble impulse wants me to come down to Kentucky and pull you out. At the same time, I know that you have no such problem and you are there because you want to be there and it was part of your life struggle and what have you. But, just a word would always be good. For the time being I have nothing more to say, so I'm sending you only this one thought—Just, I love you! (Bruteau 207)

Louis Massignon and the Seeds
of Thomas Merton's "Monastic Protest"

Gordon Oyer

During the second week of November 1964, Thomas Merton turned his thoughts toward hosting a retreat for several "peaceniks from the FOR,"[1] as he jokingly described them. Though not foreseen then, this peacemaker retreat would break new ground for interfaith collaboration in social activism and feed into later anti-war efforts. Its mix of Catholic, mainline Protestant and historic peace church voices helped to forge new relationships in peace activism and cross-fertilize theologies of social engagement. While tying down some retreat logistics with his friend Daniel Berrigan, Merton also asked if he would lead a discussion on some aspect of "spiritual roots of protest"—a phrase Merton would adopt as the retreat's theme and title. For his part, Merton shared that he would address the topic from a "monastic-desert viewpoint,"[2] or as he later named it on a handout, "The Monastic Protest. The voice in the wilderness."[3]

Merton's subject is not surprising. He was deeply invested in exploring monastic ideas and often applied desert imagery to monastic experience. Four years earlier he had published a small volume of sayings by fourth-century "desert fathers"—ascetic hermits who removed themselves to the wilderness in response to a society that conflated political power with Christian practice.[4] Regarding protest, one year earlier he had written, "It is my intention to make my entire life . . . a protest against the crimes and injustices of war and political tyranny which threaten to destroy the whole race of man and the world with him. . . . I make monastic silence a protest against the lies of politicians, propagandists and agitators. . . . [T]he faith in which I believe is also invoked by many who believe in

---

1. Thomas Merton to W. H. Ferry, n.d., Thomas Merton Center [TMC] Archives, Bellarmine University, Louisville, KY.

2. Thomas Merton to Daniel Berrigan, *The Hidden Ground of Love: Letters on Religious Experience and Social Concerns*, ed. William H. Shannon (New York: Farrar, Straus, Giroux, 1985) 85 [11/11/64]; subsequent references will be cited as "*HGL*" parenthetically in the text.

3. Thomas Merton, "Retreat, November, 1964: Spiritual Roots of Protest," in *The Nonviolent Alternative*, ed. Gordon C. Zahn (New York: Farrar, Straus, Giroux, 1981) 260; subsequent references will be cited as "*NVA*" parenthetically in the text.

4. Thomas Merton, *The Wisdom of the Desert: Sayings from the Desert Fathers of the Fourth Century* (New York: New Directions, 1960).

war, believe in racial injustices, believe in self-righteous and lying forms of tyranny. My life must, then, be a protest against these also, and perhaps against these most of all."[5] What may surprise, however, is that this monastic tradition did not of itself serve as Merton's primary resource to prepare his retreat comments. For the most part, he instead sought inspiration for this task in several writings of Louis Massignon (1886-1962), a French Catholic mystic, linguist and scholar of Islam.

Massignon, Protest and Trappist Asceticism

Louis Massignon may be most familiar to readers of Merton as having introduced him to the concept of the *point vierge*, or virginal point, which the monk described as a "point of pure truth" that is at "the center of our being" and which "belongs entirely to God."[6] As William Shannon suggests, beyond serving to enrich Merton's contemplative reflections, Massignon also influenced Merton's engagement with the world through his openness to other religions and his activism on behalf of Muslim peoples.[7] Massignon publicly challenged post-war treatment of Palestinians and supported Moroccan independence. He lobbied for fairness toward Algerians during their eight-year war for independence that began in 1954, and he publicly protested French use of internment camps and torture against them. When Paris police attacked and killed peaceful Algerian demonstrators on October 17, 1961, Massignon tried to recover bodies discarded in the River Seine to provide proper Islamic burials. His efforts elicited physical attacks at speaking engagements and criticism by embarrassed friends and family.[8]

---

5. Thomas Merton, "Preface to the Japanese Edition of *The Seven Storey Mountain*, August 1963," *"Honorable Reader": Reflections on My Work*, ed. Robert E. Daggy (New York: Crossroad, 1989) 65-66.

6. Thomas Merton, *Conjectures of a Guilty Bystander* (Garden City, NY: Doubleday, 1966) 142.

7. See Thomas Merton, *Witness to Freedom: Letters in Times of Crisis*, ed. William H. Shannon (New York: Farrar, Straus, Giroux, 1994) 275-76 (subsequent references will be cited as "*WF*" parenthetically in the text); and William H. Shannon, "Massignon, Louis," in William H. Shannon, Christine M. Bochen and Patrick F. O'Connell, *The Thomas Merton Encyclopedia* (Maryknoll, NY: Orbis, 2002) 287-88.

8. For details of Massignon's life and thought see Sidney H. Griffith, "Thomas Merton, Louis Massignon, and the Challenge of Islam," *The Merton Annual* 3 (1990) 151-72 (subsequent references will be cited as "Griffith" parenthetically in the text); Mary Louise Gude, *Louis Massignon: The Crucible of Compassion* (Notre Dame, IN: University of Notre Dame Press, 1996) (subsequent references will be cited as "Gude" parenthetically in the text); Herbert Mason, "Foreword to the English Edition," *The Passion of al-Hallaj: Mystic and Martyr of Islam. Vol. I: The Life of al-Hallaj*, trans. Herbert Mason (Princeton, NJ: Princeton University Press, 1982) ix-xlii (subsequent references

Merton's two-year correspondence with Massignon began in 1959. Massignon also forwarded publications of the *Badaliyah*, which was dedicated to prayer and fasting for Muslims, and the "Friends of Gandhi"; both were groups for which Massignon provided leadership and for whose periodicals he often wrote. Through this material and correspondence with mutual friends, Merton learned of Massignon's activism and religious views. He reported to one of these friends, Jean Daniélou, SJ, that Massignon had shared "about all the causes in which he is interested and I am going to try and do a little praying and fasting in union with him. . . . This is one way in which I can legitimately unite myself to the [testimony] and work of my brothers outside the monastery" (*HGL* 134 [4/21/1960]). After an arrest, Massignon reported to Merton that "we are laughed at for our 'non-violence,' but your approval and your prayer help us."[9]

These acts of protest that Merton vicariously followed from across the Atlantic were not inspired by inclinations toward radical politics on Massignon's part—as a prominent scholar he in many ways assumed a posture of middle-class respectability. Rather, they instead flowed naturally from Massignon's deep religious commitments. His sense of God's presence among humanity emphasized mystical substitution of one's self for others and their sins through prayer, fasting and suffering. He found this quality in the primary subject of his life's work—a ninth-century Sufi mystic named al-Hallaj, who Massignon believed mystically contributed across the ages to his own conversion experience. Massignon felt that Gandhi's life and death also embodied this trait, and the Mahatma's efforts to reconcile India's Hindu and Muslim communities offered a model for Massignon's own work to reconcile French Catholics and Algerian Muslims. As scholar Sidney Griffith commented, "To resist the [Algerian] war, to give aid to its victims was a religious act for Louis Massignon, and every demonstration or 'sit-in' where he appeared was an occasion to practice the mystical substitution that was at the heart of his devotional life" (Griffith 158).

Massignon also admired Gandhi's *satyagraha*, his willful pursuit of truth, which Massignon saw in Islam as well (Gude 128). As Herbert Mason later commented, "He didn't believe demonstrations could stop the war, but only that they could bear witness to the truth in honor and friendship. And truth meant each one's truth, not just one's own. He insisted that peaceful prayer demonstrations be said at the graves of French soldiers and policemen as well as outside political prisons. . . . Bearing witness was not a judgment, but an act of invitation to see reality through another's eyes" (Mason, "Foreword" xxxvii). In a Friends of Gandhi

---

will be cited as "Mason, 'Foreword'" parenthetically in the text).

9. Louis Massignon to Thomas Merton, May 19, 1960 (TMC archives).

newsletter article that Mason translated and published in a 1961 issue of *The Catholic Worker* (and which Merton surely read), Massignon wrote, "When we use truth as a privilege and monopoly to force an adversary to humiliate himself as a liar, then the flickering conscience which he has . . . is unable to submit to our truth, because we have refused to recognize that he has a conscience at all."[10] Mason suggests that Massignon required recognition of three truths before acting in protest: "(1) the sources of possible injustices in [one's self], (2) the humanity of [one's] opponents, (3) the real state of things existing [now] as distinguished from the state [that one's] dreams hoped to bring about" (Mason, *Memoir* 39).

Louis Massignon's appreciation for Trappist asceticism also suggested a worldview sympathetic to Merton's. Massignon saw these practices as "humanity's ultimate recourse," and he attributed the revolutionary collapses of French and Russian societies mystically to a weakening of Trappist orders in those cultures. He asserted that monastic asceticism in general "is not a private luxury preparing us for God, but is rather the profoundest work of mercy, which heals broken hearts by offering up instead its own broken bones and wounded flesh."[11] Written in 1949, his comments echo words from Merton's 1948 autobiography that reflect on a Mass during his first visit to Gethsemani: "This is the center of all the vitality that is in America. This is the cause and reason why the nation is holding together. These men, hidden in the anonymity of their choir and their white cowls, are doing for their land what no army, no congress, no president could ever do as such: they are winning for it the grace and the protection and the friendship of God."[12] A decade later, during their months of correspondence, Massignon would seek Merton's help in locating a French-speaking Trappist monastery that might dedicate themselves to prayer for Massignon's elder son, Yves, who had died in 1935.[13]

Massignon and Merton's 1964 Retreat Preparation

Merton's encounters with Massignon during the early 1960s offer insight to help unlock the cryptic notes that survive of the comments he later

10. Herbert Mason, *Memoir of a Friend: Louis Massignon* (Notre Dame, IN: University of Notre Dame Press, 1988) 40; subsequent references will be cited as "Mason, *Memoir*" parenthetically in the text.

11. Louis Massignon, "The Three Prayers of Abraham," *Testimonies and Reflections: Essays of Louis Massignon*, ed. Herbert Mason (Notre Dame, IN: University of Notre Dame Press, 1989) 3-5; subsequent references will be cited as "Massignon, 'Three Prayers'" parenthetically in the text.

12. Thomas Merton, *The Seven Storey Mountain* (New York: Harcourt, Brace, 1948) 325.

13. Massignon to Merton, July 19, 1960 (TMC archives).

gave at the 1964 retreat. His remarks there revolved around two themes: a critique of technology and a monastic view on the spiritual roots of protest. He noted technology as a discussion topic in the handout that opened the retreat, and he peppered comments on it throughout their conversations. Merton focused his comments on monastic protest, however, in a presentation given during one of their sessions. This presentation emphasized the nature of social "privilege," which drew on observations about "privileged collectivities," "judgment of the privileged," a caution that "privilege fossilizes," the role of "hope," Abraham and the story of Sodom, "substitution of oneself in the place of others before the judgment of God," and Islamic ideas on asylum and personhood. These themes recur in a one-page outline[14] that Merton used to give his presentation and in notes that Daniel Berrigan, Jim Forest and John Howard Yoder took of it.[15]

The sources of Merton's comments become most evident, however, in the pages of his 1964 "working" notebook,[16] which he used to take notes on readings or process ideas. Here Merton dedicated fourteen continuous pages to preparation for this gathering. The first five of these pages include quotations from Jacques Ellul's *The Technological Society*[17] and record a list of points that reflect Merton's own thoughts on technology. He undoubtedly wrote these pages during the first week in November 1964, about the same time as personal journal entries log his receipt of the book and capture reflections on it.[18] The nine pages that immediately follow build his case for a monastic view on the spiritual roots of protest, and they reveal that Merton explicitly referenced six different essays by Louis Massignon as he prepared. In this case, journal entries that reference some of these essays hint that he worked with them up to the day before the retreat (*DWL* 166-67 [11/16/64; 11/17 64]).

14. Thomas Merton, "Notes for F.O.R retreat. Nov. 1964," E.1 (TMC Archives).

15. Daniel Berrigan, retreat notes written on margins of mimeograph copy of Thomas Merton, "Identity Crisis and Monastic Vocation," n.d., B/98, Daniel and Philip Berrigan Collection, #4602, Division of Rare and Manuscript Collections, Cornell University; James Forest, "Gethsemani Retreat (The Spiritual Roots of Protest): Nov. 1964," 13, John Howard Yoder Papers, #H12 (TMC Archives); John Howard Yoder, "Transcription of Original Notes by J. H. Yoder, Gethsemani c/o T. Merton 18-20 November 1964," 1, John Howard Yoder Papers, #H12 (TMC Archives).

16. Thomas Merton, *Notebook 3, 1964-5*, L24-R27, Thomas Merton Papers, Special Collections Research Center, Syracuse University Library; subsequent references will be cited as "*Notebook 3*" parenthetically in the text.

17. Jaques Ellul, *The Technological Society* (New York: Alfred A. Knopf, 1964).

18. Thomas Merton, *Dancing in the Water of Life: Seeking Peace in the Hermitage. Journals, vol. 5: 1963-1965*, ed. Robert E. Daggy (San Francisco: HarperCollins, 1997) 159-61, 163 [10/30/64; 11/2/64; 11/6/64]; subsequent references will be cited as "*DWL*" parenthetically in the text.

The remainder of this paper reviews examples of how these six Massignon essays appear among Merton's notebook pages. Merton appears to be mining this material in search of Massignon's spiritual sensitivities and insights toward Muslims that motivated his protest on their behalf, insights that Merton might apply to his own American setting. The nine notebook pages that address spiritual roots of monastic protest begin with a second list of points that gathered ideas on this theme and drew in part from Massignon's essay entitled "The Three Prayers of Abraham." This essay opens by discussing a unique chain of witnesses—beginning with the patriarch Abraham and extending into the present—who provide a special, ongoing, substitutionary presence that connects humanity with the divine. For Massignon, Trappist asceticism has played a key role in sustaining this presence through its rigorous disciplines of silence and prayer.

Massignon then examines three prayers offered by Abraham that have reverberated through the ages among the three Abrahamic traditions. One, his prayer to spare Sodom if only ten just men could be found there, established an Abrahamic call to extend hospitality to others. Massignon described the city as one of "self-love which objects to the visitation of angels, of guests, of strangers, or wishes to abuse them" (Massignon, "Three Prayers" 10). Abraham's unfulfilled prayer for Sodom continues to "hover forever over societies doomed to perdition . . . that they might be spared the heavenly fire" (Massignon, "Three Prayers" 12). Another prayer, to protect Ishmael following his exile into the desert, anticipated the rise of Islam and its insights about God's inscrutability and uncompromising demand for recognition of the one true God of Abraham. The third prayer, expressed in Abraham's willingness to sacrifice Isaac, anticipated Mary's sacrifice of *her* son centuries later. Massignon laments how Abraham's descendants each presume their own privilege before God, while remaining fossilized and hardened. They crusade against and ghettoize each other, failing to recognize their common call to hospitality.

Merton's notebook list of points on spiritual roots focuses heavily on the theme of "privilege." In keeping with his handout's imagery of "the voice in the wilderness," Merton's initial point notes how the biblical prophets cautioned against the dangers of privilege and encouraged detachment from it. He also commented on the inverted "biblical dialectic" that often places spiritual privilege in unexpected hands, such as those of the stranger, the underprivileged, or the "younger son"—a likely allusion to the story of Isaac and Ishmael. Massignon's influence becomes explicit later in this list when Merton directly quotes a critique of Church institutions taken from "The Three Prayers of Abraham": "Certainly, it would be desirable in these days of social action to be able to rely upon the public testimonies of communities constituted and consecrated for this purpose. But it is precisely the abuse of their privileges which fossilizes them and deprives us of their help" (Massignon, "Three Prayers" 5). He then references "the privilege of Abraham and his intercession for Sodom" without elaborating on its significance for his topic. Merton ends this list of comments with his own definition of the *real root* of protest: "Our identification with the underprivileged," our dedication to them as an "epiphany" and "an intercessory for us." This requires our willingness to suffer, to refuse our own privilege. It also requires us to "protest against the arrogance and stupidity of the privileged" and place our "true *hope* in the spiritual privilege of the poor." Merton also named "inadequate roots," such as our identification with "the 'official policy' of any church or party" or our "servility to 'orthodoxy'" (*Notebook 3* L27-L28). Rather, Merton suggests, the fate of those who pursue the real spiritual roots of protest may instead involve living in "a sort of No Man's Land exposed to missiles on both sides."[19] This phrase also originated from Massignon, who had used it to describe the life of Jules Monchanin, a Catholic priest who spent his life in India among Hindus.

Beyond these references, Merton also turned to Massignon's comments about Charles de Foucauld (1858-1916)—a soldier turned Trappist turned hermit in the Algerian desert, where he dedicated his last years to the indigenous Muslims he lived among. Massignon had developed a close spiritual relationship with Foucauld prior to the latter's death at the hands of insurgents during World War I, and he viewed Foucauld as one of those timeless, substitutionary witnesses to God's transcendence. He also believed that Foucauld, like al-Hallaj, had mystically interceded on behalf of Massignon's own conversion in 1908. After the hermit's death, Massignon helped publish Foucauld's *Directory*, a monastic rule later used to found the Little Brothers of Jesus and other religious orders called to live among and serve the marginal. Merton cites from two essays on Foucauld,[20] particularly noting his commitment to discover the sacred in

---

19. Louis Massignon, "The Abbot Jules Monchanin," *Opera Minora: Textes Recueillis, Classés, et Présentés*, vol. III, ed. Y. Moubarac (Beruit: Dar Al-Maaref Liban S.A.L., 1963; rpt.: Paris: Presses Universitaires de France, 1969) 770, trans. Dr. Hollie Markland Harder; subsequent references to the anthology will be cited as "Massignon, *Opera Minora*" parenthetically in the text.

20. Louis Massignon, "Foucauld in the Desert before the God of Abraham, Hagar, and Ishmael," *Opera Minora* 772–84, trans. Virginie Reali (subsequent references will be cited as "Massignon, 'Foucauld'" parenthetically in the text); Louis Massignon, "An Entire Life with a Brother Who Set Out on the Desert: Charles de Foucauld," *Testimonies and Reflections: Essays of Louis Massignon*, ed. Herbert Mason (Notre Dame, IN: University

others, attend to those most abandoned, and transfer their sufferings onto himself. He copied a quotation of Foucauld that emphasized working for our own personal conversion, since our real impact depends not on what we say and do, but on the extent to which our actions are those of Jesus working in and through us.

A fifth Massignon essay that Merton cited in his notebook is titled "The Respect for the Human Person in Islam and the Priority of the Right to Asylum over the Responsibility to Wage Justified Wars."[21] Here he describes the Islamic grounding of personhood within one's personal testimony to a transcendent God, in contrast to Western notions of personhood that depend instead on social standing. He also emphasizes how through this standard Muslims grant personhood to Christians and Jews. Merton especially noted Massignon's correlation of this view of personhood to the Islamic concept of asylum, which granted refuge to foreigners during war and to fugitives. Massignon felt this priority of asylum retained the vestige of a primitive sense of hospitality, which sees the "guest" or "stranger" as one sent by God. In contrast, Western hospitality has become at best a "commercial ploy." The Christian West's abuse of Islam's primitive hospitality during their encounters reveals its own forgetfulness and contempt of the Bible. Written in 1952, the essay criticizes post-war treatment of displaced Arabic people. He prophetically noted a growing transition among refugees in camps from a "very beautiful Muslim resignation to divine will" to a growing desire to regain their land with armed force (Massignon, "Respect" 554). He also observed that "the 'biblical,' 'Abrahamic' religious meaning of hospitality toward foreigners [has diminished] because of contact with us, and increase[s] a dreadful belief in the inevitable advent of war between the rich and poor [such that] . . . I would not guarantee that [Muslim hospitality] can last a long time" (Massignon, "Respect" 545).

Massignon and Technology

Merton drew on other resources besides Louis Massignon to address spiritual roots of protest at the 1964 retreat, but none permeated Merton's preparation as he did. Moreover, Massignon also provided support for Merton's other theme, his critique of technology. Toward this end, Merton placed additional Massignon excerpts at the end of his earlier notes

---

of Notre Dame Press, 1989) 21–38.

    21. Louis Massignon, "The Respect for the Human Person in Islam and the Priority of the Right to Asylum over the Responsibility to Wage Justified Wars," *Opera Minora* 545, trans. Dr. Hollie Markland Harder; subsequent references will be cited as "Massignon, 'Respect'" parenthetically in the text.

on Ellul, rather than within the latter nine pages of material on spiritual roots. One noteworthy example addresses the *point vierge*. From one of the essays on Charles de Foucauld (Massignon, "Foucauld" 780), Merton copied a phrase that includes this term—the same essay and phrase, in fact, that introduced the term to Merton in 1960. Drawn from a public talk Massignon had given, it was first published in an issue of *Les Mardis de dar-es-Salam* (Griffith 165), the journal of a center in Cairo dedicated to Muslim-Christian dialogue, which Massignon had forwarded. Merton's personal journal entry that May shared his initial reaction to the article as a "Deeply moving prayer of Louis Massignon on the Desert, on the tears of Agar, on the Moslems, the '*point-vierge*' of the Spirit seemingly in despair, encountering God."[22] In offering his thanks for receipt of the journal, Merton quoted directly from the essay commenting, "Louis, one thing strikes me and moves me most of all. It is the idea of the '*point vierge* . . .' ['. . . the center of the soul, where despair corners the heart of the outsider']" (*WF* 278 [7/20/60]).

When drawing upon this same phrase for the peacemaker retreat, however, Merton quoted more of the original sentence, which expands the context in which Massignon had written it. In his 1964 notebook, the excerpt reads: "under pressure from a so-called Christian civilization, and technically superior, the Muslim faith reached the *point vierge*, the center of the soul, where despair corners the heart of the outsider" (Merton, *Notebook 3* R27). In other words, Massignon originally wrote it in critique of the impact that Western, technological society had on the integrity of Islam. In this brief quote, and Merton's placement of it with his technology notes, we catch a glimpse of how important one's awareness of technological society and its impact was for Merton. It helped him link technology with Massignon's concern about the privileged fossilization we risk and therefore with our complicity in crushing the *un*privileged who would help connect us to our true spiritual roots.

A more significant essay that informed Merton's view of technology was titled, "A New Sacral." Massignon wrote it in 1948 for the journal *Dieu Vivant*, which he had co-founded three years earlier. This journal gave voice to the disillusionment and desolation that engulfed Europe following World War II. Massignon shared its pessimism toward technological solutions, though as a scholar he respected the scientific method as such. His 1946 article, "The Future of Science,"[23] criticized how modern

---

22. Thomas Merton, *Turning Toward the World: The Pivotal Years. Journals, vol. 4: 1960-1963*, ed. Victor A. Kramer (San Francisco: HarperCollins, 1996) 5 [5/30/60].

23. Louis Massignon, "L'Avenir de la Science," *Opera Minora* 790-96, trans. Dr. Hollie Markland Harder.

science had begun to usurp the role of God through its ultimate claims to solve human need. He instead called us to place hope in our embrace of a "liturgical cosmos" that reflects our Creator's mind. A reader objected to this claim, suggesting we are better served by embracing "a broader sacral view that integrates science and technology," one that makes us "a very close collaborator with God." In writing "A New Sacral,"[24] Massignon reacted strongly to this suggestion. He declared, in a statement that Merton copied among his technology notes, how the "inappropriateness of this sentence irritates anyone who knows, through prayer, that God is at the root of our actions, and that he is in no way an external 'occupier' who requests the 'collaboration' of his creation. We have felt the call from God, and we resent the ridiculousness of this condescending proposal to use technical tricks to perfect the work of the Creator" (Massignon, "Sacral" 798). As the essay's translator, Dr. Hollie Markland Harder, points out, the terms "occupier" and "collaborator" carried significant emotional impact in post-war France.

Several other references to this essay in Merton's material also suggest that it bridged the spiritual roots and technology themes for him. Participants' notes of Merton's presentation cited it, and in his handout Merton juxtaposed for discussion the two extremes of viewing our technological society as either "by its very nature oriented to self-destruction, or whether it can on the contrary be regarded as a source of hope for a new 'sacral' order" (*NVA* 260). In his notebook, Merton also placed quotations from it next to his spiritual roots comments, such as a reference to Fr. (now St.) Damien, who died from leprosy while serving in a Hawaiian leper colony. But perhaps the strongest evidence of how "A New Sacral" spoke to both of Merton's retreat themes comes from his personal journal entry for November 16, two days before the retreat began. It essentially provides a synopsis of the essay and includes several of its images and allusions. This entry reads:

> Technology. No! When it comes to taking sides, I am not with the *beati* who are open mouthed in awe at the "new holiness" of a technological cosmos in which man condescends to be God's collaborator, and improve everything for Him. Not that technology is per se impious. It is simply neutral and there is no greater nonsense than taking it for an ultimate value. It is *there*, and our love and compassion for other men is now framed and scaffolded by it. Then what? We gain noth-

---

24. Louis Massignon, "Un Nouveau Sacral," *Opera Minora* 797-803, trans. Dr. Hollie Markland Harder; subsequent references will be cited as "Massignon, 'Sacral'" parenthetically in the text.

ing by surrendering to technology as if it were a ritual, a worship, a liturgy (or talking of our liturgy as if it were an expression of the "sacred" supposedly now revealed in technological power). Where impiety is in the hypostatizing of mechanical power as something to do with the Incarnation, as its fulfillment, its epiphany. When it comes to taking sides I am with Ellul, and also with Massignon (not with the Teilhardians). (*DWL* 166 [11/16/1964])

Then, perhaps with thoughts of protest fresh in mind, Merton ends this entry with a direct quotation from "A New Sacral," which reads: "We cannot fail to denounce the so-called 'harmlessness' of the 'apostles' of these technologies, which subject the spiritual to the temporal and soils life at its source in such a hypocritical way" (Massignon, "Sacral" 802; see *DWL* 166).

These examples of how Merton used Massignon to buttress his technological critique suggest a more nuanced concern for the spiritual impact of technological society than he had observed from Ellul's sociological tome. They suggest a clearer awareness of how relentlessly Western, "Christian" technological priorities impinged not merely on the interior world of participants in modern societies. Massignon seemingly reinforced for Merton the insight that this unquestioned loyalty to the advance of "progress" also forced those priorities upon other cultures encountered, violating their unique, indigenous integrity and compromising their own *point vierge*, as well as ours.

Merton's Spiritual Roots of Protest

This review of Merton's reading notes during the week before his retreat with peace advocates offers only a narrow window into his thought, one that does not fully define his ongoing priorities. In fact, only three months later Merton conceded to Daniel Berrigan that he had not yet "been able to type up the stuff from last November. . . . I have forgotten what I said and the notes aren't much help, so really I will have to start all over again" (*HGL* 86 [2/26/65])—which it appears he never did. But regardless of its lasting impact, as this paper demonstrates, Merton's exercise of preparing for this particular occasion relied heavily on Louis Massignon to express a "monastic" perspective on both protest and technology. And whatever their origin, sensitivities that echo Massignon also surface in some of Merton's later writings on protest. For example, in two of the essays that comprise *Faith and Violence*, published in 1968, Merton's comments include: "Christian non-violence does not encourage or excuse hatred of a special class, nation or social group. . . . [The Christian] will not let himself be persuaded that the adversary is totally wicked and can therefore never be reasonable or well-intentioned, and hence need never be listened to."[25] "If the 'Gospel is preached to the poor,' if the Christian message is essentially a message of hope and redemption for the poor, the oppressed, the underprivileged and those who have no power humanly speaking, how are we to reconcile ourselves to the fact that Christians belong for the most part to the rich and powerful nations of the earth?" (*FV* 20). "We must always be tolerant and fair and never simply revile others for their opinions. The way to silence error is by truth, not by various subtle forms of aggression" (*FV* 44).

> [P]erhaps our scientific and technological mentality makes us war-minded. We believe that any end can be achieved from the moment one possesses the right instruments, the right machines, the right techniques. . . . One thing that gives such a drastic character to the protest against war is the realization which the peace people have of this unjust suffering inflicted on the innocent largely as a result of our curious inner psychological needs, fomented by the climate of our technological culture. (*FV* 45-46)

Nearly thirty years after the retreat, when responding to a student paper on Thomas Merton, John Howard Yoder, a Mennonite theologian present in 1964, shared some impressions from that event, their only face-to-face encounter. Yoder agreed with those who felt Merton "came to antiwar protest slowly, after others were running with it, and that he did not anchor it deeply in what he had been thinking about before." Yoder suggested that Merton may have "felt left behind" by others tutored "in the power of the heritage of Dorothy Day."[26] We must wonder, though, whether Yoder would have felt the same had he known more of Louis Massignon's protests and Merton's exposure to them. Perhaps he may then have viewed Merton more as working to integrate his 1964 discussions into a framework of protest that Massignon had already helped him construct, rather than to simply "catch up" with others.

The comments of Herbert Mason, who knew Dorothy Day as well as Merton and Massignon, may help. Mason notes Massignon's insistence on recognizing the humanity of both victimizer and victim, on acknowledging

---

25. Thomas Merton, *Faith and Violence: Christian Teaching and Christian Practice* (Notre Dame, IN: University of Notre Dame Press, 1968) 19; subsequent references will be cited as "*FV*" parenthetically in the text.

26. John Howard Yoder to Lawrence Cunningham, 31 August 1993, 13, Yoder Papers, #H.12 (TMC archives).

that those we oppose also have a conscience,[27] and on understanding how lethal self-righteous, spiritual violence can be.[28] "[He] adhered above all . . . to the inescapable Truth, wherever [the Truth] led" (Mason, email). Mason saw Dorothy Day as driven more by ideology than Massignon, but felt that her fervor was tempered by compassion. She stood between victimizer and victim while "facing the victimizer without fear, and with an absolute refusal to meet violence with violence." Mason adds, "both radical activists were disciplined persons. Their spirits and teachings confronted fully but are not limited to their times" (Mason, "Unexpected" 12). As for Thomas Merton, Mason viewed him as a "lifelong learner of new and strange unexpected things" and a "social idealist" whose humor helped curtail his enthusiasms (Mason, email). Perhaps in the end, Merton might be seen as standing in a narrow gap between these two activists, seeking Louis Massignon's substitutional embrace of victim and victimizer, while also honoring Dorothy Day's tradition of unflinching resistance to the oppressor on behalf of the oppressed.

But however we see him, there can be no question that the vision Thomas Merton shared at this 1964 gathering drew heavily from Louis Massignon and asked for those who would protest to first radically transform their hearts and lives. The transformation he sought would dismantle our false security of privilege and status within a technological society and replace it with wisdom gained instead through identification with the underprivileged, the abandoned, the poor.

---

27. Herbert Mason, "An Unexpected Friendship," *Existenz* 7:1 (Spring 2012) 12; subsequent references will be cited as "Mason, 'Unexpected'" parenthetically in the text.

28. Herbert Mason, November 28, 2012, email to author; subsequent references will be cited as "Mason, email" parenthetically in the text.

"The Immense Mercy of God Was upon Me": Thomas Merton's Reading of the Russian Émigré Thinkers

Michael Plekon

There is no doubt that Thomas Merton absorbed a great deal from thinkers of the Eastern Church and was shaped by its liturgy and theology. In many pages of his journals and then in books he affirms his careful reading of both Eastern Fathers and contemporary Eastern Church thinkers. There are copious notes to these readings too. And there is the famous passage from his journal (also found in *Conjectures of a Guilty Bystander*):

> If I can unite *in myself*, in my own spiritual life, the thought of the East and the West of the Greek and Latin Fathers, I will create in myself a reunion of the divided Church and from that unity in myself can come the exterior and visible unity of the Church. For if we want to bring together East and West we cannot do it by imposing one upon the other. We must contain both in ourselves and transcend both in Christ.[1]

In the summer of 1957, and even earlier, Thomas Merton, had discovered the work of a remarkable collection of Russian émigré writers who lived in Paris and who, between the wars, made an enormous contribution to the renewal of theology and of liturgical and church life in the Eastern Church. Antoine Arjakovsky has provided the most exhaustive study of these thinkers and their connections to Western Church thinkers and clergy.[2] Some like Sergius Bulgakov, whom Merton read very closely, were active in ecumenical work in the 1920s and '30s and participated in the establishment of what became the World Council of Churches after World War II. The insights of others such as Nicholas Afanasiev and Paul

---

1. Thomas Merton, *A Search for Solitude: Pursuing the Monk's True Life. Journals, vol. 3: 1952-1960*, ed. Lawrence S. Cunningham (San Francisco: HarperCollins, 1996) 87 [4/28/1957] (subsequent references will be cited as "*SS*" parenthetically in the text); see also the revised version in Thomas Merton, *Conjectures of a Guilty Bystander* (Garden City, NY: Doubleday, 1966) 12 (subsequent references will be cited as "*CGB*" parenthetically in the text).

2. Antoine Arjakovsky, *The Way: Religious Thinkers of the Russian Emigration in Paris and Their Journal*, trans. Jerry Ryan, ed. John A. Jillions and Michael Plekon (Notre Dame, IN: University of Notre Dame Press, 2013). I have also profiled a number of émigré Russian figures in my study, *Living Icons: Persons of Faith in the Eastern Church* (Notre Dame, IN: University of Notre Dame Press, 2002).

Evdokimov came to shape the documents of the Second Vatican Council on the Church and on the Church in the World. Still others opened up the treasures of the Eastern Church's theology, saints, icons and liturgy— Vladimir Lossky, George Fedotov and Alexander Schmemann, all again writers with whom Merton was familiar.

In a journal entry for December 9, 1964, Thomas Merton, still novice master but already living in his hermitage, observed that as he was falling asleep the night before, he realized "that what I was, was *happy*." It was, he wrote, a "strange word" for him, but the next morning as he was coming down to the monastery:

> seeing the multitude of stars above the bare branches of the wood, I was suddenly hit, as it were, with the whole package of meaning of everything: that the immense mercy of God was upon me, that the Lord in infinite kindness had looked down on me and given me this vocation out of love, and that he had always intended this, and how foolish and trivial had been all my fears and twistings and desperation. And no matter what anyone else might do or say about it, however they might judge or evaluate it, all is irrelevant in the reality of my vocation to solitude, even though I am not a typical hermit. Quite the contrary perhaps. It does not matter how I may or may not be classified. In the light of this simple fact of God's love and the form it has taken, in the mystery of my life, classifications are ludicrous, and I have no further need to occupy my mind with them (if ever I did)—at least in this connection. The only response is to go out from yourself with all that one is, which is nothing, and pour out that nothingness in gratitude that God is who He is. All speech is impertinent, it destroys the simplicity of that nothingness before God by making it seem as if it had been "something."[3]

A few days later, on December 22, Merton records that he is reading theologian Vladimir Lossky's *La Vision de Dieu* (*DWL* 181-82). It is apparent that some of his words above echo the apophatic or negative theologizing from the Fathers that Lossky pursued. There is, at least to me, not a little humor in the fact that Merton is waxing eloquently in his journal—this is really a lovely passage—about things that language is incapable of capturing! Words about what words cannot express—but this is not so rare for Merton. I am reminded here of his sense of the unfathomable mercy and goodness of God. Think of the beautiful conclusion of *The Sign of Jonas*:

---

3. Thomas Merton, *Dancing in the Water of Life: Seeking Peace in the Hermitage. Journals, vol. 5: 1963-1965*, ed. Robert E. Daggy (San Francisco: HarperCollins, 1997) 177-78; subsequent references will be cited as "*DWL*" parenthetically in the text.

The Voice of God is heard in Paradise:

"What was vile has become precious. What is now precious was never vile. I have always known the vile as precious: for what is vile I know not at all.

"What was cruel has become merciful. What is now merciful was never cruel. I have always overshadowed Jonas with My mercy, and cruelty I know not at all. Have you had sight of Me, Jonas My child? Mercy within mercy within mercy. I have forgiven the universe without end, because I have never known sin.

"What was poor has become infinite. What is infinite was never poor. I have always known poverty as infinite: riches I love not at all. Prisons within prisons within prisons. Do not lay up for yourselves ecstasies upon earth, where time and space corrupt, where the minutes break in and steal. No more lay hold on time, Jonas, My son, lest the rivers bear you away.

"What was fragile has become powerful. I loved what was most frail. I looked upon what was nothing. I touched what was without substance, and within what was not, I am."[4]

Merton tells us, in the December 22 entry, that there in his hermitage he's returning to beginnings and that he knows where his beginning was, having the Name and Godhead of Christ preached in Corpus Christi Church, where he was baptized, close to Columbia University, where he was a student. He "heard and believed," among other things, that God had "called me freely, out of pure mercy, to His love and salvation" (*DWL* 181). In this we hear a theme that appears over and over in his writings, from the earliest, the autobiography *The Seven Storey Mountain*, to the last collection of journal entries he wrote in Thailand on his Asian journey. It is the vision that the Eastern Church liturgy expresses numerous times when God is called *Philanthropos / Chelovekolyubets*—the Lover of Mankind, the One who loves all, without limits. This is one of the major visions Merton had theologically, and I think he found it supported in the writings of the Russian émigré thinkers he devoured in roughly the last decade of his life. That was a period of amazing growth and development for him, in so many ways. It is one of a few profound insights that Merton received from the Eastern Church and made his own, part of his ecumenical and creative theological perspective. I want to present just a few of these insights or influences here, fully aware of a great deal of writing on this by Donald Allchin and others.

Merton also turns technical, theologically speaking, in this same jour-

---

4. Thomas Merton, *The Sign of Jonas* (New York: Harcourt, Brace, 1953) 362.

nal entry, noting that "contemplation" and "eschatology" are inseparable. This was the perspective of the Eastern Church for which he was indebted to Lossky. This needs some translation. For Merton, "contemplation" meant the awareness of God's presence at all times and in every aspect of one's daily existence. It is not a form of prayer but an orientation in which we listen to and hear, look for and see God both in the world and people around us as well as in our own thoughts, in our feelings, in our own selves. It would not be too much to say that Merton put forward this sense of contemplation in his best writings on prayer and the spiritual life, from *Seeds of Contemplation*[5] and *New Seeds of Contemplation*[6] through *The Inner Experience*[7] and *Contemplative Prayer*,[8] among other books.

However contemplation as a way of seeing, of living, of holiness, was there in the famous epiphany "At the corner of Fourth and Walnut" in which he described the presence of God in all the people scurrying through downtown Louisville on a busy work day (*SS* 181-82; *CGB* 140-42). I would also say contemplation was the base for his writings on social justice, civil rights, against nuclear proliferation and the Vietnam War, and for his later call for the renewal of monastic life. His lectures to student monks on the early monastics, on classic figures such as John Cassian,[9] Maximus the Confessor,[10] also on the mystics of the Byzantine and Russian Eastern Church traditions, are not mere historical exercises. Rather, he wants to document the diverse ways in which Christians have sought contemplative unity with God, the world and each other. In Lossky, as well as in the other Eastern Church writers he studies, from Solovyov and Bulgakov to Berdyaev, Fedotov, Evdokimov and Schmemann, Merton found the contemplative way rooted in a sense of the kingdom of God present now and beckoning into the future.

"Eschatology" is not just reflection on the end of time, the "last

5. Thomas Merton, *Seeds of Contemplation* (New York: New Directions, 1949); subsequent references will be cited as "*SC*" parenthetically in the text.

6. Thomas Merton, *New Seeds of Contemplation* (New York: New Directions, 1961); subsequent references will be cited as "*NSC*" parenthetically in the text.

7. Thomas Merton, *The Inner Experience: Notes on Contemplation*, ed. William H. Shannon (San Francisco: HarperCollins, 2003).

8. Thomas Merton, *Contemplative Prayer* (New York: Herder & Herder, 1969); also published as Thomas Merton, *The Climate of Monastic Prayer* (Washington, DC: Cistercian Publications, 1969).

9. See Thomas Merton, *Cassian and the Fathers: Initiation into the Monastic Tradition*, ed. Patrick F. O'Connell (Kalamazoo, MI: Cistercian Publications, 2005).

10. See Thomas Merton, *An Introduction to Christian Mysticism: Initiation into the Monastic Tradition* 3, ed. Patrick F. O'Connell (Kalamazoo, MI: Cistercian Publications, 2008) 121-36.

things," for the Eastern Church. The experience of every Eucharistic liturgy, of all the sacraments, the praying of the scriptures in the daily office—all this is to enter into the kingdom already here and now. Probably, what we see in Merton's great enthusiasm for these Russian émigré authors is a recognition by him of the same sensibilities as he saw in others who "returned to the sources." He sought in Jean Daniélou a kind of mentor and spiritual father. He did the same with Dom Jean Leclercq, with whom he also enjoyed a deep friendship. He was impressed with the work of Hans Urs von Balthasar and corresponded with him. The émigré writers of the Russian Orthodox tradition knew and worked with many others in the "nouvelle théologie"—Yves Congar, Botte, Daniélou, Henri de Lubac, among others. Arjakovsky's magnificent study of these writers reveals how many of them were published in Berdyaev's journal *Put'*, "The Way." Many attended the intellectual gatherings Berdyaev sponsored. There were connections with Sergius Bulgakov, dean of St. Sergius Theological Institute in Paris, the first Orthodox theological school in the West. Later, after World War II, the liturgical study weeks set up by Afanasiev and Kern had many Western Church participants. These scholars were cited in Alexander Schmemann's work, which eventually resulted in the formulation of a "liturgical theology" in which the *theologia prima* was the liturgy and scripture.

Merton wrote about this vision in his review of the American Orthodox priest and theologian Alexander Schmemann's book, *For the Life of the World*.[11] He praised the rejection of the sacred-secular divide and urging of the Eastern Church's sacramental vision of the world, of all reality. "Life itself is worship," Schmemann wrote, "We were created as celebrants of the sacrament of life" (Dieker & Montaldo 477). Merton thought this cosmic liturgical view was crucial for all monastics, burdened with a great deal of bad theology that segregated what was supposedly spiritual and sacred from the profane, everyday world of living. "True Christianity, and therefore true sacramental life, is the manifestation of the Living Presence of the Lord, victorious over death leading us all, with Him, through death to life" (Dieker & Montaldo 481).

The late Canon Donald Allchin, whom I had the privilege of knowing, did not introduce Merton to the Russian émigré theologians in Paris— Merton had been reading Lossky as early as 1950. But Allchin, who himself studied with these writers in Paris and was particularly close to

---

11. "Orthodoxy and the World," in Bernadette Dieker and Jonathan Montaldo, eds., *Merton & Hesychasm: The Prayer of the Heart* (Louisville, KY: Fons Vitae, 2003) 473-84 (subsequent references will be cited as "Dieker & Montaldo" parenthetically in the text); originally published in *Monastic Studies* 4 (Advent 1966) 105-15.

Vladimir Lossky and his family, was able to give Merton some personal and first-hand knowledge of the renaissance of religious thought that had occurred there. Allchin, I must acknowledge, has written extensively on Merton's reading of and commentary on these Eastern Church thinkers in his journals and books. Allchin's articles are the best on the profound influence the East had on Merton, although others who also knew Merton, such as Trappists John Eudes Bamberger and Basil Pennington, and Jim Forest and former archbishop of Canterbury Rowan Williams also have written discerning studies on this.[12] Just about every piece of Merton's own writing and notes as well as examinations of his connections with the Eastern Church have been admirably collected in *Merton & Hesychasm*.

With Allchin's essays and the rest, is there really anything else to say? It is clear that Merton read Bulgakov, Berdyaev, Evdokimov, Lossky, Florovsky, Sophrony, Olivier Clément and Alexander Schmemann very closely. He copied out a great many passages, commented on most, and included a great many of these journal entries in *Conjectures of a Guilty Bystander* as well as his introductions to books and articles. These and his comments are all now in print in volumes three and five of the journals in particular, as well as in other places. For all the challenge that Bulgakov's writing presents, especially his "sophiology," that is, his effort to show God's continuing presence in creation through the figure of Sophia, the comments surrounding quotations from Bulgakov show that Merton grasped what Bulgakov was after. Christopher Pramuk's most discerning study now shows how important, even central the figure of Sophia, Divine Wisdom, was in Merton's theological outlook.[13] There is no doubt that Sophia was an important appropriation from the Russian thinkers by Merton. Kristi Groberg notes that only after reading about Sophia in Solovyov did Merton begin to have dreams about her.[14]

Likewise with the text that Schmemann had prepared not for a

---

12. Though originally published elsewhere, these articles have been collected in *Merton & Hesychasm*: A. M. Allchin, "The Worship of the Whole Creation: Merton and the Eastern Fathers" (103-20); A. M. Allchin, "Our Lives, a Powerful Pentecost: Merton's Meeting with Russian Christianity" (121-40); John Eudes Bamberger, "Thomas Merton and the Christian East" (141-52); M. Basil Pennington, "Thomas Merton and Byzantine Spirituality" (153-68); Rowan Williams, "Bread in the Wilderness: The Monastic Ideal in Thomas Merton and Paul Evdokimov" (175-96); Jim Forest, "Thomas Merton and the Silence of the Icons" (225-33).

13. Christopher Pramuk, *Sophia: The Hidden Christ of Thomas Merton* (Collegeville, MN: Liturgical Press, 2009).

14. Kristi Groberg, "'Sweet Yielding Consent of Sophia': The Wisdom Visions of Merton via Solov'ev and Bulgakov" (panel presentation at the American Association for the Advancement of Slavic Studies, New Orleans, November 2007).

scholarly conference but for an ecumenical assembly of over three thousand Christian university students gathered at Ohio State precisely fifty years ago. William Mills has provided a fascinating historical look at this singular event, an Eastern Orthodox priest and theologian as the keynote speaker, with a study text written and distributed beforehand on the sacramental mission of the church in and for the world.[15] It was 1963, the year of the assassinations of John F. Kennedy and Medgar Evers, in many ways the beginning of the turbulent 1960s, certainly a key moment in the civil rights movement.

In his review essay of Schmemann's text, *For the Life of the World*, Merton does not dwell on the distinctive aspects of the Eastern Church, the icons and chant and splendid liturgy, the long tradition of holiness and saints and prayer. Rather, he hones in on the very heart of what the liturgy is about, precisely what Schmemann was trying to present to the gathered students. This is, for me, one of his most important intuitions from Eastern Christianity, namely that the life of God and the Kingdom, present in the Eucharist and all the sacraments, is the mission of the Church, of every Christian in the world. This wonderful openness to the world, intensely captured in Merton's Fourth and Walnut experience, was very much the experience of Paris émigré thinkers. They spoke of the "churching" of life (*votserkovenlie zhizni*), an authentic connection of faith and the world, of liturgy and life, not the production of more icons, the lighting of more candles, or the celebration of more services. This was not the resurgence of "religion" and its institutional expressions but rather real "mission," an outreach into one's world. This is what Schmemann was telling so many university students as the 1960s, as the "space race" with the Soviets and the "new frontier" of JFK were also launching, along with the already volatile civil rights movement. It was hardly a retreat from the world into the church or monastery—and here one can almost hear Merton and Schmemann in "stereo"—another trend of that time! With his prodigious reading, not only of the "return to the sources" thinkers, the Russian émigré writers and Russian mystics and ascetics, the Church Fathers, the desert monastics, Merton was experiencing his own *aggiornamento*, right alongside Vatican II. It is no wonder Merton was so enthusiastic about *For the Life of the World*, by an Eastern Orthodox priest and theologian only a few years younger than himself, someone

---

15. Michael Plekon, "Alexander Schmemann's *For the Life of the World*": A Retrospective," *Logos* (forthcoming). In his review of *For the Life of the World* (along with the anthology Schmemann edited, *Ultimate Questions*), Merton does not mention the origins of the book, something that would have been of great interest to him, the ecumenical nature of the gathering and its student base.

who had been to the Vatican Council as an ecumenical observer, someone also taking on the culture of the 1960s.

Even if Merton did not realize Schmemann's roots in the Paris of the Russian writers he was reading—Bulgakov was Schmemann's teacher, along with Afanasiev, Kern, Florovsky and the others—he clearly recognized in this American author and book the conversation, the connection between liturgy and life, between faith and culture he had learned from the émigré theologians. The importance of this "churching" dominated the Russian Christian Student Association in which Schmemann was a participant. He was educated in a climate of ecumenical and cultural openness with teachers such as Bulgakov, Afanasiev, Kartashev, Zenkovsky and Zander.[16] They were active in the Russian Christian Student Association and at St. Sergius, the Fellowship of St. Alban and St. Sergius, the first Anglican-Orthodox association, and in the ecumenical gatherings at Edinburgh and Lausanne which led to the WCC. The Eucharist, Baptism and the other sacraments are not, for him, ecclesiastical obligations or moments of intensely personal piety. Rather, the liturgy was the basis for all reflection, for it also contained the scriptures and gathered the Christian community—"The Church makes the Eucharist, the Eucharist makes the Church"—the realization of his teachers Bulgakov and Afanasiev and so many other Paris émigré writers. It should not be surprising that as early at 1937, these thinkers had entitled their manifesto of essays on the Church's engagement with the world, *Living Tradition*.[17]

The third and last Eastern Church vision Merton acquired from his study was that of holiness. He carefully studied the work of George Fedotov, now recognized for his ground-breaking renewal of hagiography by employing historiography and anthropology in interpreting the lives of the saints of Russia. The important lay theologian Elisabeth Behr-Sigel was also a student of Fedotov, and I like to think that my having had the blessing to know her links my own work on holiness in our time to Fedotov's project.[18]

---

16. On the émigrés and their contributions see Nicolas Zernov, *The Russian Religious Renaissance of the Twentieth Century* (New York: Harper & Row, 1963) and Bryn Geffert, *Eastern Orthodox and Anglicans: Diplomacy, Theology and the Politics of Interwar Ecumenism* (Notre Dame, IN: University of Notre Dame Press, 2010).

17. A number of the essays from this collection were translated and published in the anthology *Tradition Alive*, ed. Michael Plekon (Lanham MD: Rowman & Littlefield, 2003).

18. In addition to *Living Icons*, cited above, there are the other two volumes of what became a trilogy: *Hidden Holiness* (Notre Dame, IN: University of Notre Dame Press, 2009) and *Saints as They Really Are* (Notre Dame, IN: University of Notre Dame Press, 2012). See also Olga Lossky, *Toward the Endless Day: The Life of Elisabeth Behr-Sigel,* trans. Jerry Ryan, ed. Michael Plekon (Notre Dame, IN: University of Notre Dame Press, 2010).

From his earliest writing, the spiritual life was for Merton the way of holiness, the path of becoming the saint God wanted each of us to be. But as many Merton scholars have noted, including several who knew him personally, Merton's own pilgrimage toward integration, his searching for his own identity and place, his pursuit of his true self—this was none other than the revelation and the discovery of the saint he was to be. "For me to be a saint means to be myself. Therefore the problem of sanctity and salvation is in fact the problem of finding out who I am and of discovering my true self" (*SC* 26; *NSC* 31). In his introduction to Sergius Bolshokoff, *The Russian Mystics*, Merton surveyed centuries of Russian monastic spirituality (Dieker & Montaldo 333-41). He noted the Russian adoption of the classic Greek text, *The Philokalia*, as well as the contributions of spiritual writers such as Theophane the Recluse and Ignatii Brianchaninov, to name just a couple.

Yet for him the greatest example of joyful, resurrectional spirituality was Seraphim of Sarov, in many ways a figure like Francis of Assisi in the West—free, simple, poor, welcoming to all around him, full of joy in the Holy Spirit. Merton knew enough about Seraphim to realize that he was a saint of our time in his commitment to living out the Gospel in everyday life. Seraphim was intensely aware of the personal pain, the sufferings, both physical and psychological, of ordinary women and men who streamed into his monastery in the last years of his life, looking to him for counsel, prayer and healing. Though a monastic, a priest and then a hermit—how similar to Merton's own existence—Seraphim transcended all the categories and formal statuses of religious life.[19] At his hermitage he wore (as did Merton) the ordinary clothes of a Russian farmer or peasant. When he returned to the monastery, he gave up his solitude and privacy. For most of the day, to the dismay of his monastic brethren, he threw open the door of his room to all those in distress and sickness, giving them his time and compassion, his prayer and healing. Perhaps unconsciously, Merton saw in Seraphim's reluctance to be boxed in an image of his own efforts to live a simpler life. In Seraphim's reaching out to those in need, there was the same direction of concern that Merton made toward those struggling with civil rights, issues of justice and peace and ecumenical unity. I think both Seraphim's and Merton's choices were an iconic enactment of monastic and ecclesial renewal. Seraphim said that all of the activities we pursue—fasting, prayer, reading, love for the neighbor—all are so that we might acquire the Holy Spirit. Yet since

---

19. On Seraphim's distinctive transcending of ecclesiastical categories and states see *In the World, Of the Church: A Paul Evdokimov Reader*, ed. and trans. Michael Plekon and Alexis Vinogradov (Crestwood NY: St. Vladimir's Seminary Press, 2001) 131-45.

we already are given the Spirit, this had to mean that we were living in and working with the Spirit in our relationships with those around us, in everything we did in our work and our lives. In the end, is this not what Merton seemed to be driving at in the last years of his life, the recognition that every moment of living held the seeds of contemplation, the possibility of life with God?

Looking back on Merton's formidable body of writing and his fascinating, intense life, there were many influences that shaped his person and his vision. As Donald Allchin and others have said, so too I want to credit Merton's reading of the Russian émigré writers with some of his most beautiful insights on the spiritual life, such as those I have identified here. They remind us of the unity we share, Christians of the Eastern and Western Churches. They also keep us aware of the mission of the Gospel we seek to put into practice, a vision of our lives seeking God, not only for our own holiness and identity, but for the life of the world.

"The First Cistercian and the Greatest Trappist": Thomas Merton's Poems on John the Baptist

Patrick F. O'Connell

In a journal entry for June 24, 1947, the Feast of the Nativity of John the Baptist, Thomas Merton wrote, "It is the day of my great patron and friend and Protector St. John Baptist."[1] A couple of days earlier (see *ES* 86) he had begun what would turn out to be the third lengthy poem focused on this iconic figure, published in three successive volumes of verse from the latter 1940s: "St. John Baptist" in *A Man in the Divided Sea* (1946),[2] "St. John's Night" in *Figures for an Apocalypse* (1947)[3] and "The Quickening of St. John the Baptist" in *The Tears of the Blind Lions* (1949).[4] The sequence of these poems works backwards from a meditative consideration of the Baptist's ministry in the first, to a commemoration of his birth in the second, to his witness while still in the womb in the third, but in each case it is above all the solitary figure, the prophet who is also a contemplative, that attracts the poet's attention. Considered together, the series of poems on the Baptist provides evidence of why Merton found John so fascinating, and why he would consider him a patron, a friend and a protector, a subject worth the repeated attention Merton gives him in poems of considerable power and complexity.

* * * * * * *

The first and longest of the poems,[5] the three-part "St. John Baptist" apparently is structured to follow the traditional progression of monastic

---

1. Thomas Merton, *Entering the Silence: Becoming a Monk and Writer. Journals, vol. 2: 1941-1952*, ed. Jonathan Montaldo (San Francisco: HarperCollins, 1996) 87; subsequent references will be cited as "*ES*" parenthetically in the text.

2. Thomas Merton, *A Man in the Divided Sea* (New York: New Directions, 1946) 98-102; Thomas Merton, *The Collected Poems of Thomas Merton* (New York: New Directions, 1977) 122-26; subsequent references will be cited as "*CP*" parenthetically in the text.

3. Thomas Merton, *Figures for an Apocalypse* (New York: New Directions, 1947) 58-60; *CP* 171-72.

4. Thomas Merton, *The Tears of the Blind Lions* (New York: New Directions, 1949) 8-10; *CP* 199-202.

5. There is some uncertainty about the date of composition of this poem. Merton's personal copy of *A Man in the Divided Sea*, now at the Thomas Merton Center of Bellarmine University, Louisville, KY, includes handwritten dates for each of the poems; "St. John Baptist" is dated 1946. This date is repeated in a 1951 letter, written by Merton's secretary, that provides dates for almost all the poems in Merton's first three collections,

prayer[6] from *lectio*, reading of a scriptural text, to *meditatio*, reflection on its personal meaning, to *oratio*, prayerful response to the Word of God; while the fourth stage of *contemplatio* is touched on as well, it will play a more prominent role in the two subsequent poems. The first section opens with a reworking of the Lukan introduction to the ministry of the Baptist:

> When, for the fifteenth year, Tiberius Caesar
> Cursed, with his reign, the Roman World,
> Sharing the Near-East with a tribe of tetrarchs,
> The Word of God was made in far-off province:
> Deliverance from the herd of armored cattle,
> When, from the desert, John came down to Jordan. (ll. 1-6)

What in Luke 3:1-2 is simply a specification of the date by reference to the regnal year of Tiberias is now a measurement of the tyrannical rule that has oppressed the entire Roman Empire. The further elaboration in the Gospel of the emperor's subordinates has been compressed—Pilate and the high priests are omitted and Herod, Philip and Lysanias (the first of whom of course will eventually kill John) are grouped together in the rather dismissive phrase "tribe of tetrarchs," suggesting their particular identities are of no great importance, nor are the locations of the ter-

---

evidently based for *A Man in the Divided Sea* and *Thirty Poems* (reprinted as an appendix in that volume) on Merton's annotated copy (see Ross Labrie, "The Ordering of Thomas Merton's Early Poems," *Resources for American Literary Study* 8 [1979] 115-17, which includes all the dating provided by this letter; subsequent references will be cited as "Labrie, 'Ordering'" parenthetically in the text). However, a handwritten note on the typescript of "St. John Baptist" now in the archives of the Columbia University Library indicates that the poem was sent by Merton to Mark Van Doren with a group of other new poems in July 1945 (see the mention of poems being sent in Merton's July 20, 1945 letter to Van Doren [Thomas Merton, *The Road to Joy: Letters to New and Old Friends,* ed. Robert E. Daggy (New York: Farrar, Straus, Giroux, 1989) 19]), and that additional copies of these poems were mailed by Merton to Van Doren on August 8, 1945. Thus it seems more probable that the poem was composed in 1945, perhaps around the time of the Feast of John's Nativity on June 24, and that Merton had later mistakenly assumed, since this poem was one of the last in *A Man in the Divided Sea* (#54 of 56), that it was written the following year.

6. The classic description of this fourfold progression is found in the *Scala Claustralium* of Guigo the Carthusian; for Merton's own discussion of this twelfth-century work, see Appendix I in Thomas Merton, *An Introduction to Christian Mysticism: Initiation into the Monastic Tradition* 3, ed. Patrick F. O'Connell (Kalamazoo, MI: Cistercian Publications, 2008) 332-40, where he calls it "a first-class example of the medieval approach to *lectio, meditatio, oratio, contemplatio*" (332). See also William H. Shannon, *Seeking the Face of God* (New York: Crossroad, 1988), which uses Guigo's pattern (with the addition of a fifth step of *operatio* or action) as the framework for his presentation, heavily influenced by Merton, of the spiritual journey.

ritories they govern, generalized as "the Near-East." As in the Gospel, it is what is going on outside the ostensible centers of power that is of true significance—the Word of God, implicit counter to the "curse" of Tiberias, appears not in Rome but in "far-off province," on the margins of the dominant political and cultural system. The language here departs from the scriptural phrasing in an interesting way: instead of Luke's "The Word of God came to John son of Zechariah," the poem says that "The Word of God was made," which suggests a sense of dynamism, of divine activity in the prophetic word that accomplishes what it proclaims; but it also is reminiscent of the familiar Johannine formula *"Verbum caro factum est"*—"The Word was made flesh" (Jn. 1:14)—suggesting that ultimately the Word in question is not only divine revelation but divine incarnation— that the focus of the message is the coming of the Christ. But the content of the proclamation as immediately specified here—though not yet in Luke's account (only Matthew has the Baptist giving particular instruction at this juncture: "Repent for the kingdom of heaven is at hand" [Mt. 3:2])—is a message of "deliverance," presumably, in this context, from the oppressive Roman tyranny, described in the initially odd-sounding image of "the herd of armored cattle," which seemingly equates the Roman army with a kind of mindless stampede, running roughshod over the land, a subhuman trampling rather than a willful, malign attack, yet no less destructive for all that. Only at this point, concluding the first verse paragraph, is John finally mentioned explicitly, in a line that juxtaposes the opening "When" clause, focused on Tiberias, with this concluding "When" clause specifying that this is the time when (and the place where) the Word was made present in the Baptist's appearance (the trochaic rhythm of the line reinforces the effect of his "coming down" from the desert to the Jordan to begin his ministry).

If the initial note of the message is deliverance, the precondition would seem to be repentance, a requirement that is met with incomprehension and rejection:

> But his prophetic messages
> Were worded in a code the scribes were not prepared to understand.
> Where, in their lexicons, was written: "Brood of vipers,"
> Applied, that is, to them? (ll. 7-10)

The plural "messages" seems to suggest that both external liberation and internal transformation are involved, but that the authorities are willing to accept the first but not the second, not the part "applied . . . to them." "Brood of vipers" (addressed to "many of the Pharisees and Sadducees" in Matthew 3:7 and to "the crowds" in general in Luke 3:7—so closer here to Matthew than to Luke) is implicitly contrasted with the earlier "herd of cattle"—to the disadvantage of the former, as more responsible, more malicious, more guilty. The word "code" suggests political or military implications, a cipher to conceal information from the enemy, but here of course the principal "enemy" is the scribes themselves, who refuse to accept the need for personal repentance. The term "lexicon" is particularly apt for an audience of scribes, who are presented as possessing only "book knowledge," willing only to define and interpret texts rather than to appropriate the message personally; and of course the word is related etymologically to the word "*lectio*," suggesting by contrast their failure to engage reflectively with the saving Word. Instead, they react defensively and skeptically, changing the Word rather than transforming themselves:

> "Who is this Lamb, Whose love
> Shall fall upon His people like an army:
> Who is this Savior, Whose sandal-latchet
> This furious Precursor is afraid to loose?" (ll. 11-14)

The image of the Lamb is found in the Baptist's preaching in John 1:20, but the comparison of His love to an army falling upon His people is the scribes' own interpretation, suggesting they feel more threatened by the Lamb than by the Roman occupation. Likewise they distort John's own statement about being unworthy to loosen the thong of the sandals of the one who is to come by changing his humility to fear, and calling him "The furious Precursor"—filled with apocalyptic fury, a depiction that much of the rest of the poem will endeavor to refute. Here we find their "misreading" is a projection of their own feelings rather than an accurate interpretation of John's. While the title "Savior" is not found in any of the Baptist passages from the Gospels, it is associated with John in Paul's synagogue discourse in Acts 13: "God . . . has brought to Israel a savior, Jesus. John heralded his coming by proclaiming a baptism of repentance to all the people of Israel; and as John was completing his course, he would say, 'Who do you suppose that I am? I am not he. Behold one is coming after me; I am not worthy to unfasten the sandals of his feet'" (Acts 13:23-25). This technique of interweaving scriptural sources is of course a standard method of "*lectio*," spiritual reading: but here it forms a sort of counter-*lectio*, a combining of texts (John, Luke, Acts) that results in a distorted interpretation which of course could not be directly ascribed to the original audience of John at the Jordan, but as characterizing a later generation of "scribes" who employ the method only to twist the message—an indication that the failure to hear the Word properly is not restricted to John's contemporaries.

The long section that follows provides an alternate reading of the same scriptures in which wrath, violence and judgment are not the essence of the Baptist's message—quite the contrary:

> His words of mercy and of patience shall be flails
> Appointed for the separation of the wheat and chaff.
> But who shall fear the violence
> And crisis of His threshing-floor
> Except the envious and selfish heart?
> Choose to be chaff, and fear the Winnower,
> For then you never will abide His Baptism of Fire and Spirit.
> You proud and strong,
> You confident in judgment and in understanding,
> You who have weighed and measured every sin
> And have so clearly analyzed the prophecies
> As to be blinded on the day of their fulfilment:
> Your might shall crumble and fall down before Him like a wall,
> And all the needy and the poor shall enter in,
> Pass through your ruins, and possess your kingdom. (ll. 15-29)

John's words of mercy and patience, probably to be identified with his advice provided to the crowds, to tax collectors, to soldiers in Luke 3:10-14, become a threat only for those who reject the call to conversion, for those who choose to be chaff. The predicted punishment of evildoers needs to be situated in the context of the words of promise found in Luke 3:4-6 (quoted from Isaiah 40:3-5—only in Luke is the full passage given, culminating in the verse "all flesh shall see the salvation of God") and in the assertion, found only in Luke, that John "preached good news" to the people (vs. 18). Here is the counterstatement to the scribes' attribution of fear, and fury, to John himself—the fear is contingent on the rejection of the message rather than being its core. The "envious and selfish" (the have-nots and the haves) are the only ones who exclude themselves from the goodness of the news, the only ones who cannot "abide" the baptism of fire and spirit—the meaning of the Johannine term for the continuing presence of the Spirit with Jesus (1:32, 33) altered to indicate they cannot put up with, cannot stand that presence. Here is implied the true understanding of what will "fall upon His people"—the Holy Spirit and fire, both purifying and Pentecostal, which will consume the chaff but perfect and transform the wheat.

The speaker has turned to direct address with his use of the imperative as an implicit conditional: "If you choose to be chaff, then fear . . ." The audience is then identified in three sets of increasingly elaborated pairs, first simply as the "proud and strong"; then as those confident in judgment and in understanding—with the implication of course that this self-confidence is misplaced, since their judgment does not correspond to God's judgment and their understanding is in fact a misunderstanding, a misreading of the signs; finally as those who have weighed and measured every sin, that is, whose judgmental attitude has made itself the classifier of sins (of others), and those who have misplaced confidence in their understanding of the prophecies, who have analyzed them according to false criteria in a vain attempt to control the word and will of God, and so of course have missed their true import. The reference to being blinded suggests particularly the "blind guides, . . . blind fools, . . . blind ones" of Christ's discourse in Matthew 23 (vv. 16, 17, 19), which also contains another reference to the "brood of vipers" (vs. 33) just before mention of prophets being killed (of evident if unstated relevance to John as well as to Jesus himself); the discourse is immediately followed by Christ's prediction of the fall of Jerusalem and the destruction of the Temple, with not one stone left upon another, which seems to be the source of the imagery here of their might falling like a wall, made metaphorical as the "wall" excluding the poor and needy crumbles and they are able to "enter in . . and possess your kingdom"—or rather to possess the kingdom of God that the proud and strong assume is theirs by right. This fulfillment of the prophecies is suggestive of the beatitudes, especially Luke's identification of the literal poor with those who will inherit the Kingdom (Lk. 6:20), and circles back to the Baptist's proclamation of the Kingdom of heaven being at hand in Matthew 3:2 (as well as to Jesus' own first words in Mark 1:14-15 that the time is fulfilled and the kingdom at hand). This whole section then, with its recognition that the focus on salvation is primary and the consequences of rejection of salvation are subordinate, is an exercise in authentic *lectio*, a proper reading of the Word in which connections perceived between various passages add depth and richness to the principal source.

This first section of the poem concludes by shifting the focus away from the unbelieving scribes and back to the figure of John himself:

> This is the day that you shall hear and hate
> The voice of His beloved servant.
> This is the day your scrutiny shall fear
> A terrible and peaceful angel, dressed in skins,
> Knowing it is your greedy eyes, not his, that die of hunger.
> For God has known and loved him, from his mother's womb,
> Remembering his name, filling his life with grace,

Teaching him prophecy and wisdom,
To burn before the Face of Christ,
Name Him and vanish, like a proclamation. (ll. 30-39)

"This is the day" echoes and reverses the verse "This is the day that the Lord has made; let us be glad and rejoice" (Ps. 117[118]:24), while also alluding to the "great and terrible" day of the Lord in Malachi 3:24 and elsewhere, which is, for those who are willing to hear and accept the Word rather than hating it, "the day of salvation" Paul speaks of in 2 Corinthians 6:2, quoting Isaiah 49:8, a passage immediately following the second servant song and so in good *lectio* fashion recalling "the voice of His beloved servant," identified here with the Baptist, whose "voice" cries out in the wilderness (Lk. 3:4; Mt. 3:3; Mk. 1:3; Jn. 1:23; cf. Is. 40:3). The focus on hearing is complemented by an emphasis on sight in a parallel construction also beginning with "This is the day": here it is the "scrutiny" of their "greedy eyes" that perceive the Baptist as a figure inspiring fear—"A terrible and peaceful angel" in the literal sense of messenger (*angelos*: cf. Lk. 7:27,[7] quoting Mal. 3:1), evoking awe like a supernatural being, not himself aggressive or violent but making evident the hidden violence of opponents. The reference to his clothing (Mt. 3:4, Mk. 1:6; not mentioned in Luke, but contrasting to the detail about being "dressed in fine garments" from Christ's description of John in Lk. 7:25) is followed immediately by reference to his food of locusts and wild honey, but his austere diet doesn't put him in any danger of starvation; rather it is his detractors, never satisfied in their greed, who are dying spiritually; more specifically it is their eyes that die, that are blinded to their own culpability. Their scrutiny results not in clear perception but in fear that parallels the hatred engendered by what has been heard.

What they have failed to see and hear is the true identity and vocation of John, given his name from his mother's womb like the servant of the Lord (Is. 49:1-2, found in both the introit and epistle for the Feast of the Nativity of the Baptist[8]) and known by the Lord from before he was formed in the womb, like the prophet Jeremiah (Jer. 1:5, part of the epistle for the vigil and the gradual for the feast[9]), already filled with the grace of the Holy Spirit before birth (cf. Lk. 1:15), a prophet and more than a prophet (Lk. 7:26) and like Jesus himself a child of wisdom (Lk. 7:35). As in the earlier lines of this section, sight and hearing are again paired at

---

7. The Latin Vulgate of Luke 7:27 reads: *"Ecce mitto angelum meum ante te."*

8. See *Saint Joseph Daily Missal*, ed. Hugo H. Hoever, SOCist (New York: Catholic Book Publishing Co., 1959) 922, 923.

9. *Saint Joseph Daily Missal* 920, 923.

its conclusion, but here in a positive complementarity as John, described by Jesus as "a burning and shining lamp" (Jn. 5:35), burns before the face of Christ like the messenger (Elijah) of the prophet Malachi, described as like a refiner's fire and serving here as a light in which Christ can be seen, though paradoxically "he was not himself the light" (Jn. 1:8), not the light of the world to which he gave testimony; likewise his proclamation of the good news, his kerygma, is to name Christ, as he himself received his true name from God—to reveal him as the Lamb of God, and then to disappear—an allusion to the Baptist's words to his disciples in John 3:30 that he must decrease, and perhaps as well a foreshadowing of his vanishing in death at the hands of Herod. Once the proclamation has served its purpose it can disappear, and so it is with John—the final line of part one bringing him to the fulfillment of his task and then removing him from the scene, taking him from womb to tomb in the course of five lines, suggesting both his unique greatness and his subordination to the one to whom he points.

The second, longest section consists of a three-part dialogue between the poet and the Baptist. This *meditatio* moves from the reworking of the scriptural text characteristic of *lectio* to a reflection on the spiritual significance of John's experience that can be aligned with the three powers of the soul characteristically found in Ignatian meditation.[10] The memory is engaged in the petitioner's request for the prophet to reveal *"Whom you met upon the far frontier / At the defended bridge, the guarded outpost"* (ll. 40-41). The intellect or understanding is then brought to the fore with the question: *"What did you learn on the wild mountain / When hell came dancing on the noon-day rocks?"* (ll. 56-57). Finally the role of the will is brought into consideration with the final question: *"But did your eyes buy wrath and imprecation / In the red cinemas of the mirage?"* (ll. 74-75). The sense of imaginative identification between poet and prophet here allows John himself to speak, yet the inclusion of deliberately anachronistic details creates a dislocation from purely historical reconstruction

10. See *The Spiritual Exercises of St. Ignatius*, trans. Anthony Mottola (Garden City, NY: Doubleday Image, 1964) 54-56; see also Louis L. Martz, *The Poetry of Meditation*, rev. ed. (New Haven: Yale University Press, 1962) 34-39 for a classic discussion of this process as found in seventeenth-century poetry. While Merton himself is rather critical of too discursive an approach to meditation sometimes associated with the Ignatian method (see for example Thomas Merton, *Contemplative Prayer* [New York: Herder & Herder, 1969] 51), he would have been quite familiar with the application of the three powers of the soul from making the *Exercises* privately in early 1940 (see Thomas Merton, *Run to the Mountain: The Story of a Vocation. Journals, vol. 1: 1939-1941*, ed. Patrick Hart [San Francisco: HarperCollins, 1995] 135-38; Thomas Merton, *The Seven Storey Mountain* [New York: Harcourt, Brace, 1948] 268-73).

and juxtaposes past and present, John's context and that of the poet and his readers.

The initial request for the story of John's prophetic commissioning is basically a development of Luke 3:2: "The Word of God came to John son of Zechariah in the desert." But implicitly it is a two-part request: it explicitly asks "Whom you met upon the far frontier," at the margins, the liminal space at the edge of the settled area, a question already provided with its answer by the capital letter for the interrogative pronoun; but implicitly it is asking as well who was encountered at the defended bridge, the guarded outpost, with the implication that "the world" is defending itself against "invasion," not of barbarians (whatever they themselves may think) but of the Word of God that would undermine their "order." In response, John relates his journey into the wilderness:

> "I passed the guards and sentries,
> Their lances did not stay me, or the gate of spikes
>
> Or the abysses of the empty night.
> I walked on darkness
>
> To the place of the appointed meeting:
> I took my sealed instructions,
> But did not wait
> For compliment or for congratulation from my hidden Captain.
> Even at my return
> I passed unseen beside the stern defenders
> In their nests of guns,
> And while the spies were trying to decode some secret
> In my plain, true name,
> I left them like the night wind." (ll. 42-55)

The beginning of John's narration is perhaps surprising, suggesting ironically that the guards and sentries would prevent him from leaving as much as the invaders from entering. But neither they nor the "abysses of the empty night" blocked his journey: human, material obstructions and deeper spiritual hindrances were equally ineffective. The latter emerge as paradoxically more substantial, suggesting the need to come to an awareness of one's own radical nothingness, to transcend a fear of the void, in order to encounter the Word of God. Here is the Baptist's desert spirituality, the path of self-emptying, of inner purification in which one "walk[s] on darkness," that leads to an encounter with his "hidden Captain," envisioned as a covert military mission, a clandestine meeting in which he receives "sealed instructions," the assignment, of course, to "prepare the way of the Lord." It is marked both by a sense of duty and a sense of urgency, expecting and waiting for no special recognition for following orders (cf. Lk. 17:10). On his return he once again slips past enemy lines as the defenders fail to deter his entry. The deliberate anachronism of "nests of guns" is a clear indication that the description is not to be taken as literal reportage: the opposition of "the world" to John the Baptist's message is just as evident in the contemporary era, the period of the Second World War that was probably still going on when Merton wrote this poem, as it was in ancient Judea.

The misdirected efforts of the "spies" in trying to find some occult significance in John's "plain, true name" (cf. the surprise at the choice of this name at his birth [Lk. 1:59-63]) indicates a mistaken focus on the messenger rather than the message, on the precursor rather than the Messiah, the "hidden Captain" who is ignored. It is this preoccupation that allows John to pass them by "like the night wind," both suggesting the freedom of those born of the Spirit (cf. Jn. 3:8) and, in its reference to the night, indicating that there is indeed a mystery about John, but it is not what the investigators assume is mysterious. A sense of opposition and incomprehension is paramount here, but it is transcended by the experience of spiritual liberty and undermined by the foolish, absurd, even bumbling efforts to inhibit the Word of God. Worldly power is ineffectual in countering spiritual wisdom.

The second question, *"What did you learn?"* assumes an encounter in the desert with the demonic as well as with the divine, an implied parallel with Christ's own time in the desert, so that the Baptist would be a forerunner here as well. The "wild mountain," not mentioned in the Gospel, suggests a parallel with Moses and Elijah as well, perhaps especially with Elijah, since John, the new Elijah, is likewise a hearer of the "still small voice" (1 K. 19:12). The imagery also foreshadows that of the temptations of the desert fathers, above all that of the noonday demon (Ps. 90[91]:6), literally of course the full force of the desert sun at midday. The questioner presupposes an experience of threat or danger from an encounter with the world perceived as fallen and under the power of demons, but this turns out to be a misapprehension countered by John's actual experience:

> "I learned my hands could hold
> Rivers of water
> And spend them like an everlasting treasure.
> I learned to see the waking desert

> Smiling to behold me with the springs her ransom,
> Open her clear eyes in a miracle of transformation,
> And the dry wilderness
> Suddenly dressed in meadows,
> All garlanded with an embroidery of flowering orchards
> Sang with a virgin's voice,
> Descending to her wedding in these waters
> With the Prince of Life.
> All barrenness and death lie drowned
> Here in the fountains He has sanctified,
> And the deep harps of Jordan
> Play to the contrite world as sweet as heaven." (ll. 58-73)

What John actually experiences is not destruction but transformation, re-creation, renewal, a restoration of paradise. It is a visionary foresee-ing of precisely the renewal of the desert prophesied in Deutero-Isaiah (cf. Is. 41:18-20, 43:19-21, 44:3-4, 51:3). But it is not just a perception but a commission. John is called to be an agent of renewal. The water imagery of course refers most immediately to his baptismal ministry, but in the biblical perspective personal and cosmic renewal are inseparable. The initial lesson focuses on his own mission, the power to hold rivers in his hand—to hold, but not to hold on to, not to possess, but rather to (ex)spend this precious, valuable resource without its depletion—it is "everlasting" both in the sense of undiminishing and eternal. Then the scope widens to encompass the natural world in a process of reciprocal contemplation: John sees the waking desert and the desert beholds John. This mutual seeing is of course eschatological, drawing especially on Romans 8 with its recognition of the liberation of humanity from sin as intrinsically connected with the freedom of all creation. It foresees the final consummation, as the culminating reference to the wedding feast of Revelation 21:2, 9-10 makes clear (cf. also the water imagery in Rev. 21:6, 22:1-2, 17), but here not the city but the "dry wilderness" is imaged as the Bride, "dressed in meadows" and "garlanded with an embroidery of flowering orchards" as her wedding garments. The desert sings "with a virgin's voice," suggesting the song to the Lamb in Revelation 4:11, 5:9-10, 12, 13, 7:10-17, and especially the wedding song of the Lamb (Rev. 19:5-8). But the wedding "in these waters / With the Prince of Life" connects with the baptism scene as well, as the final reference to the Jordan makes clear. The union of Christ and creation is already present at the outset of his ministry. As barrenness and death itself are drowned in the fountains (thus a connection with the Exodus story as well, with the forces of death destroyed), the sound of the waters themselves accompanies the Bride's song—land and river in concert—and becomes a foreshadowing of the heavenly hymn. Earthly harmony, reflective of the "contrite," reconciled world that has been transformed by the message of repentance introduced by John and brought to completion by Jesus, foreshadows the ultimate sweetness of heaven, John's final image here.

As though he cannot quite bring himself to let go of his preconceptions of the apocalyptic implications of John's message, the questioner counters the image of hands spending the treasure of life-giving waters with that of eyes buying wrath and imprecation; but the phrase "red cinemas of the mirage," with its suggestion of an illusory vision caused by the beating down of the desert sun, actually indicates he is giving the Baptist the opportunity to refute this stereotype rather than holding it himself. This prompts John's longest and most definitive response, an unequivocal rejection of his imputed role of wrathful denouncer, judge and condemner:

> "My eyes did not consult the heat or the horizon:
> I did not imitate the spurious intrepidity
> Of that mad light full of revenge.
> God did not hide me in the desert to instruct my soul
> In the fascism of an asp or scorpion.
> The sun that burned me to an Arab taught me nothing:
> My mind is not in my skin.
> I went into the desert to receive
> The keys of my deliverance
> From image and from concept and from desire.
> I learned not wrath but love,
> Waiting in darkness for the secret stranger
> Who, like an inward fire,
> Would try me in the crucibles of His unconquerable Law:
> His heat, more searching than the breath of the Simoon,
> Separates love from hunger
> And peace from satiation,
> Burning, destroying all the matrices of anger and revenge.
> It is because my love, as strong as steel, is armed against all hate
> That those who hate their own lives fear me like a sabre." (ll. 76-95)

He begins by asserting that his eyes did not "consult" (i.e. take counsel from) either the heat (the "red cinemas") or the horizon (the mirage). The deliberately inflated terminology of "spurious intrepidity" ironically undermines and mocks the pomposity of the illusory bluster, the pretense of fearlessness that marks "that mad light full of revenge"—a spurious clarity, a pseudo-illumination that is distorted by a desire for retaliation, for a self-justifying condemnation of others, especially in response to injuries done to oneself. John shows himself here to be faithful to the teaching of the Sermon on the Mount (cf. Mt. 5:43-48)—even though it has not yet been preached. The purpose of his sojourn in the desert is not to adopt the behavior of the asp or scorpion, two poisonous creatures that strike out at whatever they perceive as threatening—he rejects this will to power and domination that is identified, in an obvious anachronism, with fascism. Such a supposition would identify God himself with a fascist attitude. He rejects a reductively naturalistic response to the desert, a purely superficial transformation like that of the skin exposed to the sun—his mind is not similarly darkened, and therefore does not act out of hostility, opposition, a narrowly "political" response.

These lines have exposed the distorted, destructive misapprehensions of the meaning of the desert experience. They depend on an absolutizing of the present, of the fallen world, a failure to perceive the eschatological transformation described in the previous section. Such reactions are totally incompatible with a vision of a restored creation. Rather, John the Baptist is properly recognized as the paradigmatic desert figure, whose apophatic experience of emptiness is a liberation from all that is not God, a release from an imprisonment in one's own self-constructed world. It is a deliverance from image—a cleansing, a purification of memory; from concept—the purification of the understanding; from desire—the purification of the will. He is able to proclaim deliverance to others (cf. l. 5) only after experiencing this deliverance, this inner freedom, himself. He expresses the completion of what he "learned" (cf. ll. 56, 58, 61) in the simple juxtaposition of wrath (cf. l. 74) and love, found in the darkness that both contrasts with the mad light of revenge and suggests that on one level there is an analogy to his darkened skin: a proper darkness of the mind means surrendering one's own images and concepts and desires to await the proper instructions (cf. l. 47) from the "secret stranger." Likewise there is an authentic, positive dimension to the imagery of heat—not the outward-directed heat of anger and hatred but the purifying "inward fire" that burns away all dross, the refiner's fire of the messenger in Malachi 3:23 which here refines the messenger himself. This heat more penetrating than the desert wind—the Simoon—suggests the breath of the Spirit that separates love from hunger—i.e. from the desire for personal fulfillment, and peace from satiation—the pseudo-satisfaction of such fulfillment. True love, John declares, is not self-directed craving, and true peace is not self-satisfied contentment. (Note the balance of phrasing here: love and peace are complementary, while hunger and satiation are mutually exclusive alternatives). What is burned up are the "matrices"—i.e. the sources, the originating forms—from which anger and revenge arise: not just the outer manifestations but the roots, the buried motivations; it is the destruction of the destructive tendencies themselves, consumed by the fire of love. All this is an explication of the simple assertion "I learned not wrath but love." Wrath, as a destructive force, is easily identified with fire. Love may have a superficial resemblance to this fire, but it is directed at that which is unreal: what is destroyed by love is illusion, above all the illusion of one's own righteousness that is the fundamental "matrix" of anger and revenge.

The final two lines of this section shift the image but confirm the point. The reason why some people mistake love for wrath is because their own hatred, above all self-hatred, self-rejection, is threatened by the power of love. Here love "strong as steel" suggests both the sword of the Spirit (cf. Eph. 6:17) and the word of God sharp as a two-edged sword (Heb. 4:12). John is feared like a sabre because love is perceived as a threat to hate—note that the opposition is to hate, not to the persons hating: they are the ones who cause their own fear by their self-contradictory stance. They hate their own lives but fear to surrender the hatred, which is their only connection to their (false) selves. Though not made explicit, this fear may well be a reference to Herod in particular, and so a veiled allusion to John's death, in which it is he, not his opponent, who is put to the sword, an apparent, but only apparent, triumph of hatred over love.

The final section of the poem, a prayer to St. John, moves from *meditatio* to *oratio*. The prayer begins with a series of four appositives in direct address, each more developed than the previous one. The first, simply "strong Baptist" (l. 96), is perhaps a reference to the power of John's hands to hold rivers (ll. 58-60); the second, "Angel before the face of the Messiah" (l. 97), recapitulates the earlier descriptions of John as a "terrible and peaceful angel" (l. 33) and as "Burn[ing] before the face of Christ" (l. 38) and so focuses on his role as messenger; the third, "Desert-dweller, knowing the solitudes that lie / Beyond anxiety and doubt" (ll. 98-99), is the key one for John as monastic model—to go into solitude is to pass through and to go beyond both the affective weakness of anxiety and the intellectual weakness of doubt; finally he is addressed as "Eagle whose flight is higher than our atmosphere / Of hesitation and surmise" (ll. 100-101), symbol of contemplation (borrowed from the traditional ascription to the other John, the evangelist): here "hesitation" represents the affective and "surmise" the intellectual difficulties that are transcended in contemplative elevation. The final identification switches from appositives to a declarative statement: "You are the first Cistercian and the greatest Trappist" (l. 102); as solitary and contemplative, John has both priority and eminence—he is the original model of the Cistercian charism and the perfect fulfillment of the Trappist vocation. The full significance of this statement is then developed in the subsequent lines, which are petitionary, making a three-fold request:

> Never abandon us, your few but faithful children,
> For we remember your amazing life,
> Where you laid down for us the form and pattern of
> Our love for Christ,
> Being so close to Him you were His twin.
> Oh buy us, by your intercession, in your mighty heaven,
> Not your great name, St. John, or ministry,
> But oh, your solitude and death:
> And most of all, gain us your great command of graces,
> Make our poor hands also fountains full of life and wonder
> Spending, in endless rivers, to the universe,
> Christ, in secret, and His Father, and His sanctifying Spirit. (ll. 103-114)

The first petition is for mutual fidelity: as the monks are John's faithful children, so, he prays, may John be committed to them; as they remember his life, so may he not forget them. John's life is seen as the form and pattern for authentic love of Christ. All that has been said so far, then, is applicable not just to the Baptist but to themselves. John's love for Christ, above all, is exemplary for them. This needs to be specified, however—his life is a template for them in some respects but not in all, as the second petition will indicate. For John is not only a model of love for Christ, but is also himself an image of Christ in a unique way. The notion of John as Christ's "twin" is a novel one, evidently to be referred not only to the kinship and birth stories but implicitly to the way the Baptist's adult life, particularly the desert sojourn and the martyr's death, parallels that of Jesus. So contemplatives find in John both a model for relating to Christ and also an inimitable identification with Christ. This, apparently is what is to be seen as "amazing" about John's life. Only at this point, in the context of prayer, is there a sudden recognition of this double dimension, a new awareness of the full significance of John's person and work. Thus the second request specifies in what way John serves as form and pattern—not in his "great name"—presumably corresponding to "strong Baptist" (l. 96); not in his ministry, also unique—corresponding to his "angelic" role (l. 97); but rather in his "solitude and death" (cf. ll. 98-99). The solitude is to be expected in the overall context of the poem thus far, but the explicit reference to his death is a new element, previously alluded to only obliquely (cf. ll. 94-95). Is it intrusive here, or is it rather the final, culminating act of fidelity to his call? It is saved for last to give it due prominence, though it is presented without any elaboration or description whatever. The reference is not, presumably, to the particular circumstances of John's martyrdom, but to death as the completion of the process of self-surrender—a death to self, a fulfillment of commitment to follow Christ "*usque ad mortem*" in the language of the Benedictine vow.[11] It is this that John is asked to "buy us," what he purchases with the "everlasting treasure" that he "spends" earlier in the poem (cf. l. 60). Finally the third petition pulls back from the ultimate example of death to the ongoing example of a fruitful, generative life. The imagery of lines 58-60 is appropriated, or at least desired, by monks—to share in John's work as a channel of grace, to have hands that serve as fountains of living water. But what is to flow forth here is identified as the very divine life of the Trinity. The role of the monk, like that of John, is ultimately to be an agent of the cosmic renewal described earlier in the poem (ll. 61-73), to be a channel of God's presence "to the universe," to "spend . . . Christ" himself. This is to be done "in secret," not as a public apostolate but by continual, constant, faithful presence in the wilderness, in the solitude of prayer and silence and obscurity. Ultimately what John gives to the contemplative and what the contemplative is to give to the universe is Christ Himself, inseparably united (as at the baptism) with the Father and with the sanctifying (not just Holy but "holy-making") Spirit. Thus the long process that has led speaker and audience from reading through meditation to prayer culminates in the petition to become, through John's intercession, not only a participant in but a mediator of the Trinitarian life that is of course intimately associated with Jesus' baptism in the Jordan by John, and with the baptismal formula by which every Christian has subsequently been initiated into life in Christ.

* * * * * * *

"St. John's Night," Merton's next poetic interpretation of the significance of the Baptist,[12] focuses on the ancient custom in southern France of

11. See Merton's discussion of the formula of monastic profession in Thomas Merton, *The Life of the Vows: Initiation into the Monastic Tradition* 6, ed. Patrick F. O'Connell (Collegeville, MN: Cistercian Publications, 2012) 235-36.

12. The dating of this poem is also problematic: according to the 1951 letter already cited above, all the poems in *Figures for an Apocalypse* were composed in 1947 (Labrie, "Ordering" 117); however this poem was presumably written around the time of the feast it commemorates, when, in 1947, according to his journal Merton was writing "The Quickening of St. John the Baptist." It is possible that Merton wrote the two poems,

lighting signal fires to celebrate the birthday of St. John on June 24,[13] a celebration of light that is of course associated with the summer solstice occurring at virtually the same time and one that in fact predates the establishment of the Christian feast itself, as Merton himself will indicate. The poem begins with the moment the fires are kindled:

> Now where the hills of Languedoc are blue with vineyards
> Swimming to the brows of the low ridges brown as shells,
> A thousand villages begin to name your night with fires. (ll. 1-3)

The scene is Languedoc, Merton's own birthplace, which creates a special connection even though it is never explicitly mentioned. The opening image, unexpectedly, is one of water, as the blue of the vineyards, grapes becoming ripe in color, suggests water "swimming" up the hillsides, where the signal fires are to be lit. This rich image of water crowned by fire immediately suggests the Baptist's own distinction between his own baptism with water and that of Christ, who will baptize with the Holy Spirit and with fire, but in fact the two are no longer to be regarded as mutually exclusive. For this is "water" that will become wine, and so recalls Christ's first miracle, while the light of the fires suggests the illumination that John will bring to his listeners, as foretold by his father Zechariah in the *"Benedictus"* (cf. Lk. 1:78-79), and here the fires are said explicitly to "name your night"—to identify this shortest night of the year as being intrinsically connected with the birth of John, referred to in the second person and so the primary audience of the poem.

In the verse paragraph that follows, the flames are personified as

---

appearing in different volumes, at virtually the same time, but unlikely, so "St. John's Night" may date from June of 1946.

13. Merton scholar Monica Weis, SSJ provides a vivid description of this celebration as experienced during a visit to Prades, Merton's birthplace: "Every year on June 23, the vigil of the feast of St. John the Baptist, a fire is lighted on Canigou, one of the highest mountains in the Pyrenees, that has on it a cross decorated with the Catalan flag. During the night many of the 'locals' keep vigil on the mountain so that early in the morning of the feast, they can take torches lit from the sacred fire and in an impressive relay ignite bonfires—estimated to be as many as 30,000—all through the Languedoc-Roussillon region. The young men of Prades, France, where Merton was born, engage in something of an Olympic marathon competition. Once their torch is aflame, each of them races down the mountain, hoping to be in the vanguard of men bringing the sacred fire to a waiting pyre in the village square. They arrive to a cheering throng about noon, after the arduous descent, winded but exuberant to be part of this ancient custom honoring the Baptist—and eager to partake of the feast prepared by the women of the village. Once they have added their torch to the huge bonfire, there is dancing and singing by all the spectators to celebrate the Baptist, a patron of France since the Crusades" (personal communication, 6/21/2013).

waking and seeing, thus transferring the power of light to make visible to the flames themselves:

> The flames that wake as wide as faith,
> Opening their fierce and innocent eyes from hill to hill
> In the midsummer nightfall,
> Burn at the ageless cross-roads these their
> Pagan and converted fires. (ll. 4-8)

This awakening of the flames on the hilltops is compared to opening the "eyes" of faith, the process of enlightenment, of illumination that is traditionally associated with baptism by the Fathers of the Church.[14] They are described as both "fierce and innocent"—dangerous only to what is false, to what prefers blindness and darkness, with the power to destroy what is illusory (cf. the fire imagery in Mt. 3:12, Lk. 3:9) but providing the light to see what is real. The spread of the fires "from hill to hill," as one is lit from another, provides a sense of successive awakening, a process of extending the light across the land. The middle line situates the event in the proper temporal frame—both midsummer, the day of greatest light, and at nightfall, the bringing of light at the point of the coming of darkness. So the fires have a paradoxical relation to natural light, both extending it and transcending it, just as faith is in continuity with but goes beyond nature, the same dynamic that is suggested in the final reference to "Pagan and converted fires." The phrase points to the origin of the custom in the pre-Christian celebration of the solstice, but the rite has been "converted," given a new meaning rather than simply rejected and condemned. The implications of the word, juxtaposed with "pagan," of course suggest conversion of the people (and implicitly their baptism) but also the more secular meaning of change of function, of purpose. So there is both continuity and change, the incorporation of an ancient traditional custom into a new framework, thereby giving it a new significance. The fires are situated not only in time but in space—"at the ageless cross-roads." After the specificity of "midsummer nightfall," "ageless" suggests a transcending of temporal limitations; it is not precisely a synonym for "timeless," but rather an indication of not becoming old, outworn, merely antiquarian, meaningful only as a relic of the past; the ritual is of perennial significance, continued relevance. In particular, it is the "cross-roads" that are so described. The fires are lit at points of intersection, of both convergence and divergence. In context there is again a suggestion of a coming together of the natural and the graced, the pagan

---

14. See Thomas Merton, *The New Man* (New York: Farrar, Straus and Cudahy, 1961) 205-17.

and the Christian, but also an implication of subsequent divergence, of discontinuity. Crossroads imply a point of decision, the need to choose the right way—aided, implicitly, by the light that represents faith, an illumination that reveals the true path, which is of course a role associated with the saint who is being celebrated by these fires.

The lines that follow focus on wheat, a complement to the mention of vineyards in the opening line (picked up again here in line 15) and thus suggesting a Eucharistic symbolism typical of so many of Merton's early landscape poems,[15] but also recall John's preaching on the wheat and the chaff (Mt. 3:12; Lk. 3:17):

> And the dark shocks of the fair summer's harvest
> Rise up in the deep fields
> Where for two thousand years, St. John,
> Your fires are young among us;
> They cry there, loud as was your desert testimony,
> Out by the grey olive groves,
> Out at the crossing of the vineyard roads
> Where once the wheat sheaves wept with blood
> In warning to the sickles of the manichees. (ll. 9-17)

The image of the harvest suggests the eschatological fulfillment being foreshadowed, but here the shocks are seen only in the firelight, a harvest that is not yet a definitive completion. They are said to "Rise up," recalling Christ's own words in John 12:24 that "Unless a grain of wheat fall to the ground and die, it remains a single grain, but if it die it will yield a rich harvest," as well as his words later in the same chapter: "And when I am lifted up from the earth, I will draw everyone to myself" (Jn. 12:32). This message is both extended through time and possessing an immediacy, as the juxtaposition of "for two thousand years" and the present tense of "Your fires are young" indicates. The recognition of time incorporates both *chronos*, the long history of Christianity, and *kairos*, the sense of present illumination, of present challenge, the now-ness of the sign being provided. As symbols of the Baptist, the fires themselves are said to "cry there," that is, to cry out like John's voice crying in the wilderness, and their message is presumably his own: "make straight the way of the Lord" (Jn. 1:23); "Prepare the way of the Lord, make straight his paths" (Mt. 3:3, Mk.1:3, Lk. 3:4). Thus another connection is made to the roads referred to again in line 15: the fires enable one to see the "way" of the Lord at the crossroads. The olive groves, grey in the twilight, recall the

---

15. See for example "Aubade: Lake Erie"; "Holy Communion: The City"; "The Communion" (*CP* 35, 39-40, 40-41).

Mount of Olives to which Jesus withdrew at this same time of day, and in which he was discovered by the light of torches having a very different function from those lit "Out at the crossing" here, suggesting not only a point of decision but of a road that will lead to the cross. The section ends with a warning against the false eschatology of the Albigensians or Cathars, the medieval manichees of Languedoc, whose sickles were not those of the final gathering of the harvest; the enigmatic syntax is a clue to the message here: where the poet sees the wheat sheaves weeping blood not "In warning of the sickles" but "In warning to the sickles"—a reminder that the false dualism that rejects the world of matter as evil, and rejects the incarnate, fully human Christ as well, takes a wrong turn at the crossroad, misinterprets the sign and so calls for an end of the world (symbolized in the book of Revelation by the cutting of the wheat by sickles [14:14-20]) that is not the fulfillment of the Gospel message but its perversion. The blood on the wheat may be a specific allusion to the murder of the Cistercian Peter of Castelnau, the papal legate assassinated by the Cathars on January 15, 1208, or perhaps a forewarning that the result of the Albigensians' intransigence would be bloodshed on a massive scale in the so-called Albigensian "Crusade," but the stress seems to be not so much on actual bloodshed (by the Cathars or of the Cathars) as on the misconstrual implied by their failure to connect the sickles to the true eschatological harvest. In any case it represents a historical wrong turn, an instance when the light provided by the fires at the crossroads did not succeed in leading these travelers in the right direction, an implicit warning to present-day pilgrims, to whom the poem now turns its attention.

In the remainder of the poem, the symbolic significance of the ritual of the St. John beacons is interiorized and applied to the lives of the poet and his fellow monks.

> And in our hearts, here in another nation
> Is made your deep midsummer night.
> It is a night of other fires,
>
> Wherein all thoughts, all wreckage of the noisy world
> Swim out of ken like leaves, or smoke upon the pools of wind.
>
> (ll. 18-22)

An analogy is seen between the fires burning on the hills in France and the interior fires burning in the hearts of the monks in choir during the night office of the Feast of the Nativity of St. John, "other fires" in "another nation." These fires are purgative, in which the vanities of secular life, the thoughts and wreckage "of the noisy world," are consumed like the leaves of autumn. Here too images of fire and of water are linked, as thoughts are said to "swim out of ken" like burning leaves rising up before being completely consumed, or like "smoke upon the pools of wind," the eddying of the smoke of those leaves that have been completely burned like swirling water—i.e. some thoughts are completely gone, others in the process of disappearing. Thus these fires are "other" not only because they are figurative, but because they are primarily purgative rather than illuminating as the beacons of France are. But this is only a preliminary understanding of the meaning of the fires, which will develop further as the poem continues.

With the disappearance of the noisy world the possibility of paying attention to the darkness, to listening in silence, emerges. The speaker calls upon his audience, himself and his fellow monks, in a triple imperative that is then matched by a triple question:

> Oh, listen to that darkness, listen to that deep darkness,
> Listen to those seas of darkness on whose shores we stand and die.
> Now can we have you, peace, now can we sleep in your will,
>   sweet God of peace?
>
> Now can we have Your Word and in Him rest? (ll. 23-26)

The triple command suggests an ever deepening penetration as the process of listening develops, from darkness to deep darkness to seas of darkness. The daylight world of rationality is gone, so hearing is the only sense operating—thus the fire here does not provide illumination but functions simply to consume false, illusory perceptions. Once again water imagery is introduced, as speaker and listeners stand on the shores waiting for the waves to engulf them, an ambiguous image that can either suggest baptismal symbolism of dying to the old self or a negative experience of dying without passing over the waters to the land of promise. The lines that follow have a similar intensification by repetition with variation, as the speaker addresses first personified peace and then the God of peace, asking for immediate possession of peace and mystical rest in the Word of God, that which is ultimately to be listened for and heard in the dark silence. Yet it seems as though the answer to the repeated question—Now can we . . .—is in fact "no"! For this is not the conclusion of the poem, merely the start of its second half. The remainder returns to address once again John the Baptist, the Precursor, the one who prepares the way. The implication is that this is still the time of preparation, not of consummation, that the impatience of the desire for peace and rest "Now" must be tempered.

> Prophet and hermit, great John-Baptist,
> You who have brought us to the door-sill of your wilderness,
> You who have won for us
> The first faint savor of the world's desertion:
> When shall we have to eat the things that we have barely tasted?
> When shall we have your own vast loneliness's holy honeycomb?
>
> (ll. 27-32)

For the first time in the poem, the focus is really on John himself, addressed as prophet and hermit. He is first identified by a pair of relative clauses, then asked a pair of parallel questions. As the one who has "brought us to the doorsill of your wilderness," John is presented as being at home in the desert, while at the same time the speaker and his companions are recognized as being only on the threshold of the wilderness, only at the starting point of their journey into the unknown, identified as "your wilderness" but not yet as theirs. This turn to John represents a reducing of the intensity of the questions asked in the previous section, a recognition of the actual stage of their spiritual journey as being a time not for rest but for patient waiting for further movement. Likewise John's providing for them only "the first faint savor of the world's desertion," a slight hint of the flavor of leaving behind the world—suggesting an experience of smelling the aroma of food while standing at the door of a house—contributes to the sense of awareness that in fact one is only at the beginning of the journey, at that liminal point where the wilderness is before one and the world behind. This first gift has been "won for us" by John's fidelity to his dual role of prophet and hermit—he has prepared the way for entering the desert, for living a genuinely contemplative life, as he has prepared the way for the rest of the Christ-life. The two questions that follow again represent a scaling back from the questions posed in the previous section, not a repeated "Now can we . . ." but the much less peremptory "When shall we . . ." The appetite for the wild honey that is John's own food in the wilderness, which can be identified with Israel's bread in the wilderness, the manna that is compared to the taste of honey in Exodus 16:31, as well as with the banquet of Wisdom that is "sweeter than the honeycomb" (Sir. 24:27), has been whetted but not satisfied. The desire is still there, but the phrasing of these questions suggests that the speaker is learning to be patient.

In the section which follows, John is recognized, surprisingly, not simply as Christ's precursor but as the mediator of the Holy Spirit:

> You hold in your two hands, lo! more than Baptism:
> The fruits and the three virtues and the seven presents.

> We wait upon your intercession:
> Or die we without mercy on the rim of those impossible shores?
> (ll. 33-36)

His present role, then, surpasses that which he exercised in his earthly ministry. No longer does he administer a baptism of repentance, but in the Christian era, from his present heavenly position, he hands on the fruits of the Spirit (Gal. 5:22), the theological virtues of faith, hope and love, the seven gifts of the Spirit (Is. 11:2), the same Spirit, of course, who led Jesus himself into the wilderness after he was baptized by John, so that implicitly the journey into the desert means following not just John but Christ himself. One cannot enter the wilderness, then, without the prompting of the Spirit, and for this they must "wait upon your intercession," wait for John's prayer that the Spirit be given to lead them on their way. Otherwise they may die without mercy on the "impossible shores," impossible because impassible by their own power just as passing through the Red Sea into the desert, or across the Jordan into the Promised Land, was impossible for the people of Israel without the guidance provided by the pillar of fire. The speaker expresses fear of being left high and dry, of not going into the desert, of being left behind in the land of enslavement.

Thus the speaker returns once more to the image of the beacon fire in asking for light to lead them into the wilderness:

> Kindle, kindle in this wilderness
> The tracks of those wonderful fires:
> Clean us and lead us in the new night, with the power of Elias
> And find us out the summits of the love and prayer
> That Wisdom wants of us, oh Bridegroom's Friend! (ll. 37-41)

Whereas the "other fires" earlier consumed the thoughts and wreckage of the noisy world, these "wonderful fires," suggestive of the "signs and wonders" associated with the Exodus journey, provide light to travel in the darkness, to enter into the desert rather than be left on the shore. What are to be kindled are actually the "tracks" of the fires: the paths made by those preceding are to be lit up. John's power is like that of Elias (cf. Lk. 1:17, the angel's words to Zechariah the father of John) who himself traveled through the wilderness to Mt. Horeb, his own recapitulation of the exodus in his escaping from Ahab and Jezebel. In asking John to "Clean us and lead us in the new night," the speaker combines the purgative and illuminative functions of fire, the "new night" suggesting the darkness in which God's people are led forward by the pillar of fire. The pattern is completed with the final request to "find us out the summits of love and prayer / That Wisdom wants of us," both spiritual equivalents of the hills of Languedoc and identified with Sinai/Horeb as well as with the mount of transfiguration where Moses and Elijah are present with Jesus. These heights are the climax of the spiritual journey, marked by contemplative union with God and a participation in the divine love for all creation, the third and final phase of the spiritual journey as traditionally presented. The final address to John as "Bridegroom's friend" (Jn. 3:29), the one who guides the bride to her spouse, suggests the wedding feast, the eschatological banquet, the fulfillment of the desire to "eat the things we have barely tasted." Here, we note, is the first explicit reference to Christ in the poem, and only as a possessive, but it is actually the climax toward which everything has been directed, an indication, as in the original passage of the Gospel from which it is taken, that John is completely oriented toward Christ.

In the final lines of the poem, the fire imagery is explicitly associated with this unitive phase as well. The speaker prays:

> And take us to the secret tents,
> The sacred, unimaginable tabernacles
> Burning upon the hills of our desire! (ll. 42-44)

The tent of meeting, the tabernacle, is the place of encounter with the Lord in Exodus (Ex. 25:8, 22; 29:42; 33:7-11; 36:8; cf. 1 Macc. 2:4-8; Rev. 15:5); it is also associated in Sirach with the dwelling place of divine Wisdom (Sir. 24:4, 7-10). Here it is envisioned, in one last parallel to the fires of Languedoc, as "Burning upon the hills of our desire." Thus the poem concludes, not with the experience of mystical union, but with a prayer for such union as the culmination of the journey into the wilderness in order ultimately to be made one with Wisdom, one with Jesus the Bridegroom, the Logos who is Wisdom become flesh, all envisaged as taking place through the agency of the Baptist who is not only the Bridegroom's friend, but, as Merton called him in his journal reflection, the "great patron and friend and Protector" of the contemplative as well.

* * * * * * *

The germ of Merton's final poem on John the Baptist[16] is found in his journal entry for June 21, 1947:

---

16. For a brief overview of this poem, see Martin J. Burne, OSB, "Some Thoughts on the Early Poetry of Thomas Merton: Reading 'The Quickening of St. John the Baptist,'" *The Merton Seasonal* 14.1 (Winter 1989) 10-14; this is apparently the only critical discussion of any length on any of the Baptist poems. In *Words and Silence: On the Poetry of Thomas Merton* (New York: New Directions, 1979) 82-83, Sr. Thérèse

After the Night Office I got an idea for a poem, or anyway an idea about the relation of contemplatives to the rest of the Church. We are hidden in her womb, but we should be mystics and mystically sense the presence of Christ, and the exultation of our experience will awaken the whole Church and she will begin to sing and preach. But instead of writing the poem, I spent the day in prayer. I only got down a couple of lines and maybe I will leave it at that. Because I can [*sic*] see how writing it will make me love God more, and it may well make me love Him less, especially if I write instead of praying. However I shall see at work tomorrow, which is the Vigil. (*ES* 86)[17]

He did, of course, go on to write the poem, "The Quickening of St. John the Baptist," with the subtitle, *"On the Contemplative Vocation."* The overall structure may initially seem rather more complicated than in the previous poems, but in fact its nine verse paragraphs have a carefully ordered pattern, with three pairs of subunits considering the Visitation scene from three different perspectives, followed by a three-segment application to monastic life.

The poem begins with two verse paragraphs addressed to Mary, the first consisting of a set of three parallel questions:

> Why do you fly from the drowned shores of Galilee,
> From the sands and the lavender water?
> Why do you leave the ordinary world, Virgin of Nazareth,
> The yellow fishing boats, the farms,
> The winesmelling yards and low cellars
> Or the oilpress, and the women by the well?
> Why do you fly those markets,
> Those suburban gardens,
> The trumpets of the jealous lilies,
> Leaving them all, lovely among the lemon trees? (ll. 1-10)

The present tense here places the speaker in the temporal frame of the scriptural story, and suggests the questions are not to be considered merely rhetorical but expressing a genuine puzzlement. The verb "fly from" suggests an effort to escape danger, as though Mary were fleeing

---

Lentfoehr provides excerpts from drafts of earlier versions of the poem.

17. Merton begins this passage by mentioning that he was "Reading St. Bernard's sermon on *St. John Baptist*" (*"In Nativitate S. Joannis Baptistae"* [J. P. Migne, ed., *Patrologiae Cursus Completus, Series Latina*, 221 vols. (Paris: Garnier, 1844-1865), vol. 183, cols. 397C-404C]), but this sermon, focused on the image of John as a burning and shining lamp (*"lucerna ardens, et lucens"* [Jn. 5:35]) does not consider the unborn John as a model for the contemplative and so does not seem to be a direct influence on the poem.

from spring flooding, but even the second line already seems to modify this interpretation, since mention of sand indicates that the shores are not completely flooded, and the "lavender" of the water, suggestive of the color of the sea at twilight, does not accord with a sense of threat, so the move to higher ground is apparently not motivated by natural conditions. The second question, substituting the less dramatic "leave" for "fly" and replacing "drowned shores" with "ordinary world," suggests that Mary's withdrawal is not to be attributed to some extraordinary external situation. She is departing from (not fleeing) common, everyday life—the workaday world of fishing boats and farms, the yards associated with wine and cellars associated with oil, the women of the village gathered as usual at the well. The direct address to Mary as "Virgin of Nazareth" both links her to this milieu and sets her apart from it, since her virginity is now not simply the normal state preceding married life but a unique element that will henceforth set her apart from the routines and rhythms of the world being described here. The third iteration of the question returns to the verb "fly," but now clearly with no suggestion of escaping physical danger; she is leaving behind the marketplace, a place for exchanging news, like the well, along with merchandise, and "suburban gardens," already outside the town, then, where are to be found lilies personified as "jealous," as though aware that their own purity is inferior to hers, and as "trumpets," instruments that are used to attract attention, to summon an audience for some sort of public proclamation. Here the question seems to point toward Mary's motive for withdrawing, a desire to avoid unwanted gossip, but the perspective is still focused on the negative, on what she is going from rather than what she is going toward.

The second of the two sections addressed to Mary is again composed of three syntactic units, but now the first two are statement rather than question:

> You have trusted no town
> With the news behind your eyes.
> You have drowned Gabriel's word in thoughts like seas
> And turned toward the stone mountain
> To the treeless places.
> Virgin of God, why are your clothes like sails? (ll. 11-16)

In the first sentence here the speaker provides his own answer to the questions he has previously raised. The "news" is of course the "good news" of her child's conception, but it is also startling information that is sure to be misunderstood by the local townspeople. The parallel sentence that follows reuses the image of drowning from the opening line in a figurative context: the angel's announcement is submerged in thoughts, not to be vocalized but kept for the time being beneath the surface, in the mind. But again there is a question whether this is an adequate interpretation on the speaker's part, as the word "drowned" suggests an effort not merely to conceal but to stifle the word, still too negative an understanding. The rest of the sentence does show Mary "turned toward" a destination, depicted as a stark landscape far removed from the busy and productive village, its treeless vistas a vivid contrast to the gardens with their lemon trees and lilies. The return to a question in the final line here indicates that the speaker himself recognizes that his formulations do not fully explain Mary's journey. Though she is moving into the mountains, the billowing of her clothes reminds him of sails, not drowning but being carried along by the wind, traditionally associated with the power of the Holy Spirit which blows where it wills. Now she is addressed not as "Virgin of Nazareth" but as "Virgin of God," suggestive of a mystery that cannot be adequately summed up in neat classifications. An image that "doesn't fit," a question that is left unanswered, guard against too simplistic, too reductive an interpretation.

The next pair of verse paragraphs is addressed to the reader, and moves the scene forward to Mary's arrival at the house of Elizabeth. The first section is again composed of questions, though now looking back from present to past:

> The day Our Lady, full of Christ,
> Entered the dooryard of her relative
> Did not her steps, light steps, lay on the paving leaves like gold?
> Did not her eyes as grey as doves
> Alight like the peace of a new world upon that house, upon
> miraculous Elizabeth? (ll. 17-21)

Mary is now "Our Lady," the familiar figure of Christian devotion, "full of Christ" after his conception as she was "full of grace" at the time of the Annunciation. But the imagery of the questions, phrased as they are to elicit a positive response, is designed to draw the audience beyond their accustomed perceptions into an imaginative and meditative response to the scene of Mary's arrival. They are asked to see Mary's footsteps, light both in weight and as illumination, gilding the very pavement on which she walks. The brightness of the golden leaves is juxtaposed with the unobtrusiveness of her grey eyes, compared to doves of peace (associated of course with the Holy Spirit as well) alighting (both settling and bringing light) on the house and on Elizabeth herself, who, the Gospel tells us (Lk. 1:41), is filled with the Spirit upon Mary's arrival, and whose own pregnancy is itself "miraculous." The good news kept behind Mary's eyes earlier in the poem can now emerge, first not as words but as a blessing that her eyes themselves bestow, the promise of a world transformed by the presence of the Redeemer. The audience is invited to make this perception their own by responding positively to these questions. In doing so, they are imaginatively transported back to the scene, so that the following lines return to the use of the present tense in a declarative sentence:

> Her salutation
> Sings in the stone valley like a Charterhouse bell:
> And the unborn saint John
> Wakes in his mother's body,
> Bounds with the echoes of discovery. (ll. 22-26)

While drawing both on the evangelist's words in Luke 1:41 and Elizabeth's response to Mary's greeting in verse 44, the speaker introduces the idea that Mary's words function like a monastic bell, as a call to prayer; and since it is the bell of a charterhouse, a Carthusian monastery, it is a call not to communal but to solitary, contemplative prayer, the first note of what will become the central theme of the remainder of the poem. It is a bell that awakens the child in Elizabeth's womb, calls him to some sort of awareness of the significance of what is happening, as the monastery bell awakens its monks to come to consciousness of the presence of God in their lives. As the monk arises from his bed, so the unborn child "Bounds," quickens, the movement itself serving as an echo, a corresponding response, to Mary's word. John now becomes the focus of attention, addressed directly in the next pair of verse paragraphs, paralleling the two opening sections addressed to Mary, and presented as a model for the contemplative life in the three sections that complete the poem.

The monastic imagery introduced by the charterhouse bell is applied to John himself as the speaker calls on John to echo Mary's song with his own:

> Sing in your cell, small anchorite!
> How did you see her in the eyeless dark?
> What secret syllable
> Woke your young faith to the mad truth
> That an unborn baby could be washed in the Spirit of God?
> Oh burning joy!
> What seas of life were planted by that voice!
> With what new sense
> Did your wise heart receive her Sacrament,
> And know her cloistered Christ? (ll. 27-36)

John's future vocation as a desert solitary is here perceived to have begun even before his birth. The womb is his first hermit cell, in which he is to sing God's praises like one of the early desert fathers. There follow two questions about how John was able to perceive Mary's presence in the darkness of the womb—the phrase "eyeless dark" actually suggests an answer to this question, as it recalls that it was the power of Mary's eyes (rather than John's) that blessed his mother, and so himself, with the peace that flowed from her own unborn child—it was not seeing but being seen that brought this awareness, this "illumination." The second question shifts from sight to hearing, asking what "secret syllable" awakened not only John himself but his faith in the truth of the presence of the Holy Spirit. The promise made to Zechariah by the angel that the child would be filled with the Holy Spirit even from his mother's womb" (Lk. 1:16) is here fulfilled, and imaged as a kind of baptismal cleansing from original sin, a "Sacrament" mediated by Mary. The questions are punctuated by a pair of exclamations, the first associating the joy that Elizabeth identifies as the motive for her child's leaping in the womb with the flame that the Spirit will much later bestow upon the apostles. The second exclamation—not a question though beginning with "What"—returns from the image of fire to that of water in a provocative, disconcertingly blatant mixed metaphor in which not seeds but "seas of life" are said to be planted by Mary's voice. But in fact the image works because it anticipates John's future ministry of baptizing that is foreshadowed by this "baptismal" experience of his own. As sight and hearing were the focus of the two previous questions, so now it is a "new sense," transcending both, that enables John not only to receive this "Sacrament" but to know "her cloistered Christ," like John himself hidden from view in his own "monastic" environment, indicating that while the focus will be on John as model for the contemplative, ultimately it is Jesus who is the pattern on whom John, and those who imitate John, depend.

The second of the two sections of direct address to John provides a transition from a focus on John's experience to an explicit recognition of the paradigmatic dimension of this experience for the contemplative:

> You need no eloquence, wild bairn,
> Exulting in your hermitage.
> Your ecstasy is your apostolate,
> For whom to kick is *contemplata tradere*.
> Your joy is the vocation
> Of Mother Church's hidden children—
> Those who by vow lie buried in the cloister or the hermitage:

> The speechless Trappist, or the grey, granite Carthusian,
> The quiet Carmelite, the barefoot Clare,
> Planted in the night of contemplation,
> Sealed in the dark and waiting to be born. (ll. 37-47)

John's way of communicating his awareness of the divine presence is not through words but by the very vitality and dynamism of the experience itself. Elizabeth is able to interpret accurately the meaning of her child's quickening, his coming to life in the womb, as an encounter with the Word made flesh in "the cloistered Christ" because she too is filled with the Holy Spirit as the child leaps in her womb (Lk. 1:41). Thus his kicking is indeed his way of passing on the fruits of contemplation; his ecstatic bounding is his way of communicating the good news. Though he is in his "hermitage" he is not isolated from the rest of the world but through his mother can have a profound if mysterious influence on it. It is here that the poet finds the essential analogy to the lives of contemplatives, as the rest of this section makes clear. While he begins by declaring that John's joy at encountering Christ, in the Spirit, is the heart of the contemplative vocation, it is the aspect of hiddenness that is developed first. As John is concealed in his mother's womb, so contemplatives, as typified by the four orders specifically mentioned, are hidden within "Mother Church," the first in each pair associated with silence, the second with simplicity and detachment. They are said to "lie buried. . . . Planted in the night of contemplation," again suggesting the seed growing secretly, a death to self as a prelude to risen life, the final, eschatological rebirth for which they wait in patient expectation—a note that will be developed in the next section, the first of three that comprise the meditative reflection and application that complete the poem.

> Night is our diocese and silence is our ministry
> Poverty our charity and helplessness our tongue-tied sermon.
> Beyond the scope of sight or sound we dwell upon the air
> Seeking the world's gain in an unthinkable experience.
> We are exiles in the far end of solitude, living as listeners
> With hearts attending to the skies we cannot understand:
> Waiting upon the first far drums of Christ the Conqueror,
> Planted like sentinels upon the world's frontier. (ll. 48-55)

No longer addressing John, the speaker now identifies himself with the contemplatives mentioned in the previous lines, using the first person plural throughout the rest of the poem. He begins with a series of paradoxes that implicitly engages with the question of how, or whether, contemplatives make a contribution to the wider Church. If night is their diocese, how are they a part of the organizational structure of the Church? Likewise the identification of silence as a ministry runs counter to the common understanding of ecclesial service, and poverty would seem to exclude rather than exemplify charity, while helplessness—i.e. spiritual poverty—makes any preaching not only awkward, the conventional sense of "tongue-tied," but quite literally unspoken, restrained from being expressed. Like John in the womb, they are said to be beyond sight and sound, yet claim to "seek the world's gain," not just their own spiritual advancement. Their contribution is characterized as "an unthinkable experience," a phrase that can be understood on one level as referring to the fact that the nature of their contribution seems inconceivable, but from another perspective it describes an experience that cannot be conceptualized or comprehended, and therefore cannot be clearly articulated—which leads back to the question of how it can be communicated and so made available to others. If they "dwell upon the air," are they simply building castles in the air without solid foundations rooted in the earth? If they are exiles set apart from the everyday world by their solitude, are they out of touch with the rest of society? Part of the response to these implicit challenges to the contemplative life is provided in the concluding lines of this section of the poem, which emphasize the eschatological dimension of their life. They are listeners rather than speakers, focused on the transcendent yet unable to comprehend it and therefore to explain it. Yet as "sentinels upon the world's frontier," they live in attentive waiting for the final arrival of the Kingdom of God, the return of Christ in glory, and so witness to the provisional quality of the present life. So this in itself is a significant contribution to wider human and ecclesial life, serving as a sign of what is not yet here by their life of silence, solitude, darkness, emptiness, detachment. They are not then simply floating in mid-air but firmly "Planted," rooted in their place like faithful guards keeping watch for the sake of the entire community, a role that has an implicit parallel to the Baptist's vocation to herald the first coming of Christ: he too was a kind of sentinel waiting for the arrival of the King.

But the next section points out that this does not encompass the entire range of the contemplative contribution to the Church as a whole. There is a present as well as a future dimension to the contemplative life, an "already" along with the "not yet," a mystical awareness as well as an eschatological expectation. It is here that the analogy to John's experience at the Visitation is explicitly developed:

> But in the days, rare days, when our Theotocos
> Flying the prosperous world

> Appears upon our mountain with her clothes like sails,
> Then, like the wise, wild baby,
> The unborn John who could not see a thing
> We wake and know the Virgin Presence
> Receive her Christ into our night
> With stabs of an intelligence as white as lightning. (ll. 56-63)

Though it happens only seldom, on "rare days," it does happen that Mary the God-bearer, the Theotocos, allows the contemplative to experience the coming of Christ here and now. Words, phrases and images already used in presenting the Visitation story are now reapplied to describe the contemplative encounter with Christ through Mary. Again she is said to "Fly the prosperous world"; again her clothes are compared to sails as she comes now to "our mountain"; John is once again characterized as both "wise" and as "wild" and also as unable to see; like John the contemplative wakes and knows and receives both Mary and her Son. Only the final line introduces a completely new image, the sudden piercing awareness, an "intelligence," of Christ's presence like a lightning flash in the darkness—not a conceptual understanding but an intuitive perception, not the result of a process of reasoning but a sudden insight, an illumination, an enlightenment. So the contemplative vocation is not only to await the final coming of Christ but to experience his present coming in spirit, still hidden but no less powerful for that. It is not the "birth" into everlasting life, but it is a quickening, a stirring that foreshadows the final consummation.

The final lines complete this analogy by returning to the double focus with which it began in lines 41-42—on joy and on the effect of contemplation on the Church as a whole:

> Cooled in the flame of God's dark fire
> Washed in His gladness like a vesture of new flame
> We burn like eagles in His invincible awareness
> And bound and bounce with happiness,
> Leap in the womb, our cloud, our faith, our element,
> Our contemplation, our anticipated heaven
> Till Mother Church sings like an Evangelist. (ll. 64-70)

The double paradox of the opening line here emphasizes the mysterious coincidence of opposites in mystical experience, where the flame of the Spirit cools and the fire remains dark, incomprehensible, even as it illuminates like the lightning flash. Like John, the contemplative is said to be washed, here bathed by God's own gladness, God's own joy, both cleansed and clothed in the fire of God's love. Borrowing an image from the first

Baptist poem, contemplatives are now compared to eagles, symbols of contemplation who burn with an awareness of the divine presence that is "invincible," a sense of assurance and confidence in the divine presence that cannot be overcome. The response is that of John—an innocent, child-like joy that had earlier been identified as the essence of the contemplative vocation (ll. 41-42), a leap in the womb that is described in a series of appositives: first a group of three that moves from the concrete image of the cloud to the theological concept of faith to the abstract term "element" (as in "being in one's element," one's authentic milieu); then the pairing of contemplation and anticipated heaven, the mystical and eschatological, promise and its fulfillment. Finally, the speaker affirms that this experience is not merely private and individualized, but has a profound effect on the entire Church. As Merton had said in his journal, "the exultation of our experience will awaken the whole Church and she will begin to sing and preach." Hidden in the very womb of the Church, the witness of the contemplative emerges from within and radiates throughout the entire body. Merging the experience of Elizabeth responding to John's joyful leap and that of Mary responding to Elizabeth's words with her own Magnificat, the final line suggests that the experience of contemplatives is one impetus, one source of inspiration, for the Church as a whole to proclaim the good news, to sing like an Evangelist. Even before birth, then, John the Baptist serves as an exemplar for the contemplative, shows himself to be a patron, a friend, a protector, a "wise, wild" model, implicitly confirming the aptness of his identification as the first Cistercian and the greatest Trappist.

"With My Hair Almost on End":
Le Point Vierge and the Dawn Birds

Monica Weis, SSJ

On June 5, Pentecost Sunday, 1960, Thomas Merton penned a lengthy journal entry in which he notes his stinging eyes after proofreading the galleys for *Disputed Questions* and reading Paul Landsperg's book on Personalism. Merton also tentatively explores his notion of commitment: was commitment to the Gospel enough, or did it need to overflow into action? Were his religious vows sufficient, or did they imply commitment to monastic policy and viewpoint? Did commitments to the Church and the Order necessarily involve countercultural living? And Merton comments on the necessity of solitude to support understanding and wisdom.[1]

This solitude, which Merton dubs a "withdrawal 'to see better'" (*TTW* 9), is interesting to probe, yet it is not the most significant lesson to be reaped from this passage written on the great feast of the Holy Spirit. I am suggesting that the solitude necessary for understanding and wisdom that Merton so ardently desires is captured not in these philosophical speculations, but experientially in his awareness of and reaction to the break of day referred to in the same passage: "With my hair almost on end and the eyes of the soul wide open I am present, without knowing it at all, in this unspeakable Paradise" (*TTW* 7). This, for sure, is a moment of true wisdom, perhaps even a mystical experience. And if it is indeed a direct encounter with the Divine, Merton will be hard pressed to satisfactorily articulate it for us. Nevertheless, his words invite us to probe a bit more.

Early in this passage, Merton's poetic eye offers us a picture of dawn: "At 2:30—no sounds except sometimes a bullfrog. Some mornings, he says Om—some days he is silent." Then he notices the whippoorwill, sometimes near, sometimes far. "The first chirps of the waking birds—'*le point vierge* [the virgin point]' of the dawn, a moment of awe and inexpressible innocence, when the Father in silence opens their eyes and they speak to Him, wondering if it is time to 'be'? And He tells them 'Yes.' Then they one by one wake and begin to sing." *This* is when Merton's hair stands almost on end. Through a spiritual encounter he can only hint at in metaphors, Merton realizes he is present at a daily creation, a daily Eden

---

1. Thomas Merton, *Turning Toward the World: The Pivotal Years. Journals, vol. 4: 1960-1963*, ed. Victor A. Kramer (San Francisco: HarperCollins, 1996) 6-9; subsequent references will be cited as "*TTW*" parenthetically in the text.

that is a "paradise of simplicity, self-awareness—and self-forgetfulness—liberty, peace." Although we don't know exactly what Merton's mystical encounter is like, we can determine that it is only when the eyes of his soul are awake that he truly sees reality and the Reality of fecund life all around him. Sadly, he notes, "even monks, shut up under fluorescent lights and face to face with the big books and the black notes" miss it. Contrast this to the single-sentence paragraph that introduces this description of his experience: "The other day (Thursday)—the *full meaning* of lauds, said against the background of waking birds and sunrise" (*TTW* 7).

A facile reading of the passage that follows this prelude statement could dismiss Merton's description of the coming of day as mere poetic fancy. However, I would argue that this passage—particularly with its reference to *le point vierge*, and primarily because of it—represents a significant spiritual, even mystical, insight into the *"full meaning* of lauds" that Merton feels compelled to describe. Readers might sense here a similarity to the Native-American vision quest. Like the indigenous seeker, Merton has been in solitude, in the woods, and through the totem or symbol of the birds he has a direct encounter with Ultimate Reality. This is what makes his hair stand on end. That many monks chanting in their enclosed chapels miss this experience—indeed, that many people seem unaware of the miracles all around them—is echoed in the writings of the great European mystics and American nature writers such as Julian of Norwich, Hildegard of Bingen, Meister Eckhart, Henry David Thoreau, John Burroughs and Annie Dillard—not to overlook gospel passages from Romans (8:14-17), 2 Corinthians (3:17-18) and Ephesians (5:14). Each of these writers calls us to greater awareness—to become more awake—the first step on any spiritual journey. This 1960 Pentecost morning is an important experience in Merton's life-long spiritual journey, even more so, because one year later on the vigil of the feast of Pentecost (May 20, 1961), Merton cross-references his earlier journal entry to affirm the "peace and certitude" he has experienced during the year by trusting in God the Father, the Church, and his superiors (*TTW* 121).

But let's look now at how the journal passage of the birds waking is presented in *Conjectures of a Guilty Bystander*,[2] the rearranged collection of journal entries Merton was working on in the early 1960s (published in 1966). In this recast version, the vignette about the birds asking the Father if it is time to be is the lead passage in the book's central section, entitled "The Night Spirit and Dawn Air," a direct reference to Meng Tzu (Mencius), the fourth-century BCE Chinese philosopher who advocated

---

2. Thomas Merton, *Conjectures of a Guilty Bystander* (Garden City, NY: Doubleday, 1966) 117-18; subsequent references will be cited as "*CGB*" parenthetically in the text.

both pause and rest in order to regenerate energy. In this reorganized version of *le point vierge*, Merton's comment about his hair standing on end is missing—perhaps because this compilation of reflections for publication is directed toward a different audience than is his personal journal. Here, in *Conjectures*, Merton's description of the bullfrog is lengthened, the whippoorwill merits more precise adjectives, and all creation "asks permission to 'be' once again, as it did on the first morning that ever was." Notice, too, that Merton's comment that the monks do not recognize this veritable paradise within their grasp is broadened to include all of his readers—us. *We* are to be chastised because we are too blinded—or imprisoned—by our lights, clocks, thermostats, electric shavers and radios. Our world is not just filled with static; we have allowed it to become static, and thus we miss the startling dynamism of ongoing creation. We miss what Gerard Manley Hopkins, one of Merton's favorite poets, celebrates: a world "charged with the grandeur of God," where "lives the dearest, freshness deep-down things . . . Where the Holy Ghost over the bent / World broods with warm breast and with ah! Bright wings."[3] One can imagine Merton shaking his head at us as he laments: "Here is an unspeakable secret: paradise is all around us and we do not understand. It is wide open. . . . 'Wisdom,' cries the dawn deacon, but we do not attend."

Yet I would call your attention to a sentence that begins a new paragraph in this section: "All wisdom seeks to collect and manifest itself at that blind sweet point" (*CGB* 117). Here, perhaps, is not only a tiny insight into Merton's direct encounter with Ultimate Reality, but also a perspective on that mysterious phrase *le point vierge*, a French phrase traceable to Sufi mystics, by way of Merton's correspondence with Islamic scholar Louis Massignon.[4] At the "blind sweet point," something indescribable, something mystical, occurs. Although virtually untranslatable, we might look at *le point vierge* this way. *Le point vierge* is the cusp, the edge, the moment of transition before a new becoming, the startling meeting of transcendence and immanence that allows a Divine breakthrough that changes everything. Allow me to propose three quick and imperfect examples from human experience that may offer a clue to the mysterious phrase *le point vierge*.

---

3. "God's Grandeur," *Gerard Manley Hopkins: The Major Works* (Oxford: Oxford University Press, 1986) 128.

4. See *TTW* 5 [5/30/1960] and Thomas Merton, *Witness to Freedom: Letters in Times of Crisis*, ed. William H. Shannon (New York: Farrar, Straus, Giroux, 1994) 278 [7/20/60 letter to Louis Massignon]; see also Sidney H. Griffith, "Thomas Merton, Louis Massignon, and the Challenge of Islam," *The Merton Annual* 3 (1990) 151-72.

In the literary world, midsummer's eve is such a moment of poise between the past and future seasons when fairy magic can alter the rhythm of the universe. Shakespeare well understood the power of this night as evidenced in his oft-performed play of mischievous love, *Midsummer's Night Dream*. In the sports world, think of the platform diver poised, toes gripping the edge, rehearsing in her imagination the double somersault and half-gainer about to be performed; or the basketball star standing at the free throw line, ball in hand, eyes focused on the net, body balanced to sink the shot that wins the game. Such is the cusp, the poise, the moment of becoming for the birds, and, as Merton adds in the *Conjectures* version, the "blind sweet point" that in some mysterious and mystical way gathers and focuses cosmic wisdom.

As if this were not enough to ponder, let us examine the second use of *le point vierge* in *Conjectures*. A mere twenty-five pages after the birds episode, and now really into the middle of this central section of *Conjectures*, Merton recounts his epiphany at Fourth and Walnut, his deep realization that he is related to all these people and that they are all walking around shining like the sun (*CGB* 140-42). For Merton, the experience of Divine Immanence, that is, Divinity incarnated in this world, is real in a new and deeper way. Now, a few years removed from that life-changing experience, recorded on March 19, 1958,[5] Merton is into a yet deeper realization of the inner beauty and unfolding being that is part of every one of us. We need to experience Merton's exact words: "Again, that expression, *le point vierge*, (I cannot translate it) comes in here. At the center of our being is a point of nothingness which is untouched by sin and by illusion, a point of pure truth, a point or spark which belongs entirely to God, which is never at our disposal, from which God disposes of our lives, which is inaccessible to the fantasies of our own mind or the brutalities of our own will. This little point of nothingness and of *absolute poverty* is the pure glory of God in us" (*CGB* 142).

Whew! All those adjectival dependent clauses in the second sentence—Merton's harried and ultimately inadequate attempt to define the indefinable; and then he collapses into a simple sentence: this little point is the glory of God in us. According to Merton, *le point vierge* is the core of our being, the creative spark of God that is pure gift—very much like the birds asking the Father if it is time to be. The birds react to this creative spark, accept being as a daily gift from God, and one by one they wake up. For the birds, this is a daily event, but Merton discerns a significant

---

5. Thomas Merton, *A Search for Solitude: Pursuing the Monk's True Life. Journals, vol. 3: 1952-1960*, ed. Lawrence S. Cunningham (San Francisco: HarperCollins, 1996) 181-82; subsequent references will be cited as "*SS*" parenthetically in the text.

difference in humans. *Le point vierge*, our inner nothingness, is not a discrete, repeatable event, but an ongoing *dwelling*. Our very center, where we find the poverty of our nothingness, is where God dwells. In humans, *le point vierge* is the sustaining spark of Divinity within that allows us to recognize our True Self, our unity with God's Self, and our unity with each other. All created and uncreated being comes together at this inner point of nothingness. Or as Meister Eckhart describes this moment of mystical enlightenment: "in this breaking-through I find that God and I are both the same."[6] Indeed, our hair *should* be standing on end.

Earlier Merton has said: "Here is an unspeakable secret: paradise is all around us and we do not understand. It is wide open. . . . 'Wisdom,' cries the dawn deacon, but we do not attend" (*CGB* 118); now he is returning to this experience of the ineffable, with a subtle and poignant insight: "I have no program for this seeing. It is only given. But the gate of heaven is everywhere" (*CGB* 142). This inner nothingness is our paradise, our meeting place with the Divine, and its gate is everywhere—if only we are aware. It seems to me that March 19, 1958, June 20, 1960, and Merton's work on the *Conjectures* manuscript in the early 1960s are all trying to drive home the same message: if we want to progress in the spiritual life, we must learn how to be awake to the glory of God that is around us and within us because transcendence and immanence are always intersecting, colliding, merging. Everything is incarnational; everything is sacrament.

Yet Merton's deep mystical insight does not occur without a larger context. For several years, he had been studying Zen Buddhism and corresponding with D. T. Suzuki, who holds that the kind of inner poverty we need in order to be empty of Self is a genuine sense that we have "Nothing to gain, nothing to lose; nothing to give, nothing to take; to be just so, and yet to be rich in inexhaustible possibilities" (*ZBA* 109). Our inner emptiness is not the emptiness of nothingness, but the emptiness of fullness (see *ZBA* 133-34). This kind of paradoxical language resonated with Merton because it reflected not only Suzuki's sincere practice of Zen, but also both men's common quest for spiritual Truth. For them it was not only a way to describe wisdom, but it created a felt communion that was beyond words. To be sure, Zen and Christian mysticism are not co-extensive; nevertheless, there is, according to world religion specialist John Carmody, a legitimate and similar profound sense of encounter with Ultimate Reality in these two religious approaches.[7]

---

6. Thomas Merton, *Zen and the Birds of Appetite* (New York: New Directions, 1968) 114; subsequent references will be cited as "*ZBA*" parenthetically in the text.

7. John Tully Carmody and Denise Lardner Carmody, *Mysticism: Holiness East and West* (New York: Oxford University Press, 1996) 17.

In addition to studying Zen, Merton was also reading Russian orthodox theologians, namely Berdyaev, Bulgakov and Evdokimov, with their emphasis on human history as a "powerful Pentecost" (*SS* 86) with the "ever-possible marriage of human and Divine Wisdom."[8] And in that study, Merton was coming to a new realization not bound by restrictive dogmas or formulas. He was discovering yet a new way of seeing. The creative theology of the Russians prompts him to write in his journal: "If I can unite *in myself*, in my own spiritual life, the thought of the East and the West of the Greek and Latin Fathers, I will create in myself a reunion of the divided Church. . . . We must contain both in ourselves and transcend both in Christ" (*SS* 87). So, Merton is reading, thinking and praying about Wisdom, especially as it is articulated in Russian sophiology, which crescendos as he approaches the feast of Pentecost. His interest in these other Eastern approaches to Wisdom becomes the backdrop for his mystical experience of the full meaning of lauds and *le point vierge*. Indeed, as Christopher Pramuk argues in his extensive study, *Sophia*, Merton's cross-cultural immersion is critical preparation for this "irruption of Sophia into Merton's theological consciousness" (Pramuk 153).

But what happens after such a mystical experience? Where does it take the person? Certainly, we know that Merton was soon to be granted his desire for more solitude in the hermitage, at first spending days there, then the occasional overnight, and in August of 1963 moving permanently to the hermitage. And we know from *Day of a Stranger*, written in May 1965, how much his immersion in nature influenced his perspective on the natural rhythm of his day, his decision "to marry the silence of the forest,"[9] and his commitment to critique American culture from its margins. This commitment to greater solitude and contemplation soon takes Merton to Asia and his meeting with Eastern mystics, and his subsequent permanent encounter with Ultimate Reality Itself.

So with the backdrop of extensive reading, a commitment to "withdrawal to see better," and extended solitude that requires focused awareness to both his natural surroundings and the landscape of his heart, Merton offers us *not a formula, but a model* of how we, too, might prepare to experience Wisdom. What appears first as delightful language, a picturesque scene of early morning is, on second reading, a profoundly mystical and dynamic passage that reveals how Merton is touched and transformed at the core of his being. And while we might prefer to consider

---

8. Christopher Pramuk, *Sophia: The Hidden Christ of Thomas Merton* (Collegeville, MN: Liturgical Press, 2009) 154; subsequent references will be cited as "Pramuk" parenthetically in the text.

9. Thomas Merton, *Day of a Stranger* (Salt Lake City: Gibbs M. Smith, 1981) 49.

the Fourth and Walnut and Polonnaruwa episodes ("all walking around shining like the sun" [*CGB* 141]; and "clarity, as if exploding from the rocks themselves" that takes him "beyond the shadow and the disguise"[10]) as the major turning points in Merton's life, I would suggest that these references to the *"full meaning* of lauds" and *le point vierge*, located as they are in the central position in *Conjectures*, are not only pregnant with meaning, but also significant transformative moments in Merton's spirituality. As a model, they invite us—nay, dare us—to "withdraw to see better," to experience the "blind sweet point" at the core of our own being, and hope to have our hair stand on end. Yet, as Merton reminds us, we can't orchestrate or program this encounter with Ultimate Reality; it is only given.

Nevertheless, "the gate of heaven is everywhere."

---

10. Thomas Merton, *The Asian Journal*, ed. Naomi Burton Stone, Brother Patrick Hart and James Laughlin (New York: New Directions, 1973) 233, 235.

Thomas Merton and Pierre Teilhard de Chardin: "The Dawning of Divine Light"

Robert Weldon Whalen

Pierre Teilhard de Chardin and Thomas Merton are two of the most extraordinary and paradoxical figures among the twentieth century's array of religious thinkers. Neither was a theologian; neither led a movement; neither was a religious official; neither was a television personality. Both in their day were accused of assorted errors and even downright heresies; both spent much of their religious lives in the ecclesiastical doghouse.[1] But their work, long after their deaths, continues to attract enormous and remarkably diverse followings. What makes Teilhard and Merton both controversial and compelling is that they were in their day "outliers," "forward thinkers," "eccentrics," who created vocabularies, concepts and counsels that, however strange they might once have sounded, have become, today, convincing to millions. Very different persons, Teilhard and Merton were both "pilgrims of the future."[2] Joseph Needham, an East Asian scholar and President of the Teilhard Centre in London, argues that Teilhard "was called to be the greatest prophet of this age."[3] Michael Higgins insists that Merton was "the twentieth century's most eloquent and accessible spiritual figure."[4]

Every significant writer has his or her following. Whole schools, and untold dissertations, have sprung up around the work of theologians like Karl Barth and Karl Rahner. The appeal of Teilhard and Merton is different. Their work attracts scholars to be sure, but it also attracts people of all sorts of persuasions, backgrounds and educations. Teilhard died in 1955, Merton in 1968. Why has their work not yet been safely entombed in the academy?

---

1. For a review of their chronic ecclesiastical trouble, see Robert Nugent, *Silence Speaks: Teilhard de Chardin, Yves Congar, John Courtney Murray, and Thomas Merton* (New York: Paulist Press, 2011).

2. Teilhard described himself as a "pilgrim of the future": see Christopher Mooney, *Teilhard de Chardin and the Mystery of Christ* (Garden City, NY: Doubleday, 1968) 35; subsequent references will be cited as "Mooney" parenthetically in the text.

3. Joseph Needham, "Foreword," in Ursula King, *Towards a New Mysticsm: Teilhard de Chardin and Eastern Religions* (New York: Seabury, 1980) 7; subsequent references will be cited as "U. King" parenthetically in the text.

4. Michael Higgins, *Heretic Blood. The Spiritual Geography of Thomas Merton* (Toronto: Stoddart, 1998) 2; subsequent references will be cited as "Higgins" parenthetically in the text.

Teilhard and Merton have lived on into their futures precisely because a profound concern with futurity was a theme these two very different people shared. Among their many gifts to us was a sacramental spirituality of what Teilhard referred to as "Ahead" and not just "Above."[5] To be sure, Teilhard and Merton fundamentally disagreed on several key issues. Where they did agree, though, was on developing what might be called a sacramental spirituality of "Ahead." Why have Teilhard and Merton remained so present so long after their deaths? They remain so present because their shared concern with futurity makes their work vibrantly contemporary.

In November 1960, Thomas Merton wrote a review of Teilhard's *Divine Milieu.* Five years after Teilhard's death, his work had begun to appear and to inspire both great curiosity and fierce debate. The fact that some of Teilhard's friends within the *nouvelle théologie* movement, such as Henri de Lubac, were emerging as key figures in the run-up to what would be Vatican II meant that taking a stand on Teilhard inevitably plunged one into heated church politics. Like everyone else, Merton was curious about Teilhard. Merton's own thought, meantime, was taking a noticeable turn. William Shannon notes that "Between 1955 and 1965 Merton became a very different kind of monk from the one who had in 1941 entered Gethsemani with the fervent desire to leave the world behind."[6] Merton was still thinking through his "Louisville epiphany" of 1958,[7] in which it suddenly dawned on him that he actually loved the people bustling along Fourth and Walnut Streets in Louisville, and that their experience and his were inextricably linked.

Categories like "action," "world" and "history," categories central, too, to Teilhard, became very important to Merton. Merton wrote his review, and when the Trappist Abbot General, Dom Gabriel Sortais, apprehensive about having one of his monks get entangled in the on-going Teilhard controversy, refused to grant Merton permission to publish the article, Merton took to his journal in high dudgeon:

> Dom Gabriel . . . has refused permission to print an article I wrote on Teilhard de Chardin's *Divine Milieu*. . . . [O]ne must not say anything in favor of T. de C. . . . It may be quite correct that T. is a theological

---

5. Citing Teilhard, Mooney notes that the young Teilhard was torn between the "God of Upward" and the "God of Forward" (32).

6. William H. Shannon, *"Something of a Rebel": Thomas Merton, His Life and Works* (Cincinnati: St. Anthony Messenger Press, 1997) 35.

7. See Thomas Merton, *A Search for Solitude: Pursuing the Monk's True Life. Journals, vol. 3: 1952-1960*, ed. Lawrence S. Cunningham (San Francisco: HarperCollins, 1996) 181-82 [3/19/1958]; Thomas Merton, *Conjectures of a Guilty Bystander* (Garden City, NY: Doubleday, 1966) 140-42.

screwball. But I refuse to form part of an indignant chorus against him, and I refuse even to form part of a silently disapproving or hostile assembly of righteous critics. I refuse to draw back from him shaking my garments. I have nothing but sympathy for his attempt to take a new view of things. I have not read anything but the *Divine Milieu*, but as far as I am concerned the book is generally healthier and more deeply, genuinely *spiritual* than anything that has ever emanated from the authoritarian mind of Dom Gabriel.[8]

Teilhard's work was not influenced by Merton. Merton was intrigued by Teilhard's thought. Merton dedicated two short essays to Teilhard, "The Universe as Epiphany" (his review of *The Divine Milieu*) and "Teilhard's Gamble."[9] In "The Universe as Epiphany," Merton identified Teilhard as a mystic, defended Teilhard's orthodoxy and applauded Teilhard's rejection of "the false notion of a *disincarnate* or *disembodied* Christianity" (*L&L* 174). In "Teilhard's Gamble," though, Merton expressed his skepticism about what he described as Teilhard's cosmic optimism. "Teilhard," Merton wrote, "does not seem to notice the wounds of mendacity and hatred which have been inexorably deepened in man by his practice of technological warfare, totalitarianism, and genocide" (*L&L* 190). (As an aside, one might note that the frequent charge that Teilhard was a naïve optimist is perhaps overstated, as Christopher Mooney points out [Mooney 19-20, 30]). Teilhard remained on Merton's mind. Boris Pasternak's cosmic mysticism reminded Merton of Teilhard.[10] Some of Albert Camus' Christian admirers thought that if Camus had read Teilhard, Camus might have been more sympathetic to Christianity. Merton doesn't think so. Though he acknowledges striking parallels between Camus' and Teilhard's thought, Merton argues that Camus (like Merton) would have criticized Teilhard's optimism.[11] Writing about John Milton, Merton thought of Teilhard. Teilhard's "splendid" "Mass on the World" reminded Merton

8. See Thomas Merton, *Turning Toward the World: The Pivotal Years. Journals, vol. 4: 1960-1963*, ed. Victor A. Kramer (San Francisco: HarperCollins, 1996) 64-65 [11/14/1960] (subsequent references will be cited as "*TTW*" parenthetically in the text); see also Higgins 104-105 and Monica Weis, *The Environmental Vision of Thomas Merton* (Lexington: University Press of Kentucky, 2011) 135.

9. Both can be found in Thomas Merton, *Love and Living*, ed. Naomi Burton Stone and Brother Patrick Hart (New York: Farrar, Straus, Giroux, 1979) 171-84; 185-202; subsequent references will be cited as "*L&L*" parenthetically in the text.

10. See Thomas Merton, "Pasternak's Letters to Georgian Friends," in *The Literary Essays of Thomas Merton*, ed. Patrick Hart, OCSO (New York: New Directions, 1981) 90; subsequent references will be cited as "*LE*" parenthetically in the text.

11. Thomas Merton, "The Plague of Albert Camus" (*LE* 216-17). Merton makes the same point in "Camus and the Church" (*LE* 265-66).

of Milton's hymn to light in *Paradise Lost*. Christ in *Paradise Lost* is, Merton remarks, a "dubious figure"; Teilhard's "Cosmic Christ" is just the sort of figure Milton tried, but failed, to create. Teilhard is, Merton argues, "in many ways a Miltonic epic 'poet.'"[12]

Teilhard and Merton were two very different people. Teilhard was thirty-four years older than Merton, and he wasn't simply part of an older generation, he was part of a different moral geography. The child of an ancient Auvergne family, Teilhard was shaped both by the traditional piety of his parents and the *Belle Epoche*'s fascination with science. Intellectually, Teilhard was an heir of Henri Bergson; like Bergson, Teilhard was fascinated by change, energy, creativity and science's astonishing discoveries. Merton, born in 1915 in the midst of the Great War, was an archetypal denizen of the terrible twentieth century. Robert Inchausti refers to Merton as "the quintessential American outsider, who defined himself in opposition to the world in both word and deed and then discovered a way back into dialogue with it and compassion for it."[13] Orphaned as a child, rootless, Merton belonged to the world which ranged from Verdun and the Somme to Auschwitz and Hiroshima. Merton's intellectual contemporaries were Heidegger, Sartre and Camus. If life was the puzzle for Teilhard, Merton and his generation were haunted by death.

Teilhard was a geologist and a paleontologist; Merton was a poet. A Jesuit, Teilhard was a world traveler; Merton, a Trappist, spent most his adult life in the Kentucky hills. Teilhard the scientist was fascinated by technology, despite the terrible uses to which it could be put; Merton, an admirer of William Blake, was suspicious of technology, though delighted that it could light up his hermitage.[14] Teilhard's was a hermeneutics of discovery; a hard-working scientist, he was amazed by what science could teach. Merton's was a hermeneutics of suspicion. Much like, for example, the writers of the Frankfurt School, Merton was appalled by the hubris of instrumental rationality. Their vocabulary was different and at times mutually incomprehensible. Teilhard, for example, meant by "world" the entire cosmos; "world" was for Teilhard a positive term. Merton meant by "world" especially humanly constructed society and more often than not what Merton saw shocked him. To be sure, Merton's much commented-on "turning toward the world" in the late 1950s inspired an occasional

---

12. Thomas Merton, "Prophetic Ambiguities: Milton and Camus" (*LE* 259).

13. Thomas Merton, *Seeds*, ed. Robert Inchausti (Boston: Shambhala, 2002) xi.

14. For a good summary of Merton on technology, see Paul Dekar, *Thomas Merton: Twentieth-Century Wisdom for Twenty-First-Century Living* (Eugene, OR: Cascade Books, 2011) 85-114 (chapter 5, "Thomas Merton, Guide to the Right Use of Technology"); subsequent references will be cited as "Dekar" parenthetically in the text.

mellowness, but to the end of his life he remained bitingly critical. Here, for instance, is a journal notation from May 27, 1967:

> I have dutifully done my bit. I have been "open to the world." That is to say I have undergone my dose of exposure to American society in the 60's. . . . I love the people I run into—but I pity them for having to live as they do, and I think the world of U.S.A. in 1967 is a world of crass, blind, overstimulated, phony, lying stupidity. The war in Asia gets slowly worse.[15]

There were, in addition, at least two other areas of serious difference. Teilhard lived much of his life in Asia, yet he remained critical of Hinduism and Buddhism, what he called "the path of the east." His objections were those William James had toward the Hinduism of Swami Vivekananda. In the late nineteenth century, Vivekananda became one of Hinduism's first representatives outside India, and William James was fascinated. But in the end, James criticized Vivekananda's thought because, James argued, Vivekananda ultimately argued against pluralism and for a kind of monism in which all difference merges into the One. Teilhard had the same concerns. He objected to Hinduism and Buddhism not because they were Asian, but because he thought that they were philosophically "monist," with little room for matter, evolution or plurality. Teilhard argued that the next crucial stage in human religious thought would emerge not so much from Christianity's encounter with Hinduism and Buddhism, but from the confrontation between science and Christianity.[16]

Merton, to the contrary, was fascinated by the "eastern path" throughout his entire life, from his spirited defense of Gandhi as a high-school student in England, until his death in Asia. Among the many attractions of the eastern path for Merton was precisely its ability to critique the scientific-technological rationality which, Merton thought, so profoundly distorted the souls of Europeans and North Americans. "We must never forget," Merton wrote, "that Christianity came to the west from the Orient."[17]

Teilhard and Merton differed as well on their understandings of mysti-

---

15. Thomas Merton, *Learning to Love: Exploring Solitude and Freedom. Journals, vol. 6: 1966-1967*, ed. Christine M. Bochen (San Francisco: HarperCollins, 1997) 239.

16. For his thoughts on William James and Vivekandanda, I thank my colleague, Professor Norris Frederick: see Norris Frederick, "William James and Swami Vivekananda: Religious Experience and Vedanta/Yoga in America" in *William James Studies* (forthcoming, 2013). On William James, Vivekananda and Teilhard, see U. King 48-50.

17. Thomas Merton, *The Road to Joy: Letters to New and Old Friends*, ed. Robert E. Daggy (New York: Farrar, Straus, Giroux, 1989) 319 [4/28/1961 letter to Joseph Tjo Tchel-oung], quoted in Dekar 157.

cism. Both were convinced that a "new mysticism" was emerging in the twentieth century. For Teilhard, this "new mysticism" was a "mysticism of knowing," as Thomas King has argued. According to King, "the real significance of Teilhard is not that he might have reconciled truths of modern science with truths of Christian faith, nor that he was a Christian mystic with a considerable scientific achievement . . . rather it is in Teilhard's exuberant claim that in the very act of scientifically achieving, he knew God." For Teilhard, King continues, "God is found in the act of knowing."[18] Thomas Merton, however, followed what William Shannon has called a "dark path."[19] Much like Theodor Adorno, for example, Merton was convinced that modern European and North American thought was dysfunctional and infected with multiple moral and epistemological viruses. The only therapy was a kind of "unthinking" which he found in the "apophatic ways" of ancient Christian mystics and Zen masters.

Teilhard and Merton had very different ideas about things. We might, though, apply to them one of Teilhard's favorite metaphors. Scientists and theologians disagree among themselves and with each other, and their concepts and methods are as irreconcilable as parallel meridians that encircle the globe around the equator. At the poles, though, the meridians increasingly come together by, as Teilhard said, a kind of "structural necessity" (Mooney 66). Maybe in heaven Teilhard's and Merton's divergent thoughts converge.

Or maybe we need not go to heaven just yet to detect a kind of convergence. To shift metaphors, we might note that even parallel lines can, in certain geometries, cross, and to understand Teilhard's and Merton's continuing appeal, one must investigate those areas in which their thought does not so much agree as intersect. Three areas are particularly striking, and the third is key to understanding Teilhard's and Merton's continuing resonance.

First, Teilhard and Merton were mystics who were convinced that a "new mysticism" was being born. Neither thought of mysticism as some sort of occult or magical phenomenon. For neither did mysticism involve visions, speaking in tongues, unhinged emotions or feats of levitation. Instead, for both, mysticism might best be described as a kind of religious phenomenology, that is, an approach to religion that attempts to suspend inherited categories and focus on lived experience. Religion includes many things: personal disciplines and community rules; statements of dogma and philosophical speculations; community prayer, covered-dish suppers and bingo games. But like Rudolf Otto, William James and Louis Dupré,

---

18. Thomas King, *Teilhard's Mysticism of Knowing* (New York: Seabury, 1981) vii.

19. See William H. Shannon, *Thomas Merton's Dark Path: The Inner Experience of a Contemplative* (New York: Farrar, Straus, Giroux, 1982).

among many others,[20] both Teilhard and Merton insisted that praxis must be religion's foundation; as Merton said about the Desert Fathers, "The word to emphasize is *experience*."[21] Each was critical of the tendency of accumulated historical and sociological debris to encrust and distort experience. Teilhard often insisted that the first religious act was "to see";[22] Merton applauded Zen's admonition to "wake up." Both Teilhard and Merton argued that the "mysticism" of the future, while drawing on the rich resources of the past, would be "new." The "newness" of the new mysticism would arise from new challenges which new generations would face. The "newness" would come, Teilhard thought, from the interplay between religious consciousness and science; it would come, Merton speculated, from the increasing interaction among all religions, and especially the interaction between Buddhism and Christianity.

Second, for Teilhard and Merton, this "new mysticism" would be intensely incarnational and sacramental. The "new mysticism" would move away from the "self," to use Merton's language, and toward the "person," and the archetype of this new person is Christ. This new person, Christ, is no abstraction; both Merton and Teilhard think of Christ explicitly in incarnational, not Platonic, terms. Both Teilhard and Merton were, moreover, "theologians of the body" *avant la lettre*. "Matter" was a fundamental category to Teilhard the geologist, and mysticism was inconceivable without matter. We are not redeemed "from matter," we are redeemed "through matter." "Matter is the matrix of Spirit," Teilhard writes, and "Spirit is the higher state of matter."[23] Merton's poetry, his photographs and calligraphy, as well as his deep love of nature, testify to his attraction to the tactile. Both included not only nature in general but sexuality specifically in their emerging understanding of a new, densely sacramental, mysticism. For all the limitations they shared with their patriarchal generations, both Teilhard and Merton were pioneers in the rethinking of gender, sexuality and sacramentality.

Third—and this is a key to understanding their continuing impact today—both Teilhard and Merton understood their new, sacramental

---

20. See Rudolf Otto, *The Idea of the Holy* (New York: Oxford University Press, 1958); William James, *The Varieties of Religious Experience* (New York: Collier, 1961); Louis Dupré, *The Other Dimension* (Garden City, NY: Doubleday, 1972).

21. Thomas Merton, *The Wisdom of the Desert: Sayings from the Desert Fathers of the Fourth Century* (New York: New Directions, 1960) 11.

22. Teilhard wrote that the whole point of his book *The Divine Milieu* was to encourage his readers to "see" (Pierre Teilhard de Chardin, *The Divine Milieu*, trans. William Collins & sons [New York: Harper and Row, 1968] 46).

23. Pierre Teilhard de Chardin, *The Heart of Matter*, trans. René Hague (New York: Harcourt Brace Jovanovich, 1978) 35.

mysticism in the light of futurity. How religion thinks about the future matters. The twentieth century's rediscovery of eschatology, for example, from Martin Luther King's Beloved Community, to Jürgen Moltmann's "theology of hope," to the visions of Liberation Theology, is well known. Both Teilhard and Merton shared this interest in "tomorrow." Together, they add, though, a distinct tone to "futurity." Born into a piety which understood God as "above," Teilhard increasingly thought of God as not only "above" but even more importantly as "ahead." We are not simply pneumatically propelled heavenward, individually, by events in the past; we are, rather, drawn, as a species, to heaven's future. The future is more than a new calendar page; it is much more than simply that which has not yet occurred. The future, for Teilhard, is charged, magnetic and intensely real. Paradoxically, the future is what both gives the impetus to cosmic evolution to begin with, and is, at the same time, the convergent "omega" toward which the entire cosmos, in all its materiality, moves. We are drawn not simply into a static and impersonal "One," but rather toward a plural, "hyper-personal," Trinity.

At first glance, "futurity" does not seem as prominent in Thomas Merton's vocabulary as it is in Teilhard's. Drawn to the past mysticisms of West and East, and deeply critical of his own present, Merton's thought often seems juxtapositional rather than evolutionary. Platonic dichotomies like false self/true self, and alienation/authenticity, and the sudden ruptures that separate them, seem more typical of Merton than do Teilhardian meditations on evolution. Merton more than once mentioned his respect for Plato; he noted in his journal, on October 24, 1960, that "I have finally come to admit to what extent I have always been a Platonist" (*TTW* 59). Merton was typically attracted to "event," not "process" (*TTW* 66). Yet the magnetic pull of the future is just as important to Merton as it is to Teilhard. Merton's famous "turn toward the world" was above all a statement of faith not in the world as he knew it, but in the world as it could become. His hopes for personal conversion, for monastic reform, for peace and social justice, were all rooted in his sense of the future. In 1958, Merton wrote an introduction to a Spanish edition of his *Obras Completas*, designed for his many readers in Latin America. In his introduction, Merton spoke of the role of the ancient Church in the New World. "We love our old traditions," he wrote,

> but we are men of the future. Our responsibility is to the future, not to the past. The past does not depend on us, but the future does. . . . [P]art of our work for the salvation of mankind must be to construct a world in which man can willingly prepare for God—with vision

of a free life on earth. The Church in this New World is more than a decorative symbol of the past. It is the mother of the future. Its members must open their eyes to the future; they must recognize the signs that point to the future.[24]

Pierre Teilhard de Chardin and Thomas Merton remain, long after their deaths, extraordinarily compelling figures. Each has inspired a rich scholarly commentary. Even more striking, each has attracted a remarkably diverse array of readers from around the world. What do Teilhard and Merton, such very different figures, share? Why do Teilhard and Merton, figures from the past, still speak so eloquently to us, their future? They speak so eloquently because we, and our heirs, are their subjects. Teilhard and Merton speak about many things, but both speak especially about the future. They both provide what Paul Dekar says about Merton, "twentieth-century wisdom for twenty-first-century living." They returned to the sources of Christianity not to examine fossils but to locate the sources of what the *nouvelle théologie* of the 1950s called "ressourcement," the rediscovery of the energies of life.[25]

"Dawn" and "light" were recurring motifs in both Teilhard and Merton. Dawn inspires Teilhard's famous "Hymn of the Universe":

Since once again, Lord—though this time not in the forests of the Aisne but in the steppes of Asia—I have neither bread, nor wine, nor altar, I will raise myself beyond these symbols, up to the pure majesty of the real itself; I, your priest, will make the whole earth my altar and on it will offer you all the labors and sufferings of the world.

Over there, on the horizon, the sun has just touched with light the outermost fringe of the eastern sky. Once again, beneath this moving sheet of fire, the living surface of the earth wakes and trembles, and once again begins its fearful travail. I will place on my paten, O God, the harvest to be won by this renewal of labor. Into my chalice I shall pour all the sap which is to be pressed out this day from the earth's fruits.[26]

On May 31, 1961, Merton jotted in his journal, "The great work of sunrise again today. The awful solemnity of it. The sacredness. Unbearable

---

24. Thomas Merton, "Preface to the Argentine Edition of *The Complete Works of Thomas Merton*" (1958), in Thomas Merton, *"Honorable Reader": Reflections on My Work*, ed. Robert E. Daggy (New York: Crossroad, 1989) 42.

25. See Jürgen Mettepenningen, *Nouvelle Théologie / New Theology* (London: T & T Clark, 2010) 91.

26. Pierre Teilhard de Chardin, *Hymn of the Universe* (New York: Harper and Row, 1965) 19.

without prayer and worship" (*TTW* 123). Two years later, on May 21, 1963, he wrote about that day's early morning light:

> Marvelous vision of the hills at 7:45 A.M. The same hills as always . . . but now catching the light in a totally new way, at once very earthly and very ethereal . . . the whole slightly veiled in mist so that it seemed to be a tropical shore, a new discovered continent. And a voice in me seemed to be crying "Look! Look!" For these are the discoveries, and it is for this that I am high on the mast of my ship (have always been), and I know that we are on the right course, for all around is the sea of paradise. (*TTW* 321-22)

Teilhard might suggest that this "dawning of the divine light" all around Merton, and that to which they both sailed, the newly discovered country, might be called the "divine milieu," or better still, the "Christic future." Jürgen Moltmann, a contemporary of Teilhard and Merton, has argued that our modern understanding of history makes us aware of the radical openness of the future. We have learned that human history is not simply a closed system of pneumatic causes and effects, but is, rather, an open system inescapably contingent and uncertain. For Christians, Moltmann writes, revelation "opens up history by the promise of something new." Revelation "presents the future." Easter, Moltmann continues, "is a light of the *novum*"; it is not only the "illumination of the real but also the opening up of the new."[27] If we agree that futurity is one of the great themes of our time, we can find few better guides to reflecting on the dawning light of the future than those two very different persons, Pierre Teilhard de Chardin and Thomas Merton.

---

27. Jürgen Moltmann, *Hope and Planning*, trans. Margaret Clarkson (New York: Harper & Row, 1968) 15, 17, 39.

Thomas Merton and the Concept of the Child-Mind: "The Only One Worth Having"

Fiona Gardner

Introduction

In *The Sign of Jonas* Thomas Merton comments on some pictures sent to the Abbey of Gethsemani from some apparently "backward" children in Milwaukee: "these wise children were drawing pictures of their own lives. They knew what was in their own depths. They were putting it all down on paper before they had a chance to grow up and forget."[1] In his poem "Grace's House"[2] Merton writes about a drawing of a house on a hill done by a four-year old girl called Grace. Merton uses the picture of a largely preverbal and unself-conscious world to locate his contemplative understanding and spiritual experience of the inner life. For Merton the drawing can be seen as a reminder of perhaps a long forgotten sense of paradise—an Edenic landscape epitomized in terms of plant and animal life where the grass is alive, the animals aware, and each blade of grass matters. The poem offers an adult commentary on the drawing, but with layers of meaning reaching back to a state of child-mind simplicity.

Patrick O'Connell offers a thorough explication of the poem,[3] presenting it as arguably one of the best of Merton's poems of sacramental awareness. Grace's drawing suggests a holistic vision grasped intuitively in a way that adults lose and forget because it is inaccessible to the analytic mind—the adult mind of verbal, conceptual thought:

> There is a name on the box, name of a family
> Not yet ready to be written in language. (ll. 27-28)

As O'Connell notes, "it can be known only from within, through love and wisdom, relational and participatory knowledge" (O'Connell 532). These qualities are all aspects of the child-mind. It was St. Thérèse who

---

1. Thomas Merton, *The Sign of Jonas* (New York: Harcourt, Brace, 1953) 341.

2. Thomas Merton, *The Collected Poems of Thomas Merton* (New York: New Directions, 1977) 330-31; subsequent references will be cited as "*CP*" parenthetically in the text.

3. Patrick F. O'Connell, "'The Surest Home Is Pointless': A Pathless Path through Merton's Poetic Corpus," *CrossCurrents*, 58.4 (2008) 522-44; subsequent references will be cited as "O'Connell" parenthetically in the text.

said, "to write is nothing—nothing at all. . . . One must be in it to know."[4] Grace draws what she knows—she is in it. Merton writes poetically about the drawing from a place of contemplative awareness and experience.

Merton's focus on the child-mind, which he writes in a letter to John Wu is "the only one worth having,"[5] reflects the firm and insistent teaching in the Synoptic Gospels that becoming like a child is essential to entry into the kingdom, that mysteries are revealed only to babies, which complements Jesus' teaching in St. John's Gospel that no one can see the kingdom unless born anew (John 3:3). Jesus did not define the child he told adults to be like. Instead each person is invited to find their own child-mind and so to discover their spiritual maturity. Jesus's parabolic teaching contrasts with the unregenerate mind of the cynical adult which is blinded and darkened. For Merton the distinction between adult ignorance and the innocent truth exemplified in Grace's drawing cannot be spanned—"It is the uncrossed crystal / Water" (ll. 35-36). However one of Jesus' teachings is to place the silent child amongst the talking disciples. As it is the silent child who teaches by example, so it is through silent contemplation that we can approach a sense of the true self. As Merton writes in *Hagia Sophia*, "We do not see the Child who is prisoner in all the people, and who says nothing" (*CP* 365).

The suggestion in this paper is that the child-mind as conveyed by Merton in his poem is a state of adult consciousness. The child-mind of the adult is not the same as the mind of the four-year-old child who drew the picture, nor is it a pathological version of it or a mawkish regression, but rather, according to Merton, the essence of mature spirituality. The poem is about recognition of an inward journeying home, "somewhere I had been as a child . . . a reunion."[6] For Merton the inner self remains a child—a dweller in paradise—but we lose our path to this inner self: "Alas, there is no road to Grace's house!" (l. 50). In this poem, Merton offers each reader a reminder and recognition of this universal state of paradise consciousness and grace—incidentally where Adam too was an infant. This is a state that like Adam is lost to us inevitably by precocity, and, as the early Fathers described it, by an act of immodest maturity or

4. St. Thérèse of Lisieux, *Autobiography of a Saint* (London and Glasgow: Collins Fontana, 1958) 18.

5. Thomas Merton, *The Hidden Ground of Love: Letters on Religious Experience and Social Concerns*, ed. William H. Shannon (New York: Farrar, Straus, Giroux, 1985) 614 [4/1/1961].

6. Thomas Merton, *Dancing in the Water of Life: Seeking Peace in the Hermitage. Journals, vol. 5: 1963-1965*, ed. Robert E. Daggy (San Francisco: HarperCollins, 1997) 202.

growing up too quickly.[7] The Christ Child reveals not simply the child-hood we have lost, but a new childhood in and through him. It is a state of connectedness and a movement towards Ultimate Unity.

It is worth noting that the mind of the four-year-old is mainly operating below ego consciousness, so whilst not strictly preverbal it is a mind largely unsophisticated and uncluttered by complex conceptual thinking. Merton saw that for adults the true self can be seen as a reality beyond the level of ego consciousness, but he did not think this made ego consciousness irrelevant. For in adults the ego contributes to contemplation by actively opening to deeper levels of awareness. This realization is exemplified in Merton's description of his epiphany at the statues of Polonnaruwa as a state of conscious awareness "beyond the shadow and the disguise,"[8] and I will be referring to this experience of spiritual maturity in this paper alongside the words from his poem about the child-mind.

There is a resistance to appreciating the child-mind as a state of spiritual maturity for obvious reasons. Perhaps it appears anti-intellectual in some ways, or an embarrassment, or an insult to our adult achievements and capabilities. There are usually ambivalent attitudes towards children linked to our own personal histories—there may be mixed messages and a lack of understanding, or a reluctance to return to what was experienced as a time of powerlessness and vulnerability. As the British psychoanalyst Donald Winnicott is reputed to have said about his own childhood, "Once was enough."[9] However what Merton's poem invites the reader to do is not to become lost in the personal past but rather to see how aspects of the child-mind can serve to bring us nearer to God and relieve us of the weight of adult care and unnatural concern about spiritual prowess. The drawing of the house and surroundings is seen by Merton as both a representation of Grace herself (her childhood spirituality) and also as a symbol of a possible state of grace—i.e. the child-mind in an adult.

I'm going to take three aspects that characterize the child-mind and that are found in the poem and reflect on them in the light of Merton's own experience of spiritual maturity at Polonnaruwa.

---

7. See John Saward, *Perfect Fools* (Oxford: Oxford University Press, 1980) 9.

8. Thomas Merton, *The Other Side of the Mountain: The End of the Journey. Journals, vol. 7: 1967-1968*, ed. Patrick Hart (San Francisco: HarperCollins, 1998) 323; subsequent references will be cited as "*OSM*" parenthetically in the text.

9. D. W. Winnicott (personal communication from a colleague who worked with DWW).

1. The Child-Mind: Relational Consciousness

The first aspect is relational consciousness, where relational refers to the importance of God, other people and creatures together with the self. It is the quality of such interdependent interactions from a spiritual perspective that Merton focuses on in the poem.

> No blade of grass is not counted,
> No blade of grass forgotten on this hill. . . .
> O paradise, O child's world!
> Where all the grass lives
> And all the animals are aware! (ll. 5-6, 37-39)

It has been noted that very young children appear naturally to have relational and conscious intuitions at a very young age; they seem to be aware of and have an implicit understanding of their relationship to their environment long before they can name it, and as has been noted, experiences that "transcended the human, pointing to something beyond."[10] Rebecca Nye writes of her very young son calling excitedly to her: "When I hurried over he pointed triumphantly out of the window and ecstatically cried out 'Grass!'"[11] "No blade of grass is not blessed" (l. 44); and from Polonnaruwa: "my feet in wet grass" (*OSM* 323). In contrast, "relational" in the adult involves a more conscious centering of the self and personal authenticity in relationship. Recent psychological understanding rejects the dominant model of spiritual maturity as autonomy, but rather equates maturity with relationship. Joann Wolski Conn writes on the intimacy of mutual interdependence, and the mature person as one who can freely surrender herself or himself, "who can risk a genuinely mutual relationship with others and with God."[12] It is as if we have to unlearn our self-centered individuality, self-preoccupation and self-containment where we are endlessly negotiating our social relationships and our relationship to God with such care and control. Spiritual maturity then means a development beyond autonomy to a balance of independence and relationship that allows genuine intimacy with God and others.

In Merton's account of Polonnaruwa he writes of his ability (and I

---

10. Elaine Champagne, "Being a Child, a Spiritual Child," *International Journal of Children's Spirituality* 8.1 (2003) 43-53, quoted in Brendan Hyde, *Children and Spirituality: Searching for Meaning and Connectedness* (London and Philadelphia: Jessica Kingsley, 2008) 54; subsequent references will be cited as "Hyde" parenthetically in the text.

11. David Hay and Rebecca Nye, *The Spirit of the Child* (London: Harper Collins, 1998) 61; subsequent references will be cited as "Hay & Nye" parenthetically in the text.

12. Joann Wolski Conn, *Spirituality and Personal Maturity* (New York: Paulist Press, 1989) 57.

don't think here he just means physical ability) "to approach the Buddhas barefoot and undisturbed" (*OSM* 323). Whilst the very taking off of shoes is reminiscent of biblical instruction of walking on holy ground (cf. Ex. 3:5), it can also stand as a metaphor for the necessary stripping away of the superficial self. Here "barefoot and undisturbed" implies in the right frame of mind, free from the past and future egoic concerns. For Merton's long journey of integration of the past, both conscious and unconscious, is part of what allows him to approach the statues unencumbered. Merton is standing freely, no longer tied to roles, structures, institutions but conscious and alive.

The "consciousness" part of relational consciousness emphasizes awareness, mystery and value-sensing. Awareness-sensing is being in the here-and-now, a state of mind which is characteristically vivid.

> The huge sun, bigger than the house
> Stands and streams with life in the east
> While in the west a thunder cloud
> Moves away for ever. (ll. 40-43)

This intensity and immediacy of awareness is referred to by psychologists such as Vygotsky,[13] who sees this experience as one characterized by the absence of marked time (past and future) and the content is highly symbolic—the language of "pure" meaning. David Hay and Rebecca Nye note that this level is normally inaccessible since, as we reconstruct it into the language of the culture to which we belong, time is "marked" and the intense quality of the original meaning is diluted (Hay & Nye 61). This is what happens with Merton's account of Polonnaruwa: he even writes that it "was such an experience that I could not write hastily of it and cannot write now, or not at all adequately" (*OSM* 321). What we read is then a diluted account of this vivid, immediate here-and-now glimpse of God. Indeed the account begins firmly located in time: "Today is Thursday," which follows "I visited . . . on Monday" (*OSM* 322). It has taken three days for the experience to be translated verbally.

Religious interest in the immediacy of awareness is taken to high levels of sophistication in Buddhism through the practice of "single-pointed" awareness, and in Christian contemplative prayer with "the sacrament of the present moment" (Caussade).[14] And this raised awareness can also be described as "tuning," which links to feeling at one with nature and any heightened aesthetic experience. Merton writes, "I don't know when in my

---

13. Lev Vygotsky, *Thought and Language* (Cambridge, MA: MIT Press, 1962) 119.

14. See Jean Pierre de Caussade, SJ, *Abandonment to Divine Providence* (London: Catholic Way Publishing, 2012).

life I have ever had such a sense of beauty and spiritual validity running together in one aesthetic illumination" (*OSM* 323). Merton's experience at Polonnaruwa also indicates the idea of flow. This is when concentrated attention gives way to a liberating feeling where action and awareness become merged. There is a sense of the activity almost managing itself or being managed by an outside influence—the whole thing transforms into a single flow: "Looking at these figures [here is the effort-filled attentiveness] I was suddenly, almost forcibly, jerked clean out of the habitual, half-tied vision of things, and an inner clearness, clarity, as if exploding from the rocks themselves, became evident and obvious" (*OSM* 323)—something transcending the self takes on the activity of looking.

A further aspect of such consciousness is that of bodily awareness or focusing, what the American philosopher and psychotherapist Eugene Gendlin calls the "felt sense":[15] "my feet in wet grass, wet sand" (*OSM* 323). Part of the awareness is mystery and the sense that part of the experience is incomprehensible. For adults to encounter the mystery of existence with feelings of wonder and awe, especially in the middle of rational activity, can be a surprise. However for young children there may be no difference between the commonplace and the profound; much of life appears incomprehensible and therefore mysterious.

> On the summit: it stands on a fair summit
> Prepared by winds . . . .
> There is no path to the summit—
> No path drawn (ll. 1-2, 8-9).

Education with its emphasis on answers to everything gradually erodes that sense of mystery.

2. The Child-Mind: Experience and Play

The second characteristic of the child-mind: one of the experiences in childhood spirituality is value-sensing. Children readily express emotion and the value of what is happening in their everyday experience. There is often an animistic tendency to attribute or project their own emotion and thoughts onto animals and things.

> Important: hidden in the foreground
> Most carefully drawn
> The dog smiles, his foreleg curled, his eye like an aster.

---

15. Eugene Gendlin, *Focusing: How to Gain Direct Access to Your Body's Knowledge: How to Open up Your Deeper Feelings and Intuition* (London: Rider 2003): www.youtube.com/watch?v=j7PEC5Mh5Fy [accessed 11/27/2013].

Nose and collar are made with great attention:
This dog is loved by Grace! (ll. 19-23)

And from Polonnaruwa: "The queer *evidence* of the reclining figure, the smile, the sad smile of Ananda standing with arms folded. . . . The rock, all matter, all life, is charged with *dharmakaya*—everything is emptiness and everything is compassion" (*OSM* 323).

This phenomenon of seeing life and feelings in creatures and objects is sometimes derided as childish or over-imaginative, but may be a precursor to the move in spiritual maturity from seeing things primarily from the perspective of personal gain and self-importance to appreciating a wider, holistic perspective. Also, Merton's theology of feeling found throughout his work is the adult equivalent to the small child's easy expression of both delight and despair.

Childhood spirituality and the child-mind of mature spirituality are characterized by the ability to trust, to experience dependence, and by an idea of ultimate goodness. This can be transmitted to young children at an early age. Peter Berger writes of the mother who can banish chaos and restore the benign shape of the world by "Don't be afraid—everything is in order, everything is all right."[16]

... and solid smoke
Rolls from the chimney like a snow cloud.
Grace's house is secure. (ll. 2-4)

However it is debatable from Merton's account of his upbringing whether this would actually have been transmitted to him. Yet it seems that he found this experience, as can happen later in life, through the order and containment of the monastic life. He writes: "the peace not of emotional resignation but of Madhyamika, of *sunyata*, that has seen through every question without trying to discredit anyone or anything—*without refuta-tion*—without establishing some other argument. For the doctrinaire, the mind that needs well-established positions, such peace, such silence, can be frightening" (*OSM* 323). Children are drawn to make meaning through play and imagination. As has been noted, "it is the imagination which governs our experience of God."[17] Winnicott writes about the space for experiencing: a space between a mother and small child where the healthy illusions of life can be housed. Research asserts that God-concepts form in

---

16. Peter Berger, *A Rumour of Angels* (London: Allen Lane/Penguin, 1970) 72.

17. Sandra Schneiders, *Women and the Word: The Gender of God in the New Testament and the Spirituality of Women* (New York: Paulist Press, 1986) 70, quoted by Christopher Pramuk, *Sophia: The Hidden Christ of Thomas Merton* (Collegeville, MN: Liturgical Press, 2009) 212.

every human being (even when parents are non-believers), and they form in an intermediate space between the infant and the outside world.[18] This is a space between inner and outer reality, between the personal and the material, between subjective and objective realities, a space to which both contribute. It is in this spiritual space that experiences are integrated and from which emotionally based concepts are formed. So through experience and playing with the experiences both emotionally and intellectually spiritual maturity develops. God-concepts are therefore initially personal constructions that form independently of formal religious instruction. This is why it is so easy to construct false idols or to domesticate God and to forget that God is more than we can easily imagine and so much more than our projections. These personal constructs, as Joyce Bellous notes,[19] must grow up to engage with and be transformed by the God who lives above mere human concepts.

> All the curtains are arranged
> Not for hiding but for seeing out.
> In one window someone looks out and winks. . . .
> From behind a corner of Grace's house
> Another creature peeks out. (ll. 11-13, 17-18)

Play deriving from the earliest games of "peek-a-boo" and hide-and-seek evolve in adult spirituality into a playing with the absence and presence of God. Jerome Berryman writes that poets and mystics are the best and most articulate players of this game. About poets he writes, "Perhaps their love for and artful use of metaphor is a kind of compressed game of hide and seek in itself, which makes them more comfortable with such play. The poets also make it quite clear that this game is not trivial."[20] Play is usually signalled by non-verbal actions and as has been noted in the section on relational consciousness children are better than adults at tracking relationships without language, because they are not yet as dependent on language as adults.

Merton writes about the Wisdom-child of Proverbs as playing in the world: "And they did not know their real identity as the Child so dear to God who, from before the beginning, was playing in His sight all days,

---

18. D. W. Winnicott, "Transitional Objects and Transitional Phenomena," *Playing and Reality* (London: Penguin, 1971) 1-30.

19. Joyce E. Bellous, Simone A. de Roos and William Summey, "A Child's Concept of God," in *Children's Spirituality: Christian Perspectives, Research and Applications*, ed. Donald Ratcliff (Eugene, OR: Cascade Books, 2004) 204; subsequent references will be cited as "Ratcliff" parenthetically in the text.

20. Jerome W. Berryman, "Children and Mature Spirituality" (Ratcliff 27).

playing in the world."[21] At Polonnaruwa he plays hide-and-seek with the figures: "And the sweep of bare rock sloping away on the other side of the hollow, where you can go back and see different aspects of the figures" (*OSM* 323).

Tobin Hart writes of the spiritual capacity in children of wisdom as a way of knowing that emerges through an opening of heart and mind and an ability to get to where feelings of wonder act as a cornerstone for the spiritual experience. He recounts one child's description of standing in the water at the beach moving back and forth with the motion of the waves. When her father had asked her what she was doing (note the adult emphasis on doing rather than being) she had stated simply she *was* the water. She was unable to explain it in any other way. The child had experienced becoming one with the Other—the child knew that the spiritual, the "other" world is embedded in the here and now.[22] "On this archetypal, cosmic hill, / This womb of mysteries (ll. 45-46). "I mean, I know and . . . have now seen and have pierced through the surface and have got beyond the shadow and the disguise" (*OSM* 323).

3. The Child-Mind: No Status and Powerlessness

The third characteristic of the child-mind:

> And there: the world!
> Mailbox number 5. . . .
> A spangled arrow there
> Points from our Coney Island
> To her green sun-hill.
>
> Between our world and hers
> Runs a sweet river . . . (ll. 24-25, 29-33)

The child's lack of worldly status means exclusion from power, participation and recognition. The child is by definition on the outside and is the one who is brought to Jesus, not one who assumes access; the child is the one who is blessed rather than the more powerful one conferring the blessing on another. Yet in a state of powerlessness and no status it is however possible for mutual blessing. This is known in mature spirituality as humility of mind. As Berryman notes, "When people forget that they are creatures and not God, they become too inflated to enter the small

---

21. Thomas Merton, *The Courage for Truth: Letters to Writers*, ed. Christine M. Bochen (New York: Farrar, Straus, Giroux, 1993) 90 [10/23/1958 letter to Boris Pasternak].

22. Tobin Hart, *The Secret Spiritual World of Children* (Makawao, HI: Inner Ocean, 2003), cited in Hyde 74.

doorway into God's domain. It is for children and the child-like, rather than for the powerful who must expand their power to find their worth" (Ratcliff 39).

Merton's reading of St. Bernard and Guerric of Igny amongst others gave him a theological frame alongside his personal spiritual experiences. Guerric writes that becoming a little child means going out of our adult mind, a state he sees characterized by weakness and foolishness but one that is akin to simplicity, humility and learned ignorance.[23] This is a life unconformed to the world. Merton writes, "Wisdom cries out in the market place—'if anyone is little let him come to me.'"[24]

The glory of the "green sun-hill" is that it is natural—it sits lightly. As Rabbi Hugo Gryn writes, "Spirituality is like a bird; if you hold it too tightly, it chokes; if you hold it too loosely, it flies away. Fundamental to spirituality, is the absence of force."[25] In spiritual maturity this is awareness of human powerlessness and personal dependence on God; the state of grace is not held to either by ownership or through self-will or force. "I was knocked over with a rush of relief and thankfulness at the *obvious* clarity of the figures. . . . The thing about all this is that there is no puzzle, no problem, and really no 'mystery'" (*OSM* 323).

Conclusion

Children are not adults and adults are not children. Adults, however, can become not childish but childlike. As Phillip Toynbee writes about the goal of life: "if there is one; if I ever reach it—will certainly be seen, *then* as something marvellously simple. Not a child's simplicity, but the simplicity of childhood regained. So many accretions to be cut out or planed away."[26] To become as small children in our spiritual life, the child-mind requires a great leap of the imagination. "Grace's House" evokes a visual description for us of a familiar childish drawing but it is the implicit meaning that draws us to understand the paradox within the adult mind of what is required of us. The model is ultimately the Christ Child who in the legend of St. Christopher is smaller than small and bigger than big—and where wholeness is of immeasurable extent, older and younger than consciousness and enfolding it in terms of time and space.[27]

23. See John Morson, *Christ the Way: The Christology of Guerric of Igny* (Kalamazoo, MI: Cistercian Publications, 1978) 39-61.

24. Thomas Merton, *Turning Toward the World: The Pivotal Years. Journals, vol. 4: 1960-1963*, ed. Victor A. Kramer (San Francisco: HarperCollins, 1996) 17.

25. Hugo Gryn, quoted in Ratcliff 1.

26. Philip Toynbee, *Part of a Journey: An Autobiographical Journal 1977-79* (London: Collins Fount, 1981) 65.

27. C. G. Jung, *The Archetypes and the Collective Unconscious*, in *The Collected*

The child-mind is an Awakening. As Elizabeth Goudge writes, "The child in us is always there, you know, and it's the best part of us, the winged part that travels furthest."[28]

Works, vol. 9 (London: Routledge and Kegan Paul, 1959) 158, 178.

28. Elizabeth Goudge, *Green Dolphin Country* (London: Hodder and Stoughton,1956) 484.

From Downtown Louisville to Buenos Aires: Victoria Ocampo as Thomas Merton's Overlooked Bridge to Latin America and the World

Mark C. Meade

In Buenos Aires in 2011, I presented a version of this paper for the book launch of *Fragmentos de un Regalo*,[1] the correspondence between Thomas Merton and Victoria Ocampo. The title of the book means "fragments of a gift." They are fragments because, even though twenty-five letters are included, twenty of which were previously unpublished, some letters are known to be missing. The "gift" is taken from Merton's first letter of reply to Victoria, stating that her letter was "a true gift from God." In Buenos Aires, Merton needed more of an introduction than Victoria Ocampo, but I will try to briefly summarize her life for this essay before discussing the significance of their correspondence. (For the lecture in Argentina, I was encouraged to refer to her as Victoria rather than Ocampo because her sister, Silvina Ocampo,[2] received notoriety of her own as a poet and writer of short fiction. I have henceforth used Victoria when not using her full name.)

Victoria Ocampo was born in 1890 to a wealthy aristocratic family in Argentina. The first of six daughters, and with no brothers, she would become heiress to her family's fortune. Later in life, Victoria used this wealth to promote the literary journal *Sur* that gained her international fame and which helped her to export Latin American literature to the world and to import world literature to Latin America. While her parents could not control her later fiscal priorities, her father, her husband and Argentine society, including peer authors, kept her in limited cultural boundaries enforced upon women of the time. Like Merton, Victoria spent much of her childhood in France. Though the girls of the family were not allowed

---

1. Thomas Merton and Victoria Ocampo, *Fragmentos de un Regalo: Correspondencia y Artículos y Reseñas Publicados en* Sur, introduction, translation and notes by Juan Javier Negri (Buenos Aires: Sur, 2011); subsequent references will be cited as "*FR*" parenthetically in the text.

2. Silvina Ocampo was married to the novelist Adolfo Bioy Casares. Robert MacGregor of New Directions Publishing sent Merton a copy of Bioy Casares's *Plan de Evasion*, and Merton responded with his thoughts about the book: see the letter of March 6, 1958 from Merton to MacGregor in *Thomas Merton and James Laughlin: Selected Letters,* ed. David D. Cooper (New York: W. W. Norton, 1997) 132-33; subsequent references will be cited as "*SL*" parenthetically in the text.

formal education outside the house, they had a French tutor. Victoria's old-money family also prohibited university matriculation, but she was allowed to attend a number of lectures at the Sorbonne. She was drawn to the theater and allowed to take private acting lessons in her youth, but her father forbade her to be publicly on stage. "[He] would later repeat: 'the day one of my daughters gets on stage is the day I put a bullet through my head.'"[3] In 1912, Victoria began a largely unhappy marriage to Monaco Estrada. She was 22. During her honeymoon, Victoria discovered a letter from her new husband to her father with assurances that "all of his daughter's fantasies of becoming an actress would disappear as soon as she became pregnant. Victoria writes: 'I married a traitor'" (Gainza and Bordelois, "Chronology"). Eight years later they separated, and Estrada would die thirteen years later in 1933.

Victoria wrote and translated throughout her career, mainly writing literary critiques beginning with a book in French highlighting the female characters in the *Divine Comedy*. She wrote biographies of Virginia Woolf and T. E. Lawrence. An admirer of Indian poet and intellectual Rabindranath Tagore, his illness while on a 1924 tour of South America gave Victoria the opportunity to host him for two months of his recovery. In 1930, Victoria would curate an exhibition of Tagore's art in France. Victoria's crowning achievement was the founding in 1931 of the journal *Sur* and in 1933 of *Sur*'s book-publishing wing. In journal and book form, she published authors with whom Merton corresponded, like Henry Miller and Octavio Paz, and those whom Merton read, such as Albert Camus. She continued to travel throughout her life and to host authors and intellectuals at her family estate, Villa Ocampo. Dying in 1979, she had donated the villa in her will to UNESCO for use as a cultural and educational center focusing on programs for children. Much of the land on the estate was sold during her lifetime to fund *Sur* and other literary projects.

Merton did not suffer the same gender-based discrimination as Victoria, but some of Victoria's best writing, like Merton's, can be found in her memoirs and in a vast correspondence with an international array of friends and intellectuals. Ivonne Bordelois describes Victoria the letter-writer as one who, not unlike Merton, possessed a mixture of cutting wit, warmth and candor emerging from the hidden realm of private correspondence with friends. For Merton, his private journals and correspondence provided sanctuary from monastic censorship and the demands of his order for a famous monk to maintain a holy public veneer. In Victoria's

---

3. María Gainza and Ivonne Bordelois, "Victoria Ocampo's Chronology: 1890-1906" (http://www.villaocampo.org/ing/historico/victoria.htm [accessed 9/10/2011]; subsequent references will be cited as "Gainza and Bordelois, 'Chronology'" parenthetically in the text).

case, the privacy freed her from certain social expectations and limitations. Bordelois writes of Victoria:

> Beyond her articles, books, and memoirs, Victoria penned a huge number of letters, the volume of which exceeds the rest of her written work put together. Her correspondence was written in silence, with her notable tenacity and a headstrong determination. As generous as Victoria was, her words often stung, and in her letters can be found a number of biting finales vis-à-vis the brilliant figures that encircled her: "Lacan struck me as a small Napoleon," she writes, or "Ravel seemed to pay no heed to Ravel," "Borges doesn't deserve the talent he has," . . . [and] "Simone de Beauvoir, who went on about Virginia Woolf's feminism, had never heard of [Three] Guineas."[4]

In 2009, Javier Negri of Victoria's literary estate began gathering manuscripts and papers related to Merton and Victoria from *Sur*'s archive, the Merton Center, and the New Directions and James Laughlin collections at Harvard. In 2011, *Fragmentos de un Regalo* was published. It contained all extant correspondence, none of Victoria's having previously been published. Some of Merton's earlier letters had not been published as they were not among the carbon copies kept at the Merton Center, the primary source for Merton's letters to Ocampo in *The Courage for Truth*.[5] Negri also included essays by Merton and reviews of Merton's books published in the journal *Sur*.

Beyond the intrinsic value of the correspondence of two diverse literary figures like Victoria and Merton, I believe their correspondence is greatly significant to Merton studies in the following ways. It has been widely noted that Merton's Fourth and Walnut experience in downtown Louisville[6] broadened his view of the type of issues he would address, namely, moving from writing exclusively personal reflections about the spiritual life and poetry centered around life at Gethsemani to writing essays and poetry that brought his religious convictions to bear on the social issues of the day and that addressed global concerns. Scholars

---

4. Ivonne Bordelois, "Villa Ocampo in the Arts: Her Essays" (http://www. villaocampo.org/ing/historico/cultura_10.htm [accessed 9/10/2011]).

5. Thomas Merton, *The Courage for Truth: Letters to Writers*, ed. Christine M. Bochen (New York: Farrar, Straus, Giroux, 1993) 207-12; subsequent references will be cited as "*CT*" parenthetically in the text.

6. See Thomas Merton, *A Search for Solitude: Pursuing the Monk's True Life. Journals, vol. 3: 1952-1960*, ed. Lawrence S. Cunningham (San Francisco: HarperCollins, 1996) 181-82 [3/19/1958] (subsequent references will be cited as "*SS*" parenthetically in the text); Thomas Merton, *Conjectures of a Guilty Bystander* (Garden City, NY: Doubleday, 1966) 140-42.

like William Shannon have noted that not long after this experience, Merton entered into dialogue with people from outside the monastery, from various places globally, and from religious and cultural traditions quite different from his own.[7] Not all have linked Merton's contact with intellectuals of the world to his experience in Louisville, but I think the newly found Victoria Ocampo correspondence helps us to see this link was more than a private revelation later published. The timing of Merton's first letter to Victoria places her squarely in the midst of a pivotal shift in Thomas Merton's writing. What Merton chose to write to Victoria and when he did it reveal new insights about Merton.

Both Victoria and Merton shared a quality of transcendence that manifested itself in various aspects of their lives. Possibly, the term transcendence be could used to describe a state inhabited those who have crossed into a metaphysical world detached from the rest of us, and further, employed with a pejorative connotation referring to those who seem to have lost contact with the material world. By transcendence, I refer to the more literal meaning of the Latin *trans-* and *scandere*, to climb across, to climb over. Merton and Victoria crossed boundaries and healed divisions. They overcame barriers in communications, culture, politics, gender dynamics and religious division. Both drew on sources new and ancient. Victoria's cosmopolitan tastes as a publisher did not deny her distinctly Argentine voice. For Merton, being a mystic meant seeing the "hidden wholeness" in all things, as he expressed in the poem *Hagia Sophia*.[8] The mystic need not lose grounding with the material world to see beyond the external differences. The true mystic does not have to lose his or her personal uniqueness and rootedness to a particular culture or faith tradition to recognize a connection to all people, to all creation and to the divine. As Merton states in an essay entitled "The Contemplative Life in the Modern World":

> Ancient and traditional societies, whether of Asia or of the West, always specifically recognized "the way" of the wise, . . . whether in art, in philosophy, in religion, or in the monastic life . . . they would so to speak bring together in themselves the divisions or complications that confused the life of their fellows. By healing the divisions in themselves they would help heal the divisions of the whole

---

7. William Shannon, *'Something of a Rebel': Thomas Merton: His Life and Works: An Introduction* (Cincinnati: St. Anthony Messenger Press, 2005) 35-38.

8. Thomas Merton, *The Collected Poems of Thomas Merton* (New York: New Directions, 1977) 363.

world. . . . This way of wisdom is no dream, no temptation and no evasion, for it is on the contrary a return to reality in its very root.[9]

For Merton, the mystic was not only continually aware of the world's problems, but one who sought to resolve the conflicts on a personal level and then to universalize reconciliation.

Victoria's mystical insights came from within and without her birth culture's Catholic milieu. Doris Meyer, in her biography of Victoria, notes that Victoria equally drew inspiration from Dante's vision in the *Divine Comedy* and the Eastern wisdom of Rabindranath Tagore. In them, Victoria discovered something akin to Merton's idea of "hidden wholeness." Meyer writes that Victoria recognized that "both Dante and Tagore aspired to achieve 'allness,' 'wholeness,' the union of finite and infinite."[10] As in *Hagia Sophia*, Merton often cited the Holy Wisdom of God manifesting itself as a feminine force, a tradition with its roots in the Hebrew Scriptures. He may have seen in Victoria reflections of these unifying and sapiential aspects.

For Merton, the path to wisdom was a long road of self-growth and discovery to achieve a spirituality that embraced the world, a journey now documented in his journals. To say that Victoria and Merton were possessed of this transcendent quality is not a novel assertion. However, I believe that it was Merton's inauguration of contact with Victoria that was one of the first human connections that put into action in Merton's life the mental shift from world-denial to world-affirmation, from self-isolation to transcendence. I can trace the significance that Victoria had on Merton from his first letter to her on July 21, 1958. The date of the letter is significant. This was the mid-point of Merton's most active years as a writer. For this chronology, I refer to the time beginning with Merton's first great success as a writer, *The Seven Storey Mountain*, in 1948, to his death in 1968. More than simply a mid-point, 1958 was a pivot point. In Merton's personal journals we can pinpoint an important revelatory experience that happened just a few months prior to his first letter to Victoria, March 18, 1958, at Fourth and Walnut Streets in Louisville. As noted, this is commonly seen as a shift for Merton away from an insular

---

9. Thomas Merton, *Faith and Violence: Christian Teaching and Christian Practice* (Notre Dame, IN: University of Notre Dame Press, 1968) 218; subsequent references will be cited as "*FV*" parenthetically in the text. This essay, written in March 1965 and originally published as the preface to the Japanese edition of *Seeds of Contemplation*, was later expanded and appeared under this title in the Indian journal *The Mountain Path* 2 (October 1965) and subsequently in *Faith and Violence*.

10. Doris Meyer, *Victoria Ocampo: Against the Wind and the Tide* (New York: G. Braziller, 1979) 64.

view of the monastic life, a view that saw the goal of monasticism and the spiritual life as denying the world outside the cloister wall in favor of an idealized life of prayer and asceticism.

I affirm this prior analysis of this event and take it a step further. In *Merton: A Film Biography* by Paul Wilkes and Audrey Glynn, Fourth and Walnut is portrayed as a cosmic reordering, a change in Merton's mental landscape which affected all of his future writing. This change forced him to reconsider his monastic vocation and to now include in it a concern for problems of the world, including racism and atomic weapon proliferation, issues he confronted in critical essays following this revelation.

What I am proposing is a link between this event and Merton commencing engagements, mainly through correspondence, with a worldwide cadre of great minds—firstly, Victoria Ocampo. Many of these types of letters were only privately published during Merton's lifetime because of the censorship he experienced from his monastic superiors on controversial subjects, especially on the subject of nuclear war, e.g., his mimeographed circulation of the "Cold War Letters,"[11] which had been barred from publication. In such letters as these, it would not just be the wall of the cloister that would be transcended, but barriers such as the Iron Curtain. One of Merton's earliest letters inaugurating a vocation of global correspondence was with Russian author Boris Pasternak in August of 1958 (*CT* 87-93). However, we now know that the first such barrier to be crossed was between the poles on a north-south axis when Merton first wrote to Victoria, one of culture and language, between the American divide, the Anglo-American north and the Latin American south.

As a clarification, Merton had contacts in Latin America prior to Victoria, but most were responsive on his part, for example, Merton responding to publishers of his books in translation in Latin America or letters written to Merton by monks and nuns there for spiritual advice. He had an interesting exchange of letters with sculptor Jaime Andrade from Ecuador[12] beginning shortly before his letters with Victoria; however, Merton had written to Andrade because he was searching for an artist to carve a statue for the chapel used by Gethsemani's novices, an increasing number of whom were coming from Latin America at that time. Not long after the time Merton and Victoria entered into dialogue, the Andrade correspondence was deepening into issues regarding global solidarity and

---

11. Thomas Merton, *Cold War Letters*, ed. Christine M. Bochen and William H. Shannon (Maryknoll, NY: Orbis, 2006).

12. Thomas Merton, *The School of Charity: Letters on Religious Renewal and Spiritual Direction*, ed. Patrick Hart (New York: Farrar, Straus, Giroux, 1990) 107-109, 111-12, 113-15, 248.

not simply the art commission. In contrast to most prior interactions with Latin Americans, Merton *initiates* correspondence with Victoria. There may have been a publishing motive in mind because Merton sends Victoria a couple of items for possible inclusion in *Sur*. However, it is clear from the tone of the first letter that there is a connection to the experience in Louisville and a theme of solidarity that would prefigure the Cold War Letters of the early 1960s.

Although their correspondence begins with Merton writing to Victoria, I should not place all of the initiative for Merton's connection with Latin America with Merton himself. In a sense, Latin America came to him. Nicaraguan poet Ernesto Cardenal had spent some time as a novice with Merton, but novices also came to Gethsemani from Colombia, Bolivia, Argentina and elsewhere in Latin America. It was through the poet Cardenal and James Laughlin at New Directions that Merton gained access to the poets of South America and fell in love with their writings. I find a first reference to Merton hearing about *Sur* through New Directions Vice-President Robert MacGregor. He offered to send Merton a novel by Adolfo Bioy Casares from *Sur*'s publishing wing.[13] Merton had asked a postulant coming to the monastery from Argentina in spring of 1958 to bring him a copy of *Sur*, and the *Sur* office sent him multiple issues (see *SS* 188 [4/4/1958]). Merton may not have realized that Victoria had by this time included reviews of three of his books in *Sur* between 1950 and 1956. These were the Latin American releases in Spanish by Editorial Sudamericana of *The Seven Storey Mountain*, *Seeds of Contemplation* and *No Man Is an Island*.[14]

According to Christine Bochen, editor of *The Courage for Truth*, the collection of Merton's letters to writers, "The earliest of these letters [to writers in Latin America] were written to Pablo Antonio Cuadra, the Nicaraguan writer and editor of *La Prensa* . . . beginning in 1958" (*CT* xiii). Although Victoria Ocampo is listed among fifteen other contacts from Latin America, Bochen was not aware at time of publication in 1993 of Merton's early correspondence with Victoria, nor was any scholar aware of this before the recent discovery of thirteen new letters, the first of which precedes that of the Cuadra correspondence (*CT* 178-95). Cuadra had already visited Merton at Gethsemani through a visit arranged by Ernesto Cardenal. However, Merton waited to write to Cuadra and first reaches out to Victoria in letter form.

Merton had other earlier global contacts prior to Victoria. For a decade

---

13. See MacGregor's November 18, 1957 letter to Merton (*SL* 134).

14. *FR* 41-57; Victoria was one of the founders of the publisher *Editorial Sudamericana* in 1939, but had left the venture by the time Merton's books were published.

Merton had been in contact with English author Evelyn Waugh following the publication of *The Seven Storey Mountain* (*CT* 3-21). Merton reached out to Waugh for the sake of a writing mentor, not to open himself to the wider world. One could argue that Merton's correspondence with Jacques Maritain in the same year, 1948, was an earlier thread of engagement with the world than with Victoria (*CT* 22-53); however, Maritain wrote first to Merton. Merton initiates contact with Erich Fromm, the German-born psychoanalyst and philosopher living in Mexico.[15] He engaged Fromm on the intellectual plane, but Merton was not yet in the mode of worldly engagement. Though claiming sympathy in opposition to war, Merton refused to sign an anti-war declaration Fromm sent in March of 1955, claiming he was ignorant of current events and that his superiors would likely object to his signing a public statement. Moreover, at this time, he claimed that he did not know of progressive Catholics who might sign, except possibly Jacques Maritain or Bishop John Wright of Springfield, Massachusetts (see *HGL* 311-12 [3/18/1955]). By the 1960s, he had signed public petitions and was in contact with many anti-war Catholics, which emphasizes the changes that Merton experienced in 1958.

Besides being a rare example of an international contact that Merton initiated and that was begun primarily for the sake of communication before late 1958, Merton's letters to Victoria are the first of such letters to follow his experience at Fourth and Walnut Streets in Louisville. The words of Merton's first letters to Victoria echoed the language expressed in his journal entry about his downtown Louisville revelation and demonstrated his desire to establish human connection with like-minded intellectuals: "I assure you of my complete agreement with all that Sur stands for, and my utter 'solidarity' with you. I say this not only as a writer but as a monk, because I realize now more than ever dedication to God in religious life cannot be pretence for attempted evasions, but on the contrary commits a man all the more irrevocably to a position and a witness in the world of this time" (*FR* 59-60). Merton called his first response to this letter, "*un vrai don de dieu*" ("a true gift from God") (*FR* 69).[16] Unfortunately, Victoria's first letters to Merton have not been discovered and likely will not be; yet, a few things are apparent. She was

---

15. Thomas Merton, *The Hidden Ground of Love: The Letters of Thomas Merton on Religious Experience and Social Concerns*, ed. William H. Shannon (New York: Farrar, Straus, Giroux, 1985) 308-24; subsequent references will be cited as "*HGL*" parenthetically in the text.

16. Merton wrote his first letter to Ocampo in English, but wrote most subsequent letters in French as both were fluent in this language; translations from the published letters from French to English are by Mark Meade, with the original texts in the footnotes.

known not to mince words, and Merton asks, "How can I thank you for the simplicity and confidence with which you tell me so frankly what you think?"[17] In her frank response, Victoria seemed to have quickly established a connection with Merton, but she was also clear that Merton's relationship with God and with the institutional Catholic Church differed from her understanding. This seemed evident from Merton's attempts at clarification. He did not back down from his essentially Christian identity as a monk, but, perhaps for the first time, tried to articulate to someone else the unifying vision he had in Louisville:

> [N]ever believe that I am some different being from you because I am here in a very quiet monastery without problems like yours. Much to the contrary, I live in the heart of your problem because I live in the heart of the Church. I do not believe myself truly a monk, or truly a priest, if I were not able to feel in myself all of the revolts and all of the anguish of modern man.[18]

Merton sent two poetic essays with his initial letter, "Prometheus: A Meditation"[19] and what he calls a "statement addressed to intellectuals," which he did not name, but which from the context was likely his "Letter to an Innocent Bystander" (*BT* 51-64), an essay in the form of an open letter. Merton named the intellectual who witnessed violence as an "innocent bystander." Though not the cause of violence, the intellectual was also not ignorant of it, was implicated through shared humanity, and must resist injustice through courageous witness. He included clergy among the bystanders called to bear witness. He would carry this theme into the title and message of his book *Conjectures of a Guilty Bystander* of 1966, the same volume that published his world-affirming revelation at Fourth and Walnut. The monk now not only must recognize the positive aspects of connectivity to the rest of humanity, but he must also implicate himself in the violence of the world and recognize that to be aware of these evils is to be a "guilty bystander." Yet, the intellectual and the monk must respond non-violently.

From available evidence, Victoria was one of the earliest people to

---

17. "Comment vous remercier de la simplicité et de la confiance avec lesquelles vous me dites si franchement ce que vous pensez?" (*FR* 69).

18. "[N]e croyez jamais que je suis un être different de vous, que je suis ici dans un monastère bien tranquille, avec aucun problème comme le vôtre. Bien au contraire, je vis au coeur même de l'Eglise. Je ne me croirais pas vraiment moine, vraiment prêtre, si je n'étais pas capable de sentir en moi même toutes les révoltes et toutes les angoisses de l'homme moderne" (*FR* 70-71).

19. Thomas Merton, *The Behavior of Titans* (New York: New Directions, 1961) 15-23; subsequent references will be cited as "*BT*" parenthetically in the text.

whom Merton had sent "Letter to an Innocent Bystander." It was published the following month in France; Victoria published it in early 1959, it was sent to Czeslaw Milosz for his journal for Polish émigrés later in 1959, and it did not appear in English until 1961. Once again, for Merton, this essay was part of a process of crossing boundaries and forming connections between intellectuals throughout the world. How better to accomplish this than to send it to Victoria because *Sur* was already at the forefront of this process?

The challenge for Merton as a monk was to engage in an authentic dialogue as a person of faith with those, such as Victoria, who may have been drawn to things spiritual, but who operated outside of religious institutions and traditional roles. This was especially true for Merton as a Catholic in dialogue with intellectuals from Latin America, whose struggles with the institutional Church were cast against a history of colonial exploitation. At a meeting of the International Thomas Merton Society in 1995, Miguel Grinberg spoke of how he counseled Merton in his "Message to Poets"[20] to neutralize certain clerical language.[21] Merton was writing this message for a meeting in Mexico City in 1964 of poets, most of whom were from Latin America. Merton went to the extent of signing the piece with a familiar form of his monastic name, Louis, but changing his title from "Father" to "Uncle Louie." In his January 1959 letter to Victoria, Merton was clear that when he speaks to her of God, it was a dialogue, not a sermon, refuting the assumption that by having taken vows or being an ordained cleric, he had all of the answers. If Merton did not already know of Victoria's interest in Tagore, he would have seen in the pages of *Sur* openness to varied religious traditions. We see references to the Buddha and to the *Bhagavad Gita* in the reviews of Merton's books of the 1950s, well before Merton himself had published on traditions of the East.

Merton also sensed that to stand with the intellectual, he had to acknowledge a rift between the secular and religious worlds. He wrote in his first letter, "it seems to me that I am bound, by the circumstances of my own life and background, to do something to heal the prodigious and unpardonable breach that has arisen between the Church and the intellectual world of our time" (*FR* 60). Merton would many times revisit this style of dialogue that he first exhibits with Victoria. Such letters to friends and some writ-

---

20. Thomas Merton, *Raids on the Unspeakable* (New York: New Directions, 1966) 155-61.

21. Miguel Grinberg, "Thomas Merton and the New World Kairos," audio recording from the Fourth General Meeting of the Thomas Merton Society (Boulder, CO: Sounds True Recordings, 1995).

ten as essays in the form of open letters followed the theme of the "guilty bystander," self-inclusion in systems of violence and miscommunication that lead to division. An example is his "Apologies to an Unbeliever" (*FV* 205-14), an attempt at respectful dialogue between the monk and the atheist or agnostic. Another is his "Letters to a White Liberal,"[22] which is addressed to fellow white progressives engaged in the struggle for equal civil rights for black Americans in the United States. Merton claimed that these "white liberals," though viewing themselves as working for a just cause, were undermining equality by their own prejudiced assumptions. Merton was concerned about a subtle condescension that existed among whites that defined equality by unfairly projecting that blacks would need to be recreated in the image of whites to be equal.

Though Victoria clearly identified as a feminist, she was sometimes critical of the movement in a way that resonates with many of today's feminists. Like Merton's "white liberal," she felt that progressive women and their male allies may have hurt the women's movement by expecting that women must become just like men to achieve equality, even taking on many faults inherent to patriarchy. She recognized the liberated woman might lead in different ways than a man in power and might carry herself differently. An expression of this belief was her admiration of business-woman Coco Chanel and the world of high fashion that she revolutionized:

> Although she admired and shared the writer Susan Sontag's positions of the rights of women, Victoria diverged from her North America counterpart with regard to fashion. Sontag maintained that the dictates of style were frivolous, and advised women to stop worrying about their physical appearance. Victoria, in contrast, reflected that 'it would be a shame for them to do away with the spectacle of a well-dressed woman.'[23]

Merton's and Victoria's dialogue did not progress to such a discussion on the topic of feminism, but we can see Merton expressing similar ideas in some of the conferences he gave for religious sisters in 1968. He discussed "The Feminine Mystique" in a conference published posthumously in *Springs of Contemplation*.[24] Despite the title, I do not find evidence he

---

22. Thomas Merton, *Seeds of Destruction* (New York: Farrar, Straus & Giroux, 1964) 3-71; subsequent references will be cited as "*SD*" parenthetically in the text.

23. María Gainza and Ivonne Bordelois, "Villa Ocampo in the Arts: Fashion" (http://www.villaocampo.org/ing/historico/cultura_8.htm [accessed 9/10/2011]).

24. Thomas Merton, *The Springs of Contemplation: A Retreat at the Abbey of Gethsemani*, ed. Jane Marie Richardson, SL (New York: Farrar, Straus, Giroux, 1992) 161-76.

actually read Betty Friedan's book *The Feminine Mystique*, though he may well have known about it. He referred mainly to Mary Daly's book *The Church and the Second Sex*, describing the "feminine mystique" as an idealization of women which also harms them through patriarchal distortion of their true nature.

Of course, it was in a spirit of international solidarity, especially between North and South America, that Merton found some of his truest resonance with Victoria. Both made connections across hemispheric borders and helped foster a sense of unified American identity across continents through literature. As Merton wrote for a commemorative volume about Victoria, "she symbolizes America in the broad sense, the only sense, in which I am proud to be numbered among Americans" (*SD* 284).

The paradox of lives of transcendence, of establishing deep bonds of love which can bring great joy, is the parallel pain when these bonds are severed by death. Merton and Victoria had the ability to realize on an intuitive level a broader perspective on death, not just the negative. Yet, both still felt deeply the pain of their own losses and could empathize with the pain of another. Victoria revealed to Merton the heartache caused by three family deaths. In a letter of July 4, 1959 (not extant), she told Merton of the death by suicide of her niece Angélica Bengolea Ocampo, not yet 32 years of age, whom she called "Bebita." We know only of the letter through Merton's answer. He did not minimize the pain of the loss or claim to be able to explain why suicide or the death of young people happened. Instead, he connected her death to a larger illness shared by humanity. Merton wrote, "everyone, the whole world, is very sick. If Bebita has died, it is because we are all very sick in one way or another."[25] In less than a year, Victoria would lose two sisters. When she informed Merton in December of 1967 of the death of her sister Francisca, she spoke of her sister's long sufferings as a caregiver for her husband contrasted with the mercy of only a brief illness and sudden death. She wrote, "The unexpected death (merciful to her) was cruel for us, for my sisters."[26] The following June another sister died suddenly, Rosa, the mother of the young woman who had committed suicide. Maybe because of Rosa's continued suffering over the loss of her daughter or for other reasons, Victoria again described her death as "merciful." However, this did not diminish her pain. She continued, "Why can we not understand or accept death as

---

25. "Si Bebita est morte, c'est que nous sommes tous malades, d'une façon ou d'une autre" (*FR* 123).

26. "Cette morte imprévue (miséricordieuse pour elle) a été cruelle pour nous, pour mes soeurs" (*FR* 300).

something as natural as birth? It is still incomprehensible and horrible."[27]

Merton was all too familiar with the impact of the death of loved ones, having lost his mother at six and father at fifteen, as well as his brother during the Second World War. Not long after responding to Victoria in her loss, he would depart for a journey to Asia. This trip would be his greatest achievement in his lifelong task of building bridges. This time it was to enter dialogue with the religions of the East. He would speak at an interreligious conference and meet the Dalai Lama. As I mentioned before, transcendence need not imply a severing of one's roots. Merton's embrace of Buddhism did not imply a breaking of ties with his identity as a Christian monk. He had received permission to travel to Asia by his abbot, and while there, he prayed the psalms and celebrated Mass each day.

It was his Asian trip that also brought him face-to-face with the mystery and inevitability of death, both natural and incomprehensible as Victoria described. Just a week before the tragic accident that would take his life, he describes in his Asian journal a powerful experience, maybe as powerful as the one he experienced a decade prior in Louisville, while he visited the Buddha statues of Polonnaruwa in Ceylon.[28]

Facing his death soon after, we will never know if Merton's 1968 revelation at the Buddha statues of Polonnaruwa would have made the same type of transformation in his writings as his 1958 revelation in Louisville. However, I am confident that Victoria would have been a person with whom he could have shared the experience had he returned from Asia—someone who understood transcending the limits of country and culture, and a person who searched for God in novel ways.

In conclusion, Victoria Ocampo and Thomas Merton continue to inform and inspire a broken world, a world in need of wisdom, art and the kind of vision that transcends the differences that cause global unrest. Theirs was also a friendship that could offer mutual support during personal loss. In troubled yet exciting times, Merton and Victoria forged a bond of healing that was, at first, a joy to one another and has now become a gift, or at least the fragments of a gift, for us to piece together. They were the pioneers, but, ultimately, it is up to us to take the fragments they left us and to learn how they can be pieced together in the process of global reconciliation.

---

27. "Pourquoi est-ce qu'on ne peut pas comprendre ni accepter la mort comme une chose aussi naturelle que la naissance? Elle est tourjours incomprehensible et affreuse" (*FR* 306).

28. Thomas Merton, *The Other Side of the Mountain: The End of the Journey. Journals, vol. 7: 1967-1968*, ed. Patrick Hart (San Francisco: HarperCollins, 1998) 321-23.

Merton and Barth in Dialogue
on Faith and Understanding:
A Hermeneutics of Freedom and Ambiguity

Raymond Carr

"I am not a pro." This confession occurred in a letter of Thomas Merton written in 1966 to Rabbi Abraham Joshua Heschel, addressing Merton's ability to persuasively write a book about opening the Bible. In the letter Merton expresses his confusion about the expectations surrounding the writing of the book; he admits his skepticism about the project, especially as it related to the mass-media; and he questions his capacity to write such a text—because as noted, he is "not a pro."[1] His reference to expertise is aimed at the vocation of a "professional biblical scholar." To be sure, it was not unusual for Merton to express his reservations about biblical scholarship; in fact, in the very next year—in a letter to the feminist theologian Rosemary Radford Ruether—he admits to rarely reading much of "the new stuff" about the Bible "because there is just too much."[2]

Merton's overall mind-set in relation to the modern professionalization of biblical scholarship is significant. Indeed, his attitude offers illumination of the theme of this year's Merton Society conference, "Living Together with Wisdom." Merton's posture, especially in dialogue with Karl Barth, arguably the greatest Protestant theologian of the twentieth century, raises important questions about faith and understanding, about *human* wisdom as it relates to opening the Bible. A dialogue between these two theologians privileges unknowing rather than knowing, questions more than answers, and presses us to a dimension of depth, grounding human identity in the faithfulness of God rather than human wisdom in relation to historical complexities. At any rate, I will begin by first addressing the background of my own relationship with Barth and Merton, respectively, in terms of how I discovered these two theologians.

---

1. Thomas Merton, *The Hidden Ground of Love: Letters on Religious Experience and Social Concerns*, ed. William H. Shannon (New York: Farrar, Straus, Giroux, 1985) 435 [12/12/1966 letter to Abraham Joshua Heschel]; subsequent references will be cited as "*HGL*" parenthetically in the text.

2. Thomas Merton and Rosemary Radford Ruether, *At Home in the World: The Letters of Thomas Merton & Rosemary Radford Ruether*, ed. Mary Tardiff (Maryknoll, NY: Orbis, 1995) 17.

First Impressions: Meeting Karl Barth and Thomas Merton

During undergraduate studies at Lubbock Christian University in Texas, I stumbled upon Karl Barth's most famous commentary, *The Epistle to Romans*, a book often described as falling like a "bomb in the playground of the theologians." Even today I cannot recall the degree to which I used his commentary in my paper, but I do remember Barth's unusual style. His book did not read like the typical historico-critical commentary, i.e., like a report. It read like a confession, a witness. Of course it critically engaged the latest historical resources of his day; and he clearly wrote in a way that reflected a critical engagement with the modern church.[3] Still, more delicately, Barth's appeal to historical methodology did not overshadow his appeal to encounter. And gratefully it would not be my only encounter with Barth. Eventually, I wrote a paper called "Karl Barth: The Humble Contributor," with my reference to his humility being in actuality an allusion to Barth's understanding of the theologian as one *set in question* by the *Sache* [subject matter] of the biblical text, which functions as the *terminus a quo* ("the limit from which") of Barth's subsequent thought. The result is that for Barth there are no great theologians. I still remember the response of my professor, who quipped, "German theologians are rarely humble." He had missed a dimension of depth in Barth.

My encounter with Merton followed a similar trajectory. At some point around 2005, I was glancing at books in a used bookstore in Berkeley, California when the spine of *Opening the Bible* caught my attention.[4] During this time, I was an adjunct at Pepperdine University, teaching an introductory Hebrew Bible class and as a result, the problem of an open Bible occupied attention. As I stood there perusing Merton's brief text, an hour or so quickly passed. It was my first introduction to Merton, and I was captivated by his approach. Merton, like Barth, wrote in a confessional way, and his attention to the "implicit contrast between the dry, academic and official learning *about* religion and the living power of the word" (*OB* 9-10) was refreshing to me, and the resonance of that moment remains with me. Moreover, his inviting tone and "unapologetic" style (in the classical sense of apologetics) have a dimension of depth as their pillar, rather than rhetorical flourish or sophisticated arguments. Essentially, Merton's approach reveals his efforts to seriously respond to the *true subject matter* of scripture, focusing on the identity of humanity

---

3. Eberhard Busch, "What Does It Mean for the Christian Church to Confess and to Reject?" *The Princeton Seminary Bulletin* 25.2 (2004) 183.

4. Thomas Merton, *Opening the Bible* (Collegeville, MN: Liturgical Press, 1970); subsequent references will be cited as "*OB*" parenthetically in the text.

as the *terminus ad quem* ("limit to which"). To be sure, his understanding of this "ultimate freedom" which he calls a "non-word" provides not merely the ground and source of humankind's being; it provides the very foundation for Merton's whole approach to biblical spirituality. For Merton the subject matter of scripture, i.e., God, "fills the whole Bible like the smoke that fills Solomon's temple" (*OB* 16). It is this God who lights the spark of identity in human beings.

I soon adopted *Opening the Bible* for my classes at Pepperdine, and as I gained insight into the theology of Barth and Merton, I came to the conclusion that they not only represent the best of post-war theology, but that both theologians promote a theological vision that transcends the impasse between faith and understanding, assenting not merely to a "religious identity" but to an authentic encounter with the word of God. In fact, their theological approach can be properly categorized under the phrase "theological hermeneutics"—being a hermeneutical strategy which takes its cue from the mysterious content of scripture, i.e. "God"—a non-word for Merton and likewise several terms for Barth, including the "third dimension" and the "strange new world, the world of God."[5]

Merton's identification with Barth at this point is not coincidental. In fact, in key sections of *Opening the Bible* Merton draws heavily on Barth, appealing primarily to Barth's early essays called *The Word of God and the Word of Man*—a collection which reveals Barth's effort to establish a sharp distinction between the world of the Bible and human history, morality and religion (see Barth, *Word* 28-50).[6] Theology, understood as an academic science, provides one of the primary polemical contexts for Barth's development and therefore the "strange world" within the Bible—in the minds of those who champion historical critical studies—tacitly makes Barth a so-called enemy of historical studies. In other words, the privileging of God in scripture relativizes human knowing, thus making Barth an enemy. Merton's identification with Barth places him in a similar category. At any rate, Barth's and Merton's approach can be described as a shift from "knowing to unknowing."[7]

---

5. Karl Barth, *The Word of God and Word of Man*, trans. Douglas Horton (Gloucester, MA: Peter Smith, 1978) 32-33, 53; subsequent references will be cited as "Barth, *Word*" parenthetically in the text; see also *OB,* 17, 25-26, 75.

6. See also Eberhard Busch, *Karl Barth: His Life from Letters and Autobiographical Texts*, trans. John Bowden (Philadelphia: Fortress Press, 1994) 100-102.

7. Here I am using the language of knowing as a way of describing Enlightenment rationality which marginalizes the sense of mystery by reducing God in its biblical approach to the treatment of an object.

Pilgrimaging from Knowing to Unknowing

In order to move the reader from knowing to unknowing, Merton appeals to the *Revelatio Dei* which he views as being born out of the deeper concern of the biblical text, being evidenced in invasions, happenings and breakthroughs in a "life-giving power" to our world (see *OB* 8-15). Consequently, Merton understands that the implicit claim of the Bible is to reveal the inexplicable reality of God as the pervasive presence in the Bible and the world (see *OB* 16-17). Merton views the ultimate identity of "God" as being in tension with human beings. For him God sets humanity in question, outstripping our knowing and providing the true ground for humankind's identity. God resists human efforts to use static logic to master or control God as the supreme criterion or content of scripture; God furthermore remains the foundational criterion within the text. Understood this way, Merton's fundamental appeal to the mysterious nature of revelation is the primary reason for his theological dialectics and the inspiration for the sense of *aporia* one experiences when reading in his suggested manner.

The term *aporia*, often used of Plato's writings, especially in the works of Socrates, refers to a type of puzzlement occasioned by the raising of questions or objections without proffering solutions. Merton excels at inviting questions, using various reference points or allusions to raise questions about what it means to open the Bible, being principally concerned with God's answer (or lack thereof), which paradoxically pushes the reader back to the pertinence of his or her questions. (For example, when addressing the "problem of suffering," Merton appeals to the fact that the Bible does not view suffering as a problem.) In this encounter our questions are paradoxically intensified, and Merton aims to bring the reader not merely to a place of doubt, but to the real ground and center of being. In this way, human assurances or certitudes are not in human answers, but ultimately in God's answer. When understood as such, human faith witnesses to the transforming power of God which transcends human ambiguities.

Merton's methodology is in keeping with Barth's theology. In his first essays and earliest cycle of dogmatic theology, Barth argued that humanity must know itself as it is known by God.[8] Indeed, he argued, "there are questions we could not ask if the answers were not already at hand, questions which we could not even approach without the courage

---

8. Karl Barth, *Gottingen Dogmatics*, vol. 1, ed. Hannelotte Reiffen, trans. Geoffrey W. Bromily (Grand Rapids, MI: Eerdmans, 1991) 83; subsequent references will be cited as "Barth, *Gottingen*" parenthetically in the text.

of the Augustinian thought, you would not seek me had you not already found me" (Barth, *Word* 274).[9] Barth's point, akin to Merton's, is to define humanity with reference to knowing God who is already at hand at the beginning of our pursuit of God; thus we can only *ask after* (*nachdenken!*) God while humbly acknowledging our limitations. God has placed humanity in contradiction. God is the first datum, not man.[10] Such a theological approach not only resists the methods of historical-critical scholars, but more importantly it reorients faith to its true ground, i.e., the faithfulness of God. Aporetically, knowledge of God should always be understood as a gift. Human faithfulness, therefore, is not based on objective, abstract knowing, but rather grounded in the faithfulness of God and witnessed in the subjective human response to the Unknown God. The ambiguity of human knowing finds its security in the spiritual framework of this other, and for Merton freedom is found in this tension with God's unlimited freedom. God indeed is the *ultimate root* of human freedom (see *OB* 24, 74).

To be sure, especially in light of Barth's later theology, one can ask if there is any constituent factor which theology should be founded on other than God. Epistemologically, this valorizes a methodological approach and ethics which resist disciplinary restrictions that focus on principles of morality, casuistry or rigid sacramentalism; and it may be the reason many theologians cease following Barth, assuming he sacrifices too much ethically. The truth of the matter is that such ethical disagreement with Barth stems from his view of the *Revelatio Dei*. It is, moreover, this view of divine freedom that sets up the tension with historical-critical studies since Merton and Barth are not seeking an answer (it is at hand); they are responding to it.

Relentless Questioning in a Different Direction

Merton's and Barth's aporetic methodology, or to put it differently, their so-called preoccupation with "unknowing," shapes the whole of their "theological hermeneutics." They offer a challenge to the modern scientific agenda because it moves in the opposite direction. Preconceived, abstract, reductionist or stereotyped readings do not open up to God.

---

9. See also the *Gottingen Dogmatics*, where Barth attributes this statement to Pascal rather than Augustine.

10. See Barth, *Gottingen* 81; see also Karl Barth, *The Holy Spirit and the Christian Life*, trans. R. Birch Hoyle (Louisville, KY: John Knox Press, 1993) 5: in this earlier text Barth engages in dialogue with Catholic thought and uses the language of *dandum* rather than *datum* to reinforce revelation of God as being *from* God to man rather than the other way around; hence knowledge of God always "comes to us" and is not a quality we possess.

Perhaps one could argue that they end up in an anthropological cul-de-sac. Ironically, neither Barth nor Merton is an enemy of historical criticism or philosophy in general, and both engage in biblical thinking without sacrificing historical studies at the altar of naivety, and thus advocating fideism. And while their line and direction challenges historical criticism—because scientific approaches often remain at the level of words, details and surface complexities—the primary goal is to understand faith as taking seriously what Merton calls "the many-dimensional, the paradoxical, the conflicting elements of the Bible as well as those of life itself" (*OB* 59); thus the move to freedom occurs in the direction of what can be described as ambiguity.

Similarly, Barth sought a methodology whereby knowledge of God and knowledge of self could emerge out of the radical openness to the question of God which could not, in his view, be evaded nor settled (see Barth, *Gottingen* 69-76). Even the grand scope of Barth's *Church Dogmatics* can be understood as the *intellectus fidei* of a joyful mind in pursuit of God. Ironically, from the beginning Barth understood historical criticism as a positive development. Historical criticism, in his opinion, could liberate the Church from traditionalism of the past. It was a touchstone in the work of perhaps his most important teacher, Wilhelm Herrmann, to distinguish revelation from tradition; thus faith understood as the transmission of ideas could not bring about genuine religious conviction.[11] For this reason he did not envision critical studies as a pillar for the rise of some type of new liberal tradition.[12] He summed up his attitude toward these studies with one of his more famous quotes among Barth scholars, i.e., "the critical historian needs to be more critical," meaning their questions were not aimed at the question of the text, but born of some other concern.[13] Unfortunately, Barth's emphasis led many historico-critical scholars to see him as an "enemy of historical criticism."[14] As Eberhard Jüngel points out, Barth's metacritical approach was the declaration of

---

11. Karl Barth, "Principles of Dogmatics According to Wilhelm Hermman," *Theology and Church: Shorter Writings 1920-1928*, trans. Louise P. Smith (New York: Harper & Row, 1962) 248; subsequent references will be cited as "Barth, *Theology*" parenthetically in the text.

12. Karl Barth, *Revolutionary Theology in the Making: Barth-Thurneysen Correspondence—1914-1925*, trans. James D. Smart (Richmond, VA: John Knox Press, 1964) 36.

13. Karl Barth, *The Epistle to the Romans*, trans. Edwyn C. Hoskyns (London: Oxford University Press, 1957) 8; subsequent references will be cited as "Barth, *Romans*" parenthetically in the text.

14. See Barth's discussion of this problem in "The Preface to the Second Edition" of *The Epistle to the Romans* 6-13.

a hermeneutical criterion and many viewed it as a declaration of war.[15] Their attacks, to be sure, concealed the modern preoccupation with historical reconstruction and vapid scientific investigations, rather than an authentic concern for living faith.

This difference opens up one way of thinking about the relationship between freedom and ambiguity. For ambiguity is often spoken of as deprecation, as loss; however, this distinction misses both Barth's and Merton's way of understanding human existence. Following Merton, ambiguity is not a weakness; it is a site for learning to live. In this way, even mythopoetic sections of the biblical text—often ignored, dismissed or marginalized by many historical scholars—offer profound insight into human life, differing from more discursive modalities. The philosopher Hans-Georg Gadamer argues that the poet and prophet illuminate truth in a way which honors the imagination and transcends the limitations of our more technical and critical ways of knowing. Gadamer further writes, "it is not the weakness, but the strength of the oracle that it is ambiguous."[16] In this regard, poetic, prophetic and paradoxical modes of thought open one up to life, outstripping final answers. Such imaginative literature is observed, for instance, in the apocalyptic imagery in the Book of Revelation. This type of language resists our attempts to capture God, language which beckons us to use the imagination.

Understood this way, ambiguity can complement a movement of a thinker who revels in a questioning posture, not a posture open towards nothing, but a questioning posture—a life, a person who radically opens up to God, responding to God's answer which is already present in the beauty and the ambiguity of life. Such ambiguity, when attended properly, both conceals and reveals something deeper about humanity that moves beyond the mundane and moves in the direction of our deeper ground.

Merton, in keeping with Barth, expresses a concern for this inner meaning of the text. Understood in a more remote twentieth-century context, Merton's approach corresponds to "dialectical theologians," including Barth, Rudolf Bultmann, Paul Tillich, Friedrich Gogarten, Emil Brunner and others.[17] Barth arguably was simply its most prolific spokesperson. So methodologically, then, Merton properly belongs in continuity with the early dialectical school of theology since he too dis-

---

15. Eberhard Jüngel, *Karl Barth: A Theological Legacy* (Philadelphia: Westminster Press, 1986) 71.

16. Hans-Georg Gadamer, *Truth and Method*, trans. Joel Weinsheimer and Donald G. Marshall (New York: Crossroad, 1988) 444.

17. See James M. Robinson, ed., *The Beginnings of Dialectic Theology*, vol. 1, trans. Keith R. Crim and Louis De Grazia (Richmond, VA: John Knox Press, 1968).

tinguishes the first, more superficial level of reading—concerned with objective knowledge—from the deeper more personal level of encounter of the "*inner content* which challenges the reader and demands of him a personal engagement, a decision and commitment of his freedom, a judgment regarding an ultimate question" (*OB* 61; emphasis added). He correctly perceived that "the passage to personal relatedness and insight" (*OB* 62) is at the heart of what it means to open the Bible. Consequently, as we shall see in the next section, Merton explicitly addresses the inner life, and he does so in a much more direct way than Barth, who uses more of an oblique style.

Nevertheless, both Barth and Merton desire to question the text in the way that acknowledges the limits of their personal readings. Barth in fact called for a "wider intelligence than that which moves within the boundaries of [one's] own natural appreciation" (Barth, *Romans* 8). Their obtuseness to this limitation, in Barth's opinion, was part of the problem with historical scholars who gave short shrift to the biblical text. Barth sought something deeper by which to be "driven on till I stand with nothing before me but the enigma of the matter; till the document seems hardly to exist as a document" (Barth, *Romans* 8).

Merton actualizes it through his interlocutors in the world of the 1960s. By engaging in such dialogue Merton amplifies the sense of *aporia* one can experience when truly encountering the Christ-self. In other words, he demonstrates the relatedness of God to all things by increasing the range of his conversation partners. Merton does this by referencing *here* and *there,* appealing to Protestants, Catholics, agnostics, Marxists, Zen Buddhists, Taoists, literary scholars, philosophers, historians of religion, filmmakers and of course theologians (Barth, Bultmann, Bonheoffer) *et al.* His liberal appeal is in keeping with his understanding of the world in the 1960s.[18] In fact *Opening the Bible* models the same theological underpinning and conversational intent as *Conjectures of a Guilty Bystander,* where Merton described his writing as an implicit dialogue with other minds, a dialogue which consummates in a more authentic identity.

In short, Merton's redundant appeal to various "dialogue partners" in *Opening the Bible* functions in two ways. First, it implicates the reader in life itself, serving to reinforce the relatedness of the Bible to the world and the world to the Bible. He even writes, "The Bible is a 'worldly' book" (*OB* 55), meaning that God is at the center of human life and not at the periphery. The periphery is the place of idols. Abstract intellectual

---

18. See Thomas Merton, *Conjectures of a Guilty Bystander* (Garden City, NY: Doubleday, 1966) v; subsequent references will be cited as "*CGB*" parenthetically in the text.

knowledge of God overlooks the reader's mental impositions on the biblical text and often functions idolatrously, isolating the reader from her or his true center—and from the world in which s/he lives. Thus Merton's methodology unmasks modern thinking for its versatile attempts to master the contents of scripture, leading many readers to become "lords of the word." Merton, by contrast, can ultimately be interpreted as attempting to free the Bible from our feigned control. And allow me to only whisper this next statement: *I think Merton is deeply suspicious of our wisdom.*

Merton's suspicion of course is not aimed at divorcing man from his questions. They are designed to encourage encounter which is beyond the "surface of the Bible" toward a deeper identification with God. When the reader moves beyond the surface s/he is "no longer simply questioning the book but being questioned by it" (*OB* 18). So, here again Merton presses us in a paradoxical direction toward the true ground of being, and naturally for Merton, a more rich, more robust and more imaginative faith does not occur by fetishizing or escaping the biblical text, but rather by attending to it with openness and refusing to allow a substitute ground for God; thus for Merton religious understanding thrives on imaginative encounter born of life's real questions. He states this succinctly: "In the progress toward religious understanding, one does not go from answer to answer but from question to question. One's questions are answered, not by clear, definitive answers, but by more pertinent and more crucial questions" (*OB* 19-20). Hence, only hearts open to crucial questions experience what Merton believes is the fundamental aim of Bible, "a full realization of our own identity" (*OB* 20).

From Unknowing to Knowing (Oneself)

As stated, criticism of various methodological approaches to the Bible is not the primary aim of Merton's or Barth's theological hermeneutics. Merton's goal, observed in the redundancy of his explanations as to what it means to open the Bible, is seen in his emphasis on *identity*. He wants to challenge readers to own up to their finitude and respond to the deeper ground of their freedom (see *OB* 20). Of course this would reorient and redefine what we mean by freedom. Moreover, to an audience like the one in the 1960s, experiencing one of the more turbulent periods in American history, freedom would resonate deeply with their needs and concerns, and Merton would also demonstrate that the Bible is a book fundamentally concerned with the world. And for Merton the problem of identity occurs in several places with the first concern being his effort to connect his vocation more deeply to the social reality. "[D]o not expect to find 'my answers.' I do not have clear answers to current questions. I do have questions, and, as a matter of fact, I think a man is known better by his questions than by his answers. To make known one's questions is, no doubt, to come out in the open oneself" (*CGB* v). "Coming out in the open" seems to be one of the primary reasons for Merton's approach to the Bible. In fact, his questioning posture juxtaposed with his understanding of the Bible as "worldly book" is a critique of a type of "unworldly" faith which would relegate God to some ethereal place in the great beyond. By contrast, Merton emphasizes that God is the "very ground of our existence and reality." God, moreover, is neither dismissive of the world nor interested in endorsing an easy conformity to the world. Of course this argument would fit Merton's profound interest in the Bible being a *transforming agent* and the recognition of the word of God thereby. The transforming message of the biblical text would therefore resist substitutes, including morality, aesthetics, philosophical-ethical systems and even religion (see *OB* 57-58).[19] It seems that Merton is not merely concerned with "coming out in the open," but he is concerned with coming to oneself seen in having one's identity truly wrapped up in God (see *OB* 57).

Merton epitomizes this openness in how he understands the vocation of the monk. For him the vocation of the monk did not place the "contemplative" on a higher level than others, "elevating him [or her] to a privileged state among the spiritually pure, as if he were almost an angel, untouched by matter and passion, and no longer familiar with the economy of sacraments, charity and the Cross."[20] To the contrary the life of the contemplative implicates one even more deeply in the world. In Merton's case his vocation represented a paradoxical turn. Thomas Merton, this man of the world, an artist, a writer, impetuous, urbane, and even, arguably, worldly, actualizes his identity as a Trappist monk, constantly breaking new ground while submitting himself to the careful advice of his abbot, of course.

Barth also privileges the fundamental human situation. Being profoundly aware of the dilemma of the subjective, modern mind of the nineteenth century, God's freedom in revelation coincides with Barth's later emphasis on theology as a form of theoanthropology.[21] In using this language, Barth aims at understanding humanity in light of revelation.

---

19. See also *OB* 74-79 for a lengthy discussion of religion and Merton's justification for why he attends to religion as closely as he does.

20. Merton mentions this in several places. See for example Thomas Merton, *Contemplative Prayer* (New York: Herder & Herder, 1969) 25.

21. Karl Barth, *Introduction to Evangelical Theology* (Grand Rapids, MI: Eerdmans, 1963) 12.

Christ is understood as being deeply connected to the world of man. As a result theology transcends human dichotomies and false identifications which abstractly distort the relationship between God, the world and humanity. In Barth's words such a view of God is "unionistic," witnessing to deeper unity between us and God:

> Christomonism would mean that Christ alone is real and that all other men are only apparently real. But that would be in contradiction with what the name of Jesus-Christ means, namely, union between God and man. This union between God and man has not been made only in Jesus Christ but in him as our representative for the benefit of all men. Jesus Christ as God's servant is true God and true man, but at the same time also our servant and the servant of all men.[22]

Barth to be sure emphasized what he described as a Christological concentration. Revelation and the world are not false alternatives. God understood in this way becomes free for the world, speaking a "yes" in a mystery at the heart of the world—understood as promise.[23] Ironically, Barth articulated the relationship between God and the world through natural theology, the view he was often accused of rejecting. In Barth's view, however, natural theology (*theologia naturalis*) must be understood in light of revelation (*theologia revelata*). As a result, God's claim on humanity is not determined by the fallenness of the world or by what Merton may term the "shallow self, the ego-self" (*OB* 70). To the contrary God affirms human "life in communion with himself [God]."[24] In sum for Barth, Christ's universal Lordship provides the center and ground of the external world and therefore he understood himself as offering a "more natural theology" which of course has implications for how one understands nation, culture and race.[25]

In Barth's understanding the whole world is charged with the potential to be a witness to the glory of God. As a matter of fact, we should never reduce "what God can do" to what the Church itself is commissioned to do.[26] The freedom of the word of God opens up to the world in a way that transcends the borders of the Church. Barth, of course, develops this understanding more fully in his discussion of revelation, where he appeals repeatedly to the word of God *extra muros ecclesiae* [outside the

---

22. Karl Barth, "A Theological Dialogue," *Theology Today* 19.2 (1962) 172.

23. Karl Barth, "Church and Culture" (Barth, *Theology* 343-44).

24. Karl Barth, "Church and Culture" (*Theology* 342-43).

25. Eberhard Jüngel, *Christ, Justice and Peace: Toward a Theology of the State*, trans. D. Bruce Hamill and Alan J. Torrance (Edinburgh: T & T Clark, 1992) 26-27.

26. Karl Barth, *Church Dogmatics* (London: T & T Clark, 1975) I.1, 54.

walls of the Church]. This appeal is deeply reminiscent of Merton's own concern for spirituality understood as *le point vierge* [the virgin point], a point described by Merton as "never at our disposal" (*CGB* 142).

And while Barth's description of the freedom of God can be interpreted as giving way to radical political dimensions of God in relation to the world—since the free God transcends the limitations of humanity—his theology (in light of the subjectivism) also represents a more objective view of God's "otherness." Merton, by contrast, identifies God more closely to the inner subjective world of humanity, describing God as the ultimate center of our being. He nevertheless still speaks of God in a way that preserves God's mystery, which of course can be interpreted as the preservation of transcendence since God is beyond the fractured nature of our illusions and the dominance of our will (see *CGB* 142). For me Merton indeed raises an important question. Should we view Merton as offering in fact a pneumatological theology, a theology of the Holy Spirit which offers a Catholic answer to a Protestant dilemma? Is Merton's theology the answer to subjectivism?

Solidarity with the Godless

At any rate, both Barth and Merton point to a transcendent reality which transcends even the unbelief of humanity. And when understood in this way I realized I missed a dimension of depth in Merton since for many years, when teaching Merton's concession to non-believers in his little book, I assumed his position was based solely on the unbeliever's willingness to wrestle with the text; or the unbeliever's "honest disagreement" versus the believer's "dishonest submission."[27] However, no matter what one thinks about honest disagreement this position simply places the believer and unbeliever in a kind of competition with one another. While the unbeliever may demonstrate a greater freedom in reading, the Bible has as its ground the free God who claims all human beings. I have since come to the conclusion that the deeper impetus behind Merton's solidarity with unbelievers, an attitude most clearly expressed in Merton's usage of thinkers "outside the framework of official belief" (including Pasolini, the Marxist filmmaker, and Erich Fromm, the agnostic psychoanalyst) is the *Revelatio Dei*. To be sure, Merton agreed with Fromm's contention that there is "an unconscious faith in God which you might find in the atheist and an unconscious lack of faith which you might find in a practicing Catholic" (*HGL* 320). He even concedes that the priest has to contend with this, both in others and in him or herself. However, in Merton's view we all rely on "the Holy Spirit's action and grace, which keep working to

---

27. "The Bible prefers honest disagreement to a dishonest submission" (*OB* 34).

break the institutional crust" (*HGL* 321 [10/8/1963]). Certainly, if God is ready to break the ecclesiastical crust of the believer, God must also be working in the crusty soil of the non-believer!?!

Here Merton's fondness for Barth is perhaps more evident than anywhere else. Since Barth is often mistakenly understood as an exclusivist, it comes as a surprise (perhaps it should not) that Merton recognizes this intuition in Barth's theology. And Merton was so impressed he writes in *Conjectures* that "this is one of the great intuitions of Protestantism" (*CGB* 303), and knowing Merton the question of solidarity with the world was not simply a central motivation for his vocation, but central to his reasons for writing *Opening the Bible*, accenting the reading of nonbelievers. Considering the world of the 1960s and even the great exodus from the Church during that time Merton is again bringing perspective to the world, and he uses what he considers to be "one of the central intuitions of evangelical Christianity" to do it (*CGB* 304). In following this direction Merton echoes Barth's emphasis on a "provisional" or "virtual" brother, rather than an anonymous Christian. Barth's intuition here is that "every man [person] has his destiny in Christ"[28] and that in pointing this out he is "not telling him anything new or remote but something familiar and close, something that is already his" (Barth, *Gottingen* 84-85). Merton of course articulates a similar concern: "I honestly think that there *is* a presence of Christ to the unbeliever, especially in our day, and that this presence, which is not formally 'religious' and which escapes definition (hence the inadequacy of terms like 'invisible church' or 'latent church'), *is perhaps the deepest most cogent mystery of our time*" (*CGB* 297-98).

In conclusion, especially at this point Merton raises the specter of his relationship to Karl Barth, and it is clear that he appeals to Barth in a way which demonstrates a profound familiarity and appreciation for Barth's theology. He expresses very clearly his "fondness for Barth," despite his arguments that Bonheoffer is perhaps closer to the Catholic viewpoint. And at every point we have discussed above—from the word of God as the beginning of our knowing to the move toward identity—Thomas Merton identifies with Karl Barth. Even when addressing our solidarity with the godless, Merton appeals to Barth's theology. What do we learn from Merton? While this certainly does not mean Merton had an inordinate dependence on Barth, it should encourage us to think more deeply about the impasse that separates Catholics and Protestants. Perhaps what Merton and Barth are teaching us—especially about faith and understanding—is that we should move not only beyond the subjective and objective

---

28. See *Karl Barth's Table Talk*, recorded and edited by John D. Godsey, *Scottish Journal of Theology Occasional Papers* 10 (Edinburgh: Oliver and Boyd, 1963) 14-16.

dichotomy that plagues our theology, but that we should surrender to the ground, source and center of reality and turn to God as the gateway for us all. It is in such *faith* that we transcend human fragmentations and violences; it is in such *understanding* that we transcend human certitudes and authorities; and it is in such *freedom* that we transcend ambiguities and immaturity. *Hominum Confusione et Dei Providentia Regitur!*

2012 Bibliographic Review Essay
Thomas Merton, Escape Artist

David Joseph Belcastro

"In times like these, escape is the only way
to stay alive and keep dreaming."

Henry Laborit

Introduction

I first came upon the above quotation by Laborit while viewing *Mediterraneo*. The film opens with this line as an epigraph providing the viewer with a particular focus on the story that follows. Gabriele Salvatores' antiwar film takes place on a Greek island where a unit of Italian soldiers find refuge after their ship is sunk by the British during the Second World War. As the line suggests, their escape from the insanity of war brings them to a place where life is restored, the deepest dimensions of human experience are explored, and the lives of men and villagers are allowed to naturally flourish.

It so happened that the viewing of this film and my reading of Charles Taylor's *A Secular Age* converged, and in such a way to suggest the title and composition of this essay. Taylor views the modern world as "the final triumph of the Hollow Men, who, knowing the price of everything and the value of nothing, had lost the ability to *feel* or *think* deeply about anything." That loss, he believes, contributed significantly to the construction of flat societies that are "confining, even stifling" of human life. All this, Taylor points out, eventually "led some prominent converts to break out of it." He identifies two of those converts: Thomas Merton and Jacques Maritain.[1]

This "breaking out" eventually became the hallmark of Merton's vocation. Consequently, it is appropriate to post the line from Laborit as an epigraph to this essay, thereby providing the reader with a perspective on the books under review in this volume of *The Merton Annual* and briefly noted here. These books published in 2012 address various aspects of Merton's escape from the multiple confinements that incarcerate the human spirit.

We begin with Merton's formation as a monk and author. For Merton

---

1. Charles Taylor, *A Secular Age* (Cambridge, MA: Harvard University Press, 2007) 734.

the work of prayer and writing drew upon three commitments: the tradition of the Roman Catholic Church, the current affairs of the modern world and his formation as a Trappist monk in that world.[2] With the new publications of Merton's talks and essays on contemplation, as well as articles that clarify his relation to the world, we are invited to consider the nature and purpose of his unique vocation. Even though his interior life was formed in the silence and solitude of a monastic tradition, his work took place in collaboration with men and woman outside and far beyond the cloistered walls of the abbey. We once again find an interesting collection of publications that focus on friends with whom Merton shared the search for freedom, friendships that formed a solidarity of resistance and hope for a new world. Next, we turn to two publications that represent two of the many confinements from which Merton escaped—the emerging age of technology and the well-established puritanical world of porn.[3] In neither case do we find a rejection of either modern technology or human sexuality. On the contrary, Merton's escape is never simply an escape *from* confinement but an escape *to* new possibilities in which the human spirit is free to thrive. Finally, one last work represents a genre often overlooked: compilations of Merton texts can be too easily dismissed as simply that and nothing more. *Precious Thoughts* provides an opportunity to reappraise our opinion of "fabricated" books. Here we find a publication that continues Merton's legacy of integrating past traditions with concerns for the modern world and the formation of interior life—*our* interior lives as each of us searches for the freedom that is necessary for living authentically.

Formation

Oscar Wilde wrote, "Nothing that is worth knowing can be taught." While the statement strikes one as true, it raises questions regarding the vocation of teaching. What is intended when a person assumes the role of teacher in a classroom? What is considered worth knowing? What kind of knowing is implied? Clearly for Wilde it is more than the transmission of information from teacher to student. Perhaps Wilde is suggesting that true learning occurs only when the inquiry is *shared* by both teacher and student, in such a way that both are opened to discovering in their own

---

2. See Thomas Merton, *No Man Is an Island* (New York: Harcourt, Brace, 1955) xiv.

3. "Puritanical world of porn" refers to the state of sexuality in today's world. It is the result of a puritanical understanding of sex as "unclean" and the porn industry's response to market demands, albeit hidden, for "dirty" sex books and films. In other words, sexuality in the modern world has been ill-defined and significantly limited by the convergence of these two opposing forces.

experiences that which is worth knowing. As one listens to Merton's talks on old cassette tapes or new CDs[4] or reads the six volumes of notes for those talks, one immediately recognizes that Merton's integrated approach to teaching flows out of his experience with religious traditions, sacred and secular texts and the contemplative life. Thus the talks represent both his gift to others and his own inquiry, an inquiry that was less about information and more about formation, his own and that of those he addressed.

Patrick O'Connell has committed his fine skills and comprehensive knowledge of Merton to the daunting task of editing Merton's monastic conferences. During the past decade, O'Connell has edited five volumes of talks on initiation into the monastic tradition.[5] In 2012, Cistercian Publications released the sixth volume, *The Life of the Vows*.[6] While previous volumes in this series provide readers an opportunity to observe the pastoral concern of Merton at work as spiritual master and teacher, this new addition to the series underscores the importance of vows that shaped not only the lives of the monks under his care but Merton's vocation and perspective on the world he sought to serve. Even though the talks represent a pre-Vatican II understanding of monasticism, they are nonetheless of importance to both scholars and general readers of Merton.

This valuable contribution to the Merton corpus offers scholars notes previously unpublished. The indices are a helpful aid to researchers who hope to gain a true, deep and multifaceted understanding of Merton's thoughts on issues ranging from *abandonment* to *Zebedee, sons of*. Merton's threefold commitment to the ancient traditions of the Roman Catholic Church, the cultural and religious diversity of the contemporary world and the formation of persons in Christ prepared to serve that world is most evident in these notes that represent dedicated hours of preparation. And

---

4. See the review by Patrick O'Connell of the recent release of CDs by Now You Know Media in this volume of *The Merton Annual*.

5. See Thomas Merton, *Cassian and the Fathers: Initiation into the Monastic Tradition*, ed. Patrick F. O'Connell, Monastic Wisdom [MW] vol. 1 (Kalamazoo, MI: Cistercian Publications, 2005); Thomas Merton, *Pre-Benedictine Monasticism: Initiation into the Monastic Tradition 2*, ed. Patrick F. O'Connell, MW 9 (Kalamazoo, MI: Cistercian Publications, 2006); Thomas Merton, *An Introduction to Christian Mysticism: Initiation into the Monastic Tradition 3*, ed. Patrick F. O'Connell, MW 13 (Kalamazoo, MI: Cistercian Publications, 2008); Thomas Merton, *The Rule of Saint Benedict: Initiation into the Monastic Tradition 4*, ed. Patrick F. O'Connell, MW 19 (Collegeville, MN: Cistercian Publications, 2009); Thomas Merton, *Monastic Observances: Initiation into the Monastic Tradition 5*, ed. Patrick F. O'Connell, MW 25 (Collegeville, MN: Cistercian Publications, 2010).

6. Thomas Merton, *The Life of the Vows: Initiation into the Monastic Tradition 6*, ed. Patrick F. O'Connell, MW 30 (Collegeville, MN: Cistercian Publications, 2012); subsequent references will be cited as *"LV"* parenthetically in the text.

of course, the notes witness to his impressive capacity to think deeply about everything, questioning everything, and thereby cultivating within his students the growth and formation needed for their lives as monks.

This formation is of both private and public significance. Each monk accepts these vows in the solitude of a monastic cell for the purpose of restoring an authentic identity in the divine image. While this is done alone, the intention of the vows is not confinement from the world but freedom to love the world. That is to say, the vows are the disciplines necessary to escape the binding vices that imprison the human spirit and thereby prevent a virtuous life from flourishing in the freedom of God's grace. It is on this point that the importance of this book for the general reader becomes clear. Inside or outside the monastery, the task of and obstacles to formation in Christ is an ever-present challenge. This Merton knew and appreciated. Consequently, his vocation required him to climb over the walls of his own monastic enclosure to assist laypersons in their lives in Christ. Resisting those who believed that the contemplative life was limited to a select few, Merton's instructions on formation became public, his pastoral concern for restoring our true identity in Christ became public, his call to life emancipated from the seemingly endless entrapments of the world became public. Of course, we must keep in mind the original audience of these particular talks, i.e. cloistered monks. Even so, we will find in these notes moments when Merton's voice extends beyond a classroom in the monastery on a given day:

> the religious state is one in which men and women give themselves exclusively to the love and service of God, in lives totally impregnated with prayer and sacrifice. There are many different kinds of religious observance—some active, some contemplative, some apostolic; all have this in common—that they are consecrated to God exclusively and permanently and that this consecration is offered predominantly in a spirit of sacrifice and prayer, and the ones who are thus called seek to make themselves perfect in the friendship of God by love. (*LV* 107)

As we move on to the next two books under consideration, a passage by Merton included at the outset of *On Christian Contemplation* provides a link to the previous paragraph. Merton writes:

> Can contemplation still find a place in the world of technology and conflict which is ours? Does it belong only to the past? The answer to this is that, since the direct and pure experience of reality in its ultimate root is man's deepest need, contemplation must be possible if man is to remain human. If contemplation is no longer possible,

then man's life has lost the spiritual orientation upon which everything else—order, peace, happiness, sanity—must depend. But
true contemplation is an austere and exacting vocation. Those who
seek it are few and those who find it fewer still. Nevertheless, their
presence [bears] witness to the fact that contemplation remains both
necessary and possible.[7]

On Christian Contemplation and *On Eastern Meditation*[8] are compilations of Merton's thoughts on the nature and purpose of contemplation in
the modern world and the importance of being open to the wisdom that
is offered by Eastern traditions on meditation. Together, they represent
an important aspect of Merton's endeavor to scale the walls of history
that separate East and West. While one may rightfully read these books
as meditations on prayer, at a deeper level they represent Merton's endeavor to liberate humankind from those destructive conflicts that divide
humanity into opposing camps. Along with his Asian pilgrimage, these
writings witness to his commitment to unite within himself every division
within the world and thereby awaken within humanity an awareness of
the contemplative dimension wherein is discovered the essential oneness
of all humanity in the Hidden Ground of Love.

One might ask, is there anything new here? Bonnie Thurston, editor
of *On Eastern Meditation*, expresses some reservations regarding the
compiling of excerpts out of context, but finds reassurance in remembering Merton's similar practice in *The Wisdom of the Desert*, *Gandhi on
Non-Violence* and *The Way of Chuang Tzu* (xvi). Even so, the weaving
together of texts can be something of a challenge to the reader. As Mark
Meade notes in his review of these two books published in this volume
of *The Merton Annual*, there is some frustration with and slight confusion
from constantly looking up the references when one is interested in the
original context of the passage. These concerns are of course valid. There
is, however, another way to approach these books. Recall for example that
The Rule of St. Benedict is a compilation. This is also true for *Patanjali's
Yoga Sutras*. While weaving together texts from the past, both composi-
tions stand on their own and have provided an invaluable service to the
life of various religious communities throughout history. These were texts
that drew on collective wisdom of the past with the intention of creating
a text that would engage new generations in the ongoing exploration of

---

7. Thomas Merton, *On Christian Contemplation* edited with a preface by Paul M.
Pearson (New York: New Directions, 2012) 5.

8. Thomas Merton, *On Eastern Meditation* edited with an introduction by Bonnie
Thurston (New York: New Directions, 2012).

the spiritual dimensions of the human experience.

Could the same be said of these two publications? I believe so. First, they are skillfully edited. In other words, neither is simply a filing of Merton excerpts with little or no attention to the overall composition. Pearson's and Thurston's arrangements, while different, are carefully crafted. Since both editors provide clear explanations of their formats in the introductions, I will say nothing more here other than to stress the importance of taking the time to understand and appreciate the *new* approaches to and presentations of Merton's thoughts on contemplation. Even though there is something new here, it is important to underscore a second point. Both books were edited by scholars who know their Merton. In other words, the works are, from an academic point of view, solid. There is no misrepresentation of Merton's thought. On the contrary, I imagine that Merton would recognize in Pearson and Thurston kindred souls with whom he shares much in common. There is one significance difference, however, between the editors and Merton. So a third point: the times have changed. While both editors are committed to the Merton legacy, they are also concerned with a new generation that may find in Merton what they need to live the Christian life in the twenty-first century. As Pearson explains, the purpose of *On Christian Contemplation*

> is to encourage the reader on their spiritual journey and, for those new to the work of Thomas Merton, to open up some of the insights of this modern spiritual master. It should not be read as a manual or textbook on the life of prayer but as a "primer" on meditation and contemplation to be read, as Merton himself suggests, "quietly" and "in such a way that when you get something to chew on you stop and chew" in the manner of *lectio divina*, spiritual reading. (xiv)

These are books for the *new monastics* seeking guidance for their journeys in an age of revolutionary change. As such, they contribute to the Merton legacy by addressing the question raised above by Merton in the affirmative: "Can contemplation still find a place in the world of technology and conflict which is ours?"

As noted previously in this essay, it is impossible to address Merton's formation of young monks and laypersons without becoming aware that we are also observing the formation of his vocation. **Thomas Merton: Monk on the Edge**,[9] co-edited by Ross Labrie and Angus Stuart, presents various perspectives on Merton's vocation that converge to highlight his place in the modern world. For Merton to be fully appreciated and

---

9. *Thomas Merton: Monk on the Edge* edited by Ross Labrie and Angus Stuart (North Vancouver, BC: Thomas Merton Society of Canada, 2012).

understood it is necessary to clarify the location and importance of his hermitage, a hermitage that now transcends the monastic grounds of the Abbey of Gethsemani and thereby serves the world in a way recognized, obscurely perhaps, on the edge. What that means becomes clear as one reads through the Introduction, ten articles and concluding Afterword. Each piece reveals a different insight into Merton's view of the world from the edge, a view that is desperately needed as humanity finds its way into a new millennium.

Paul Dekar's article entitled "Technology and the Loss of Paradise" begins by focusing attention on Merton's hermitage. For Merton, Dekar explains, "The hermitage was paradise on earth where he could recover his truest personhood" (65). If viewed in light of Ross Labrie's Introduction to this volume, it is clear that the hermitage was also a breaking out of the institutional inertia of Christianity that affirmed rather than challenged the status quo of the modern world (9). The juxtaposition of these two images, paradise on earth and breaking out, may seem at first glance contrary to everything that we know about Merton. Even so, it is a common misunderstanding of monks and hermits as individuals who create a paradise of their own in an effort to escape the harsh realities of this world. This, however, is not the case with Merton. *Thomas Merton: Monk on the Edge* corrects this misunderstanding and thereby establishes the need for monks and hermits who live on the edge. Merton's flight from the world to this remote location was not a withdrawal from society and its problems but was rather intended, as Michael Higgins points out in his article entitled "Prophecy and Contemplation," to bring something to the world that was missing.

The issues facing the modern world are sufficiently complex and perplexing to require an outsider's perspective. The hermitage provided that. Within the walls of this cinderblock building, Merton's interest in the world expanded, rather than contracted. As one simply scans the titles of the articles in this collection, one becomes aware of a monk whose years as a student at Columbia University situated him, as Stuart's article on "Merton and the Beats" points out, within the counter-culture movement of the Beats. While Merton's road trip from New York stopped at Gethsemani, he would eventually make the pilgrimage to City Lights Bookstore in San Francisco. Consequently, we should not be surprised to find on the bookshelf in the hermitage works by Albert Camus, a writer greatly respected by Merton and the Beats. Labrie's article entitled "Merton on Atheism in Camus" shows the seriousness with which Merton wrestled with the theological turmoil of the 1960s that drew into question the existence of God. What more needs to be said? This paradise on earth was a busy place. Ron Dart's

"Peacemaker," Ryan Scrugg's "Merton and Interreligious Dialogue" and Dekar's already mentioned article on technology reveal the hermitage as a center for interreligious dialogue, an observation post for environmental studies and a retreat house for peace activists.

The root cause of the problems facing the modern world is to be found in the heart of humanity. To address these problems, a person is required who understands what troubles the human spirit. Merton's life formed by the *Rule* of Benedict provided this. And it was a perspective of the world gained from years of discipline that he brought to the world. His vision, mystical and apocalyptic, provides a way out of the prison the modern world created for itself. It is a vision of the world redeemed in Christ. That vision is skillfully teased out by Michael Higgin in "Prophecy and Contemplation," Susan McCaslin in "Merton's Mystical Visions: a Widening Circle," Bruce Ward in "Apocalypse and Modernity," Donald Grayston in "Merton in Asia: The Polonnaruwa Illumination" and Lynn Szabo in "The Mystical Ecology of Merton's Poetics."

Collaborators

Merton's attempts to escape were executed in collaboration with accomplices who also sought freedom. At the center of this endeavor was his capacity for deep and abiding friendships. The opening articles and interview in this volume of *The Merton Annual* bring to our attention the friendship that existed between Merton and James Laughlin. This and other relationships were personally important for Merton and essential to his intention to find an authentic way of *being* in the modern world. As Merton explains in a letter to Czeslaw Milosz dated May 21, 1959:

> as far as solidarity with other people goes, I am committed to nothing except a very simple and elemental kind of solidarity, which is perhaps without significance politically, but which is I feel the only kind which works at all. That is to pick out the people whom I recognize in a crowd and hail them and rejoice with them for a moment that we speak the same language. Whether they be communists or whatever else they may be. Whatever they may believe on the surface, whatever may be the formulas to which they are committed. I am less and less worried by what people say or think they say: and more and more concerned with what they and I are able to be.[10]

The publications noted below draw our attention to persons with whom Merton found a "simple and elemental kind of solidarity." These friend-

10. *Striving Towards Being: The Letters of Thomas Merton and Czeslaw Milosz* edited with an introduction by Robert Faggen (New York: Farrar, Straus, Giroux, 1997) 40.

ships not only enriched his life but indicate the crossing of social and religious divisions. This statement needs qualification. You will notice that one of the reviews includes a person Merton never met. I will return to this point at the end of this essay when we consider another book in which we are able to observe the ongoing collaboration of Merton with "friends" he would never meet. Perhaps death is another confinement from which it can be said Merton escaped?

   Thomas Merton and Thérèse Lentfoehr: The Story of a Friendship[11] and ***Denise Levertov: A Poet's Life***[12] are new additions to the publications regarding Merton's relations with women. While the first book is, as the title indicates, a story of their friendship, the second focuses on Levertov's life with only four references to Merton. Even so, it is clear that both women contributed in various ways to Merton's life and work. Lentfoehr's attention to Merton's writings as his first archivist and self-appointed publicist is notable. Their exchange of materials and letters was impressive. And while the friendship was mutually beneficial, Christine Bochen in her fine review of the book questions whether the relationship was of greater importance to Lentfoehr than it was to Merton.[13] Even though the contact between Levertov and Merton was significantly less than it was with Lentfoehr, it was nonetheless significant in its own right. These two poets, Merton and Levertov, were engaged in the same endeavor, to reveal the spiritual dimensions of this life and express it in their poetry. You will find excellent reviews by Deborah Kehoe of both books in this volume of *The Merton Annual* that further clarify the importance of these relationships. It will suffice here simply to note Paul Pearson's comment in the Preface to the Lentfoehr book. After recalling publications that address Merton's friendships, Pearson rightly points out:

> Clearly missing from this list though are Merton's friendships with women. Some attention has been given to some of those relationships from the sixties such as Mary Luke Tobin, Rosemary Radford Ruether and, of course, the nurse he fell in love with in 1966. But his lifelong friendships with women have been overlooked thus far, and I think in particular of his friendships with women such as Naomi Burton and the subject of this volume, Sr. Thérèse Lentfoehr. (xv)

---

11. Robert Nugent, SDS, *Thomas Merton and Thérèse Lentfoehr: The Story of a Friendship* (New York: St Pauls, 2012).

12. Dana Greene, *Denise Levertov: A Poet's Life* (Urbana: University of Illinois Press, 2012).

13. See Christine Bochen, "A Mutually Enriching Relationship," *The Merton Seasonal* 38.3 (Fall 2013) 26.

This oversight is significant. The omission of Merton's relationship with women leaves a gaping hole in our understanding of his life *and* work. Furthermore, it is an important issue to address because this hole echoes an attitude toward woman that prevailed in Merton's time. The monastic walls and signs forbidding women within the enclosure most certainly enforced the division. There is no reason to claim that Merton was a budding feminist. On the contrary, he was in many ways a "man" of his times. Those times, however, were marked by significant change. That change engaged and challenged Merton. So it is reasonable to suggest that something was unfolding in his life with regard to women that deserves attention.

Glenn Hinson's *A Miracle of Grace: An Autobiography*[14] is another welcome addition to the collection of books that recall friendships that were important to Merton during his lifetime. Like so many who take seriously the Christian life as a spiritual pilgrimage, Hinson found in Merton a mentor whose wisdom greatly influenced his life and work. The relation began with Hinson's trips to Gethsemani with his students from the Baptist seminary in Louisville. Conferences were held with Merton. While the division between Catholics and Protestants is less pronounced today, at that time it was quite significant. The commitment to ecumenical discussions and the courage of these two men to cross this line is much to be admired. Erlinda Paguio's fine review of *Miracle of Grace* in this volume of *The Merton Annual* underscores the importance of Hinson's life story for Merton studies.

John Wu, Jr.'s *You Know My Soul: Reflections on Merton's Prayers*[15] draws our attention to the way in which Merton's interest in and journey to the East forged a lasting friendship. The text witnesses to the uniting of East and West, with English and Chinese on facing pages. Merton's presence is there, as is that of the author, son of Merton's close friend and collaborator and himself a Merton visitor and correspondent as a young man, as he reveals in his introductory personal reminiscences here. Wu's reflections on sixteen prayers by Merton reveal an intimacy that transcends both time and space. That transcendence is important. The escape Merton engineered was from confinements that prevent humanity from discovering its essential oneness. This is what drew Wu to Merton. It is this transcendent oneness that he seeks to share with the reader. As one moves through the prayers, reflections and drawings, there is a sense of "emptiness and freedom" that

---

14. E. Glenn Hinson, *A Miracle of Grace: An Autobiography* (Macon, GA: Mercer University Press, 2012).

15. John Wu, Jr., *You Know My Soul: Reflections on Merton's Prayers* (New Taipei City, Taiwan: Costantinian Press, 2012).

"lasts only for a short time, yet [is] enough for a lifetime" (207).

We conclude with two publications on the life and work of Leonard Cohen. This is the "friend" I mentioned that Merton never met. Donald Grayston's review of **The Holy or the Broken** and **I'm Your Man: The Life of Leonard Cohen**[16] in this volume of *The Merton Annual* clarifies the relation between these two men. As Grayston points out, Cohen made a pilgrimage to Gethsemani and Merton's grave. That is significant. More significant, however, is the similarity of their lives, spirits and messages. Both men climbed over the wall that separates the secular from the sacred. This is no small matter in a world where the meaning of life seems so elusive. It is only when the sacred and secular are reunited that the meaning will once again become apparent. Merton says as much in that delightfully funny poem about the five virgins who get into the wedding of the Lamb because they are good-looking and know how to dance. Had Merton known Cohen, I believe that he would have been included in the poem. Why not? A Jewish-Buddhist songwriter and performer from Canada fits quite well in Merton's inclusive, eclectic world. Besides, Cohen's "Our Lady of Solitude" is a beautiful song of devotion to Mary that everyone at the wedding, including Merton, would have greatly enjoyed.

> All summer long she touched me
> She gathered in my soul
> From many a thorn, from many thickets
> Her fingers, like a weaver's
> Quick and cool
>
> And the light came from her body
> And the night went through her grace
> All summer long she touched me
> And I knew her, I knew her
> Face to face
>
> And her dress was blue and silver
> And her words were few and small
> She is the vessel of the whole wide world
> Mistress, oh mistress, of us all
>
> Dear Lady; Queen of Solitude
> I thank you with my heart
> For keeping me so close to thee

---

16. Alan Light, *The Holy or the Broken: Leonard Cohen, Jeff Buckley and the Unlikely Ascent of "Hallelujah"* (New York: Simon & Schuster, 2012); Silvie Simmons, *I'm Your Man: The Life of Leonard Cohen* (New York: HarperCollins, 2012).

While so many, oh so many, stood apart

And the light came from her body
And the night went through her grace
All summer long she touched me
I knew her, I knew her
Face to face[17]

Freedom

As we have already noted, the freedom that Merton sought and found was inclusive of all aspects of society that limit humanity's capacity for freedom in which life might flourish. Two books here noted bring to our attention two areas of present concern.

Returning to Reality: Thomas Merton's Wisdom for a Technological World [18] is a significant contribution to Merton studies that offers an invaluable perspective on a pressing contemporary issue. Phillip Thompson, author of this excellent book, heads the introduction with a quotation from Merton that straightaway focuses the inquiry that follows:

> There is no escaping technology. . . . It isn't just that we have got a lot of machines. But that the entire life of man is being totally revolutionized by technology. This has to be made very clear. We are not at all living just in an age where we have more tools, more complicated tools, and things are a little more efficient, that kind of thing. It's a totally new kind of society we're living in. (xiii)

That "new kind of society" raised concerns for Merton even as a monk and hermit with limited experience of technology. Nevertheless, he was quick to pick up on the implications. Simple shifts in language were alerts, warning of a new understanding of what it meant to be human, an understanding that had infiltrated the Church and his own monastic community. Merton took notice of Pope Paul VI's reference to contemplatives as "aviators of the spirit," thereby suggesting "an 'illusion' that contemplatives knew the mechanisms guiding the 'secrets of interior life' and could use them" (xvii).

What troubled Merton about this emerging shift in humankind's understanding of itself was the demeaning of humanity to a material existence in service to a totalitarian world. In this new era, an important

---

17. Leonard Cohen, *The Lyrics of Leonard Cohen* (London/New York: Ominbus Press, 2009) 103.

18. Phillip M. Thompson, *Returning to Reality: Thomas Merton's Wisdom for a Technological World* (Eugene, OR: Cascade Books, 2012).

question arises: will contemplatives be able to live in such a world? In order to fully appreciate the significance of this question, we must recognize that the existence of monks and monasteries is not the only concern, but also that deeper dimension of life which is essential to the freedom of the human spirit. In other words, our true self was once again at risk of being obscured. This time, however, technology not only threatens annihilation by nuclear holocaust but more subtly via the deluge of data from multiple forms of communication. Thompson addresses both of these challenges and a third, the manufacturing of transhumans.

Thompson skillfully weaves together texts from various sources to reveal Merton's vision of contemplative life in a technological world and then brings the wisdom inherent in that vision to the three challenges noted above. He does so recognizing what was "lacking then was the wisdom to know how to accept the undeniable utility of technology without violating the requirements for a fully human life, a life that praises God, aids other people, and nurtures creativity and freedom" (xvi). As one might expect, the search for a life that "nurtures creativity and freedom" eventually leads the reader to the woods, not a metaphorical woods, but a real forest where seekers have throughout history retreated, as did Merton, first to the abbey and later to the hermitage. Thompson rightfully concludes the book here, recognizing as he does that Merton was a "forest dweller" who understood that nature provides the grace necessary to restore human society when it becomes too walled off from life (81).

Once again we find a book on Merton's relationship with M. that fails to rise to the task.[19] ***Thomas Merton—The Exquisite Risk of Love: The Chronicle of a Monastic Romance***[20] fails but not for lack of trying. It is simply a daunting task. As the author himself points out: "For too long, Merton scholars have shied away from addressing Merton's love for M." (2-3). This shying away from the relationship has been for good reason. It was and remains a private matter and is simply none of our business. Furthermore, it may be impossible to chronicle a romance without sounding like a Hollywood movie or an enticing cover story for a tabloid. There is, however, another way of looking at this. A more productive approach would be to *not* focus on the relationship. If we focus our attention on Merton's inquiry into the disconnect between spirituality and sexuality in the modern world, I believe that we would come up with something

19. See Christine Bochen's review in this volume of *The Merton Annual*; Deborah Kehoe, "A Miscalculated Risk," *The Merton Seasonal* 32.2 (Summer 2013) 42-43; and Patrick F. O'Connell's review in *The Merton Journal* 20.2 (Advent 2013) 46-49.

20. Robert Waldron, *Thomas Merton—The Exquisite Risk of Love: The Chronicle of a Monastic Romance* (London: Darton, Longman, Todd, 2012).

of importance. There are sufficient references to this issue throughout Merton's essays, correspondence, notes, journals and poetry to retrace the steps of his journey into one of the most perplexing problems of our day. But the task will require the knowledge and understanding of someone like Thomas Moore, whose book *The Soul of Sex: Cultivating Lives as an Act of Love*, digs deep into the nature of human sexuality to reveal the sacredness of Eros. The profaning of this sacredness is to be lamented. It has deprived us of one of the most precious graces afforded to us. Should we be surprised that even on this issue Merton has something to offer us? After years of reflecting on his experience of Eros, he shares with us the following spiritual direction:

> The act of sexual love should by its very nature be joyous, uncon-strained, alive, leisurely, inventive, and full of a special delight which the lovers have learned by experience to create for one another. There is no more beautiful gift of God than the little secret world of creative love and expression in which two persons who have totally surrendered to each other manifest and celebrate their mutual gift. *It is precisely in this spirit of celebration, gratitude, and joy that true purity is found.* The pure heart is not one that is terrified of eros but one that, with confidence and abandon of a child of God, accepts this gift as a sacred trust, for sex, too, is one of the talents which Christ has left us to trade with until He returns.[21]

Here is the place to begin an inquiry into Merton's contemplative vision of Eros for a world entrapped in a narrow and negative understanding of sexu-ality, an understanding that prevents discussions on gender, homosexuality and sexual abuse from opening onto new ways for humanity to reclaim this most "beautiful gift." Perhaps now is the time for a conference on Merton & Human Sexuality? If so, someone would contribute significantly to the discussion with a study of Czeslaw Milosz's poem entitled "In Krakow." Here, Merton's old friend, late in life, in his last collection of poems, included lines that witness to the beauty of Eros and inadvertently laments its loss:

> The nakedness of a woman meets the nakedness of a man
> And completes itself with its second half
> Carnal, or even divine,
> Which is likely the same thing,
> As revealed to us in the Song of Songs.

---

21. Thomas Merton, *Love and Living*, ed. Naomi Burton Stone and Brother Patrick Hart (New York: Farrar, Straus, Giroux, 1979) 117-18; subsequent references will be cited as "*L&L*" parenthetically in the text.

And must not every one of them nestle down into the Eternally
    Living,
Into His scent of apples, saffron, cloves, and incense,
Into Him who is and is coming
With the brightness of glowing wax candles?
And He, divisible, separate for each of them,
Receives them, him and her, in a wafer, into their own flame.[22]

Conclusion

We conclude with one last book. While ***Precious Thoughts: Daily Readings from the Correspondence of Thomas Merton***[23] edited by Fiona Gardner could be simply understood as another compilation of texts, lifted out of context, and set aside as less worthy of attention, I found something more than a "fabricated book."[24] Here is another example of collaboration. As noted earlier with regard to the two books on meditation edited by Pearson and Thurston, I am of the opinion that it is time to view these works in a new light. I sense from his review of *Precious Thoughts* in this volume of *The Merton Annual* that Jonathan Montaldo would agree. Since Montaldo has provided an excellent review of the book, I will focus on the way this book extends Merton's gift of friendship and pastoral care to those seeking freedom to grow in the grace of God.

It is important to note that Gardner is a psychotherapist and spiritual director. Her skillful selection of excerpts from Merton's letters was influenced by the expertise that she brought to the task. As a person committed to a caring profession, she approached the letters with a concern for a world perplexed about the purpose of life and thus in "search . . . for inspiration, nuggets of hope, fragments of faith" (10). Knowing that Merton understood the alienation and fragmentation of the modern world, she sorted out excerpts into daily readings believing "one at a time, day by day, over a year" (12) readers are gradually directed in their journey to God.

As a book intended for formation and freedom it fulfills the intentions expressed by Merton in an essay posthumously published:

The purpose of education is to show a person how to define himself authentically and spontaneously in relation to his world—not to impose a prefabricated definition of the world, still less an arbitrary

---

22. Czeslaw Milosz, *Second Space* (New York: Harper Collins, 2004) 6.

23.*Precious Thoughts: Daily Readings from the Correspondence of Thomas Merton* selected and edited by Fiona Gardner (London: Darton, Longman, Todd, 2011).

24. See Jonathan Montaldo's review of *Precious Thoughts* in this volume of *The Merton Annual* where he mentions Robert Giroux's thoughts on books "fabricated" from Merton texts.

definition of the individual himself. The world is made up of the people who area fully alive in it: that is, of the people who can be themselves in it and can enter into a living and fruitful relationship with each other in it. The world, is therefore, more real in proportion as the people in it are able to be more fully and more humanly alive: that is to say, better able to make a lucid and conscious use of their freedom. Basically, this freedom must consist first of all in the capacity to choose their own lives, to find themselves on the deepest possible level. (*L&L* 3)

Gardner selected the title for the book from a letter by Boris Pasternak to John Harris in which Pasternak expresses his appreciation for Merton's "precious thoughts and dear bottomless letters" which had enriched his life (9). So the title invokes memories of another time and place in which the human spirit was imprisoned. And, now, Merton's letters come to us with the same intent: to assist us in times like these, when escape is the only way to stay alive and keep dreaming.

Reviews

MERTON, Thomas, *The Life of the Vows: Initiation into the Monastic Tradition* 6, edited with an Introduction by Patrick F. O'Connell, Preface by Augustine Roberts, OCSO, Monastic Wisdom, vol. 30 (Collegeville, MN: Cistercian Publications, 2012), pp. lxxxi + 604. ISBN 978-0-87907-030-4 (paper) $44.95.

From October, 1955 until April, 1965 Thomas Merton gave weekly conferences to Gethsemani's young monks on the Benedictine vows of obedience, stability and conversion of life. With clarity and gentle exactitude, Merton scholar Patrick O'Connell has edited this work not only of monastic interest, but, since Merton thought that "The ultimate purpose of the vows . . . is to be understood as the restoration of one's authentic identity as made in the divine image and the unconditional gift of this true self to its Creator" (liii) and that "the essence of the vows is not restriction but liberation" (lv), of general interest to serious Christians as well. Vows deal with the "struggle against the habits of the world, the vices, the passions and everything that can draw us away from God, and a life of continual effort to acquire virtues" (279). These are struggles we all face.

These conferences are among Merton's most systematic theological works. The "Index of Contents" (3-6) illustrates their careful organization. Part I (7-105) introduces "the basic principles of Christian theology about man and his striving for his last end" (7). Merton closely follows the thought of St. Thomas Aquinas in this most dense writing in the book. Part II (105-51) treats the "States of Life: The State of Perfection." It begins with the assertion "that man's life should be nothing else but a friendship with God, a communion in the divine nature, a divinization by grace" (105). Here Merton's thought seems especially pre-Vatican II in its treatment of religious life as the most perfect choice; religious are "objects of a special love and election on the part of God" (105). I suspect I will not be the only reader who finds this "monastic triumphalism" (see, for example, the conclusions on page 127) a bit tiresome. In any case, in Parts I and II Merton lays the theological foundations for what follows and is the heart of the book.

Part III (151-234) is a general treatment of vows, understood less as a "juridical act of profession" than as an interior conversion (151) embracing renunciation of the former life and imitation of Christ, incorporation into

211

a society of love, the religious family and consecration to God by vows (152). Part IV (234-480), which Merton calls "the most important part of our study" (234), illustrates how this is worked out in the Benedictine vows of obedience ("the *most important of the vows*" because it "establishes us in a stable condition in the religious state" [237]), conversion of manners (which includes chastity and poverty treated in separate subsections) and stability, which Merton describes as "essentially simple and uncomplicated" (447). For each vow, Merton provides general principles, theological (again relying on St. Thomas) and biblical foundations, and practical material on keeping the vow. (Current readers may find details of which failures to keep a vow are sin, and of the sins which are mortal or venial, dated and off-putting.) While "the vow of obedience is the most important . . . from the point of view of *discipline*," Merton thinks that "the vow of conversion of manners . . . *is what really makes the monk*" (295).

I encourage the general reader not to be put off by the book's subject or size. Its careful outline indicates where one can dip in for material of personal interest (though page numbers in the outline do not always correspond exactly to page numbers in the text). Of practical general interest is Merton's distinction between servility and obedience (271). His long treatment of conversion of manners (274-447) is of interest both to monastics and lay Christians, and the theologically grounded monastic understanding of sexuality provides both balance and welcome relief from the attitudes of a sex-crazed society. Merton well knew that the vow of poverty "is especially crucial today, in America" (380). His discussion of that vow may have the most radical implications of any of the conferences. This collection is the most complete summary of Merton's thought on the purpose of monasticism as it is practically expressed in its vows. If like Merton's correspondent Rosemary Radford Ruether, one questions monasticism's "relevance,"[1] his scathing analysis of contemporary society (7-9) and presentation of monasticism's alternative "way" provides ample justification.

O'Connell's long introduction (xiii-lxxxi) is an excellent overview of Merton's thinking about monasticism, the subject that led to some of the monk's most scholarly and careful writing. (Appendix C [549] lists Merton's other books on monasticism.) O'Connell's evaluative summary of Merton's writing on monasticism (lii-lxxiv) is especially fine. The introduction also highlights a number of Merton's later themes that are first articulated here, provides both the sources of Merton's teachings and their limitations (see for example pages xx, xxviii, xxxii) and compares

---

1. See Thomas Merton and Rosemary Radford Ruether, *At Home in the World: The Letters of Thomas Merton & Rosemary Radford Ruether*, ed. Mary Tardiff (Maryknoll, NY: Orbis, 1995).

the development of his ideas over a period of years (see for example pages xlvi, li). I found O'Connell's insights into Merton's texts, its editions and the editing process fascinating reading. His exactitude is evident in the editing itself and in Appendices A and B (the textual notes and the table of correspondences with Merton's taped conferences). His immense learning is humbly hidden in the extensive and illuminating footnotes. This is exactly the sort of work we expect of O'Connell, to whom Merton scholars and readers owe a great debt of gratitude for bringing Merton's monastic conferences into print.

This is a book of conferences given by one who loved monastic life (I leave evaluation of his own observance of it to others) and edited by one who understands its author and his subject. While perhaps not the easiest introduction to Merton's monastic thought, it is one of the most comprehensive and engaging, and comes highly recommended for its contents and their implication for both monks and serious Christians. Because, as Merton wrote, they "are to enable us to *be* someone, not to do something" (9), monastic vows turn western society's quest for money, sex and power on its head. And at least some of us think that is exactly where such a quest belongs.

Bonnie Bowman Thurston

MERTON, Thomas, *On Christian Contemplation*, edited with a Preface by Paul M. Pearson (New York: New Directions, 2012), pp. xiv + 82. ISBN 978-0-8112-1996-9 (paper) $13.95.

MERTON, Thomas, *On Eastern Meditation*, edited with an Introduction by Bonnie Thurston (New York: New Directions, 2012), pp. xviii + 76. ISBN 978-0-8112-1994-5 (paper) $13.95.

> "Honestly I do not think it matters a bit
> whether one can sit cross-legged or not."

In this strange new world in which even the pope has an account on the online social network Twitter, I wondered, "Would Merton tweet?" and if so, "What would Merton tweet?" This line from *On Eastern Meditation* (59) would meet the standard of brevity required by Twitter's 140-character limit on messages. Though the above passage is the complete selection, it is one of the shorter ones from this volume. Still, most quotations from *On Eastern Meditation* are a few sentences or shorter. Knowing this, and seeing another volume of the same size and look from the same publisher, one might expect the same format inside *On Christian Contemplation*. This is not the case. Both volumes are well-chosen selections of Merton's writings. Yet Editor Paul Pearson chose generally longer selections of text in *On Christian Contemplation* rather than Editor Bonnie Thurston's brief but well-organized excerpts in *On Eastern Meditation*. This means a very different reading experience for each volume, each having advantages. To be sure, both books are brief and the selections in *On Christian Contemplation* are only long in comparison with the even shorter selections in *On Eastern Meditation*.

My professional background as a librarian and archivist predisposes me to be mindful of a source even before I have read its corresponding excerpt. Because of this, it took a little getting used to the system of citing sources in *On Eastern Meditation*. Drawing from nine of Merton's books, selections are followed by a two- or three-letter code to designate the source book followed by its page number. The wisdom of this method is that, with many brief quotations per page, it lessens the interruption of the flow of text and prevents the annoyance of flipping to endnotes at the back of the book, or the poor aesthetics and overly academic look of footnotes. I quickly became accustomed to this system. Nevertheless, other questions arose. For example, the code "*HGL*" means the source is Merton's volume of letters *The Hidden Ground of Love*, but I immediately wanted to know to whom the letter was written and when. Maybe this is the genius of the work of the editor. I knew enough to find the source if curious, and if a well-chosen selection, I would be motivated to do so. (In fact, I now know the recipient of Merton's letter about whether it is important if one can sit cross-legged. However, I will not divulge this identity but will leave that to those curious enough to pursue this reference.)

Slight confusion regarding sources in *On Eastern Meditation* did not end for me in knowing which book was being quoted. I had forgotten a particular statement in the introduction that provided important clarification and had to revisit it later: "When a quotation is itself a quotation (Merton quoting Gandhi, for example) the reference includes Merton's citation" (xvi-xvii). As indicated, excerpts from *Gandhi on Non-Violence* are the most potentially confusing. One third of this book is an essay by Merton on Gandhi and the rest of the book contains Merton's selections from Gandhi's two-volume collection *Non-Violence in Peace and War*. If the reader misses the above line from the introduction of *On Eastern Meditation*, the difference between a quotation by Merton or by Gandhi may not be clear. In these citation examples, the former is by Merton and the latter by Gandhi: (*GNV* 22) and (II-151, *GNV* 47). If you understand the citation style, it is quite simple, but woe to those who skip book introductions because even the "Key to Abbreviations" provides no more clarification on this front.

Despite my quibbling over very small details, I really enjoyed Bonnie Thurston's selections in *On Eastern Meditation*. I found the volume well organized, and sometimes more systematic in organizing Merton's thoughts than Merton was for himself. To evoke again the model of Twitter, I found the "tweet" or "tweet and a half" sized selections to be useful. This is a treasure trove of brief bits of quotable Merton, which is much in demand in the Internet age. Returning to the "cross-legged" line from the beginning, Thurston places Merton's humorous quip about ambivalence regarding prayer posture from the letters next to a brief passage from *The Asian Journal* regarding contrary ideas in Zen and Tibetan Buddhism on the importance of sitting in a particular way. Not only did Thurston's ordering of the selections provide interesting connections, it was also useful to have a segment of a longer work lifted from its source context and framed on its own for emphasis. Surrounding what you want to give meaning with silence reminds me of the white space in a gallery around a work of art. Richard Rohr puts it more poetically, and I find it an apt description of the art of Thurston's work as an editor: "Beauty emerges from the silence around it. . . . If something is not surrounded by this ontological identity of silence and space, it is hard to appreciate something as singular and beautiful."[1] Again, "Silence is what surrounds *everything*, if you look long enough. It is the space between letters, words, and paragraphs that makes them decipherable and meaningful. When you can train yourself to reverence the silence around things, you first begin to see things in themselves and for themselves."[2]

I turn now to Paul Pearson's comparatively longer selections in *On Christian Contemplation*. There are some selections of no more than a paragraph, but most excerpts range from one to three of the small pages of this volume. Pearson draws from a diverse array of seventeen books, which include poetry, journals, volumes of letters and books of essays and spiritual writings. He also includes some previously unpublished material from the Merton Center's archives, a rare gift in a book of selected writings (see "Notes on Meditation" [63]), and draws from a few essays that had only been published in serial form and that had not been included in subsequent books until now (see "Toward a Theology of Prayer"; "Notes on Prayer and Action"; and "The Contemplative Life: Its Meaning and Necessity" [19-24, 53-55, 56]).

---

1. Richard Rohr, "Find God in the Depths of Silence," a lecture given at Festival of Faiths: Sacred Silence, May 15, 2013 in Louisville, KY (http://www.youtube.com/watch?v=uaMVKnpsDA8: accessed September 25, 2013).

2. Richard Rohr, "Finding God in the Midst of Silence," *Sojourners* 42.3 (March 2013) 18.

Pearson intersperses Merton's reflections on contemplation with Merton's contemplative poetry. This style breaks up the contemplative notes and essays in a valuable way and helps to move the reader away from approaching contemplation as a completely mental exercise of the rational mind. As Pearson quotes from a conference by Merton in Alaska, "Mental prayer is only a phrase—you cannot pray with your mind" (25). Another essay Pearson includes further addresses this point: "How does the theology of prayer approach this problem? Not by reasoning but by symbol, by poetic insight, leading directly to those depths of the heart where these matters are experienced and where such conflicts are re-solved" (from "Toward a Theology of Prayer" [20]). As with Thurston's volume, Pearson has arranged complementary selections. His alternation of poetry and prose also illustrates the point Merton is making about con-templation's need to lead from the mind to the heart and to the imagination.

Each of these slim volumes should appeal to both the new and sea-soned Merton reader. Those new to Merton will find many hooks to lead them into his other works. Long-time readers will see something they have read before in a new light in Thurston's framing and juxtaposition of the quotations, and may find new gems in Pearson's thoughtful and diverse selections. Just do not expect, judging a book by its cover, to find each book to read like its companion. In constructing a book of thoughtful meditations, there are many ways to get it right, not unlike in prayer and meditation itself. As Merton puts it in *On Christian Contemplation*, "It isn't a question of there being one right way to pray, or one right answer to the question of prayer, and we should be perfectly free to explore all sorts of avenues and ways of prayer" (25).

Mark C. Meade

Thomas Merton, *Precious Thoughts: Daily Reading from the Correspon-dence of Thomas Merton*, selected and edited by Fiona Gardner (London: Darton, Longman, Todd, 2011), pp. 175. ISBN 978-0-232-52883-1 (paper) £10.99.

Robert Giroux, during his tenure as a trustee for the Merton Legacy Trust, often voiced his disapproval to fellow trustees Anne McCormick and Tommie O'Callaghan of what he called "fabricated books" that were put together by editing selections or excerpts from across Merton's writing. He disliked these "re-packagings" because he judged these col-lections threatened to deflect from the integrity of Merton's presentation of himself and his ideas in the more complete context of the books he had actually written for publication in his lifetime. While Giroux would not have called "fabricated" *The Asian Journal of Thomas Merton*[1] or Patrick O'Connell's recent edition of Merton's *Selected Essays*,[2] I doubt he was amused, for instance, at my own edited selections from Merton's work, like *Choosing to Love the World*[3] and *Thomas Merton in His Own Words*.[4] Fiona Gardner's *Precious Thoughts* is another example in that burgeoning genre of selections from Merton's literature to make a book that is earning one of Bob Giroux's now posthumous frowns.

While ignoring (although not without respectful qualms) the judgment of this powerful guardian-dragon of Merton's legacy, I can still appreciate Gardner's service to Merton's readers, whether ripened or fresh, in providing instances of his gifts for spiritual direction embedded within his correspondence. Gardner underlines expressions of important themes that can easily be overlooked when plowing through Merton's correspondence selected and published in five volumes by Farrar, Straus & Giroux. In his letters to persons of high or low estate, the monk was prodigal in his gifts for expressing intimacy with a correspondent. His letters aim to produce right words for a particular correspondent's real-time concerns and questions. Merton is a prime example of a "living text" for studying the ancient monastic tradition of spiritual mothers and fathers who responded to requests to provide a "word of salvation" by an interlocutor in crisis who needed immediate advice: "Amma, what should I do?" As Gardner is a practicing psychotherapist, she professionally appreciates this tradition and has made a book of excerpts from Merton's letters that provide still cogent samples of his general counsel for those wanting to live an everyday spiritual life. The book's title is taken from an observation by Boris Pasternak, winner of the Nobel Prize and author of *Doctor Zhivago*, who valued the "precious thoughts" that studded the letters he had received from Thomas Merton. Gardner organizes her compilation of Merton's "precious thoughts" by mining nuggets of insight for day-to-day reflections through a year's twelve months. Although a Merton drawing precedes each month's reflections, she has chosen to forego giving directive "chapter titles." In her introduction she provides only the most general pointers with which to approach the themes of her selections, but a close reading provides ample recurring themes that manifest her professional interest in the spiritual

1. Thomas Merton, *The Asian Journal*, ed. Naomi Burton Stone, Brother Patrick Hart and James Laughlin (New York: New Directions, 1973).

2. Thomas Merton, *Selected Essays*, ed. Patrick F. O'Connell (Maryknoll, NY: Orbis, 2013).

3. Thomas Merton, *Choosing to Love the World: On Contemplation*, ed. Jonathan Montaldo (Boulder, CO: Sounds True, 2008).

4. Thomas Merton, *In My Own Words*, ed. Jonathan Montaldo (Liguori, MO: Liguori, 2007).

advice embedded in Merton's correspondence. None of these recurring themes can receive full examination in a review, but I have chosen three to stand out that might offer a potential reader an invitation to make further explorations into Gardner's entire text. These three themes of Merton's practical advice are: clinging to a simple faith in God's mercy; realizing God's will in the unique contours of a personal spiritual life; and maintaining the proper climate of heart and mind to facilitate daily interior prayer and union with God through all vicissitudes, through a human life's patterned flow of ups and downs.

No virtue receives more stress in this compilation than does that of keeping faith. God's presence to one's life is palpable only if one adopts a way of faith, the virtue that is "the basis of all interior prayer" (17 [7 January]). Faith is the lived experience of accepting all the most individual and personal elements of one's life, persons and events for instance, as significant epiphanies of God providential mercy in one's life (19 [15 January]). Only in faith does the desire for God's voice achieve the erotic moments of hearing it: "Faith is the virtue which really puts us in contact with God: the true God, the living God. . . . He is always there, even when He is not felt" (128 [22 October]). These pious truths simply expressed are balanced by Merton's admission that faith provides no easy answers. Faith can never "serve merely as a happiness pill" (138 [18 November]). Merton's assertions about the world in the excerpts of this book default to his habitual responses to his memories of experiencing and interpreting the world as a dark, chaotic and challenging place: "The air of the world is foul with lies, hypocrisy, falsity, and life is short, death approaches" (21 [20 January]). Thus Merton's advice to a correspondent is never overly optimistic: "The times are difficult. They call for courage and faith. Faith is in the end a lonely virtue. Lonely especially where a deeply authentic community of love is not an accomplished fact, but a job to be begun over and over" (145 [1 December]).

Merton's advice on how to know the will of God centers consistently on accepting everything that happens in a person's everyday life as a potential opening to knowing God's will for that person in its particulars: "The concrete existential situation you are in here and now, whatever it is, contains for you God's will, reality. Your only job is to accept it as it is" (15 [2 January]). "You have a concrete situation to face and accept as positively and constructively as possible" (27 [1 February]). The will of God is experienced, not by excessive analysis, but by an attentive listening for the signals of the direction to which the tasks of the day call one forth to love the life you are leading with courage and acceptance. "[W]e have to start from where we are, and respond to grace as we are, within our own communities and we have to take one step at a time. The main thing is to be ready to refuse nothing when the call really comes, and to be open to each little thing, each new opportunity to make our life more real and less of a systematic and mechanical routine" (41 [7 March]).

In his giving advice on the challenges to practicing interior prayer, Merton can be abrupt. In so many words he can tell his correspondent to relax, shut up and be un-self-conscious, "not thinking about yourself and not trying to figure everything out" (33 [18 February]). The irony here, of course, is that Merton always needed to follow his own advice. Actually, all of Merton's admonitions in this book can be interpreted as his best advice for himself based on his own hard, previous experience: "In our prayer we should avoid everything that makes us uselessly examine and analyze ourselves, and simply go to Him in faith, even if it means that we have to be very patient with a form of prayer that seems dark and arid" (29 [9 February]). Merton on prayer adheres closely to the teachings of the Benedictine John Chapman who advised his readers to "pray as you can, not as you can't." Merton echoes Chapman's advice: "Our interior prayer is simply the most intimate and personal way in which we seek the Face of God" (30 [10 February]). We must learn to pray, in a phrase from Merton's autobiography, "out of the roots of our own life."

Rowan Williams has published a small collection of insightful essays on Merton under the title, *A Silent Action*. In the first essay of the collection he amusingly opines that the monk has become "one of the most wearisomely familiar names in the canon of modern spiritual writing, and the whole industry of Merton Studies has blossomed (if that is the word) and shows no sign of diminution. Indeed, I am busily contributing to it as I write these words."[5] Fiona Gardner's *Precious Thoughts* is another flowering within that section of the Merton Studies greenhouse that exhibits re-constructed books that mix and match strands from Merton's thinking. These efforts at highlighting Merton's work should not receive uncritical applause, but my own opinion is Maoist in the matter. I prefer to let ten thousand flowers bloom.

After all, I remind myself that probably every month someone in the world is encountering a Merton work for the first time, most likely *The Seven Storey Mountain* or *New Seeds of Contemplation*. Some of these new readers continue to be wowed by Merton's words. A book like *Precious Thoughts* can serve as an invitation for readers with little time now to promise themselves further exploration of the full texts of Merton's letters "when they retire." And then Merton believed in "book

---

5. Rowan Williams, *A Silent Action: Engagements with Thomas Merton* (Louisville, KY: Fons Vitae, 2011) 17.

providence"—the book you need to read falls into your hands at just the right moment of your needing to read it. Who knows the good that a small volume like *Precious Thoughts* will do?

In discerning the value of all the Merton secondary literature (all of it selected perspectives—it could all be called "fabricated") the market for really useful secondary paths into Merton's mind will eventually sift out the wheat from the chaff. Unlike Thomas Merton's original books, some of which appear to bear indefinite expiration dates, the secondary literature is mostly destined for no-longer-in-print oblivion (although James Finley, whose *Merton's Palace of Nowhere* is headed for its thirtieth anniversary in print, can rightly chuckle at this assertion[6]).

"Without contact with living examples, we soon get lost or give out. We need to be sustained in the interior work that we alone can do, with God's grace: but still there is need of the push that comes from others who do the same, and who can, in the briefest signals, communicate some of their directions to us" (141 [27 November]). Gardner's *Precious Thoughts*, her compilation of brief "signals," provided by one always pushing forward through all his experiences to find his identity with all his relations "in Christ," will provide "push" and direction for those who choose to linger over her selected texts. Is her compilation further evidence of the continued "blossoming" of Merton Studies, if one can use that word, or is her book yet another epiphany of unwanted weeds in the garden? Who am I to judge? I can only report that, on most pages of this new "fabrication," this Merton-reading old dog was re-enchanted enough to stop and sniff the roses.

Jonathan Montaldo

MERTON, Thomas, *Thomas Merton on Contemplation* (Introduction by Fr. Anthony Ciorra + 5 Lectures: 4 CDs); *Finding True Meaning and Beauty* (4 Lectures: 2 CDs); *Thomas Merton's Great Sermons* (Introduction by Fr. Anthony Ciorra + 4 Lectures: 2 CDs); *Vatican II: The Sacred Liturgy and the Religious Life* (7 Lectures: 4 CDs); *Thomas Merton on Sufism* (Introduction by Fr. Anthony Ciorra + 13 Lectures: 7 CDs); *Ways of Prayer: A Desert Father's Wisdom* (Introduction by Fr. Anthony Ciorra + 13 Lectures: 7 CDs); *Thomas Merton on the 12 Degrees of Humility* (Introduction by Fr. Anthony Ciorra + 16 Lectures: 8 CDs); *Solitude and Togetherness* (Introduction by Fr. Anthony Ciorra + 11 Lectures: 11 CDs); *The Prophet's Freedom* (Introduction by Fr. Anthony Ciorra + 8 Lectures: 8 CDs) (Rockville, MD: Now You Know Media, 2012).

---

6. James Finley, *Merton's Palace of Nowhere: A Search for God through Awareness of the True Self* (Notre Dame, IN: Ave Maria Press, 1978).

Thomas Merton's conferences as novice master began to be recorded on audiotape in late April 1962, initially so that the brothers at the Abbey of Gethsemani (who at the time had a separate novitiate) could listen to them as they worked in the monastery kitchen. The practice continued throughout the rest of Merton's term as novice master, and subsequently his regular Sunday afternoon talks to the community during the final three years of his life, while he was living as a hermit, were also taped. Eventually more than six hundred recordings were made and preserved, including talks Merton himself taped at the hermitage to be sent to various audiences, presentations at different meetings held at Gethsemani and even the talks given in 1968 in California, Alaska and India.

Some of these recordings began to be made available commercially as early as the 1970s, when Electronic Paperbacks produced three sets of twelve cassettes each, a total of seventy-two conferences; later Credence Cassettes (renamed Credence Communications with the advent of the compact disc) issued just over one hundred cassettes, most of them two-sided (some of the later ones released as CDs as well). Recently Now You Know Media, a relatively new company specializing in original audio and video courses by well-known Catholic scholars, has begun an ambitious program of marketing Merton conferences in thematic sets, unlike the previous companies' practice in which each cassette was sold separately and without any stated connection with the others. In 2012, the first year in which these Merton recordings were produced by Now You Know, nine different sets, ranging from four conferences on two CDs to sixteen conferences on eight CDs were issued, a total of 81 for this single year (available as well in MP3 format). All but two sets include introductions to the material by Fr. Anthony Ciorra, presenter of the generally well-received 2011 Now You Know series of twelve lectures entitled *Thomas Merton: A Spiritual Guide for the Twenty-first Century*. While the list price for many of the lengthier series is quite high, all of them seem to be perpetually on sale for a considerably reduced cost. Given the limited space available, this "omnibus" review of the 2012 sets will focus somewhat less on the matter of Merton's presentations than on the manner of Now You Know's innovative packaging, which has had somewhat mixed results thus far but is a very promising and exciting beginning to what one may hope will become a major contribution to making Merton's message more widely available through the medium of the spoken word.

The first set to be issued, given the rather generic title *Thomas Merton on Contemplation*, is actually a kind of "grab-bag," or sampler, consisting of five conferences (a better term for the rather informal classes than "lectures," used by the publisher), only two of which actually mention contemplatives and the contemplative life explicitly, and even these only in passing. The talks have no intrinsic connection with one another and are presented in no clearly discernible order, whether thematic or chronological, but the first three, at least, do serve as a fine introduction to Merton's teaching style and content. The first (numbered 2 after Fr. Ciorra's introduction), "Prayer and Meditation on the Meaning of Life," given on January 28, 1964, reflects on the recent community retreat and emphasizes the importance of authentic self-knowledge, as distinguished from introspective self-absorption, as the fruit of prayer; the next, "Monastic Spirituality: Life Is a Journey," is more than a year older, from January 16, 1963, and presents Abraham as a paradigm for the Christian and monastic life as a journey into the unknown to find God beyond the boundaries of familiar and comfortable patterns and habits; the third, "Cassian on Prayer," part of Merton's course on "Pre-Benedictine Monasticism" and dating from May 19, 1963, considers Cassian's teaching on constant prayer and the various kinds of prayer, including the "prayer of fire" that is beyond words; the last, entitled "Religious Silence," one of a small group on that topic and dating from December 14, 1963, consists largely of interactions with the novices on the topic of silence and makes a rather odd culmination to this heterogeneous group. The fourth presentation, "God-centered Prayer," is actually not from Merton's conferences to his novices at all; it was his first attempt to produce a tape for a non-Gethsemani audience, made in January 1967 for novices at the nearby motherhouse of the Sisters of Loretto with whom Merton had developed a warm relationship through their superior, Sr. Mary Luke Tobin; it discusses the life of prayer and answers some questions the novices had forwarded to him, on the role of emotions, the existence of hell, spiritual virginity—ending rather abruptly as the tape runs out but to be continued on the reverse side (not included here but found in a set issued in 2013 in which this recording is repeated[1]). Fr. Ciorra's introductory comments provide a fine overview of Merton's main writings on contemplation and on his teaching on the importance of attentiveness and awareness of the divine presence, concluding with a beautiful passage from *The New Man*; but he touches only briefly on each of the five talks themselves, and refers to them as "Thomas Merton's conferences on contemplation" as though this were Merton's own intentional focus in this disparate group, which is clearly not the case. Fr. Ciorra does not deal at any length with the topic of Merton's novitiate conferences in general, nor does he provide any information on the chronology (unlike some of the subsequent sets,

---

1. Thomas Merton, *Prayer and Growth in Christian Life* (13 presentations on 5 CDs) (Rockville, MD: Now You Know Media, 2013).

this one does not indicate the dates of presentation on the case cover, but the publisher promises this omission will be remedied), so the listener has no way of knowing when the talks were given nor in what sequence. More context, both in general and in connection with these particular presentations, would have been of greater assistance and relevance than the introductory overview of contemplation drawn mainly from Merton's writings.

The set entitled *Finding True Meaning and Beauty* has no introduction by Fr. Ciorra, probably because the pair of conferences on beauty was initially slated to be issued alone, and the second pair on "Your Search for Meaning" was added only shortly before the set appeared. The two groupings have no intrinsic chronological or thematic connection with one another and were apparently packaged together only for convenience in marketing. The two conferences on meaning, from February 11 and 18 (mistakenly dated "13" on the case), 1968, are actually part of Merton's lengthy series of weekly presentations discussing Sufism, along with Hasidism, which began in April 1967 and continued, with various interruptions, through June 1968. They draw both on the Iranian-American psychologist Reza Arasteh's book on *Final Integration* (well known from Merton's essay-review "Final Integration: Toward a 'Monastic Therapy'"[2]) and on Martin Buber's collection of Hasidic tales, a number of which Merton reads and comments on in the course of the two presentations. From both sources Merton draws the lesson that authentic human wholeness cannot be simply adjustment to social and cultural norms but must involve a breakthrough to transcendent meaning that confronts the issues of mortality and meaningful creativity, which the Christian recognizes as the acceptance of the cross. The two conferences on beauty date from August 1964 and are actually the initial presentations from a series on art that will continue with a number of conferences on Celtic art, in particular, and then move on to the long sequence of talks on poetry that will continue through April of 1965. Merton emphasizes beauty as an intrinsic aspect of the being of any object, not merely a property of its generic essence but also the radiance of each particular being. The beauty of art is presented as "the splendor of being shining forth from a thing well made," which provides a delight that transcends sensual pleasure as well as the pleasure of knowing that involves the communication of information. He concludes his second conference with a brief look at contemporary art, contrasting the more subjective approach of expressionism with the objectivity of constructivist or conceptual art, which rejects the idea that the purpose

---

2. Thomas Merton, *Contemplation in a World of Action* (Garden City, NY: Doubleday, 1971) 205-17.

of a work of art is to provide a picture (of something other than itself)—citing his friend Ad Reinhardt as exemplifying this position. Both pairs of presentations in this set are valuable and stimulating (though not to the degree of the hyperbolic "spellbinding lectures . . . [d]elivered with unrivaled brilliance and insight" as claimed on the case cover) but they have little actual connection with one another and would have been better issued as part of the sequences in which Merton originally presented them.

The least satisfactory of the 2012 releases is *Thomas Merton's Great Sermons*. The four presentations included are neither all great, nor are they all sermons! In his introduction Fr. Ciorra encourages the audience to imagine themselves sitting in the pews of the choir in the abbey church as Merton is presiding and preaching at the liturgy, but in fact only one of these talks was given in the church, and at none of them was Merton the principal celebrant at Mass. The first, "Thomas Merton's Sermon on the Trinity," is only eight minutes long and was excerpted from a recording of a Mass celebrated at Gethsemani by Merton's friend Dan Walsh on May 21, 1967, one week after he had been ordained. It focuses on the gospel reading from Matthew 28, the "great commission" to preach the good news to the ends of the earth and baptize in the name of the Father, Son and Holy Spirit, and applies this instruction to the monastic community, whose members obey this command through their openness to the other—for example to the poor and to those of other religious traditions—and to the future. This recording had been immediately preceded by two others in which Merton reflects on the feast and on the homily he is preparing; including these reflections would have complemented the actual sermon as delivered. The second selection, "Thomas Merton's Sermon on the Feast of the Immaculate Conception," was presented in the chapter room by Merton on December 8, 1962, when he had been assigned to give the feast-day sermon.[3] It was later published in a considerably revised form as "A Homily on Light and the Virgin Mary" in Merton's *Seasons of Celebration*,[4] and a comparison of the two versions is quite instructive in revealing how Merton transformed an oral presentation very much rooted in the readings of the monastic office for the feast into a more general written meditation on Mary as "the perfect rekindling of the pure light which had been extinguished by the sin of Adam" (*SC* 163), no longer tied explicitly to the Feast of the Immaculate Conception. The final item, "Thomas Merton's Sermon on Easter," was never

3. See Thomas Merton, *Turning Toward the World: The Pivotal Years. Journals, vol. 4: 1960-1963*, ed. Victor A. Kramer (San Francisco: HarperCollins, 1996) 271.

4. Thomas Merton, *Seasons of Celebration* (New York: Farrar, Straus & Giroux, 1965) 158-70; subsequent references will be cited as "*SC*" parenthetically in the text.

preached at all: it is the recording made at the hermitage on September 14, 1967 for Argus Communications that was subsequently published as a small booklet entitled *He Is Risen*,[5] and is identical to the published text except for minor omissions in the latter. As for the third presentation, "Prose and Poetry on the Passion of Christ," it is in fact not a sermon but a novitiate conference focusing on material from Pascal's *Pensées* on the Agony in the Garden, a brief Irish poem on the crucifixion and the medieval English lyric "Quia Amore Langueo" ("Because I languish for love"), given on April 8, 1965 as part of Merton's series of conferences on poetry (and will in fact be included in the set of these conferences released in 2013[6]—with no mention that it had already been issued as a sermon the previous year). Fr. Ciorra is apparently unaware of any of this information on the provenance of the material, and while he supplies an interesting commentary on Merton's Christology in his introduction, it is of peripheral relevance to the material in these talks.

The seven conferences comprising the set entitled *Vatican II: The Sacred Liturgy and the Religious Life* come from two different time periods—December 1963, at the conclusion of the Council's second session, and early 1965, shortly after the third session. There is no introductory overview by Fr. Ciorra, somewhat surprisingly as he himself has presented an entire series of talks for Now You Know on Vatican II.[7] (An introduction is to be added to a revised version of this set.) The first three of Merton's conferences were given in a single week (December 16, 18, 20, 1963) after he had received a copy of *The New York Times* with the text of the recently promulgated *Sacrosanctum Concilium*, the Dogmatic Constitution on the Liturgy. (He jokes a couple of times that this is the first time he's given conferences from a newspaper.) He tells the novices that implementation of this constitution will result in the biggest change in the liturgy in 1600 years, and stresses the focus on full, conscious and active participation by all as the hallmark of liturgical reform. He speculates about the effect of these changes on monastic liturgy, the divine office as well as the Mass, and assures his audience that there will be no English office in monasteries (!). In the third of these conferences he provides a close reading of selected sections of the document, noting the emphasis

5. Thomas Merton, *He Is Risen* (Niles, IL: Argus, 1975); for details see Thomas Merton, *Learning to Love: Exploring Solitude and Freedom. Journals, vol. 6: 1966-1967*, ed. Christine M. Bochen (San Francisco: HarperCollins, 1997) 291.

6. Thomas Merton, *Seeing the World in a Grain of Sand: Thomas Merton on Poetry* (Rockville, MD: Now You Know Media, 2013) #16.

7. Fr. Anthony Ciorra, *The Spirituality of Vatican II* (Rockville, MD: Now You Know Media, 2012).

on the presence of Christ in the assembly, the word, the priest and the sacrament, as well as the shift from the traditional concern with juridical power of the priest operative in the Mass to the ontological power of the Holy Spirit at work in the entire community. The fourth presentation briefly considers the other document approved at the Council's second session, the Decree on Social Communications, which Merton considers to have raised some important issues about the need to keep people informed concerning crucial moral and religious questions and events, but he concludes that overall the text is "rather dull." These remarks are actually only off-the-cuff prefatory comments, less than fifteen minutes in length, at the beginning of a regularly scheduled conference on St. Anselm, as is evident from Merton's words as the selected excerpt fades out (though dated 12/26/63 on the case cover, it almost certainly comes from Sunday, December 22, 1963, since it is part of an hour-long conference that was only given on Sundays, and continues a discussion on Anselm's notion of stability that had begun on December 8). Unlike the three conferences from December 1963, the three from January 17 and 31 and February 7, 1965 discuss a document that had not yet been passed by the Council—the decree on renewal of religious life. Merton points out that the preliminary schema for this had been summarily rejected as inadequate, and in successive conferences he considers an article on the schema by the Dominican theologian and Council *peritus* J.-M. Tillard, the "*modi*" (proposed revisions) drawn up by Cardinal Suenens and other conciliar reformers, and a similar series of suggested changes made by French experts. (Though he does not say so, Merton probably obtained copies of the latter two sources through his friend Sr. Luke Tobin, who was one of the few official women observers at the Council and was deeply involved in the process of revising the document.) Merton notes here, as with the liturgy document, the importance of a shift, as proposed by the reformers, from a focus on law to an emphasis on the role of the Holy Spirit, as well as the need for "adult and active participation of all members" of a religious community in authentic renewal, and in a deeper understanding of the contemporary meaning of obedience. He also highlights the role of religious life as an eschatological sign, especially a sign of the presence of the Kingdom of God here and now—an expression of the realized eschatology that was increasingly important to Merton in the 1960s. Though given more than a year apart, the two groups of conferences in this set have a coherence of focus and a consistency of perspective that makes this a valuable compilation. Though one may regret that Merton never discussed with the novices some of the other major Council documents, such as the Pastoral Constitution on the Church in the Modern World (about which he did write extensively[8]) or the Decree on Non-Christian Religions (he was no longer novice master when these were issued at the end of the fourth and final session of the Council in December 1965), his comments in these conferences do complement well the insights on Vatican II expressed in his journals and letters and various essays.

The thirteen conferences included in *Thomas Merton on Sufism* (undated on the case cover) come from the Sunday conferences Merton gave weekly to the novices and any other community members who wished to attend during the years he lived as a hermit. This series continued for more than a year, off and on, beginning in April 1967 and running through June 1968. Unfortunately the set is incomplete, omitting not only the pair of conferences included in the *Finding True Meaning and Beauty* set but the introductory conference on varieties of Islamic thought and practice and at least four other presentations in the series; these gaps are at times evident in the presentations themselves, as Merton refers back to material in a previous lecture that does not appear in the recordings as provided here. The title is also somewhat misleading, as Merton frequently interwove material from Jewish Hasidism with that from Sufism, as well as bringing in various other disparate sources he was currently reading, so that if the listener is expecting a systematic explication of Sufi doctrine and practice he or she is bound to be disappointed (as Merton's friend and correspondent Abdul Aziz reportedly was when he heard these recordings[9]). Merton is clearly interested mainly in providing instruction on monastic practice and on the life of prayer for his intended audience, drawing on Sufi and Hasidic teaching along with whatever else he found relevant at the moment. Still, these conferences are filled with insightful comments on various aspects of Islamic and particularly Sufi theory and practice—on the inner meaning of the *shahada*, the basic proclamation of Islamic belief, that only God is fully real; on all reality as the self-manifestation of God; on the names of God and finding one's own name for God; on the centrality of the heart, the center of the self for the Sufi; on the practice of *dhikr*, or remembrance, as fundamental to Sufism; on the experience of divine mercy and compassion in authentic experience

---

8. See Thomas Merton, "Christian Humanism in the Nuclear Era," in *Love and Living*, ed. Naomi Burton Stone and Brother Patrick Hart (New York: Farrar, Straus, Giroux, 1979) 151-70.

9. See Sidney H. Griffith, "'As One Spiritual Man to Another': The Merton-Abdul Aziz Correspondence," in Rob Baker and Gray Henry eds., *Merton & Sufism: The Untold Story* (Louisville, KY: Fons Vitae, 1999) 121; subsequent references will be cited as "Baker & Henry" parenthetically in the text.

of God; on the movement from *fana* to *baqa*, disintegration and reintegration of the self; on the importance of the spiritual guide, the *sheikh*, in the personal transmission of wisdom to the disciple. Though he remains rather vague about the particular circumstances in which this series of conferences was presented (he says only that they were given "to novices and juniors" in the 1960s), Fr. Ciorra's introduction contextualizes Merton's growing attraction to Sufism by reference to his contacts with Herbert Mason, Louis Massignon and Abdul Aziz; he highlights the importance of the visit of the Sufi master Sidi Abdeslam to Gethsemani in 1966; he indicates the importance of the Sufi concept of the "inner jihad," the conflict with the lower self, along with the relevance of the Sufi focus on trials and bewilderment to monastic life, contemporary monastic life in particular; he refers his audience to the collection *Merton & Sufism: The Untold Story* as a fundamental resource for this topic (though he neglects to mention that key excerpts from the Sufism conferences are transcribed in that volume [see Baker & Henry 130-62]). All in all, Fr. Ciorra's introduction to this set is perhaps the most helpful of any of the 2102 releases.

The two other most extensive sets of conferences released in 2012 are each complete sequences of the final sections of courses that Merton was giving the novices when taping began in the spring of 1962. *Ways of Prayer: A Desert Father's Wisdom* includes thirteen conferences presented between April 28 and August 4, 1962, focused on John Cassian's fourth, ninth and tenth conferences. This was the culmination of Merton's extensive course on *Cassian and the Fathers* that included a preliminary discussion of "Monastic Spirituality and the Early Fathers from Apostolic Fathers to Evagrius Ponticus," followed by "Lectures on Cassian," which considered in detail the life and influence of this major transmitter of the tradition of Egyptian desert monasticism to the West, thoroughly summarized the teaching of Cassian's *Institutes*, his treatise on monastic formation and observances and on the eight principal vices (which would be the major source for subsequent teaching on the "seven deadly sins"), and finally reflected on the more contemplative teaching found in Cassian's *Conferences*. Merton had already discussed the first Conference, on the immediate objective (purity of heart) and final end (the Kingdom of God) of the monastic life, and the second Conference, on the crucial importance of discretion, at the point when the recordings begin. After a single class on the fourth Conference, concerned with concupiscence and the psychology of temptation and noting the importance of balance and moderation even in spiritual desire, Merton spends the rest of his time on the two Conferences on prayer that complete the first part of Cassian's treatise. He discusses Cassian's overview of the life of prayer as rooted in purity of heart, the instability of mind and addiction to busyness that lead to distractions in prayer, the four kinds of prayer (supplications, vows, intercessions and thanksgiving) that can sometimes be transformed into the contemplative "prayer of fire," and Cassian's extensive meditation on the Lord's Prayer; he concludes with consideration of Cassian's teaching on constant prayer, rooted in the practice of repetition of a brief invocation (for Cassian especially the phrase "O God come to my assistance, O Lord make haste to help me" from Psalm 69[70]). Since Merton's own teaching notes for these conference have now been published,[10] it is possible to compare the lively oral presentation of these conferences with the more detailed written version of the same material and so obtain a deeper appreciation both of Merton's approach to teaching his novices and of his own immersion in the material he has prepared. In his Introduction to this set Fr. Ciorra provides a helpful overview of Merton as a teacher, with a stress on his wisdom-oriented approach that emphasizes the appropriation of spiritual experience rather than the accumulation of factual information (though he himself is a bit careless with facts, stating that John Eudes Bamberger had been a student of Merton as a novice— rather than as a scholastic, and that Merton had taught at St. Bonaventure from 1938 to 1941 rather than 1940-41); he also gives his own brief but quite competent overview of Cassian's life and teaching. What he does not do, however, is focus at all on what Merton himself has to say about Cassian in these particular conferences, or give any indication that these are part of a much longer series of classes that provide the novices with a thorough introduction to the spirituality of Cassian and some of his predecessors. Neither the context nor the content of these talks receive any detailed attention.

Similar criticism can be made of Fr. Ciorra's Introduction to the second series of conferences from the same period, the final sixteen classes of Merton's course on the Benedictine *Rule*, given between July 11 and December 19, 1962 and released as *Thomas Merton on the 12 Degrees of Humility*. Fr. Ciorra again begins with an almost identical overview of Merton as teacher (including the same factual errors) and goes on to provide his own synopsis of the life of St. Benedict as related by St. Gregory the Great and his own overview of some principal points about the *Rule*, including the central importance of chapter 7 on humility, the focus of these recorded conferences. But once again, perhaps because he

---

10. Thomas Merton, *Cassian and the Fathers: Initiation into the Monastic Tradition*, ed. Patrick F. O'Connell (Kalamazoo, MI: Cistercian Publications, 2005); for a comparison of oral and written versions see xlvii-liv.

does not want simply to summarize what Merton himself will be saying, Fr. Ciorra pays little explicit attention to the content of the presentations, and once again he provides no information about the course as a whole—also available in a published text[11]—which includes extensive discussion of Gregory's *Life*, detailed treatment of the Prologue to the *Rule* as the theological foundation of Benedict's teaching, discussion of the four kinds of monks Benedict describes in chapter 1, and consideration of selected chapters of the *Rule* that focus on the abbot, the monastic community, its various officers, the importance of manual labor, and the centrality of poverty for monastic life, before coming to what Merton considers the heart of the spiritual teaching of the *Rule*, the degrees of humility. Merton emphasizes the necessity for monks to learn the main points of this chapter "by heart"—not only to memorize them but to interiorize them, to take them to heart. He looks at the archetypal image of the ladder, found not only here but in St. John Climacus and in St. Bernard's reversal of Benedict's progression in *The Steps of Humility and Pride*. He associates the way of humility with the way of the cross, which is the way to paradise. He points out that humility is the key to living out the Benedictine vow of conversion of manners. He then leads the novices on a step-by-step journey through the twelve degrees, at times providing a word-by-word analysis of St. Benedict's formulations, consistently applying the teaching of the sixth-century text to the circumstances of his twentieth-century audience. Again a comparison of oral and written versions of the material calls attention to Merton's pedagogical practice, his use of humor (often directed at himself), of apt stories and sayings borrowed from other traditions, including Zen, his references to current events, such as the Cuban Missile Crisis, which took place in the midst of these presentations, above all his repeated emphasis on the relevance of Benedict's teaching on humility to Christian and specifically monastic discipleship.

The last two sets of 2012 releases to be considered, entitled *Solitude and Togetherness* and *The Prophet's Freedom*, turn out to be the recordings of the two retreats that Merton organized and presented at Gethsemani for contemplative prioresses in December 1967 and May 1968, though there is no indication of this in the summaries provided on the case covers. Fr. Ciorra does identify the occasion in his introduction to *Solitude and Togetherness* but never mentions that the transcripts of the retreats

---

11. Thomas Merton, *The Rule of Saint Benedict: Initiation into the Monastic Tradition* 4, ed. Patrick F. O'Connell (Collegeville, MN: Cistercian Publications, 2009); for a comparison of oral and written versions, see xlii-xlvi.

have been published in the volume *The Springs of Contemplation*,[12] and speaks vaguely of their being held in the "two-year period" 1967-68 whereas in fact the two retreats were less than six months apart. He discusses Merton's booklet *Loretto and Gethsemani*[13] without making clear that while Sr. Luke Tobin was present at many of the sessions, Loretto is not a contemplative community, leaving open the possibility of misunderstanding. His introduction to *The Prophet's Freedom* seems to presuppose that his listeners have already heard the preceding introduction as he simply refers off-hand to "these conversations," and his discussion of Merton and Vatican II would have been more apropos for the set of conferences on Merton and the Council. In neither introduction does he identify the two sets as the recordings of the December 1967 and the May 1968 conferences, respectively, and he makes no use of Merton's journal comments on the retreats, for example when he calls the first "the best retreat I ever made in my life."[14] The recordings themselves, nine from the 1967 retreat (with two more containing Merton's subsequent reflections, made for the nuns in the days immediately following), and eight from 1968, make clear that the first retreat was focused more on internal issues of religious life itself while the second was more concerned with relations with the world beyond the cloister, hence the respective titles of the two sets. Unfortunately the series are once again incomplete: material from the chapter of *The Springs of Contemplation* entitled "Collaboration, Penance, Celibacy" (*SpC* 231-41) is missing completely, and sections of three other chapters (*SpC* 74-77, 88-90, 221-29) are also omitted; all these segments involve a great deal of dialogue and interaction, which may have prompted their exclusion (though much conversation characterizes all the conferences of both retreats). Nonetheless, the recordings prove to be an invaluable corrective to *The Springs of Contemplation*, which is revealed by comparison to be a far from reliable text. It was already evident from a reference to the death of Martin Luther King in one of the chapters included in the 1967 section of the book that there was some inaccuracy in placement, but it is now clear as well that the two final chapters in the 1968 section actually belong to the 1967 retreat (as the chapter missing in the recordings probably does as well). The recordings also reveal that

12. Thomas Merton, *The Springs of Contemplation: A Retreat at the Abbey of Gethsemani*, ed. Jane Marie Richardson, SL (New York: Farrar, Straus, Giroux, 1992); subsequent references will be cited as "*SpC*" parenthetically in the text.

13. Thomas Merton, *Loretto and Gethsemani* (Trappist, KY: Abbey of Gethsemani, 1962); this text is also included as an appendix in *Springs of Contemplation* (275-85).

14. Thomas Merton, *The Other Side of the Mountain: The End of the Journey. Journals, vol. 7: 1967-1968*, ed. Patrick Hart (San Francisco: HarperCollins, 1998) 21 [12/7/1968].

the transcription goes beyond simply removing redundancies and verbal tics to extensive paraphrase and even rewriting of Merton's words; that the material is often radically reordered—material from the third 1967 conference, for example, being scattered over four different chapters, including the second last in the entire book; that some sections are radically condensed, and a number of large segments of the material are simply omitted, whether deliberately or inadvertently—for example forty minutes of the conclusion of Merton's presentation on Hasidism and thirty minutes of the opening segment of his discussion of Yoga in the following conference (probably his most extensive treatment of the major tenets of Hinduism); that quotations from sources Merton is reading (e.g. an article by Joost Meerloo [*SpC* 5-6]) are sometimes presented as Merton's own words (and transcribed just as loosely). Errors are introduced: a reference to St. Thérèse of Lisieux is mistakenly transferred to St. Teresa of Avila (*SpC* 17); when Merton refers to Fr. Thomas Philippe's teaching on Mary as "marvelous stuff," in *Springs of Contemplation* this material is erroneously attributed to "Paul Philippe, formerly secretary of the congregation for religious" (*SpC* 49-50), whereas what Merton actually said was that Thomas Philippe was "no relation to Paul Philippe, who used to be the secretary of the congregation." It will be essential henceforth to consult these recordings rather than simply relying on *Springs of Contemplation* for any references to or citations of these important retreats.

Now You Know Media is to be highly commended for embarking on this daunting project. Though of the 59 actual "novitiate" recordings (not counting the retreats and other more specialized taping), 44 had been previously available commercially (18 of these from both Electronic Paperbacks and Credence), the decision to issue these recordings in coherently related sets, even if realized only imperfectly for some of these releases, marks a revolutionary advance in giving listeners the opportunity to comprehend and appreciate what Merton was actually about in the novice conferences, in his weekly talks during the hermitage period, with their rather different purpose and dynamics, and in the various other types of presentations also preserved on tape during these last seven years of Merton's life. It is to be hoped that Now You Know will continue its project—with carefully assembled complete groupings and with introductory commentary more oriented toward situating the material in specific chronological and topical contexts—until virtually all the "oral Merton" has become available to a wide general audience.

Patrick F. O'Connell

NUGENT, Robert, SDS, *Thomas Merton and Thérèse Lentfoehr: The Story of a Friendship* (New York: St Pauls Editions, 2012), pp. xxiv + 194. ISBN 978-0-8189-1339-6 (paper) $14.95.

When a slender, unimposing volume of biographical study manages to deliver a wealth of pertinent facts as well as engaging revelations about its subjects—including the one I thought I already knew—that book earns my respect. Quoting generously from what he calls a "clockwork correspondence" (18) of approximately twenty years between Father M. Louis and Sister Thérèse, the formal terms with which they addressed each other throughout their acquaintance (as noted by Paul Pearson on page xvii), Robert Nugent skillfully traces the arc of this remarkable relationship. The book is a boon to Merton studies for many reasons.

First, as Pearson also points out in the Preface, this study takes a significant step toward filling the need for more extensive explorations of Merton's associations with influential women. Sister Thérèse Lentfoehr, SDS, author of *Words and Silence: On the Poetry of Thomas Merton*, an in-depth analysis of Merton's verse, invaluable for the personal insights of a friend and fellow poet into his craft, is indisputably one of those women. Additionally, key people who were close to Sister Thérèse have advocated for scholarly treatment of her poetics and of her friendship with Merton. In fact, in the introduction, Nugent explains good-naturedly that he found his impetus for the book in the words of one of Thérèse Lentfoehr's former Salvatorian Sisters calling for someone to "crawl out from somewhere . . . and write about her alone" (xix). While not about Sister Thérèse alone (as Nugent carefully notes), the book at its core is a detailed biographical chronicle of her life, vocation and death. This running narrative creates the context in which the sister's friendship with the famous monk is explored. This structure accomplishes two purposes: it tells the heretofore untold story of who Sister Thérèse was in her own right and offers "Merton aficionados . . . one more side of [his] multi-layered personality" (1). It is indeed enlightening to see Merton from this angle, that is, in relationship with a woman who, like himself, was an intensely multi-faceted character and a devoted correspondent who both gave to and asked much of their friendship.

The title of the introduction, "Listening In," suggests that rather than assume the dominant voice of the text, Nugent will allow the words of Lentfoehr and Merton to advance the narrative with minimal authorial commentary. The book's 422 endnotes, referencing numerous primary sources, largely letters and journals, attest to the success of this strategy. The fact that the two friends met face to face only twice in twenty years

(21) underscores the extraordinary significance of the written word as the bonding agent of their relationship. The author cites these references within a framework of seven chapters based on the chronology of Thérèse Lentfoehr's life and the evolution of her relationship with Merton, including a chapter on her early life (she was born in 1902), her entrance into religious life, her literary and academic work, and her life after Merton until her own death in 1981.

From this "listening in" the author assembles a vivid and balanced portrait of the two main characters, with no trace of effusion or slant. Thus Nugent succeeds admirably at achieving his purpose, stated in the introduction, that readers will "gain some insight into a more informal side of Merton and will meet and come to know one of Merton's closest friends, who . . . has never received the due recognition for the part she played in his life and work" (xxiv). One of the first lessons the reader learns about the two friends is that their lives contained memorable parallels beyond the obvious connection of their religious vocations, common experiences that one could reasonably assume deepened the bond between them. Thérèse Lentfoehr, like Thomas Merton, was the child of an artist. Also like Merton, she was formally educated in literature, earning a Master's degree in English from Marquette University, and was a classroom teacher of English composition and literature. Very pertinent is the fact that she was, also like Merton, a recognized poet (she published five volumes of verse) and a literary critic. Significantly, while the accounts of their initial contact vary somewhat, the consistent element of the different versions of how Father Louis "met" Sister Thérèse is that the contact was occasioned by poetry, written by one and admired by the other. There is apparently no extant artifact to clarify the details (16-17). (Perhaps the ambiguity concerning this first meeting of minds has its own poetic resonance?)

The first documented exchange aptly enough also centered upon poetry, edidted by Lentfoehr, one selection of which was reviewed by Merton in what Thérèse considered "unnecessary and sophomoric" (18) terms—and she wrote to tell him so. Not long after that tense encounter, however, she wrote to him again, this time to praise his recently published *The Seven Storey Mountain*. When Merton replied by sending her an original typescript of the book, he, as Nugent puts it, planted "the seed" of what would become Sister Thérèse's "Merton collection" (18), a passionately maintained, single collector's archive, unmatched in its expansiveness, a testimony of her lifelong devotion to his life and work.

Commendably, Nugent does not omit the idiosyncrasies and vulnerabilities of each party in the friendship nor the difficult moments that these traits occasionally caused. For example, while he is careful to render

Sister Thérèse as a loyal supporter of Merton's career, he also shows that she apparently could be possessive and relentless, sometimes exasperatingly so, when it came to procuring artifacts for her Merton collection, particularly photographs of him, especially in the early days. Nugent also relates an incident wherein Sister Thérèse insisted on straightening up Merton's hermitage during a visit there in 1967, audacity that rankled in Merton and prompted Tommie O'Callaghan to remind him that "Thérèse was his 'first fan' and knew more about him and his work than anyone else" and to entreat him to be more patient with her (159-60). Finally, Nugent includes details showing how Sister Thérèse's commitment to Merton had an element of emotional instability, such as her reaction to learning about Merton and M. Nugent writes that according to one of her former students, "the revelation threw her into a royal tizzy so that she had wept almost hysterically when she told him about it" (141-42). The fact that she destroyed the letters in which Merton apparently confided the affair to her (and noted emphatically that she did so) (142) further evokes the fierce intensity of her attachment to Merton.

Nor does Nugent's story depict a perfect Merton. The author notes that in addition to frequent gifts of relics and other sacred objects that Thérèse bestowed on Merton, she also willingly offered her services as a typist, an act of generosity to which Merton on occasion responded, in Nugent's word, "disingenuously" (hinting, albeit gently, that Merton was taking advantage of her), such as when Merton wrote to her: "I only permit myself to impose on you because you say the work is entertaining and that it amuses you" (79). A more powerful implication of Merton's capacity for insensitivity regarding Thérèse is Nugent's account of how in 1972, in preparation to write her previously mentioned book on Merton's poetry for New Directions, she traveled to Bellarmine where she was denied access to Merton's private materials because Merton had not listed her among those who had permission to read them, and how this experience led to an outburst of grief and anger overheard by others in the guesthouse where she was staying during her visit to Louisville. An apologetic James Laughlin tried to assuage her feelings in a letter several months after the incident, by telling her "that Tom was just daydreaming when he wrote that part of the trust Indenture, and did not name you" (169).

Overall, what resounds most forcefully in this study are the affirming portrayals of Merton and Lentfoehr's friendship. The book is rich with passages from their letters conveying the true nature of this bond between two friends sharing a life of total submission to God, yet not free of the anguish that is common to people who walk by faith. The following excerpt is but one illustration. Writing to Thérèse on what he mistakenly thought was the anniversary of her vows (missing it by one day), Merton reassures her: "He loves you very much, you know, and He has proved it by letting you suffer. . . . If there were one present I would really like to give you it would be this: that you be overwhelmed with the sense that whatever may be your infirmities they, and they most of all, are your most infallible claim upon His infinite love. That is one grace I want for myself too, I certainly have plenty of infirmity to cash in on" (65). These and similar statements of spiritual counsel recorded throughout the book radiate love; although the words come from Merton, the empathy they imply bespeaks a trusting, open soul on the receiving end, saying almost as much about the listener as the speaker.

Thomas Merton and Sister Thérèse Lentfoehr: The Story of a Friendship ends with an Afterword by Sister Carol Thresher, SDS, in which she describes Sister Thérèse as a "living legend" (173), a transcendent artistic spirit and a person of rare selflessness, who embodied the Salvatorian charism (175). The Afterword is followed by a 1974 poem of Lentfoehr's called "Song for a Marriage" (177-78) in which can be heard the voice of a gifted poet celebrating love as the heart of creation. The choice to conclude the book in this way fortifies Nugent's intentions to confer on the accomplishments of Sister Thérèse Lentfoehr their rightful consideration.

Deborah Kehoe

WALDRON, Robert, *Thomas Merton—The Exquisite Risk of Love: The Chronicle of a Monastic Romance* (London: Darton, Longman, Todd, 2012) pp. x + 146. ISBN 978-0-232-52924-1 (paper) £12.99.

The title of Robert Waldron's book, *The Exquisite Risk of Love: The Chronicle of a Monastic Romance*, the image of a nude Eve, sporting a sparse but discreetly positioned spray of leaves, and the name of Thomas Merton—all work together to create a cover designed to catch the reader's attention. Observing that scholars have "shied away" from addressing Merton's love for M., Waldron undertakes to do just that by examining the poems Merton wrote in 1966 after falling in love with a young woman assigned to care for him while he was hospitalized for back surgery. Waldron "cross-references" the poems with entries in the personal journal Merton was keeping at the time to illustrate how, in both poems and journal entries, Merton celebrates the passionate love he feels for M. even as he struggles to reconcile that love with his life as a monk.

A few words about Waldron's sources—both the poems and the journal—may help to place his book in context. Merton entrusted the poems, inspired by his love for M., to the care of his friend and publisher

James Laughlin, who printed the poems in 1985 in an expensive, limited edition of 250 copies, simply entitled *Eighteen Poems*.[1] By that time, three of the poems had already been published in 1977 in *The Collected Poems of Thomas Merton*.[2] Five others would later appear in the sixth volume of Merton's journal, *Learning to Love*,[3] published in 1997. More recently, Lynn R. Szabo included thirteen of the eighteen poems in *In the Dark before Dawn: New Selected Poems of Thomas Merton*,[4] published in 2005. In addition, excerpts from the poems have appeared in Michael Mott's biography, *The Seven Mountains of Thomas Merton*,[5] and in various articles, essays and books, as well as in Patrick F. O'Connell's entry on *Eighteen Poems* in *The Thomas Merton Encyclopedia*.[6] However, Waldron's book marks the first publication of all eighteen poems in a single trade volume and includes two poems that until now were only available in the limited edition published by Laughlin: "Two Songs for M." and "Gethsemani, May 19, 1966."

The journal *Learning to Love: Exploring Solitude and Freedom* (a title chosen by the editor, who is also the author of this review), is the sixth of seven volumes of Merton's private journals and spans the period from January 2, 1966 to October 8, 1967. The volume includes three appendices: "A Midsummer Diary for M." (*LL* 303-48), a short journal written in June 1966, which Merton shared with M. and a copy of which he entrusted

---

1. Thomas Merton, *Eighteen Poems* (New York: New Directions, 1985).

2. Thomas Merton, *The Collected Poems of Thomas Merton* (New York: New Directions, 1977) 447-48, 615-18, 801-802.

3. Thomas Merton, *Learning to Love: Exploring Solitude and Freedom. Journals, vol. 6: 1966-1967*, ed. Christine M. Bochen (San Francisco: HarperCollins, 1997) 52-54, 56-57, 59-61, 64-65, 131-33; subsequent references will be cited as "*LL*" parenthetically in the text.

4. Thomas Merton, *In the Dark before Dawn: New Selected Poems*, ed. Lynn R. Szabo (New York: New Directions, 2005) 188-219.

5. Michael Mott, *The Seven Mountains of Thomas Merton* (Boston: Houghton Mifflin, 1984) 454, 456.

6. Patrick F. O'Connell, "*Eighteen Poems*," in William H. Shannon, Christine M. Bochen and Patrick F. O'Connell, *The Thomas Merton Encyclopedia* (Maryknoll, NY: Orbis, 2002) 128-32. O'Connell concludes the entry with a concise and cogent description of *Eighteen Poems* that may be especially helpful to readers of this review who are unfamiliar with the collection: "the sequence as a whole traces the pattern of the relationship from an initial experience of holistic 'paradise-consciousness,' a sense of oneness not only with one another but also with the natural world, and with its divine source, through a period of anguish caused by the fact of physical separation and by the tension between commitment to another person and commitment to a solitary vocation, to a tenuous yet genuine resolution that both embraces the bond of shared experience and accepts the necessity of letting go of the other and of the possibilities she embodies" (132).

to the safekeeping of James Laughlin; "Some Personal Notes, January-March 1966" (*LL* 351-67), which Merton kept in a small spiral notebook; and "A Postscript" (*LL* 371), an entry, dated April 14, 1966, from one of Merton's reading notebooks. The titles of the second and third of these appendices were given to the selections by the journal editor. Although Waldron is "cross-referencing" the poems with the journal, he does not quote directly from the journal; instead he paraphrases Merton's journal entries. The only exceptions are "A Postscript" for which Waldron cites the notebook, housed in the Merton collection at Syracuse University, rather than *Learning to Love*, and a single direct quotation.

The Exquisite Risk of Love consists of an Introduction and eighteen short chapters—each bearing the title of one of the eighteen poems. The stanzas (and in the case of the prose poem "Certain Proverbs Arise out of Dreams," the paragraphs), are interspersed with Waldron's explication and commentary. In addition to making references to Merton's journal, Waldron introduces and discusses a host of topics related to Merton's life and work that, in Waldron's view, shed light on the poems. For example, while introducing the first of the poems, "With the World in My Bloodstream," Waldron considers the significance of having a home, likening Merton to Henri Nouwen and Gerard Manley Hopkins. Thus Waldron observes that Nouwen found a home at L'Arche, Hopkins in the Society of Jesus, and Merton at the Trappist Abbey of Gethsemani where, Waldron notes, no women were allowed; where, in an all-male community, a monk often finds "a substitute" for the absence of the feminine in Mary; and where one renounces life's vital aspect of "touch." These observations about the monastic life set a context for Waldron's reading of Merton's relationship with M. Waldron compares Merton's experience and poems with those of writers such as Hart Crane, John Donne, George Herbert and T. S. Eliot and makes reference to religious figures such as St. Bonaventure, St. John of the Cross and Meister Eckhart. Waldron reads Merton through the lens of Carl Jung who, Waldron writes, would describe Merton "as an unbalanced man" who "has allowed his intellect to dominate his personality at the expense of his emotional life" (124).

The book reads like a labor of love on Waldron's part. His excitement for the project and his conviction about the significance of the poems is apparent throughout. Waldron's voice as a writer comes though vividly which makes the tone of the book conversational. As I was reading, I had the feeling that Waldron was "speaking" to me and other readers. In fact, I could imagine each chapter as a short talk. As a result, Waldron's style is certainly readable and the content is thought-provoking.

Having said that, I must add that there are several aspects of the book that warrant caution on the part of the reader. Some are matters of fact, others matters of interpretation. Here is an instance in which both fact and interpretation are problematic: Waldron quotes Merton reflecting on his purpose in writing in a paragraph Merton wrote in a notebook entry of April 14, 1966—a passage published as "A Postscript" in *Learning to Love*:

> For to write is to love: it is to inquire and to praise, or to confess, or to appeal. This testimony of love remains necessary. Not to reassure myself that I am ("I write therefore I am"), but simply to pay my debt to life, to the world, to other men. To speak out with an open heart and say what seems to me to have meaning.

Waldron mistakenly states that the passage was written a year after Merton met M. (9) even though his note correctly identifies the date of the entry as April 14, 1966 (16). While error in dating is a relatively minor matter, Waldron uses erroneous dating to support his view that "Merton's writing perspective suffered a tremendous sea change when he met M." (9). Waldron characterizes the "sea change" this way:

> Prior to M., Merton's writing was much involved in Catholic apologia. As he [Merton] describes it, his writing was too dogmatic; too much a list of things one had to obey and do. Not good writing because, although many admired it, it was fraught with compassion. The best writing is direct admission without embellishment. (9)

There is no compelling evidence to support the thesis of a "sea change" in Merton's writing, before and after M., nor is there reason to accept Waldron's characterization of Merton's writing before M. as "apologia." While some have observed that Merton's best-selling autobiography, *The Seven Storey Mountain*, published in 1948, is marked by a triumphalistic view of Catholicism, neither the autobiography nor Merton's subsequent writing can be construed as "apologia." I simply do not know what to make of Waldron's statement that Merton's writing prior to 1966 was not good writing "because it was fraught with compassion." A typo perhaps? What Merton wrote in the notebook on April 14, 1966 was this:

> The bad writing I have done has all been authoritarian, the declaration of musts, and the announcement of punishments. Bad because it implies a lack of love, good insofar as there may yet have been some love in it. The best stuff has been more straight confession and witness. (*LL* 371)

It is worth noting here that when Merton assessed his own writing in a graph he constructed in 1967, he identified only one book as "awful" (*What Are These Wounds?*), one as "very poor" (*Exile Ends in Glory*), and one as "poor" (*Figures for an Apocalypse*). Other categories included "less good," "good," "better" and "best." He did not place any books in the category of "best." Interestingly, he rates *The Seven Storey Mountain* as "better."[7]

Waldron extends the before and after comparison to Merton's poetry. In the Introduction to *The Exquisite Risk of Love*, Waldron asserts that Merton's "poetry prior to *Eighteen Poems* was romantic and traditional with a preference for rhymed poems. The major exception of his poetic opus is the nearly unreadable *The Geography of Lograire*" (3). Even a quick perusal of *In the Dark before Dawn*, the collection of Merton poems selected and edited by Lynn Szabo, offers ample evidence to the contrary. The collection, arranged thematically and chronologically, highlights the breadth and depth of Merton's poetry from the '40s, through the '50s and into the '60s. Certainly, Merton developed as a poet over time and the poems inspired by Merton's love for M. are part of his story and his poetry. As Szabo illustrates, these poems explore the theme of what it means to be human—one theme among many in Merton's poetic corpus. Over the years, Merton explored the landscapes of geography and of the sacred within. He was also writing poems about history's watershed events at Hiroshima, Nagasaki and Auschwitz and engaging the issues of the world and its cultures. But I find nothing to suggest that *Eighteen Poems* signals the turning point that Waldron suggests.

There are other points on which Waldron and I differ. For example, he writes, "As a monk, he was of the mind that one must win God's love by one's actions" (22). This statement clashes with what I read Merton to be saying about his experience of Christian faith and more precisely his experience of God. God's love and mercy are grace—pure gift. On other occasions, Waldron wrestles with the state of Merton's soul and whether or not and how he has "violated his vow": "And so we are then forced to ask ourselves if he is committing a mortal sin, thereby endangering his immortal soul" (122). Is this really a question we need to ask ourselves?

In his last chapter, Waldron observes that "It is enriching to read both the *Eighteen Poems* and *Learning to Love* simultaneously." Then he adds: "But if I had to choose which of the two is the finer chronicle of Merton's love for M., I would have to say that it is found in his poetry" (145). I resist characterizing either one as the finer chronicle. In my view, both are powerful expressions of Merton's experience and insight—clearly

---

7. Thomas Merton, *"Honorable Reader": Reflections on My Work*, ed. Robert E. Daggy (New York: Crossroad, 1989) 150-51.

different modes of expression. After reading Waldron's book and other considerations of Merton's love for M., I can't help thinking Merton is better served by our reading the poems and the journal first-hand.

Waldron's book makes it possible for us to do just that. To do justice to Merton's poems, I would recommend reading each poem through from start to finish before reading Waldron's explication and commentary. I would also encourage readers to take the time to read the journal passages that Waldron paraphrases. Certainly, he is intent on being faithful to Merton's meaning. Nevertheless, paraphrasing has its limits and, often the journal context—what precedes or follows the passage—is integral to understanding Merton's meaning. One additional example from the book may serve to make my point. Reflecting on a promise Merton makes to Abbot James Fox, Waldron writes: "To understand the extent of the power Gethsemani and its abbot had over Merton, Merton allowed himself to be coaxed into writing and signing, on 8 September 1966, a commitment that he would never live anywhere but Gethsemani, and that he would continue to live the life of a hermit and never marry." Waldron adds: "We [*sic*] cannot help feeling, since Merton at the time of this signing was studying the absurdist Albert Camus, that Merton's signing of this written vow is absurd: absurd for the abbot to suggest it, and absurd for Merton to agree to it" (89). In his journal, Merton put it this way:

> Thursday the 8th I made my commitment—read the short formula I had written (simplest possible form). Dom James signed it with me content that he now had me in the bank as an asset that would not go out and lose itself in some crap game (is he sure—? The awful crap game of love!). A commitment "to live in solitude for the rest of my life in so far as health may permit" (i.e. if I grow old and get too crippled an infirmary room will count as solitude??).

Merton's tone is sardonic to be sure but the next line is not: "After that I was at peace and said Mass with great joy" (*LL* 129). Reading Waldron's words and then Merton's helps me to appreciate just how difficult it is put what Merton writes into our own words—and this is as true of Merton's poems as it is of his journals.

Christine M. Bochen

THOMPSON, Phillip M., *Returning to Reality: Thomas Merton's Wisdom for a Technological World* (Eugene, OR: Cascade Books, 2012), pp. xxi + 112. ISBN 978-1-62032-252-9 (paper) $17.00.

Once, during shared *lectio divina* in the hallowed Merton Hall of Genesee

Abbey, a Trappist monastery in Piffard, New York, Brother Anthony told me that the monks were open to new technologies as long as they passed one crucial test. If the technology facilitated their journey toward God, they kept it; and if it didn't, they let it go. Thomas Merton, as we're reminded in Phillip Thompson's provocative new book, had similar thoughts: "Technology can elevate and improve man's life only [if] it remains subservient to his real interests; that it respects his true being; that it remembers that the origin and goal of all being is in God" (53). If Merton were to sit down and trace out the complex weave of influences on his technological thoughts, from the Desert Fathers and Mothers to space-age physicists, if he were to use his piercing insights to name the modern idolatries and twisted psychologies that lead to harmful digital media addictions and the looming specter of deathless transhumans, if he were to teach us his methods for nurturing that inner solitude that's beyond the noise of even the most torrential digital deluge, then Thompson's book is the nexus for that coherent Catholic vision.

Indeed, that Thompson provides a *coherent* vision of Merton's nuanced contemplative response to technology is one of the most remarkable aspects of the book because Merton, as Thompson reminds us, never—outside notes and novice lectures—wrote a comprehensive essay or a book-length project explicitly dealing with his critique of technology. Gathering Merton's comments interspersed throughout articles, books, letters, lectures, unpublished essays and poems, Thompson creates a complex mosaic of Merton's ambivalent reaction to mechanized modernity, always bringing us back, after explicating Merton's response and advice, to a central contemporary question: "how do we pursue our daily lives in this technological world?" (74).

In pursuit of that question, Thompson divides his book into five chapters, the first one serving as an overview of Merton's thoughtful response to modern technology and the communities—both sacred and secular—that helped form his conscience. The next three chapters represent the analytic center of the book, in which Thompson transitions from past to present to future in order to explore how Merton's beliefs relate to three types of technologies: Cold War nuclear capabilities (past), the blooming, buzzing confusion of always-on digital media (present), and the transhumanist agenda of biotechnology (future). Each of these three chapters has a bifurcated organizing structure, in which Thompson first defines the implications of the problem at hand, and then details Merton's contemplative critique and advice. The final chapter shares specific methods Merton's writings provide for developing what Merton called a "mental ecology," a vibrant consciousness of solitude amidst our technologically mediated lives. Throughout, Thompson expertly handles the tension inherent between extracting useful Mertonian guidelines and portraying Merton's dynamic, developing, always-questioning and in-dialogue process of grappling with technology, which is the kind of mentality that led Merton in 1967, referring to his tape recorder and camera, to assert "that he might need to 'take back some of the things that I have said about technology'" (80).

The first chapter represents a highly textured tapestry of Merton's heuristic beliefs, the intellectual terms and ways of seeing technology that he borrowed and made his own, and the community of like-minded individuals—from novelists to Zen Buddhists—that provided Merton a sense of solidarity. Thompson locates the fount of Merton's technological critique within one question: how will this technology affect my connection with God, the source and summit of my existence? At the center of Merton's contemplative wisdom, Thompson explains, are the two foundational ways in which Merton connected with God: the simplicity of the early Christian desert community's movement toward "purity of heart" and the seventh-century Eastern Christian theologian Saint Maximus the Confessor's concept of *theoria physike*, or contemplation of nature. The problem for Thompson and Merton isn't about challenging some reductive technology-is-inherently-bad view, but about challenging what Thompson calls a "technological mentality," in which mechanistic efficiency and expediency are reified above everything else, and true community degrades into false collectivity, which Thompson aligns with the desire for pleasure, wealth and power (xx, 15). Although Thompson makes the admirable distinction between technology and the technological mentality, this is a distinction that, unfortunately, becomes quite tenuous later on—and even appears to disappear altogether—at certain places within the text. One cannot help but think that Thompson could have more explicitly revealed the distinction between community-building forms of technology and the Taylorist scientific labor management philosophy of standardization. Frederick Winslow Taylor, whom Thompson uses for an epigraph to the first chapter (1), championed a philosophy of labor in the late nineteenth and early twentieth century that sought to reduce humans to machines who churned out products in a regularized fashion, and it's specifically Taylor's philosophy that looms unacknowledged behind much of Thompson's technological bugbear. And yet, despite at times erasing the distinction between technology and the technological mentality, Thompson commendably always returns to the idea that, rather than some essential perversity within technology itself, it's what we *do* (or choose not to do) with technology that counts.

The second chapter is the most historically concrete and least specu-lative chapter in the book because it deals with a problem—the threat of nuclear war—that Merton directly contemplated in its fullness, as opposed to the increasingly hypothetical language in chapter three, about the con-temporary communications glut, and chapter four, about the transhumanist future. From the start, when Thompson compassionately retells the story of John Paul Merton's tragic death during World War II, which Thompson frames as the source of Merton's visceral reaction to war, we receive the image of Merton engaging with the wider world, whether that means his conscientious objection in 1941, his ongoing dialogue with nuclear sci-entists, or his willingness to challenge the Church's concept of the "just war," a heuristic from a pre-nuclear era. Thompson adroitly weaves all these strands together to uncover the spiritual meaning of a world forever subjected to the threat of total, technologically mindless annihilation: "This state of affairs regarding nuclear weapons was a direct denial of our humanity, of our vocations as children of God" (34).

The third chapter applies Merton's twentieth-century insights on technology to the twenty-first century tsunami of digital communication technologies. Coalescing statistics about technology use, Thompson argues that the modern flood of Tweets, emails and other digital media might create a culture of mental instability and shallowness. "[A] case can be made," says Thompson, "that the new communication technologies are on balance detrimental to our cognitive capacities" (42). Extrapolating from Merton's views on communication technologies, Thompson then offers some useful and reasonable methods for nurturing spiritual vitality, such as moderating the time we spend using digital media, developing a prayer life, seeking supportive allies and making time for exercise and relaxation. The main limitation with this chapter is that, in order to ap-ply Merton's twentieth-century advice to our twenty-first-century digital deluge, Thompson has to frame the contemporary technological explo-sion as a difference in degree, rather than a difference in kind, which, at times, leads to some shaky hypothetical statements, such as: "If Merton skewered the idols of television, imagine what he would think of the cur-rent flood of superficial messages coursing from a host of information technologies" (47). It's important to remember how active (as opposed to the passivity of television) and radically new (a difference in kind, not just degree) such phenomena as the rise of open-source programming and commons-based peer-production are, which see large groups of people col-laborating online on projects for the benefit of many. Although Thompson acknowledges that "There are wonderful instances of charity and human connection" with modern digital media, the two paragraphs he devotes to that subject seem rather peremptory, and one is left wishing that he had provided more instances of a vibrant, supportive, multi-modal Catholic online community (39). (In full disclosure, I should admit that Thompson critiques my professor and sometime co-author, Cathy Davidson, a digital pedagogy expert and Duke English professor, arguing that "there is little to no social or biological science to support" her claims that "Our brains are being rewired to capture . . . rich diversity and multiple possibilities" [42].) Despite a limited sense of the possibilities of a genuine Catholic online presence, Thompson's reflections on the harmful over-use of digital media and the contemplative methods to deal with this flood of digital data are both compelling and tremendously helpful for anyone looking for a Catholic response to our contemporary digital environment.

The fourth chapter explores how the bio-industrial complex is actively working to transform humans into transhumans. Focusing on the eugenics side of transhumanism, Thompson defines transhumanism as "a wide range of biotechnologies that will enable a radical evolution of human biology beyond its current capacities and limitations," such as nanotechnology that seeks to render humans immortal (57). Thompson allows Merton to weigh in on transhumanism by focusing on Merton's conception of death as a reminder of the human/divine barrier, which means that the transhumanist goal of the deathless human represents the reification of human experience (à la "Atlas and the Fat Man"[1]) and a rejection of our reunion after death with the source of our being. This is a highly compelling, imaginative and provocative chapter in which Thompson skillfully applies the roots of Merton's wisdom to a potential future reality.

The final chapter is a distillation of some of the most important ways Merton suggests that we can reintegrate our humanity and avoid technological overload. Thompson provides five suggestions for cultivating what Merton calls a "mental ecology": (1) practicing sane forms of work; (2) embracing small-scale technology; (3) learning a craft; (4) rejuvenating ourselves in nature; and (5) living a "philosophy of solitude" in which we seek "a 'spiritual and simple oneness' in ourselves" (85). If you're looking for a Catholic way to thrive amidst technology, this is a perceptive, smart and decidedly practical list. Although Thompson is wonderful at taking Merton's beliefs and turning them into practical suggestions, a major limitation in this chapter—and throughout the book—is his tendency to not explore specific ways in which *technology* can help us avoid technological overload within our contemporary data-driven lives. He certainly

---

1. Thomas Merton, *Raids on the Unspeakable* (New York: New Directions, 1966) 91-107.

gestures toward the possibility of using technology to help us deal with the digital deluge, such as when he says that "technology is not only part of the solution but also part of the problem" (73), or that "Some experts on communication technologies offer additional tips" for balancing our digitally-mediated lives (54). Thus a useful supplement to Thompson's elegant book would be Howard Rheingold's *Net Smart: How to Thrive Online*, in which the famed Stanford and Berkeley social-media lecturer explains how one can use Buddhist meditation techniques to successfully navigate the flood of digital media, outlining five fundamental digital literacies: attention, critical consumption of information, participation, collaboration and network smarts. Aside from fostering the essential digital literacy of attention, or mindfulness, Rheingold's book can show how to set up the appropriate filters, dashboards and news radars that would enable the computer to handle the digital deluge, providing both time for solitude and the opportunity to create a meaningful, community-based, Catholic online experience. If Phillip Thompson's book is essential for any Catholic seeking to discover Merton's practical advice for dealing with our always-on digital media, then Howard Rheingold's book is essential for any Buddhist; and as Merton said before leaving for his fateful Asian trip, "I intend to become as good a Buddhist as I can."[2]

Patrick Thomas Morgan

Thomas Merton: Monk on the Edge, edited by Ross Labrie and Angus Stuart (North Vancouver, BC: Thomas Merton Society of Canada, 2012), pp. 199. ISBN: 978-1-927512-02-9 (paper) $25.00 Can.

Thomas Merton was a monk on the edge of the monastery, on the edge of the Church as well as on the margins of society. The edge motif was one that Merton cultivated and promoted. Long before it became fashionable to be marginal he had confronted the monastic appellation known as singularity and its overtones of being marginal, special or peculiar. Imagine walking around a Trappist monastery with a best-selling autobiography under your name, at the age of thirty-three. Things began to get complicated. Merton entered Gethsemani in 1941. By 1948 he had published *The Seven Storey Mountain*. By 1955 he was novice master, a job he held for ten years. By 1965 he was a hermit, and by the end of 1968 he was dead at the age of 53. During this short span he achieved an enormous amount of writing and publishing. He also happened to live at a time of rapid and unprecedented change. How he fitted himself into all

    2. David Steindl-Rast, "Recollections of Thomas Merton's Last Days in the West," *Monastic Studies* 7 (1969) 10.

this is what the authors here investigate, and why the concept of the edge and the margin so aptly frames Merton's life and legacy.

The Canadian Merton Society has put together a collection of a wide variety of studies on the life and work of Thomas Merton. One is always fascinated by the way scholars come up with yet one more study of an intriguing subject, how they dig up and develop themes that may not have been addressed, at least in certain directions. This book is a good example. The volume opens with a Foreword by Patrick Hart (1) and an Introduction by Ross Labrie (3-12). Both are helpful and centering, as we have come to expect from these authors.

In "Prophecy and Contemplation" (13-22), Michael W. Higgins tells us that to prophesy is not to predict, but to seize upon reality in its moment of highest expectation and tension toward the new. To prophesy is not to calculate; it is to perceive. And Higgins tells us too that Merton came to see the contemplative life as a dependence on God. And contemplation for Merton was nothing less than the perfect and ultimate guarantor of human freedom.

"Merton's Mystical Visions: a Widening Circle" (23-44) by Susan McCaslin deals with what she terms four of Merton's most important mystical experiences. These took place in Rome, Cuba, Louisville and Sri Lanka. And she goes on to investigate and define how these four visionary experiences manifest and express the importance of being in relationship to all that is human. This provides a map of Merton's progression to a mature humanism.

"Apocalypse and Modernity" (45-63) by Bruce K. Ward investigates whether or not apocalypse has any interest or relevance in our time. Here, we get a short review of apocalypticism as expounded by such figures as Dante, Blake and Dostoevsky, as well as several Church Fathers. Pasternak and Girard are recruited as well. Ward tells us that allusions to the apocalyptic abound in Merton's writings.

"Technology and the Loss of Paradise" (65-78) by Paul Dekar deals with Merton's approach to a technological age and some of the dangers and advantages involved. (The author does not mention it, but ironically it was the technological malfunction of an electric fan that led to Merton's blazing entry into paradise.)

"Merton and the Beats" (79-100) by Angus Stuart is an interesting and curious attempt to situate Merton in the mentality and life-style of a certain marginal segment of the culture, the beat generation. Stuart lays out what it means to be a beat not just in the etymology of the word, but in its cultural manifestation. Some of the major beat figures, such as Jack Kerouac and Allen Ginsberg, are marshaled to the cause. Here Merton's affinity for the edge and the margin, and the countercultural, both civil and religious, is investigated and examined at length.

"Peacemaker" (101-15), by Ron Dart, divides Merton's life journey into four distinct yet overlapping phases, and claims it is in the fourth season that Merton's peacemaking vocation became the clearest and most mature. It seems that Merton was a pacifist, with reservations. How this struggle manifested itself and worked itself out is the thrust of this exhaustive and complete study of one of Merton's most intriguing identities as peacemaker—taking on war, violence and protest. This stance positioned Merton on the edge of civil and religious culture of his time. Merton had his share of troubles with bans and censorship, and in that sense shared with those in the front lines of a new movement that was often opposed and even attacked.

"Merton and Interreligious Dialogue" (117-34) by Ryan Scruggs studies Merton's interaction and discussion with interreligious contacts of other traditions. The three major monotheistic religions were familiar territory for Merton. Christianity attracted his attention, and especially its particular form in Catholicism. Merton in *Seven Storey Mountain* explains this attraction. The author touches briefly on the topic of whether or not Merton would have moved beyond his faith commitment. Would he have moved beyond the bounds he had known since his conversion, beyond his priesthood, beyond his monastic commitment?

"Merton in Asia: The Polonnaruwa Illumination" (135-54) by Donald Grayston discusses the experiences, mystical and otherwise, of Merton's encounter with the Buddha statues, and Merton's illuminating experiences. The themes of pilgrimage and journey are treated in depth and detail as well, providing thereby a thorough analysis of Merton's interest in Asia.

In "The Mystical Ecology of Merton's Poetics" (155-68), Lynn R. Szabo tells us that Merton's immense love for the natural world, as he discovered it in his Kentucky surroundings, grounded his poetry in a mystical ecology. Some Merton scholars consider his early monastic poetry as among his best, and his poems about the monastery are among his most quoted and memorable. The author gives many examples of Merton's spiritual sensibilities brought to life in his poetry as a mystical response to the natural world.

"Merton on Atheism in Camus" (169-89) by Ross Labrie brings the volume to a close, and give us an excellent introduction not only to the topic of atheism in the writings of Camus, but also a detailed account of Merton's Camus studies, and of Merton's own struggles with the concepts of belief, and of the place and role of God in human affairs. Merton's reading of Camus sparked many reflections on organized religion and its response to the plight of the human condition.

The book ends with a perceptive Afterword (191-95) by Susan Mc-Caslin, and brief descriptions of the contributors (197-99), all Canadians. And so we have here Merton on the edge. Paradoxically, the edge moved him to the center in many ways. It seems that of all the edges from which we have to choose—far, cutting, rough, leading, sharp—Merton as fully expected fits them all.

Richard Weber, OCSO

MCDONALD, Mary M., *It Draws Me: The Art of Contemplation* (Liguori, MO: Liguori, 2012), pp. xx + 76. ISBN 978-0-7648-2179-0 (paper) $14.99.

Our postmodern world explodes with a sense of widespread exhaustion, a vision of wars, storms and devastation. Many realize that world peace begins with one's own inner peace and this book makes the case that the silence of artworks (icons and Chinese Song landscapes) promotes inner peace. Dr. McDonald's goal for this practical book is to help us use such art in our daily prayer. She asks in the Introduction: "Can meditating with great works of art help you to pray better?" (xi). The book affirms this and achieves much more: it presents convincing evidence that use of these images can reveal a model for understanding our own life's meaning. As the author puts it, "How much more powerful would an insight [into some important aspect of our lives] be if an image could help . . . live that knowledge?" (vii).

Inspired by the challenge to develop college students' insight, Dr. Mc-Donald finds the praxis of "reading" and abiding with images. "[C]onnection and application" and "listening through reading" are key monastic principles the author stresses (5). The book clearly aims to train readers in life-giving ways to become more truly themselves. McDonald's contribution to the literature on inner-journaling is, I believe, precisely this well-structured training, which Merton aficionados will find most appealing. The book features previously unpublished lecture notes on *lectio divina* by Merton, and the 32-page illustration section includes a photo of Merton plus Song Dynasty paintings and Russian icons.

The Dedication page mentions being taught "to always enjoy yellow leaves against a gray sky" (iii). McDonald displays here the same visual-verbal sensitivity shot through Thomas Merton's journals, that reveals him as one dedicated to closely observing (reading) nature, her colors and textures. To delight in creation is to affirm oneness with it, a special joy in contemplating the Chinese tenth-to-thirteenth-century landscapes

reproduced in the center of this book. Orthodox icons' stately composi-
tions, by contrast, give access to mysteries of the Christian tradition, and
Dr. McDonald guides us in reading them. The very term "iconographer"
means one who "writes an image," and thus how to read the image needs
to be learned. From personal experience, I can attest to the power of
icons when used regularly in one's prayer time. Such an image becomes
a living presence, a friend unlike any other, "alive and challenging," as
McDonald says (8).

The author presents her research compactly and her selections of
Merton quotations feature as images as well as text, reaffirming how her
book trains us to read the other classic spiritual images. Merton's words
build powerfully in McDonald's arrangement; they take us from a casual
but common misreading of contemplation's escapist value, juxtaposed
to: "The contemplative enters into God in order to be created" (A3).
These choices pack a punch, and provoke one to look much further into
his work. As a man tempered by the Depression and the Second World
War, the existentialist Merton concludes that "it is not humanly possible
to live a life without significance and remain healthy" (A31). To live in
a state of compassion: this is the goal of the truly human life.

There are other manuals for art-journaling (like Marianne Hieb's fine
Inner Journeying through Art-Journaling [Jessica Kingsley Publishers,
2005]), and for training in how to use art images in prayer, but McDonald's
It Draws Me is the one each Merton fan should add to the "Praxis" section
of a personal library. It satisfies those who would follow up on her scholarly
sources, as well, because the author discreetly uses endnotes. McDonald
points out that "We have inherited a sense of reading as informative and a
sense of art as inert, and both prevent us from fully reflecting on and applying the messages that contemplative artists long to give" (5). The essential
task is to actively "read" the art work, as in *lectio*, and listen to the message,
the communication from the spirit of the divine within.

Active listening is the crucial skill in any learning environment, as
teachers know, and McDonald brings the reader through a concise and
intriguing history of this praxis for ancient monastic experts, from the fifth
century on. She even introduces us to Greek terms for the "technology"
of such reading. The expectation for an active listener/reader was that this
practice would change the reader, as the text's (or image's) message was
applied in the life of the reader. It is fascinating to know that "Medieval
physicians assigned reading [aloud] as another form of exercise, like they
would assign walking or running" (6). St. Bernard of Clairvaux reports
not getting beyond the third chapter of the Song of Songs, when writing
over thirteen years his eighty-six sermons on this topic. What an example

for us of deep reading! Our author follows this chestnut with a vision of Merton writing with such haste that "many syntactic errors" provoked the Cistercian censors to send him handbooks. Her analysis seems right on the mark here: more than mere rushing to get into print, Merton "was also in a way following monastic beliefs about the real goals of reading and writing" (7). Merton's unpublished notes are a real treat. They explain the forgotten liturgy of Septuagesima Sunday in its historical context which is especially relevant to our contemporary world situation; this reviewer feels a special value in this entire chapter.

The contrast between monastic reading and that for a "university culture" is illuminating in this text. As McDonald states, Merton noted that "reading for *wisdom*" was one practice lost with the rise of the university in the thirteenth century. Clearly, the latter grew secular and systematic, promoting knowledge rather than communication with the divine. We need to relearn the monastic practice, if we hope to "read" icons or the Chinese meditative landscapes in the way they were intended. To look at an image as "a challenge" to our worldly habits is not the way art history, for example, is taught, but it is critical in the contemplative atmosphere McDonald encourages. There is much to learn in this book, and much to practice. As she puts it, "The most interesting aspect of this process of reading is that each moment asks for connection. The text is connected to the reader's own life, to the community, to the divine. The reader was meant to grow in respect and love of the divine and others through this often solitary reading experience" (8).

A visionary phrase presents the reader with the ultimate goal of a truly human life: "that knowledge which flows from love and leads to more love" (9). A teacher who aims to train her students in life-affirming values and habits will find this book a substantive help. In a world where, as Merton taught in his final talk, persons must learn "to stand on their own feet" (see vii), Mary McDonald recognizes that many more people wish to know how rich these contemplative art resources are. If we recapture the insights within this book, her promise may indeed be fulfilled: "to experience more community, insight, and joy" (xi).

Margaret B. Betz

HINSON, E. Glenn, *A Miracle of Grace: An Autobiography* (Macon, GA: Mercer University Press, 2012), pp. 448. ISBN 978-0-88146-394-1 (cloth) $35.00.

E. Glenn Hinson's candid recollection of his life is a grateful appreciation of the gift of life that he received from God, an unexpected gift he called "a miracle of grace." Growing up in an impoverished and dysfunctional family in the Ozarks of Missouri during the Great Depression, he experienced much loneliness and pain from an alcoholic and abusive father, whom his mother eventually divorced. His older brother, who left home, also became an alcoholic. Reflecting on how he survived his childhood experiences and acquired a useful and fruitful life, Hinson believed that God mysteriously channeled grace into his life and helped him to respond appropriately to the grace of each present moment. Through hard work and determination, he acquired an excellent education from Washington University in St. Louis, Southern Baptist Theological Seminary in Louisville and Oxford University. He taught successfully in some of the most distinguished educational institutions in the United States: Southern Baptist Theological Seminary, Wake Forest University, Catholic University of America, the University of Notre Dame and Emory University.

Two of the many providences that Hinson is grateful for were his switching the focus of his studies from New Testament to Church History and taking his first Church history students to the Abbey of Gethsemani in November 1960 to expose them to the Middle Ages. He met the monk, poet and spiritual writer Thomas Merton at that time. When one of his students asked Merton what he was doing wasting his time in a place like the monastery, Merton responded that he believed in prayer and that prayer was his vocation. Hinson was much impressed that Merton would consider prayer as a vocation. After that first meeting. Hinson took his students to Gethsemani every semester. In his journal, *Turning Toward the World*, Merton referred to Hinson as "the Church history man" and described him as "a good and sincere person."[1] Merton had a good rapport with the Southern Baptist Seminary students and Hinson. Merton appreciated his contact with them and thought that having them come to the hermitage was a mystifying game in which God would make things well.

Hinson found a deep spiritual foundation in Merton. Hinson perceived that his students needed more than just information; they wanted and needed spiritual formation just as he did. He gradually discovered the foundations of contemplative prayer. Contacts with Merton and Douglas Steere, a Quaker philosopher, scholar and ecumenist, greatly helped Hinson in his spiritual formation and in developing courses in "Teaching Classics of Christian Devotion" and "Prayer in Christian History."

Hinson saw the convergence of the opening of the Second Vatican Council and the launching of his career as a professor of Church history as very providential. He became involved with the Ecumenical Institute

---

1. Thomas Merton, *Turning Toward the World: The Pivotal Years. Journals, vol. 4: 1960-1963*, ed. Victor A. Kramer (San Francisco: HarperCollins, 1996) 109 [4/18/1961].

of Spirituality and was engaged in many ecumenical conversations in the Faith and Order Commission of the World Council of Churches. He was also invited to speak on the subject of spirituality. In the course of his teaching career, he discerned a calling to do something about the spiritual formation or preparation of ministers. He helped shape a curriculum with a focus on spiritual formation for ministry as the integrative factor in the training of ministers.

Hinson's memoir is a hefty book of 448 pages. It contains thirty-two pictures from his childhood, marriage, career and retirement. The last two sentences in the first paragraph on page 91 were not well proofed and need some revision. Appendix A provides his succinct response for the Academic Personnel Committee and Board of Trustees of the Baptist Theological Seminary on February 3, 1992. The next three appendices present a chronology of his major engagements from 1985 to the present. There is also a list of all of Hinson's publications arranged chronologically within types of publications. His detailed description of his life experiences can sometimes be difficult to read; yet it is also an inspiration to see how he lived through and overcame some of his sufferings. He is unabashed in relating how overwhelmed and unprepared he was to becoming deaf and losing his voice. In coping with these he felt the genuine concern of many persons who truly cared for him and he also discovered more keenly God's presence—God's joining him in these vulnerabilities. "What comforts me," he writes, "is that God is with me in my deafness or whatever else I confront in life" (362).

A Miracle of Grace is an indispensable primary resource in understanding Hinson's side in the fundamentalist efforts to remove him from the faculty of Southern Seminary where he taught for more than thirty years. He was encouraged to write his autobiography by his academic colleagues and friends who were familiar with the fundamentalist attacks he received. Hinson shares with his readers his experience of this most devastating interruption in his life. He notes that fundamentalists focused their attention on him for the first time in 1979 and 1980. Paige Patterson, who was then president of Criswell Bible College in Dallas, was critical of Hinson's book *Jesus Christ*, and had misrepresented what Hinson wrote in his book. In Patterson's interview with the editor of the *Baptist Standard* on April 14, 1980, Patterson listed Hinson as one of seven "liberals" in Southern Baptist life. Hinson provides a clear and consistent defense against Patterson's attack.

On August 22, 1980, Bailey Smith, then president of the Southern Baptist Convention, remarked that "Almighty God did not hear the prayer of a Jew." Smith refused to apologize for his offensive statement. None of Hinson's colleagues responded to Bailey Smith's statement. Hinson wrote an open letter to Smith showing the problems he saw in Smith's remark. Hinson noted that Jesus was a Jew, lived and died a Jew. He showed how Smith's remark not only disenfranchised Jesus' prayer, but the prayers of everyone from Abraham to Jesus. Hinson's last sentence asserted that statements such as the ones Smith made "are the stuff from which holocausts come" (237). He agonized about publishing the letter but he realized that the time to speak out was then, so he sent it to the Kentucky Baptist state paper. His open letter to Bailey Smith created an explosive incident that made Hinson a "marked man among fundamentalists." The interfaith community, however, distributed copies of his letter to its members. He was told that the *Jerusalem Post* noted that if it were not for his letter, the Jewish Knesset would have kicked all Southern Baptist missionaries out of Jerusalem.

Hinson wrote in his journal on September 17, 1980, that the Bailey Smith incident strengthened his decision to leave Southern Baptist Seminary, but the final nudge that pushed him to move to the religion department of Wake Forest University was the news of his colleague Dale Moody being forced into retirement from Southern. Moody's position that it was possible for Christians to fall from grace conflicted with the Southern Baptists' belief on the absolute security of the believer.

Hinson stayed at Wake Forest University from 1982 to 1984. He was much excited by the number of people who sought his guidance on the subject of spirituality. His book, *A Serious Call to a Contemplative Lifestyle*, was well read in colleges, universities and churches and Hinson did many retreats based on the book. He went deeper and combined spirituality with peacemaking and continued his ecumenical activities. He left Wake Forest and returned to Southern Baptist Theological Seminary in 1984. He thought that by returning to Southern Seminary he could forestall the fundamentalist takeover of that institution. He calls the period from 1984 to 1991 "the lean years" in which he tried as best he could to be attentive to the presence of God while a crusade to get him out of Southern Seminary was initiated by James Stroud, the pastor of a small congregation in Knoxville, Tennessee. In 1991, Hinson was invited to teach at the International Baptist Seminary in Rushlikon, Switzerland. While he was making plans for his students' field trip to historical sites, he was told that the Foreign Mission Board of the Southern Baptist Convention had defunded Rushlikon. It seemed that it was the end of Hinson's career, but casting his cares to God got him through that and other situations. He felt God's presence in the courage and support his family, students and friends in other religious institutions gave to him. He wrote: "God was there in my connections with the church in all of its multiple expressions—as local congregations, denominations, international assemblies, academic meetings and endless other expressions" (272). Hinson hopes that after reading his autobiography, his readers may learn more about the way God enters an ordinary human life.

Erlinda G. Paguio

GREENE, DANA, *Denise Levertov: A Poet's Life* (Urbana: University of Illinois Press, 2012), pp. xiv + 307. ISBN 978-0-252-03710-8 (cloth) $35.00.

Writing a cradle-to-grave life story of any accomplished public figure must be a feat of consuming research, methodical organization and purposeful composition. The effective biographer selects and arranges details of formative factors, developments, conflicts and resolutions to produce a comprehensive, credible profile of one individual's time on earth. The literary biographer perhaps faces an additional challenge, for no narrative of a writer's life can effectively illuminate that person's character unless the author also integrates the writer's works into the story. And if the writer is a poet, the task of rendering a life on paper must be further complicated by the characteristic complexity of the genre. And while Wordsworth's claim that "Poets in [their] youth begin in gladness; / But thereof come in the end despondency and madness" may not describe the exact trajectory of every poet's life, the not uncommon psychic intensity of the committed poet presents the biographer with yet more intricate territory to navigate in order to capture her subject for the reader. Dana Greene, Dean Emerita of Oxford College of Emory University, meets such challenges masterfully in this first full-length study of the life of Denise Levertov (1923-1997), aptly subtitled *A Poet's Life*.

The poet whom Thomas Merton in 1961 called "splendid"[1] led a rich and energetic life from her early days in her native country of England to her last days in Seattle, Washington, where she died from lymphoma, a disease she optimistically and stoically bore, choosing to conceal it from even some of her closest friends. Moreover, from the beginning, hers was a searcher's life, a determined journey to find love, to promote peace, to discover union with God, and to convey truth through poetry, perhaps the central source of connection between Levertov and Merton, a feature that makes Dana Greene's biography an especially valuable read for both

---

1. Thomas Merton, *The Courage for Truth: Letters to Writers*, ed. Christine M. Bochen (New York: Farrar, Straus, Giroux, 1993) 127 [10/14/1961 letter to Ernesto Cardenal].

Levertov and Merton enthusiasts.

Greene divides her work into a prologue, twelve chapters, an epilogue, notes, a selected bibliography and an index. The fact that half of the chapter titles consist of direct quotations from Levertov's works and that the endnotes occupy forty-five of the book's 307 pages demonstrates upon first glance that the study is well documented by both primary and secondary sources. In the beginning, Greene acknowledges her debt to the many people who gave interviews for the book and to those who supported her project. On the list are names that readers of *The Merton Annual* will surely recognize, such as Wendell Berry, John Dear, Kathleen Norris and Bonnie Thurston, to name but a few.

Chapter 1, "A Definite and Peculiar Destiny," begins the narrative with an account of Levertov's ancestry (her birth name was Levertoff) and of her youth wherein early indicators of her life's path and vocation appear. For example, one learns that her father was a convert from Judaism to Christianity and eventually became an Anglican priest, that both of her parents and her older sister were also writers, and that, as an adolescent, young Denise sent her poems to T. S. Eliot, who responded with encouragement "to learn languages, do translations, and above all continue to write" (11), advice which she would follow throughout her life.

Chapter 3, "The Making of a Poet," details the period in Levertov's life when her ambition to write poetry took on a previously unmatched fervor and productivity. Greene explains that Levertov, who, because of her first name, felt an affiliation with Dionysus, chose the shrine to Apollo at Delphi as the site where she would take "her 'final vows' to poetry" in a ritual complete with song and dance (and intestinal sickness, brought on by an ill-advised decision to drink the water from a nearby stream). The chapter makes clear that as her penchant for grand romantic gestures suggests, Levertov believed that poetry possesses immense power, power to transcend, transport and transform both writer and reader. In the years immediately preceding her Delphic experience, 1956 to 1961, during which time she lived in New York, New England and Mexico—a peripatetic pattern that would characterize most of her life—Levertov produced four volumes of poetry, an accomplishment which confirmed her status as a new poet on the rise. Greene goes on to attribute this recognition not only to Levertov's remarkable talent and drive but also to her good fortune in having abundant support from other poets and publishers, such as New Directions' James Laughlin.

Chapters 4 and 5, "A Cataract Filming Over My Inner Eyes" and "Staying Alive," delineate Levertov's passionate opposition to the Vietnam War. Her intense feelings propelled her to join prominent activists of the era, such as Daniel Berrigan, in speaking out for peace and justice; she was also driven to write poems, not only in protest against the war, but in hope of awakening readers to their own natural revulsion to its horrors. Levertov responded fully to the revolutionary atmosphere of the 1960s and established herself as a "poet in the world," a relational identity which she would continue to revise throughout her life. It was also during this time that Levertov met Merton at his hermitage, where they spoke of war protests and poetry. Merton recorded the meeting in his journal entry of December 10, 1967, noting simply: "I like Denise very much."[2]

In Chapter 6, Greene writes how the Vietnam War "dominated Levertov's consciousness for eight years" (114) and ultimately pushed her emotional involvement to the boiling point, compelling her to travel to North Vietnam and to come home intent on chronicling before the U.S. government the abominations she witnessed there (her intentions were foiled and led to her arrest for an act of civil disobedience on the Senate floor). Furthermore, because of the impotent anger roiling within her, along with the conviction that she was, by virtue of her common humanity, complicit in the atrocity of war, she produced poetry marked by disturbing fantasies of retribution, such as "A Poem at Christmas, 1972, during the Terror-Bombing of North Vietnam" with its exclamation: "*O, to kill the killers!*"

However, as the title of the chapter "Endings" establishes, this bitterness eventually abated, possibly from utter exhaustion. What followed was a phenomenon reminiscent of the contemplative's path in pursuit of mystical union. Levertov's vision of human suffering expanded, and her poetic expression of that vision evidenced an embrace of paradox and reconciliation of the apparent contraries in the human condition. To illustrate, Greene points to the poem "Modes of Being," which opens "Joy / is real, torture / is real . . . " a work in which, as Greene observes, Levertov "juxtaposes the suffering of war with the joys of nature" and recognizes "the need to bridge the poles of joy and sorrow" (114).

Throughout the book, Dana Greene fluidly interweaves accounts of Levertov the poet and Levertov the woman. For example, the "endings" to which Greene refers in the title of Chapter 6 include more than the turning point in Levertov's poetic response to the war in Vietnam. More personal finalities took place then as well, perhaps most notably the rancorous dissolution of Levertov's long friendship with poet and mentor Robert Duncan and her divorce from Mitchell Goodman, whom she had married young and with whom she had one son, Nikolai. Apparently, Levertov

2. Thomas Merton, *The Other Side of the Mountain: The End of the Journey. Journals, vol. 7: 1967-1968*, ed. Patrick Hart (San Francisco: HarperCollins, 1998) 22 [12/10/1967].

never felt a genuine bond with either husband or child.

Additionally, in relating personal details, Greene strikes a balance between forthrightness and discretion, authorial involvement and detachment. She renders truthfully, but without gratuitous elaboration, the more sensitive aspects of Levertov's personality: her considerable and long-lived sexual appetite; her "complex attitudes toward homosexuality" (136), which manifested in curiously cold treatment of gay friends and associates; her obliviousness "to the demands she made on others" (136); and her general capacity to be "irksome" (168). Greene also writes, however, that "Levertov was charming, cosmopolitan, and articulate" (168) and consistently reports that she was prodigiously generous. Evidently, Levertov was a faithful source of financial and professional support for family members (including her former husband and his new wife), students and aspiring artists.

The most engaging element of this biography for this reader is the unfolding narrative of Levertov's spiritual journey, a pilgrimage of some hesitations and interior hindrances that culminated in her reception into the Catholic Church when she was 67 years old, a decision which mystified many of her friends. Greene quotes Levertov's comments as to which strain of Catholicism she embraced: "I believe myself to have thrown in my lot with the tradition of the CW [Catholic Worker] & Tom Merton" (190); she was not what Greene describes as "a triumphalistic Catholic," but one who was able to profess her faith only when she "allowed her poetic images to take precedence over intellectual doubt about belief" (190).

Greene traces Levertov's faith odyssey with ample references to her poetry, going back, for instance, to one of Levertov's 1960s works in which the poet speaks of a mysterious pulling sensation as "a stirring / of wonder" and which Greene chooses as the title for Chapter 8, "The Thread." Chapter 9, "Making Peace," suggests that the early tugging of the thread eventually became an audible force compelling the poet to take on what might be called an eschatological mission achievable through the mystical properties of language. In the poem by the same title, the speaker announces: "A voice from the dark called out, / The poets must give us / imagination of peace," and that peace "can't be known except / in the words of its making." (Readers of *The Merton Annual* may perceive here a striking parallel with Merton's poetics.)

Greene comments that the time of the poem "Making Peace," the late 1980s, was a period of "personal tranquility" and "generally positive" circumstances that made it possible for her to "plumb her interior life in ways she had never done before" (163) and to forge "a link between her vocation as poet and Christian" (163). In the years leading up to the onset of her sickness and imminent death, Levertov continued to find reconciling forces in her interpersonal relationships and in her poetry.

In the final chapter entitled "Once Only," taken from a late poem that evokes a sense of existential urgency, Greene relates that Levertov spent her last years as a poet much as she did her emerging years: working and living as fully as possible. Greene notes poignantly that Levertov's "last poems offer few considerations of death, except indirectly as a longing for life" (221) and asserts that while the poems published posthumously as *This Great Unknowing* have no unifying theme, many are "particularly tender" (221) pieces that resonate with human "and divine interaction" (222).

Dana Greene closes the book by reflecting on the challenges of writing Denise Levertov's biography. Chief among them is the poet's ambivalent attitude toward the genre and her professed reluctance to have her life studied independently of her poems: "She wanted to be remembered for her poetry, the 'autonomous structures' that would be appreciated on their own terms and would last," as opposed to her "fleeting and insignificant" existence (231). Yet, Greene continues, Levertov made the seemingly contradictory move of offering her diaries and letters to be archived at Stanford (one of many institutions where she taught). Possibly, a belief that no responsible biographer could conscientiously dismiss such mixed signals from her subject accounts for the centrality of the poetic evidence of Levertov's life in *Denise Levertov: A Poet's Life*.

Greene persuasively communicates the elusive nature of her subject and concludes that the project of definitively preserving the life of Denise Levertov in a single book is simply not possible. Perhaps the appearance of Donna Krolik Hollenberg's *A Poet's Revolution: The Life of Denise Levertov* only one year after Greene's work was published underscores the prophetic nature of Dana Greene's final words; perhaps, the epilogue to this first full-length life story of Denise Levertov is merely prologue to future illuminations.

Deborah Kehoe

SIMMONS, Sylvie, *I'm Your Man: The Life of Leonard Cohen* (New York: Ecco/HarperCollins, 2012), pp. 570. ISBN 978-0-06-199498-2 (cloth) $27.99 US; $35.00 Can.

LIGHT, Alan. *The Holy or the Broken: Leonard Cohen, Jeff Buckley and the Unlikely Ascent of "Hallelujah"* (New York: Atria/Simon and Schuster, 2012), pp. xxiii + 254. ISBN 978-1-4516-5784-5 (cloth) $25.00 US; $28.99 Can.

A review of two books about Leonard Cohen in *The Merton Annual*?

Why not? Merton and Cohen are soul-brothers. Leonard Cohen (b. 1934), Canadian poet and song-writer, is the greatest balladeer in English of the twentieth/twenty-first centuries (so acknowledged by Bob Dylan), a Jew with a deep affinity for Catholicism. Thomas Merton (1915-1968), French-born American poet and public intellectual who once commented that he often felt that he wanted to be "a true Jew under my Catholic skin,"[1] is regarded by many as the most creative Christian spiritual-cultural writer of his time. They share so many points of contact. Both of them were born in French-speaking cultures (France and Québec); were/are characterized by a strongly European sensibility; lost their fathers (and Merton his mother) at an early age; are poets, and both loved Spanish poet Federico García Lorca; went to Columbia—only Merton did any work there; went to Cuba; went to India; had a long-unresolved sense of their own sexuality; were/are trickster/coyote figures; grew from serious immaturity into great maturity; were/are very interested in Buddhism, Zen especially; had some difficulty at particular times with alcohol; spent time in monasteries—Leonard five years, Merton 27; were given monastic names—Jikan ("the silent one") and Father Louis; were/are "monastic in their own way"; were/are strongly anchored in their own religious tradition *and* deeply interested in other traditions; were/are 5'8"; were/are 4s on the Enneagram; and both became transreligious-transcultural spiritual teachers.

Manifestly, some of these points of similarity are more substantial than others. Nonetheless, I hunch that had they met, there would have been an extended conversation between them that would have rivaled the 11-hour initial meeting of Freud and Jung. The closest they came was when Cohen and his Zen teacher, Joshu Sasaki Roshi, visiting Gethsemani in 1974, paid their respects at Merton's grave.[2] They came together in my own understanding when as the first Canadian to be president of the ITMS I was looking for Canadian content for my presidential address at its Eleventh General Meeting in Rochester, NY in June 2009. Fortunately, I remembered reading Sarah Hampson's comment in her 2007 *Globe and Mail* interview with Cohen, that he was "monastic in his [own] way."[3]

---

1. Thomas Merton, *The Hidden Ground of Love: Letters on Religious Experience and Social Concerns*, ed. William H. Shannon (New York: Farrar, Straus, Giroux, 1985) 434-35 [9/9/1964 letter to Abraham Joshua Heschel].

2. Ira B. Nadel, *Various Positions: A Life of Leonard Cohen* (Toronto: Random House, 1996) 231-32 (Gethsemani is there spelled Gethsemane, the usual English spelling, but not the one in use at Merton's abbey).

3. Sarah Hampson, "Life of a Ladies' Man," *The Globe and Mail* (May 26, 2007), R1, R6-7. The phrase is an inside-page title, spanning pages R6 and 7. For the address, see Donald Grayston, "Monastic in His Own Way: Thomas Merton and Leonard Cohen,"

And who else was monastic in *his* own way if not Thomas Merton?

Merton we know (or think we know—he continues to surprise us). What to say of Cohen? Born in 1934 in Montréal, he was educated there, and later attended Columbia. He essayed a literary career; but having decided that he couldn't thereby make a living, began to develop his musical abilities, and with the release of his first album in 1967 launched the career as singer-songwriter that has continued to this day. There was a notable time aside from his career, between 1994 and 1999, when he lived a kind of adjunct monastic life at Mount Baldy, near Los Angeles, continuing during this time to write, but not to perform. It was a time of healing for him (he went there because he was depressed and had been drinking too much). After leaving the monastery, he discovered that his longtime manager had stolen almost all his money. Eventually this resulted in a decision to tour again; and so in May 2008 he began the first of the series of world tours which continue to this day. The reviews of these concerts have been consistently laudatory, even venerational; if you want to see and hear for yourself what he is offering in these concerts, I recommend the DVD *Leonard Cohen Live in London* (2008).

Of all the points of contact or comparison between them, the most substantial is a role which neither of them sought, but which both of them accepted (not that either of them would claim the term for himself), that of a transreligious and transcultural spiritual teacher. We live in a post-post-modern time, in which religious institutions are in rapid numerical decline, and in which the "spiritual but not religious" cohort increases daily.[4] Cohen, however, remains rooted in his Judaism as Merton was in his Catholicism; neither denies his religious identity, and both have given substantial attention to religious traditions other than their own. But they transcend the limitations of those religions by the way they present themselves, Cohen through his music, Merton through his books, both exemplifying the validity of Ken Wilber's maxim, "include and transcend." Merton's comment in the preface to *New Seeds of Contemplation* is instructive here:

> There are very many religious people who have no need for a book like this, because theirs is a different kind of spirituality. If to them this book is without meaning, they should not feel concerned. On the other hand, there are perhaps people without formal religious affiliations who will find in these pages something that appeals to

The Merton Seasonal 34.3 (Fall 2009) 3-9; see also leonardcohenfiles.com/grayston.pdf.

4. Sandra M. Schneiders, "Religion vs. Spirituality: A Contemporary Conundrum," *Spiritus* 3.2 (Fall 2003) 163-85.

them. If they do, I am glad, as I feel myself a debtor to them more than to the others.[5]

Cohen, similarly, reaches out through his concerts to those "without formal religious affiliations" while also continuing to attract those who continue to maintain a religious identity.

They are also both transcultural, in two senses. Cohen's music transcends language, and he remains popular in many nations, notably Norway and Poland among the non-English-speaking countries; and Merton's books have been translated into more than 30 languages. But they are also transcultural in the deeper sense on which Merton reflects in "Final Integration: Toward a 'Monastic Therapy'":

> Final integration is a state of transcultural maturity far beyond mere social adjustment. . . . The man who is "fully born" . . . apprehends his life fully and wholly from an inner ground that is at once more universal than the empirical ego and yet entirely his own. . . . He has attained a deeper, fuller identity than that of his limited ego-self which is only a fragment of his being. . . . He is in a certain sense identified with everybody. . . . He is able to experience their joys and sufferings as his own, without however becoming dominated by them. He has attained to a deep inner freedom [and so becomes] a potential instrument for unusual creativity.[6]

I take Merton's statement here to mean that finally-integrated persons are those who have lived their own teaching, undertaken thereby the journey of the hero, and emerged from that process to be recognized as spiritual teachers. This is a process analogous to the process of shamanic initiation necessary before the new shaman's recognition as spiritual teacher by the clan or tribe. Having walked the walk, they are listened to when they talk the talk. Their basic way of teaching, deeper than the music or the books, and what accounts for their wide appeal, is their own authenticity in following the path that they offer to others. Without asserting any kind of perfection for either of them, I am ready to recognize in them what Merton means by final integration.

To the books, then. Sylvie Simmons is a respected British music journalist who has previously written biographies of Neil Young and Serge Gainsbourg. Her book has been very favorably reviewed by, among oth-

---

5. Thomas Merton, *New Seeds of Contemplation* (New York: New Directions, 1961) xi.

6. Thomas Merton, *Contemplation in a World of Action* (Garden City, NY: Doubleday, 1971) 211-12.

ers, A. M. Homes in *The New York Times*, Mark Lepage in *The Montreal Gazette* and James Adams in *The Globe and Mail*.[7] It is variously described in those reviews as definitive, comprehensive, deft, exhaustive, insightful and compulsively readable—all terms I can support. Certainly the book, which contains many verbatim interviews with Cohen, evidences a relaxed and free-flowing relationship between author and subject.

Her treatment of Cohen's albums is indeed exhaustive: she has something to say about every song on every album. The book could function very well, in fact, as a listener's companion to all seventeen of the studio and concert albums in *The Complete Columbia Albums Collection* (2011). As A. M. Homes says in his review, "Among the book's side effects is that it sends you back to the source material; as you're reading, you find yourself craving Cohen's music in the background." She faithfully records Cohen's emotional ups and downs, but doesn't indulge in pop psychoanalysis: we are left to come to our own conclusions about his emotional journey. Nor does she claim for him what I am suggesting in calling him a transreligious-transcultural spiritual teacher; but more than sufficient raw material for such an assessment is there—his religious explorations, his vulnerability, his spiritual and emotional struggles, his time in the monastery at Mount Baldy with Sasaki Roshi, and his time in India with spiritual teacher Ramesh Balsekar in which his lifelong depression simply lifted (418-26). She also acknowledges the religious elements which others have observed in his concerts—the presence of ritual actions (kneeling, for example, during some of the songs), and the blessing of the departing concertgoers (his name, Cohen, does mean "priest" in Hebrew). It is in this context that she credits him, through his music, and in the response of his fans, with dissolving "all boundaries between word and song, and between the song and the truth, and the truth and himself, his heart and its aching" (508)—if accurate, a transcendent achievement.

Alan Light's *The Holy or the Broken,* the story of the slow ascent of Cohen's great song "Hallelujah" to its present popularity, is another fine example of music journalism, and has also been positively reviewed. It was when Light heard it sung at a Yom Kippur service (xxx-xxxii) that he recognized the cultural reach of the song, and decided to write the book. The song was first recorded on Cohen's 1984 album, *Various Positions,*

---

7. A. M. Homes, "Crazy for Love," *The New York Times* (October 12, 2012) (nytimes.com/2012/10/14/books/review/im-your-man-leonard-cohen-bio-by-sylvie-simmons.html); Mark Lepage, "The Good, the Bad, the Mysteries of Leonard Cohen," *The Montreal Gazette* (October 21, 2012) (montrealgazette.com/story_print.html); James Adams, "Cohen Bio Gives Us Everything: The Women, the Drugs, the Metaphysics," *The Globe and Mail* (October 26, 2012) (theglobeandmail.com/arts/books-and-media/book-reviews).

which Columbia decided not to distribute, and which sank like a stone. However, John Cale's 1991 recovery and recording of it brought it close to its now-classic form; and Jeff Buckley's 1994 very romantic rendition (made all the more so by his accidental death in 1997) took it the next step. It has now been covered by more than 300 singers, and was chosen in the year 2002 as the best song ever written by a Canadian.[8]

And what is the song about? Here are some of Light's takes on it. He quotes Cohen as saying that it represents "absolute surrender in a situation you cannot fix or dominate" (xxv); it's "a hymn to being alive" (66); "the definitive representation of sadness for a new generation" (114); "a song for when you don't have answers"—quoting singer Kate Voegele (123); and "perhaps the great prayer of the modern age" (228). It has sacred, sexual and secular dimensions: it is a song for all seasons and for all sorts and conditions of hearers. Churches and synagogues feel free to change some of the words and sing it as a hymn; brides and grooms choose it for their weddings and mourners for funerals. Light says that the process of its ongoing interpretation and re-interpretation is a continuing one, with people still finding "new meanings and new structure for it that work."[9]

My only quibble with Light is his title: *The Holy* or *the Broken*. I acknowledge that in choosing that title he is quoting Cohen directly. But reading the song in its entirety moves me to favor a title which would speak of both the holy *and* the broken. The song asks us to hold together the sacred dimension of life and our own difficulty in honoring it. We can't really choose between the holy and the broken; both dimensions are ineluctable parts of our experience. I find this viewpoint supported by a sign which hangs above the desk of the director of First United Church in Vancouver, a mission in the poorest and most desperate part of the city: "Hallelujah anyway!"

Warmly recommended, both.

Donald Grayston

---

8. Brad Wheeler, "Hallelujah! Cohen takes Europe," *The Globe and Mail* (December 16, 2008) R1; or, as Michael Lista suggests, perhaps even the greatest song written globally in our time: "Lyrics as Poetry: Leonard Cohen's 'Hallelujah'" (posted on the CBC Radio 3 blog, February 20, 2012).

9. Ian McGillis, "The Hallelujah Phenomenon," *The Montreal Gazette* (December 12, 2012) (montrealgazette.com/touch/story.html).

Contributors

David Joseph Belcastro is co-editor of *The Merton Annual* and current President of the International Thomas Merton Society. He is Professor of Religious Studies at Capital University, Bexley, Ohio, and has presented and published papers on Merton for the past twenty-five years.

Margaret B. Betz has taught courses in Modernist Art, Russian Art, Art and Spirituality, Picasso, Kandinsky, Malevich, Chagall and Art Criticism. Currently on the faculty of Savannah College of Art and Design, she has taught at Ohio State University, Queens College-CUNY and the School of the Visual Arts. Her articles have appeared in *ArtNews*, *Artforum*, *SoHo News*, *The Merton Annual* and other journals. Her dissertation focused on the caricatures and cartoons of the 1905 Russian Revolution. Her article on Merton's drawings and icons appeared in *The Merton Annual* 13 (2000).

Christine M. Bochen is Professor of Religious Studies and holder of the William H. Shannon Chair of Catholic Studies at Nazareth College, Rochester, New York. She has edited numerous works by Thomas Merton, including *The Courage for Truth*, the fourth volume of Merton's collected letters, and *Learning to Love*, the sixth volume of his complete journals; she co-edited, with William H. Shannon, *Thomas Merton: A Life in Letters* and *Cold War Letters* and is coauthor, with William H. Shannon and Patrick F. O'Connell, of *The Thomas Merton Encyclopedia*.

Raymond Carr is an Assistant Professor of Theology and Ethics in the Religion Division at Pepperdine University. A US Air Force veteran from Petersburg, Virginia, he received his Ph.D. from the Graduate Theological Union in Systematic and Philosophical Theology. His current research explores pneumatology and the relationship between Karl Barth, arguably the most important theologian of the twentieth century, and James Cone, the "father" of Black Theology, whose theology draws on the thought and praxis of Martin Luther King, Jr. and Malcolm X.

Peggy L. Fox is the former president of New Directions Publishing Corporation, for which she began working in 1975, and the literary executor of New Directions founder James Laughlin. She has been a trustee of the Thomas Merton Legacy Trust since 2008.

Fiona Gardner currently works as award leader for the MA in Counseling and Psychotherapy Practice at Bath Spa University, England. She is co-editor of *The Merton Journal*, former chair of The Thomas Merton Society of Great Britain and Ireland, and UK advisor for the International Thomas Merton Society. She trained and has worked as a social worker, a psychoanalytic psychotherapist and more recently as a spiritual director. She is a published writer and her latest book is *Precious Thoughts: Daily Readings from the Correspondence of Thomas Merton* (Darton, Longman, Todd, 2011).

Donald Grayston, an Anglican priest, was the eleventh president of the ITMS (2007-09). He taught Religious Studies at Simon Fraser University in Vancouver, British Columbia from 1989 to 2004. Currently he is working in the Consonantia Program, a joint offering of the Thomas Merton Society of Canada and St Andrew's United Church in North Vancouver, BC. He is also active in Building Bridges Vancouver (a public education project on the Israeli-Palestinian conflict) and in the Canadian Network for a Moral Economy.

Edward K. Kaplan is Kaiserman Professor in the Humanities at Brandeis University, where he has taught courses on French and comparative literature and religious studies since 1978. He organized the conference on Merton and Judaism that was published in a volume of the same name (edited by Beatrice Bruteau) and published an award-winning biography of Abraham Joshua Heschel (1907-1972), the Jewish theologian and social activist. In Spring 2012, he taught a seminar on Merton and Heschel at the Pontifical Gregorian University in Rome.

Deborah Kehoe lives in Oxford, Mississippi, and teaches English composition, world literature and professional writing at Northeast Community College and the University of Mississippi. She is a regular presenter at Merton Society conferences and has contributed articles and reviews to both *The Merton Annual* and *The Merton Seasonal*.

James Laughlin (1914-1997) was the founding publisher of New Directions Books and a close friend and correspondent of Thomas Merton; New Directions published more than two dozen books by Thomas Merton, including all his volumes of poetry as well as such titles as *Seeds of Contemplation*, *Bread in the Wilderness*, *New Seeds of Contemplation*, *The Way of Chuang Tzu*, *Zen and the Birds of Appetite*, *The Asian Journal* and *The Literary Essays of Thomas Merton*.

Ian S. MacNiven is Professor Emeritus of Humanities at the Maritime College of the State University of New York, and has written the authorized biography of James Laughlin, which will be published in 2014. He is also the author of the official biography of Lawrence Durrell and editor of the correspondence of Durrell with Henry Miller.

Mark C. Meade is a member of the Academy of Certified Archivists and is the Assistant Director of the Thomas Merton Center at Bellarmine University, serving on the faculty since 2003. In 2011, he was the featured lecturer for the book launch of *Fragmentos de un Regalo* at the American Embassy in Buenos Aires and has since presented on Thomas Merton and Victoria Ocampo at the 2013 International Thomas Merton Society General Meeting in Fairfield, Connecticut. He is a member of the National Council of the Fellowship of Reconciliation and a board member of the Kentucky Coalition to Abolish the Death Penalty. He has published essays in *The Merton Seasonal* regarding Thomas Merton's reflections on Albert Camus' seminal work on the death penalty, "Reflections on the Guillotine." In addition, his reviews and essays have appeared in *U.S. Catholic* and *Cistercian Studies Quarterly*.

Jonathan Montaldo, former Director of the Thomas Merton Center of Bellarmine University, has edited numerous volumes of Merton's work including *The Intimate Merton* (with Patrick Hart), *Dialogues with Silence* and *A Year with Thomas Merton*. He created a ten-booklet series for small group dialogue, *Bridges to Contemplative Living with Thomas Merton*. He serves as General Editor (with Gray Henry) of the Fons Vitae Thomas Merton series, of which the most recent volume is *Merton & the Tao: Dialogues with John Wu and the Ancient Sages*.

Patrick Thomas Morgan is currently a Ph.D. student in English at Duke University. His research focuses on theories of nature and the human within American literature of the long nineteenth century, with an emphasis on the intersection of geology and aesthetics. He has contributed to *American Literature*, *The Merton Seasonal* and *The Concord Saunterer: A Journal of Thoreau Studies*. A 2011 Daggy Scholar, he presented his essay, "Dying Together with Wisdom: The Aesthetics of Loss in Thomas Merton's Poetry," at the 2013 ITMS General Meeting.

Patrick F. O'Connell, professor of English and Theology at Gannon University, Erie, PA, is a founding member and former president of the International Thomas Merton Society and editor of *The Merton Seasonal*. He is co-author (with William H. Shannon and Christine M. Bochen) of *The Thomas Merton Encyclopedia* (2002) and has edited six volumes of Merton's monastic conferences as well as the *Selected Essays* of Thomas Merton (2013).

Gordon Oyer is past editor of *Illinois Mennonite Heritage Quarterly* and an administrator at the University of Illinois, from which he earned an MA in history. He has also written various articles on Mennonite history and served on regional Mennonite historical committees. His article in this volume is based on research conducted for his forthcoming book, *Pursuing the Spiritual Roots of Protest: Merton, Berrigan, Yoder, and Muste at the Gethsemani Abbey Peacemaker Retreat*.

Erlinda G. Paguio is former President of the International Thomas Merton Society. She served as Program Chair for the ITMS Tenth General Meeting in Memphis, Tennessee and has presented papers at Merton conferences in the U.S., Great Britain and Spain. She recently retired as Director of Development Research at the University of Louisville.

Paul M. Pearson is Director of the Thomas Merton Center at Bellarmine University, Louisville, Kentucky, Chief of Research for the Merton Legacy Trust, and Resident Secretary of the International Thomas Merton Society. He has edited *Seeking Paradise: Thomas Merton and the Shakers* (Orbis, 2003), *A Meeting of Angels: The Correspondence of Thomas Merton with Edward Deming and Faith Andrews* (Broadstone, 2008) and *Thomas Merton on Christian Contemplation* (New Directions, 2012).

Michael Plekon is a professor in the department of Sociology/Anthropology and the Program in Religion and Culture of Baruch College of the City University of New York. He is a priest in the Orthodox Church in America. His recent work has been on persons of faith—writers, activists and others—searching for identity, meaning and God: *Living Icons*, *Hidden Holiness* and *Saints as They Really Are*.

Christopher Pramuk teaches theology and spirituality at Xavier University, Cincinnati, Ohio and is a member of the Board of Directors of the International Thomas Merton Society. His essays have appeared in *America*, *Cross Currents*, *Horizons*, *Theological Studies* and other journals. He is the author of four books, including *Hope Sings, So Beautiful: Graced Encounters across the Color Line* (Liturgical Press, 2013) and *Sophia: The Hidden Christ of Thomas Merton* (Liturgical Press, 2009), which received an ITMS "Louie" Award in 2011. His essay in this volume was a plenary presentation at the ITMS Thirteenth General Meeting at Sacred Heart University, Fairfield, Connecticut in June 2013.

Joseph Quinn Raab is associate professor of religious studies and director of the Liberal Arts Studies Program at Siena Heights University in Adrian, Michigan. He has presented papers at Thomas Merton Society of

Great Britain and Ireland and ITMS General Meetings and has published articles in *Theology Today*, *The Journal of Religious Education* and *The Merton Annual*, for which he currently serves as co-editor.

Bonnie Bowman Thurston wrote her Ph.D. dissertation on Thomas Merton, was a founding member of the International Thomas Merton Society and served as its third president. She has written many scholarly articles on Merton, given retreats and lectured on Merton widely in the U.S., Canada, the U.K. and Europe. She has edited *Thomas Merton & Buddhism* (Fons Vitae, 2007), *Hidden in the Same Mystery: Thomas Merton & Loretto* (Fons Vitae, 2010) and *Thomas Merton on Eastern Meditation* (New Directions, 2012). In 2002 she resigned the William F. Orr Professorship in New Testament at Pittsburgh Theological Seminary to live quietly in her home state of West Virginia. Her most recent book is *O Taste and See: A Biblical Reflection on Experiencing God* (Paraclete Press, 2013).

Richard Weber, OCSO has been a member of the Gethsemani community in Kentucky since 1964. Thomas Merton was his novice master, and gave him the name Columban in religion. He has published items of Merton interest in popular and scholarly journals.

Monica Weis, SSJ, Professor of English at Nazareth College, Rochester NY, teaches American literature and rhetoric. She is a former Vice President of ITMS, a frequent contributor to scholarly journals and conferences, and the author of *Landscapes of Paradise: Thomas Merton's Gethsemani* (University Press of Kentucky, 2005) and *The Environmental Vision of Thomas Merton* (UPK, 2011). She is a member of the Program Committee for the IMTS Fourteenth General Meeting and has begun research for a book on Merton and Celtic spirituality.

Robert Weldon Whalen is the Carolyn G. and Sam H. McMahon Professor of History at Queens University of Charlotte and Visiting Professor of Church History at Union Theological Seminary in Charlotte, North Carolina.

Paul Wilkes is the author of numerous books including *In Mysterious Ways: The Death and Life of a Parish Priest* (1990); *The Good Enough Catholic: A Guide for the Perplexed* (1996); *The Seven Secrets of Successful Catholics* (1998); *Beyond the Walls: Monastic Wisdom for Everyday Life* (1999); *Excellent Catholic Parishes: The Guide to Best Places and Practices* (2001); his highly regarded memoir *In Due Season: A Catholic Life* (2009); and most recently *The Art of Confession: Renewing Yourself through the Practice of Honesty* (2012). He was the writer and director of *Merton: A Film Biography* (1984) and edited *Merton By Those Who Knew Him Best* (1984).

Index

A

Abdeslam, Sidi 228
Andrade, Jaime 173
Asian Journal, The (Merton) 8, 13, 16, 20, 22, 30, 31, 32, 43, 44, 46, 47, 49, 52, 53, 146, 215, 217, 266
Augustine, St. 28, 185
Aziz, Abdul 56, 227, 228

B

Barnes, Djuna 18
Barth, Karl 11, 58, 147, 181–194
Behavior of Titans, The (Merton) 176
Belcastro, David Joseph 11, 195, 265
Bernanos, Georges 69
Bernard of Clairvaux, St. 131, 166, 230, 250
Berrigan, Daniel 77, 84, 88, 94, 257, 268
Betz, Margaret Bridget 72, 251, 265
Bioy Casares, Adolfo 168, 174
Blake, William 29, 150, 247
Bochen, Christine M. 21, 29, 35, 40, 81, 85, 151, 165, 170, 173, 174, 203, 207, 225, 237, 241, 255, 265, 267
Bordelois, Ivonne 169, 170, 178
Bread in the Wilderness (Merton) 12, 17, 102, 266
Buber, Martin 223
Buckley, Jeff 205, 259, 264
Bulgakov, Sergius 9, 64, 68, 72, 97, 100, 101, 102, 104, 145
Burne, Martin J., OSB 130
Burns, Flavian 20, 44, 45
Busch, Eberhard 182, 183
Byways: A Memoir (Laughlin) 16

C

Camus, Albert 17, 149, 150, 169, 201, 241, 248, 267
Cardenal, Ernesto 174, 255
Carnegie, Andrew 14
Carr, Raymond 11, 181, 265
Cassian and the Fathers: Initiation into the Monastic Tradition (Merton)
100, 197, 228, 229
Cassian, John 100, 197, 222, 228, 229
Céline, Louis-Ferdinand 19
Chakravarty, Amiya 48
Chatral Rimpoche 23
Chenu, Marie-Dominique 60
Choate Academy 14
Ciorra, Anthony 220–232
City Lights Bookstore 201
Clement of Alexandria 36
Cohen, Leonard 205, 206, 259–264
Cold War Letters, The (Merton) 19, 35, 173, 174, 265
Collected Poems of Thomas Merton, The (Merton) 12, 38, 107, 157, 171, 237
Columbia *Jester* 38
Columbia *Spectator* 38
Conjectures of a Guilty Bystander (Merton) 10, 73, 85, 97, 102, 141, 148, 170, 176, 188
Contemplation in a World of Action (Merton) 223, 262
Contemplative Prayer (Merton) 81, 100, 114, 190
Cooper, David D. 13, 22, 45, 168
Courage for Truth, The: Letters to Writers (Merton) 40, 165, 170, 174, 255, 265
Cuadra, Pablo Antonio 174
Cunningham, Lawrence 29, 72, 95, 97, 143, 148, 170

D

Daggy, Robert E. 29, 43, 45, 72, 77, 85, 88, 98, 108, 151, 155, 158, 240, 267, 283
Dancing in the Water of Life (Merton) 29, 45, 72, 77, 88, 98, 158
Dante 172, 247
Dart, Ron 201, 248
Day of a Stranger (Merton) 145
de Foucauld, Charles 90, 91, 92

271

Dekar, Paul R. 150, 151, 155, 201, 202, 247
Delp, Fr. Alfred 8, 54
Desert Fathers 12, 84, 153, 242
Dhammapada 30
dharmakaya 31, 163
Disputed Questions (Merton) 57, 140
Dostoevsky, Feodor 247

E

ecumenism 30
Eliot, T. S. 14, 238, 256
Ellul, Jacques 88, 92, 94
Emblems of a Season of Fury (Merton) 18, 38, 55
Evdokimov, Paul 9, 98, 100, 102, 105, 145

F

Faggen, Robert 202
Faulkner, William 17
Fedotov, George 9, 98, 100, 104
Ferry, W. H. 19, 34, 84
Figures for an Apocalypse (Merton) 17, 107, 122, 240
Finley, James 220
Fitts, Dudley 14
Ford Foundation 19, 47
Ford, John 22
Fox, James 17, 19, 45, 48, 241
Fox, Peggy L. 7, 11, 12, 13, 42, 44, 46, 265
Frankl, Victor 68

G

Gadamer, Hans-Georg 187
Galian, Laurence 73
Gandhi, Mahatma 63, 86, 151, 199, 214
Gardner, Fiona 10, 157, 209, 210, 216–220, 217, 265
Geography of Lograire, The (Merton) 22, 39, 40, 41, 46, 50, 240
Ginsberg, Alan 247
Giroux, Robert 17, 27, 209, 216, 217
Glynn, Audrey 52, 173
Grayston, Donald 202, 205, 248, 260, 264, 266
Greeley, Andrew 56
Greene, Dana 203, 255–259
Gregory the Great, St. 229, 230

Griffith, Sidney H. 85, 86, 92, 142, 227
Grinberg, Miguel 177
Guigo the Carthusian 108

H

Hagia Sophia (Merton) 8, 55, 56, 57, 59, 60, 67, 158, 171, 172
al-Hallaj 85, 86, 90
Harris, John 210
Hart, Patrick 13, 29, 32, 43, 44, 48, 52, 114, 146, 149, 159, 165, 173, 180, 208, 217, 227, 231, 238, 247, 257, 267
Henry, Gray 73, 227, 267
Herbert, George 36, 38, 238
Hidden Ground of Love, The: Letters on Religious Experience and Social Concerns (Merton) 56, 75, 84, 158, 175, 181, 199, 214, 260
Higgins, Michael 147, 149, 201, 247
Hillesum, Etty 54, 61–68
Hinson, E. Glenn 204, 251–255
Homer, Winslow 35

I

Ibn Battuta 47
Inner Experience, The: Notes on Contemplation (Merton) 100

J

James, Henry 14
John Climacus, St. 230
Joyce, James 14
Julian of Norwich 72, 141
Jüngel, Eberhard 186, 187, 191

K

Kafka, Franz 17
Kaplan, Edward K. 9, 10, 74, 75, 79, 81, 266
Kehoe, Deborah 203, 207, 236, 259, 266
Kennedy, John Fitzgerald 14, 19, 103
Kerouac, Jack 247
King, Martin Luther, Jr. 154, 231, 265
Kramer, Victor A. 10, 29, 77, 92, 140, 149, 166, 224, 252

L

Labrie, Ross 108, 122, 200, 201, 246, 247, 248
Laughlin, James 7, 12–23, 24–42, 43–53, 146, 168, 170, 174, 202, 266

Learning to Love: Exploring Solitude and Freedom (Merton) 21, 29, 151, 225, 237, 238, 239, 240, 265
Leclercq, Jean 20, 101
lectio divina 200, 241, 249
Lentfoehr, Thérèse 46, 130, 203, 233–236
le point vierge 9, 10, 140–146, 192
Letters to a White Liberal (Merton) 178
Levertov, Denise 203, 255–259
Life of the Vows, The (Merton) 122, 197, 211
Light, Alan 205, 263, 264
Literary Essays of Thomas Merton, The (Merton) 29, 149, 266
Love and Living (Merton) 149, 208, 227
Loyola, St. Ignatius 114

M

M. 21–23, 207, 236–241
MacGregor, Robert 168, 174
MacNiven, Ian S. 8, 13, 14, 20, 21, 43, 48, 52, 266
Madhyamika 31, 163
Man in the Divided Sea, A (Merton) 17, 107, 108
Maritain, Jacques 33, 175, 195
Mason, Herbert 85, 86, 87, 90, 95, 96, 228
Massignon, Louis 9, 84–96, 142, 228
McCaslin, Susan 59, 202, 247, 249
McDonald, Mary 249–251
McGillis, Ian 264
Meade, Mark C. 11, 168, 175, 199, 216, 267
meditatio 108, 114, 120
Menendez, Frank 21
Merton Legacy Trust, The 13, 22, 29, 216, 265, 268
Meyer, Doris 172
Miller, Henry 18, 21, 169, 267
Milosz, Czeslaw 177, 202, 208, 209
Montaldo, Jonathan 29, 59, 72, 101, 105, 107, 209, 217, 220, 267
Morgan, Patrick Thomas 246, 267
Mott, Michael 237

N

Nasr, Seyyed Hossein 73

Negr. Javieri 168, 170
Neruda, Pablo 19
New Man, The (Merton) 79, 124, 222
New Seeds of Contemplation (Merton) 12, 100, 219, 261, 262, 266
No Man Is an Island (Merton) 174, 196
Nugent, Robert 147, 203, 233–236

O

O'Callaghan, Tommie 22, 216, 235
Ocampo, Silvina 168
Ocampo, Victoria 11, 168–180
O'Connell, Patrick F. 9, 10, 11, 70, 81, 85, 100, 107, 108, 122, 157, 197, 207, 211, 212, 213, 217, 229, 230, 232, 237, 265, 267
Opening the Bible (Merton) 182, 183, 188, 193
oratio 108, 120
Other Side of the Mountain, The: The End of the Journey (Merton) 29, 43, 44, 159, 180, 231, 257
Oyer, Gordon 9, 84, 268

P

Paguio, Erlinda G. 204, 255, 268
Parra, Nicanor 33, 40
Pasternak, Boris 57, 70, 149, 165, 173, 210, 217, 247
Pearson, Paul M. 8, 11, 24, 199, 200, 203, 209, 213, 214, 215, 216, 233, 268
Plekon, Michael 9, 97, 103, 104, 105, 268
Ponticus, Evagrius 228
Pound, Ezra 14, 46
Pramuk, Christopher 8, 54, 55, 56, 58, 60, 71, 73, 102, 145, 163, 268

R

Raab, Joseph Quinn 7, 268
Rahner, Karl 147
Raids on the Unspeakable (Merton) 20, 63, 177, 245
Raphael, Melissa 64–68, 70
Rice, Edward 53
Rilke, Rainer Maria 17
Road to Joy, The: Letters to New and Old Friends (Merton) 108, 151
Rohr, Richard 215

Run to the Mountain: The Story of Vocation (Merton) 29, 114

S

Schachter-Shalomi, Zalman 9, 74–83
Schneiders, Sandra M. 163, 261
School of Charity, The: Letters on Religious Renewal and Spiritual Direction (Merton) 173
Scruggs, Ryan 248
Search for Solitude, A: Pursuing the Monk's True Life (Merton) 29, 72, 97, 143, 148, 170
Seeds of Contemplation (Merton) 17, 28, 100, 172, 174, 266
Seeds of Destruction (Merton) 178
Seven Mountains of Thomas Merton, The (Mott) 237
Seven Storey Mountain, The (Merton) 12, 17, 26, 27, 28, 34, 35, 51, 53, 85, 87, 99, 114, 172, 174, 175, 219, 234, 239, 240, 246, 248
Shakers 37
Shannon, William H. 35, 56, 75, 78, 81, 84, 85, 100, 108, 142, 148, 152, 158, 171, 173, 175, 181, 237, 260, 265, 267, 283
Sign of Jonas, The (Merton) 15, 16, 57, 98, 99, 157
Simmons, Sylvie 205, 262
Smith, Bailey 253, 254
Sophia 7, 9, 10, 11, 54–73, 102, 145, 163
Sortais, Dom Gabriel 19, 148
Spiritual Exercises of St. Ignatius, The (Loyola) 114
Springs of Contemplation, The: A Retreat at the Abbey of Gethsemani (Merton) 178, 231, 232
Steindl-Rast, David 246
Stein, Gertrude 14, 46
Stone, Naomi Burton 13, 22, 32, 43, 48, 52, 146, 149, 208, 217, 227
Strange Islands, The (Merton) 18
Stuart, Angus 200, 201, 246, 247
Sur 168, 169, 170, 174, 175, 177
Suzuki, D. T. 19, 20, 45, 144
Szabo, Lynn 12, 202, 237, 240, 248, 283

T

Tagore, Rabindranath 169, 172, 177
Taylor, Charles 195
Tears of the Blind Lions, The (Merton) 17, 107
Teilhard de Chardin, Pierre 10, 147–156
Thérèsa of Lisieux, St. 158, 232
Thirty Poems (Merton) 12, 15, 17, 25, 108
Thomas Merton in Alaska: The Alaskan Conferences, Journals and Letters (Merton) 43
Thompson, Phillip M. 206, 207, 241–246
Thresher. Sr. Carol 236
Thurston, Bonnie Bowman 73, 199, 200, 209, 213, 214, 215, 216, 256, 269
tikkun 67, 70
tulku 23, 44
Turning Toward the World: The Pivotal Years (Merton) 10, 29, 77, 92, 140, 149, 166, 224, 252

V

Van Doren, Mark 15, 24, 108

W

Waldron, Robert 207, 236–241
Ward, Bruce K. 202, 247
Waugh, Evelyn 175
Weber, Richard, OSCO 249, 269
Weinberger, Eliot 12, 13
Weis, Monica, SSJ 10, 123, 140, 149, 269, 274
Whalen, Robert Weldon 10, 147, 269, 274
Wheeler, Brad 264
Wiesel, Dr. Benjamin 52
Wilber, Ken 261
Wilkes, Paul 8, 13, 24, 52, 173, 269, 274
Williams, Rowan 57, 58, 60, 102, 219
Williams, Tennessee 13, 28
Wisdom of the Desert, The (Merton) 12, 19, 84, 153, 199
Woods, Shore, Desert (Merton) 43
Woolf, Virginia 169, 170
Wu, John Jr. 158, 204, 267
Wygal, Jim 17

Y

Yeats, W. B. 14
Yoder, John Howard 88, 95, 268

Z

Zahn, Gordon C. 84
Zen and the Birds of Appetite (Merton)
20, 45, 144, 266

The International Thomas Merton Society

The ITMS came into being in 1987 to promote a greater knowledge of the life and writings of Thomas Merton, one of the most influential religious figures of our time. The Society sponsors a biennial conference devoted to Merton and his work and supports the writing of general-interest and scholarly books and articles about Merton. In addition, the ITMS regularly awards grants to researchers and scholarships to young people. It encourages a variety of activities such as Merton retreats. Local Chapters of the ITMS throughout the world reflect a wide range of personal interest and approaches to Thomas Merton.

Finding the ITMS has been among the most enriching experiences of my life as a student and teacher of Thomas Merton. None who have been fed by Merton should deny themselves the banquet of the ITMS. None should refuse the Society the fruits of their Merton insights.

Walt Chura
Albany, NY

ITMS Members Benefits

Members of the ITMS receive information on a regular basis about events connected with Thomas Merton at international, national, regional, and local levels. Members receive *The Merton Seasonal* quarterly (which includes the ITMS *Newsletter* twice a year).

An enhanced membership package also includes *The Merton Annual* at a reduced rate. Both publications contain articles and updated bibliographies giving members access to the most recent thinking about Merton. Members are entitled to reduced rates for General Meetings and have access to the rich collection of Merton manuscripts, photographs, drawings, and memorabilia at the Thomas Merton Center at Bellarmine University in Louisville, Kentucky.

ITMS Conferences

The ITMS holds a General Meeting every other year. These forums produce lively exchanges, spiritual renewal and new scholarly Merton research on an international scale.

ITMS Fellowships and Scholaships

Shannon Fellowships

. . . Are awarded annually to enable qualified researchers to visit the Thomas Merton Center archives at Bellarmine University in Louisville, Kentucky, or other repositories of Merton materials, such as Columbia University, Harvard University and St. Bonaventure University. The awards are named in honor of William H. Shannon, founding President of the International Thomas Merton Society.

The ITMS has played an essential role in my studies of Thomas Merton's works, beginning with the Shannon Fellowship which launched my research at the archives in Louisville. Since then, I have met a host of fascinating colleagues who work together to further Merton studies and many friends who share in the causes of peace and spiritual hospitality promoted by the ITMS.

> *Lynn Szabo*
> *Langley, British Columbia*
> *Shannon Fellow*

Daggy Youth/Student Scholarships

. . . Enable young people (ages 14-29) to participate in an ITMS General Meeting, thereby inspiring the next generation of Merton readers and scholars. These scholarships honor the late Robert E. Daggy, founding member and second president of the ITMS.

A fascinating experience to be surrounded by such deep minds and wise souls. Merton is serving as a marvelous vehicle for bringing people of intellect and spirit together to share knowledge, stories, and life. Not least among these were the Daggy scholars, who simply astounded me with their abilities and their concern for our world. No more intriguing and inspiring group of young people have I been a part of.

> *David W. Golemboski*
> *Louisville, Kentucky*
> *Daggy Scholar*

It was a great spiritual blessing for me to have shared this faith affirming experience with such a diverse crowd, people also interested in what Merton was so successful at doing in his own life: transforming the deep silence of faith into real, audible, and tangible action.

> *Rob Peach*
> *Philadelphia, Pennsylvania*
> *Daggy Scholar*

20